THE HEART OF AFRICA

THE
Heart
OF
Africa

Alexander Campbell

1954   ALFRED A. KNOPF   *NEW YORK*

L. C. catalog card number: 54–5263

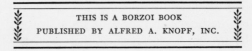

THIS IS A BORZOI BOOK
PUBLISHED BY ALFRED A. KNOPF, INC.

35057   FIRST EDITION

INTRODUCTION

JANE AND I arrived in Africa in 1937. We were married only a few days before we sailed, so we faced a new life and a new continent together. And we have lived there ever since.

We could therefore now call ourselves Africans, except that this would be a dangerous thing to do. In South Africa, for example, it might mean having to carry a "pass" and live in a "location." In Africa, a white person is a "European," even if he was born in Africa and has never been to Europe. A white American in Africa becomes a "European," whether he likes it or not. If he insists that he is not a European, he may find himself riding hard-class on the railroads and being arrested for sitting on public benches marked "For Europeans Only."

The first thing we were told was that nobody could understand Africa's complex problems who had not lived in Africa at least five years. When we had been there five years we ventured to express such opinions as that Negroes were not biologically inferior to white men. "You people from overseas don't understand," we were told.

It is true that there are many misconceptions about Africa, but perhaps the biggest of these is the firm belief of the white people who live there (Europeans) that they understand the natives (Africans). Few of them speak any African language, have ever visited Africans in their homes, or have the least idea what Africans are thinking.

Another misconception is the firm belief of the white people who do not live there that the whites in Africa are hardy pioneers who shoot big game and live open-air lives. Most of them in fact live in cities, ride in streetcars, work in offices, and have never seen a lion outside a zoo. Those who live outside the cities ride around in Chevrolets and Buicks, and read mail-order catalogues. Big-game shooting is mostly left to tourists.

Jane and I lived for some years in East London, where our

v

first two children were born, and where I worked for a newspaper, the *Daily Dispatch*. East London is a wool port in the Cape Province of South Africa, and has about as much relation to the Africa of *King Solomon's Mines* as a small town in Connecticut. Nevertheless I learned a good deal about the real Africa from my editor, Jock Barber, a pugnacious Yorkshireman who wrote flaming editorials in his shirtsleeves and habitually wore a green pork-pie hat. The *Daily Dispatch* is a newspaper of strong, vigorous, independent views, on every topic from the fallacy of white supremacy to British appeasement of Boers. Barber believed that the Boers would first weaken the English, then crush the Negroes and rule as a *Herrenvolk*. He said of the English that while they feared the Boers, they feared the Negroes more, so they were reduced to the status of piano-players in the brothel who preferred to shut their eyes to what was going on.

With Barber's blessing, I finally moved from East London to Johannesburg, and from the *Daily Dispatch* to the Johannesburg *Star*. Johannesburg, the "City of Gold," is a tough mining-camp that got rich quick and acquired a thin, a very thin, veneer of sophistication. It has always been a city of tension, and sharpening race conflicts are fast turning it into a city living in terror. It has vast Negro slums and an extraordinary crime rate; it also has stock-market "tickey-snatchers" who rise to be millionaires, and millionaire company promoters who become jailbirds. It is an outrageously vulgar, gutsy, and fascinating city, and on the whole Jane and I love it.

The *Star* was, and still is, a sound conservative newspaper of great calm and dignity. I found it a considerable change from the *Daily Dispatch*, which was housed in a building that had once been a wool warehouse. The *Star* has marble staircases, and when I first visited it, it was the lunch-hour, and the marble staircases were thronged with young men wearing black Homburg hats and carrying rolled umbrellas, hurrying out to lunch. These were the reporters. The *Star* stood amid the Johannesburg tumult like a guarantee of sanity and preached a mild tolerance. But the Boer Nationalists, who came to power in

South Africa in 1948, slowly turned the screw tighter on everyone, including the press, just as Barber had predicted they would. I worked for some happy years on the *Star*, but when I was offered the job of reporting Africa for *Time* and *Life*, I gladly accepted.

When I told my boss, Horace Flather, of my decision, he congratulated me. Flather had already declared publicly that being a newspaperman in South Africa was more hazardous than in any other country outside the Iron Curtain. The *Star* is the largest and most influential paper in South Africa, and as its editor he ought to know. "But now," he told me, "you will be able to tell the truth about what you see, without fear or favor. I hope you will."

In the course of my work for the *Star* I had several times journeyed beyond South Africa's borders, but now, though my home remained in Johannesburg, I traveled much farther and oftener afield. Almost the whole of the African continent was in my bailiwick, and I was determined to see as much of it as I could. I began an odyssey that has taken me into some strange places.

South Africa is by far the richest country in Africa. It also has the largest white population. Beyond the Limpopo I found the whites more thinly spread. I also found them entertaining some strange ideas.

The British are still in control of much of Africa. Those parts of Africa which are most distinctively British are ruled by a glacial official caste. Protocol is all. At the top of the tree is the Governor, who is always formally addressed as "Your Excellency" and referred to in his absence as "H.E." After H.E. come descending layers of chief and assistant secretaries. Despite this pomp, the real power is usually in the hands of whites who have no official position but who own land and employ cheap black labor. At Government House the African is an object of tender verbal solicitude. Among the other whites he is a coon, a nig, a *munt*, and a black sonofabitch. In these territories it is the officials who are the piano-players in the brothel.

I found none of those territories much developed. The Union

of South Africa is far ahead of them. Most of the trade is carried on by Indians. The whites live in crazy bungalows and creaking hotels and drink too much gin, but have absolutely no doubts about the divine right of whites to rule blacks. They are deeply suspicious of outsiders, especially journalists.

Busy with our three children, Jane was seldom able to accompany me on those journeys. That is why, in this book, the reader will find Jane appearing, only to disappear again, from time to time. I traveled alone among the white *bwanas*, keeping my mouth as tightly buttoned up as a detective in a story by Raymond Chandler. I often felt I was exploring the same sort of crazy world. It was always a relief to return to Jane, who preserves a sane good humor whether dealing with tarantulas or with the more inscrutable workings of the minds of whites whose simple solution for all Africa's problems is to cut off Africans' ears to teach them the meaning of the white man's justice.

Reporting Africa now is like keeping watch on a series of overheated boilers. Some have safety-valves, some not. But on all of them the gauge reads "Danger." The trick is to guess which one will blow up first.

Between September 1952, when the Mau Mau war against the white man turned Kenya into another Malaya, and September 1953, when a second African war threatened to develop in Nyasaland, I traveled 21,000 miles by air and 3,700 miles by road in Africa. But even the airplane is now too slow to catch up with African events. I flew from Kenya to South Africa almost in time to see the East London shootings I have reported in Chapter iv; but I missed the Lari massacre that occurred in Kenya three months later, in March 1953, and I also missed the battle outside the ancient walls of Kano that toppled the Constitution of Nigeria. The pace is getting steadily hotter.

Parts of this book were written in airplanes, and these introductory remarks are no exception. On my right, close at hand, looms the great African mountain of Kilimanjaro. The snows made famous by Mr. Hemingway—he is up there in Kenya now, hunting elephant—glisten whitely against the blue sky. Presently this plane will descend into the steamy coastal heat of Dar es Salaam.

In writing this book I have chosen to take the reader on a straightforward tour of the parts of Africa I know best, commencing in South Africa and finishing in Nigeria. The book thus assumes the form of a journey through Africa's actual and potential hot spots. I did, in fact, make this journey on my last swing through the continent, and have described what I saw and heard; but the book also incorporates material gathered in the course of a great many other journeys, a constant coming and going between these different places and territories. It sums up the experiences and impressions gained during the sixteen years that I have lived in Africa. In the course of the long, most recent journey through the continent which I have used as the backbone of the book, I set current impressions against the background of the impressions and experiences derived from my earlier trips.

Nicholas Monsarrat, author of *The Cruel Sea*, suggested this book, and will probably be appalled by it. Harold Strauss, of Alfred A. Knopf, Inc., has not simply acted as midwife to it; he has taken such pains and initiated so many improvements in both style and content that I now feel the credit for such merits as it possesses belongs more to him than to me. And of course there would have been no book at all if it had not been for the journeys I was encouraged to make by my employers and editors at *Time* and *Life*, to whom I am deeply grateful.

CONTENTS

CONTENTS

xii

ILLUSTRATIONS

(FOLLOWING PAGE 240)

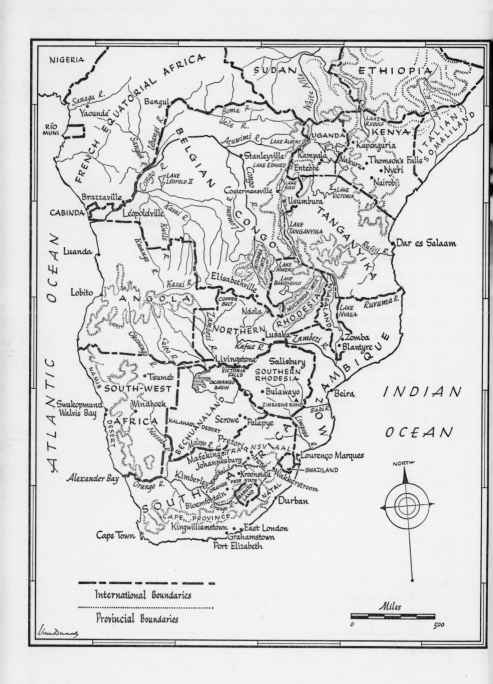

International Boundaries

Provincial Boundaries

Miles
0 ——— 500

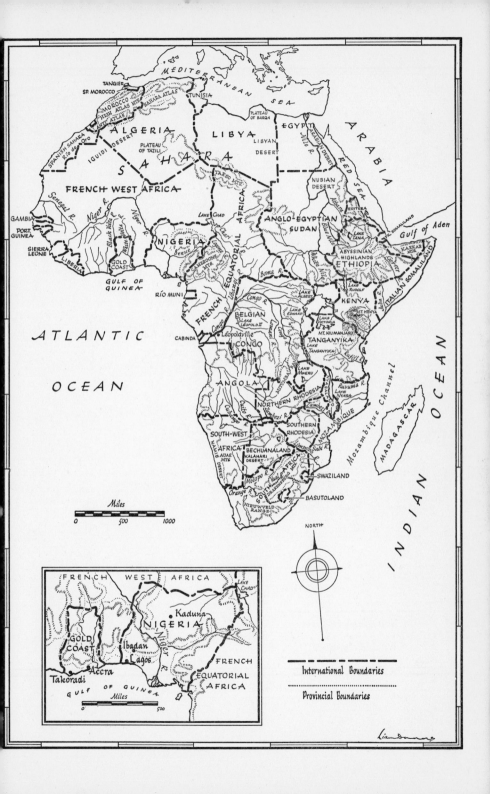

International Boundaries

Provincial Boundaries

THE HEART OF AFRICA

I

MR. PATEL GOES HOME

WHEN I look back on that sea voyage, I remember trying hard not to look at du Plooy's fingernails, after Stacey's warning. Above all, I remember what happened to Mr. Patel. I realize now that there was a neat symbolism about it, but at the time it was a hell of a honeymoon.

The day I asked Jane to marry me, I had twenty-five pounds in the bank and fine prospects. As an editorial writer on a Scottish newspaper, I could look forward to becoming in time an assistant editor. All I had to do was wait twenty years or so for the men ahead of me to die or retire.

At this juncture I received a letter from Bob Lindsay, who had emigrated to South Africa. He described the prospects there glowingly and said he could find me a job. It seemed like the finger of destiny.

When I told my editor what I proposed to do, he revolved like a top in slow motion, a favorite gesture of his. He was a ruddy-faced man with a Johnsonian cast of features and a Johnsonian habit of speech.

"I would deprecate such a move as being rash."

"Yes, sir," I said humbly.

"I would offer you a financial inducement to remain here, but it could not in the nature of things be large."

"I've already accepted this other offer, sir."

He sighed heavily. "I don't like to think of a young man ruining what might be a not unpromising career by emigrating to the colonies."

3

"No, sir," I said gloomily, but managed to repeat that the die was cast.

I felt that only ingrained Scottish caution prevented his saying more. He was already visualizing me as a gin-sodden wreck combing an African beach.

"The voyage out should be pleasant, however," he said, trying to look on the brighter side.

The news editor was less inhibited. He was a large man, with hair on the back of his hands and hair growing out of his ears. When I produced the traditional bottle of whisky for my farewell, he protested that he still had three editions to get out and had to stay sober. "Just a tot, laddie; I'll say when."

But when I began to pour, he turned his back on me and kept an eye fixed on the ceiling until the tumbler was brimming over with raw spirit. Then he turned again, cried: "Canny, laddie, canny!" downed the tumblerful in one gulp, and solemnly shook hands.

"Tell me," he asked, "do you like pigsticking and such sports?"

"Not much," I confessed, puzzled.

"Ah!" he said gloomily, "then you'll not be liking South Africa."

Jane and I were going to a place called East London, in the Cape Province of South Africa. An old gazetteer, which was all we could lay our hands on at short notice, merely reported: "East London: sheep and goats." The prospect seemed a little bleak, but I had burned my boats.

: 2 :

WE BEGAN our honeymoon in London. In Russell Square I interviewed a tall, thin gentleman whose otherwise dark office was sunny with bright posters. He had a drooping mustache and a rheumy eye that kept shifting wistfully from his fog-blurred windows to the posters showing golden beaches and blue ocean.

4

"Ah, how I envy you!" he sighed. "Haven't been in the Union for years. It's a young man's country. You'll like East London. Give my regards to Colonel Cox."

"He raises sheep?" I asked.

"He is retired. He raised a troop of horse in the Boer War. You'll find him very sound on politics. You should read his pamphlet, *One Hundred Years of Treachery, or Beware False Brother Boer*. Of course, just at present we've all got to stand together on the color issue. I don't myself trust the Boers, but they do know how to handle Kaffirs, and we must never forget the Indian menace."

He rose. "Well, good luck to you. You'll find South Africa a great and growing country. A man can stand up there. And the people are just one big, happy family."

The boat-train from Waterloo Station was crowded. Jane and I found ourselves sharing a compartment with an emigrating family, a gaitered bishop, and a lady traveling alone whose luggage labels announced she was bound for Rhodesia. The emigrating family consisted of a large man with smooth red cheeks like molded jelly, his wife, and two small children. The large man planted his hands on his knees and addressed the compartment at large.

"All going to South Africa, I suppose." He fixed a pale blue eye on the bishop. "You, sir?"

"Nyasaland," said the bishop testily, interrupted in his reading of the *Times*. He cast an apprehensive eye at the two children, who were examining his gaiters and whispering together.

"Ah," said the large man, "I suppose that's a good bit off from Cape Town, then. Cape Town is where *we're* going. (Leave the gentleman's hat alone, Albert.) I've got a brother there. He's a builder. I suppose Nyasaland's a pretty wild spot. Lots of heathen niggers, eh?"

"We call the aboriginal population Africans," said the bishop coldly.

"Thus encouraging them to be impertinent, in my view," said the Rhodesian lady, speaking for the first time. She looked at

5

the bishop severely. She was a small, hard-faced woman who wore her gray hair in tight curls. "The natives are becoming more dreadful every day. They lie and steal."

"We must remember that they are still like children," said the bishop. "We must be charitable." He laid aside his *Times*. "You live in Rhodesia, dear lady?"

"I do. I farm there."

"A most attractive life."

"Nonsense. It is an extremely hard life. One works from morning to night. The natives are quite impossible."

The bishop looked disconcerted. "Your husband has a large labor force? Many of our Nyasa boys go to work in Rhodesia. They tell me—"

"I have no husband," said the Rhodesian lady crisply. "I am a widow. My husband died ten years ago. I manage the farm single-handed. The Nyasa boys are the worst, thanks to the missions. I frequently thrash them with a sjambok."

The bishop hurriedly buried himself in his *Times*.

"I suppose," the large man's wife said timidly, "Africa's a difficult place to bring up children?"

"One has to exercise care and enforce discipline," said the Rhodesian lady. She became chatty. "My small boy was always crawling near the fire in my living-room. He would not listen when I warned him of the danger. Whipping did no good either. I had to leave the child alone a good deal, and the native nannies are quite hopeless. I did the only thing possible: I pressed his little baby fingers against the hot bars. He no longer had any inclination to go near the fire."

This anecdote temporarily quenched everyone's desire for further conversation, including even the large man's.

The train rattled on toward Southampton.

: 3 :

MR. PATEL came apologetically along the deck.

"Good morning," we said.

6

"Good morning, good morning," said Mr. Patel. "A lovely morning."

He bowed to Jane. Then he apologized silently to the rail before leaning on it and gazed sadly over the ship's side.

Mr. Patel was a plump and not very prepossessing young Indian who had been studying in Britain and was now returning to his home in Durban. He had bad teeth, and his brown skin was always breaking out in little pustules. He fussed nervously with his gold-rimmed spectacles, and was painfully shy.

Mr. Patel had adopted us on sight. It was like being adopted by a stray dog. When we came on deck, Mr. Patel was lurking in wait for us. When we entered the dining saloon, Mr. Patel was waiting to pull out Jane's chair for her. His delight knew no bounds when he found I had been at Edinburgh University. Mr. Patel also had been at Edinburgh University. "Auld Reekie!" he cried, imitating a Scottish accent. Beaming confidently round a table of disapproving faces, he gave a toast:

> *"Here's tae us,*
> *Whae's like us?*
> *De'il the few,*
> *And tae hell wi' them!"*

From then on, Mr. Patel regarded us three as inseparable. "Now we will sing a song of Sir Harry Lauder's," he would say. He would start to sing "I Belong to Glasgow," then break off and look reproachful. "Jane, you are not singing!" With Mr. Patel as the constant companion, it was turning out to be an odd honeymoon, but we hated to offend him.

He was easily offended. When not being merry, he tended to brood. At such times he went about silently apologizing for his existence. He talked darkly about the attitude of some of the other passengers toward him. "They do not like Indians. They think I should not be allowed on the same ship with them!" As he gazed sadly over the rail, I could see he was brooding now.

" 'Here's tae us, whae's like us?' " I said, to cheer him up.

7

He gave me a wan smile. "Soon we shall reach Cape Town," he said.

"Won't you be glad to be home?"

He ignored the question. "Things will be quite different then," he said gloomily. "Perhaps even before. You will see."

There were a good many South Africans on board. The men drank a lot of beer and talked knowingly about wool prices, gold mines, and diamond shares. The women's skins were coarsened by long exposure to the African sun, but they dressed well and played a skillful game of bridge. The men were jolly, hearty chaps, always dashing about and organizing deck games and plunging into the swimming-pool. When they emerged, their torsos gleaming, they lay on the edge and talked about shooting buck or even lion.

"Man," one of them would say, "you should have seen this fellow. He came bounding out at us from the bush. My nigger was scared as hell. If I hadn't grabbed the gun from him, we'd both have been goners. *Siss!* I got him right between the eyes."

"The nigger or the lion?"

Everyone roared with laughter.

Stacey listened with a thin smile. Stacey was a tall Englishman with aquiline features and a clipped black mustache. He wore tweed jackets even in the warmest weather. He looked like a Man of Distinction. You expected to find him walking the deck with a gun tucked under his arm and a retriever at his heels.

"The only lions most of them have ever seen," he said, "were in the Kruger National Park. They're Johannesburgers: you can tell by that accent—half English, half Dutch. A motley crew."

Stacey came from Cape Town. He talked familiarly about Table Mountain and the Mount Nelson Hotel. "I like the real Dutchman—he's a tough old son of a gun—but I can't stand those 'Anglikaners.' "

An exception to the general muscularity was a slim-hipped young man named du Plooy. He had dark spaniel's eyes, long sideburns, and a white-toothed smile. He only needed a Gaucho hat to look like a reincarnation of Rudolph Valentino. Jane said he tangoed divinely.

Patel shared our table. With us also were Stacey, the grim-faced Rhodesian lady from the boat-train, whose name was Mrs. Humphrey, and a couple called Forrester. Forrester was a sugar-planter in Natal, a tall, red-faced man with a bald head and a blond mustache. His wife was equally large and equally blond.

"You'll like it out there," Forrester assured us, "once you get used to the wogs." He kept a pale-blue eye fixed on Patel as he spoke. " 'Jim Fish' is all right, though. There's nothing wrong with a coon if you handle him right. The Zulu in his raw state is a fine, upstanding gentleman. He's got a natural dignity."

"I don't know how you can say that," protested Mrs. Forrester. "They're all dirty black beasts."

"Only when they get half-educated," said Forrester. "Only when some people start putting ideas in their heads."

"There is the menace from the East," said Mrs. Humphrey.

"Ah, that's true," said Forrester. "We've got to watch out for that." He looked forbiddingly at Patel, as if suspecting him of harboring a gunboat up his sleeve. "That's where the old country let us down. I noticed in London this trip there were wogs everywhere."

Mr. Patel laughed nervously. "What is a wog, Mr. Forrester?"

"A wily Oriental gentleman who lives on the smell of an oil-rag," said Forrester. "Some more coffee, dear?"

Mr. Patel became agitated, and his spectacles were misted with emotion. "You're not fair, Mr. Forrester. You generalize. There are good Indians and bad Indians, just as there are good white men and bad white men. Would you say Mahatma Gandhi was a bad man?"

"Who was talking about Indians?" asked Forrester blandly. He became immensely dignified. "Let's have no scenes, please, Mr. Patel. If you can't control yourself, you'd better find an-

9

other table." He rose. "But, since you ask me, I think Gandhi is a damned agitator. Come, dear."

"I should not have said that," Mr. Patel moaned when the Forresters had left us. "I should have kept silent."

"I thought you kept your temper very well."

"There will be trouble."

"Nonsense."

Most nights there was a ship's dance. The ship's band played lively South African dance tunes. I was watching the dancers and waiting for Jane to join me. Mr. Patel never danced, but sometimes he sat with us. Tonight, however, he had not put in an appearance. I wasn't sorry. I had nothing against Patel, and I resented Forrester's attitude, but, after all, Jane and I were on our honeymoon.

The handsome du Plooy dropped gracefully into a chair beside me and lit a cigarette. "Not dancing tonight?" he asked.

"I'm waiting for my wife."

"Where's your Indian friend?"

"I haven't seen him."

Du Plooy leaned forward and looked at me with his brilliant eyes. "Old man," he said softly, "I don't want to barge into what is none of my business, but some of these bastards are talking."

He was palpably ill at ease. He kept looking at me and flashing his white-toothed smile on and off, like someone playing idly with an electric-light switch. I waited.

"It's about the coolie," he said.

"The what?"

"The coolie—the Indian. We just don't like the way he's always hanging about your wife."

"Who's 'we'?" I asked coldly.

"We other men."

"Of all the damned cheek!" I said. "What the hell has it got to do with any of you?"

He looked sulky and frightened at the same time. "White men don't talk to coolies," he said. "And coolies don't talk to white women, if they know what's good for them."

I was still digesting this and trying vainly to frame a suitable reply when Jane came up.

Du Plooy jumped to his feet. "Can I have this dance?" he cried. Jane smiled at me, shrugged, and allowed du Plooy to lead her out on the dance floor.

I was watching them morosely and contemplating mayhem when Stacey approached and took the chair du Plooy had vacated. He nodded silently and fingered his clipped mustache. For Stacey, this was a sign of extreme perturbation. I thought I knew what was coming. Apparently they had decided to approach me one by one, to warn me off my habit of encouraging coolies. My wrath grew.

"I see your wife is dancing with that fellow du Plooy," said Stacey severely.

I stared at him.

"None of my business, of course," said Stacey somberly, "but, you know, she shouldn't. Realize you're new to the country and all that, but it just isn't done."

"I don't understand," I said feebly.

Stacey struggled within himself. He was having a horrible time, breaking out of his shell like this. But he had a duty to perform.

"Please don't think it's because he's got a Dutch name," he said at length. "I told you, I like Afrikaners. But—oh, I'll explain some time."

"Better explain now," I said.

He sighed and tugged fretfully at his mustache. "It's damned delicate."

I waited.

"There's absolutely no proof, of course. I could be had up for slander, I suppose. But, you know, we chaps who live out there, we can always tell."

"Go on," I said. "Tell what?"

"He's colored," said Stacey bluntly. "Anyway, there's colored blood there. It's quite common in Cape Town. He'd never admit it, of course, but I bet he's got a few cousins or even brothers tucked away who're either half-castes or full Kaffirs."

11

He rose, laying a fatherly hand on my shoulder. "Think it over."

I laughed. "Just one big, happy family," I said.

Stacey stared at me, disconcerted. "What?"

"Nothing," I said.

The band had stopped playing. Du Plooy steered Jane back to the table. He looked suspiciously after the departing Stacey, then quickly at me. I met his eye blandly.

"Sit down and join us awhile," I invited him.

Du Plooy sat down uncomfortably. He had long, slim hands; I found myself trying not to look at his fingernails.

"You live in Cape Town, don't you?" I asked.

He nodded.

"So does Stacey," I said.

Du Plooy laughed nervously. His voice had a high edge. "A lot of people do," he said.

"I suppose your family have lived a long time in Cape Town?" I asked.

His eyes grew hot. "We are one of the oldest Cape Town families," he said, loudly.

"Stacey was telling me something about those old Cape Town families," I said. Then I grew disgusted with it. "Forget it. Have a drink."

"No, thanks," said du Plooy. He rose quickly. "Excuse me," he muttered to Jane. Then he fled.

Jane looked bewildered. "Now, what brought that on?"

"It's damned delicate," I said. "Let's dance, shall we?"

: 4 :

THE MORNING Mr. Patel did not come to breakfast, I thought little of it. The ship had been heaving a little, and Patel did not look like a good sailor. But he did not come to lunch either, and at dinner his place was still empty.

"Our Indian friend seems to have deserted us," said Forrester. His voice was smug.

After dinner I went to Patel's cabin. He was lying on his bunk, reading. His brown eyes behind the gold-rimmed spectacles looked tired.

"Aren't you feeling well?" I asked, trying to put solicitude into my voice. At sight of him, prone and helpless in the stuffy cabin, I felt only disgust.

Mr. Patel jumped up and began to apologize for existing. He said he was feeling quite well. He was sorry to give me trouble. It was so good of me to call on him. He hoped I was well. How was Jane?

"You didn't come to dinner," I said briefly.

Mr. Patel sagged back on the bunk, and his hand fumbled for his spectacles. I had never seen his complexion so bad.

"No, no." He laughed hollowly. "I had a slight headache."

"Then you'll be with us again tomorrow?"

"Perhaps," said Mr. Patel feebly.

"Look, Patel," I said, "something's up. What is it?"

"I do not want to give any trouble," said Mr. Patel listlessly. "Mr. Forrester suggested that it would be better if I had my meals here in my cabin." After a pause he added: "It is quite understandable."

"Not to me," I said.

Mr. Patel looked me straight in the eyes. Suddenly his round face, despite the bad teeth and the pustules, was dignified. "You have not lived in Durban," he said.

"What goes on in Durban?" I asked, and then wished I hadn't. Mr. Patel gave himself over to paroxysms of self-pity. He must have been bottling a lot of it up inside himself for some time. He rolled on the bunk, beat his hand childishly against the wall, and began to weep.

"I should never have gone to England. My father warned me. He said coming back afterwards would be bad—intolerable. I would not listen. I have been in England now four years. I worked hard and was happy, I was accepted. There were little teas."

From university days, not so long before, I remembered these little teas, given by the kindly professors and their angular

13

kindly wives. Sometimes you allowed yourself to be inveigled to them, on a wet Sunday afternoon; more often you said you'd go and didn't. But always, if you did go, the grave-faced Indian and African students were there. They listened eagerly, reverently, and talked shyly. They drank their tea delicately and nibbled the tasteless little cakes. Their dark faces were solemnly aglow. You were bored, and incredulous of their actually enjoying it. You dismissed them as a dully serious lot. They all worked much too hard.

Now I began to understand just what it had meant to them, the little teas and the kindly professors and professors' wives.

Meanwhile Mr. Patel was babbling on. "I had forgotten what it would be like to go back. You do not understand. When I return to Durban—"

He stopped.

"Well?" I said. "You've got your degree. Won't you get a job?"

"Oh, yes, I shall have a job." Mr. Patel spoke bitterly. "I shall teach, in an overcrowded Indian school, in a bad slum."

"But helping your own people," I said—"that's what you did it for, isn't it?"

"I do not mind the poor pay and the bad school. Please do not think so. But, you see, it would make no difference if I were a rich merchant. I could make money, yes, but I would still be shut out—from everything that matters. All the rest of my life, because I am an Indian, I shall be shut up in a ghetto." Mr. Patel sat up again, and his voice became shrill. "All the rest of my life it will be as it is on this ship. 'Please to keep out of the dining-room, coolie! Please stay in your cabin! Please keep off the deck, stinking Indian!' "

"Look," I said, "you've been away four years. Things may have changed—"

Mr. Patel laughed. "It looks like it, doesn't it? No; I had forgotten, but it has not changed."

"All right," I said, "but *you've* changed. If you were accepted in Edinburgh, why shouldn't you be accepted in the city where you were born? Force them to accept you."

14

"No," said Mr. Patel with an infinite sadness, "it is psychologically impossible. Already I am changing back. Oh, I had the same thoughts! I would walk upright and defy them! But it is no use. I cringe—I know it, I know it. But I cannot help it. In a day or two," he said, "I shall be saying 'sir' when they speak to me."

"They can't just order you out of the dining saloon, or off the deck, or anywhere," I said. "There isn't a color-bar on this ship. It's all in your mind. Take your place at table tomorrow as if nothing had happened." I hesitated. "We'll back you up."

Mr. Patel shuddered. "There would be trouble! You would be involved—perhaps your future jeopardized! No, no, I could never do it." He peered round the cabin and smiled up at me ingratiatingly. "After all, it is not bad. I am quite comfortable here!"

"If you don't do it now," I said, "you never will. Then all the rest of your life will be just what you've said it would be."

Mr. Patel shook his head deprecatingly. "I think you are exaggerating," he said.

He was beginning to look positively cheerful. I could have struck him. And then I realized it was worse than that. You couldn't strike him. It would have been like hitting a sack of bad rice. So I left the cabin, closing the door gently after me.

: 5 :

"YOU SEE," Forrester explained, sitting back comfortably and sipping his beer, "we were really acting in the coolie's own best interests. We felt sorry for the chap."

Stacey grunted approval. Mrs. Humphrey nodded.

"The trouble is," Forrester went on severely, addressing Jane and me, "you people from overseas simply don't understand. In Africa," he proceeded, "and especially in South Africa, these people are accustomed to a rigid color-bar. They don't really resent it; they're actually grateful for it. They know it's neces-

15

sary. But when white people themselves ignore it, the colored people are made unsettled and unhappy.

"Now, take this coolie!" cried Forrester. "Just think what you people may have done to him! Remember, he has to live in South Africa the rest of his life—under the color-bar. But you've encouraged him, made friends with him, treated him as if he were an equal. The result is bound to be bad. For all we know, he may have begun to get ideas already—begun to get above himself. When he gets back to Durban, he may start behaving as if he really were the equal of a white man. Why, he might even—I don't say he will, but he might—think himself good enough to want to marry a *white girl!*"

Mrs. Forrester shuddered. "Don't, dear," she said. "Just the thought of that black hand!"

Even Stacey gave her a startled glance. Jane giggled.

A flushed face joined the group. It was du Plooy.

"You," he accused us, "come from a part of the world where white people are *safe*, where they're secure. You can afford to be 'liberal.' But we whites who live in Africa, we're outnumbered by these colored people. And, by God, we intend to go on ruling them, as we've always done. A white skin is a white skin, and colored skins are colored. Never the twain shall meet!"

Stacey's mouth fell open. He looked sharply, suspiciously, at du Plooy. But du Plooy was perfectly, passionately sincere.

Stacey gulped.

"Absolutely, old man!" boomed Forrester.

: 6 :

AT CAPE TOWN the majority of the passengers left the ship. They were swept away in a tide of welcoming friends and relatives. Negro and half-caste porters, dressed in rags, swarmed over their luggage and bore it down the gangplanks like an army of hungry ants. The ship's corridors stank with them.

Amid this abundance of cheap, half-naked labor the South

16

Africans bloomed like the resurrection plant, which shrivels until it is placed in water, when it instantly revives and starts to grow again. Watching the tattered Negroes, Forrester swelled to twice life-size. "Good old 'Jim Fish,'" he said emotionally. "God, it's good to be back!"

The immediate reaction of passengers who were seeing "Jim Fish" for the first time was to draw back from his body-smell and his ragged half-nakedness. But luggage had to be got ashore; trains were waiting; cables had to be dispatched and phone-calls made. Everyone became anxious to secure a porter. The way to get one, it seemed, was to raise your voice and at the same time put a rough edge on it, as if you were addressing deaf and mentally defective children. "Hey, you there, boy!" you shouted. Then you pointed peremptorily to a piece of luggage. "That's mine! Get it ashore! Hurry up, now!" And it was gratifying to see how the "boys" obeyed, how they hurried to get your luggage, lifting it on a black shoulder only partly covered by a torn shirt, and showing big yellow teeth between thick lips as they eagerly answered: "Yes, *baas!* Coming, *baas!*" Afterwards, when the luggage was safely ashore, they came up, sweating and grinning, holding out not one hand but both hands close together, the palms cupped. And into the cupped palms you dropped a "tickey," the South African threepenny piece, feeling a glow of satisfaction at your easy command of such docile, easily pleased labor.

This glow is the aura that constantly surrounds every white person in Africa. It is the reward for being white. It is why many whites come to Africa in the first place.

Cape Town was the home of the first real white settlers in Africa. The Dutch flag was planted there three centuries ago. The city's steep, cobbled streets lie directly under the frowning slopes of flat-topped Table Mountain. At night the lights gleam halfway up the mountain, like ropes of pearls. There are curving golden beaches, laid like scimitars against the blue throat of the sea; and in the warm valleys are fat vineyards. The Dutch built graceful high-gabled white houses, with thick walls and deep window recesses, and great oak beams and teak floors within, so that you passed from the sun's white glare into the cool shadow of polished dark wood and soft yellow light.

Jane and I went in the cable-car to the top of Table Mountain, swaying perilously, toylike, on a thread of steel over a vast drop toward the sheer face of a granite cliff. Lizards scampered over the bare sun-baked rocks. Down below, on one side, were the city's white buildings, like pretty shells rimming the blue bay, where toy cranes busily unloaded toy ships. On the other side of the mountain, Africa stretched as far as eye could reach, a vast gray plain, wrinkled like an elephant's hide.

But we had to return to the ship, for our destination was farther along the coast. A new lot of passengers had come on board, South Africans traveling by sea to Port Elizabeth, East London, and Durban.

Mr. Patel was still with us. But now that the ship was in South African waters, there ceased to be any ambiguity about his status. And this, strangely enough, made things easier for him. When he appeared on deck, or hovered momentarily in the doorway of a lounge or smoking-room, no one said anything about "coolies" or bristled at his presence. Everyone simply treated him as if he were invisible.

He contrived very skillfully to avoid us, so that we never succeeded in speaking to him again. Manifestly we were a source of embarrassment to him, for Mr. Patel's readjustment was now complete. Once he entered the smoking-room with a cigarette in his mouth and fumbled in his pocket for a match. I wondered if he would ask me for one, but instead he approached a group of strangers at a table. When a man glanced up, Mr. Patel asked him humbly for a light.

Without any expression on his face except polite boredom, the man picked up a box of matches from the table and handed it to him. When Patel offered to return the matches, the man said quickly, without looking up: "You can keep them." Mr. Patel hesitated, with the box in his hand. Then he said: "Thank you, sir," and walked away. Mr. Patel was home.

II

SOUTH AFRICA:
BATS IN THE FIG TREES

Hurry up, there, please!" a ship's officer implored, keeping an anxious eye on the bobbing launch below. "The people down there are getting seasick."

Obediently we filed into our big basket.

East London at that time, 1937, did not yet have a dock that liners could enter. The ship anchored in the roadstead, and a launch came out to take passengers ashore. To get them from the ship down into the launch, the crew rigged up a large basket affair. The disembarking passengers entered the basket in batches, and the basket was then lowered over the ship's side to the launch. It seemed a melancholy way to arrive, finally, at our destination.

Our first glimpse of our new home was of a long, low shore, with thick green bush behind yellow beaches. Out of the bush peeped whitewashed buildings with glaring red-painted iron roofs.

Our luggage was brought ashore and piled in a waterfront shed. The customs officer was an ancient with an ear-trumpet, into which one bawled, usually in vain.

"A young man's country," quoted Jane sarcastically.

Finally we got clearance and were driven off to the hotel where a room had been reserved for us. It contained, not one, but two double beds, and had an odd, musty smell, as if mummies had long lain there. We kept on waking up in the night and glancing toward the other, shadowy bed. We could both have sworn it had an occupant.

19

In the morning the hotel manager asked me, a little apprehensively, if we had slept well.

"No," said Jane, in her forthright way. "What *happened* in that room?"

The manager mopped his brow. "I'll give you another room, immediately."

"Thank you. But what was it that scared us?"

"He was a Jewish gentleman," said the manager. "He was buried on Saturday. He—ah—committed suicide."

East London will always be associated in our minds with bats and fig trees. The fig trees lined both sides of the main street, in the upper, residential section. These trees were the homes of hundreds of bats. During the day, the bats hung motionless from the branches of the fig trees. But when night fell, they came to life and flew up and down the street, wheeling madly around the electric-light standards, like large, leathery moths. There were so many bats that the town had a bat-smell, which blended with the smell of decaying figs.

Though we were given another room in the hotel, which flanked the broad street running steeply downhill to the seafront, we felt that the deceased Jewish gentleman still vaguely pursued us. As soon as possible we got a small apartment in a block that was still in process of being built. When we moved in, they were still installing the baths.

We had at first no servant, but Jane secured a large black washerwoman who came once a week, removed the washing, and brought it back next day, balanced on her head. It returned snowy white, and Jane was highly pleased with this arrangement until one day she asked where the washing was done.

She was conducted to a huddle of tin huts, well concealed from the public gaze behind thick bush. This was the "location," where the black folk lived. Women were scrubbing clothes in a large stone trough near the communal privies. This was where the white folks' washing was done.

"You'll get used to it," Jane was comfortably assured.

Almost every white family had a motor-car and at least one black servant. Nevertheless life had its primitive aspect. In the sprawling suburbs, the "death-carts" rolled at the midnight hour along unlit, unpaved roads, made ghostly by a flickering lantern carried by a Negro wearing a burlap sack who sat on top of the cart. The "death-cart," horse-drawn, was the night-soil remover. Most of the suburban homes had bucket sanitation. After one of our first social evenings, in the depths of the unlit suburbs, Jane reported indignantly: "I was sitting in that damned place when suddenly a tarantula the size of a soup-plate appeared on the wall within a foot of me. It was *watching* me, malignantly. I was too petrified to move."

"Never mind," I consoled her. "It might have been a snake."

"Where would I have applied the tourniquet?"

We kept some packing-cases, in which our household goods had traveled, in an outside storehouse. After they had been there a few weeks, I discovered they were providing a home for huge, tarantula-like spiders. I had to tip them over one by one and kill the spiders with a hammer as they emerged.

A snake cast its skin on our doorstep. Armies of black ants moved briskly across our living-room walls. One day Jane found small, intelligent-looking creatures sitting up in rows on her pantry shelves, cleaning their whiskers. They seemed conspicuously harmless, and she was enchanted with them, until she discovered what they were: boll-weevils.

The people with homes in the suburbs had cunningly placed themselves outside the municipal area. In this way they avoided having to pay local taxes. But the plan had its disadvantages, besides unlit and unpaved streets, and bucket sanitation. The town's red fire-engine was housed in a large shed down near the beach. The firemen got tired of rushing out to the homes of people who, since they were paying no municipal taxes, were not paying the firemen's wages. The next time there was a fire in the suburbs, the fire-engine stayed at the municipal boundary, and the firemen sat smoking their pipes, watching the conflagration, unmoved by the frenzied appeals of the suburbanite.

East Londoners were hospitable. They gave frequent cocktail parties, called "sundowners." There the unpleasant habits of the Kaffirs were minutely dissected. But, to hold one's audience, one had to be able to produce clinching proof that one's own Kaffirs were viler than anyone else's. Amid the sundowner babble, one caught fascinating snatches of servant biography.

"I *thought* there was something funny," said a woman in a bobbing red hat. "But she denied it, and of course it never seems to show on them. Then last night, in the middle of my party, she had the baby right there on the kitchen floor."

"My dear, what did you *do*?"

"I didn't do anything. Herbert threw her out. Said she wasn't going to saddle *us* with another mouth to feed."

East London had no theater, but it had cinemas, called "bioscopes." The films were changed once a week. A new film was an important social event. People rolled up in large cars. The men wore evening dress, and the women wore evening gowns and furs. It was like a Hollywood première. The furs had to be kept in refrigerators when not worn, to prevent the damp heat getting at them. The cinema programs consisted of ten minutes of advertisements ("filmads"), a month-old news-reel, and a cartoon. Then there was an intermission. Everyone flocked out to chat in the foyer. After the intermission, there were more "filmads," then a feature. The proceedings closed with *God Save the King,* and everyone stood stiffly at attention.

Another social function was the "morning tea." Men, thank God, were never invited. Jane returned from her first morning tea a shattered woman. She dropped limply into a chair and regarded me with revulsion, for it was I who had brought her to this snug little paradise.

"Golly!" she said.

"But what do they talk about?" I asked.

"Scandal, and the servant problem," said Jane promptly. "Did you know that a certain city councilor is having an affair with his secretary? But mainly the servant problem—on and on and on."

The morning tea was a very necessary institution. The white ladies of the town had simply no other means of occupying their overabundant leisure. All their work was done for them by Kaffirs. There was a "boy" to work in the garden, a "girl" to cook, wash, and scrub, and a "nanny" to look after the children. After breakfast, with her children taken off her hands by the white-starched black nanny, the housewife saw the long, hot day stretching emptily before her, until cocktail and party time. So the morning tea had been invented. Jane perforce attended and in return gave so many morning teas that every detail of the grisly ritual is etched upon her heart and soul.

Preparations for a morning tea were fairly simple. On every square inch of polished surface in your immaculate living-room you put out plates heaped with little sandwiches, cream scones, and cakes. The guests began to arrive about eleven o'clock, and the affair went on until nearly lunch-time. Then you bade your friends an affectionate, smiling farewell, made a firm date for the next morning tea, and retired to bed with a splitting headache while the Kaffirs removed the debris of half-nibbled food, washed the cups and plates, and emptied the overflowing ashtrays.

East London, in addition to being a wool port, was a holiday resort. There was a beach where visitors on vacation from upcountry bathed, and a "marine drive," which was always crawling with slow-moving automobiles.

The chief recreation of the townspeople, especially at weekends, was to drive along the beach front, park their cars facing the sea, and sit there, watching the waves while black nannies took the children out of the cars and let them play on the sand. After an hour or so of this the happy families packed the nannies and the children back into the cars and drove home, well satisfied to be assured that the Indian Ocean was still there. Once a ship that ventured too close inshore stuck fast on a rock, a pebble's throw from the beach. The crew waded safely ashore, and the cargo was salvaged, but the ship could not be moved. Thereafter, every weekend, the townsfolk motored out to the wreck and, sitting in their automobiles, watched it with deep interest. Very slowly, under the battering of wind and waves, the rust-red hulk disintegrated. Years later, when only a buckled scrap of metal still adhered to the rocks, the motor-cars were still lined up facing the sea every Sunday afternoon, and the people were still watching.

There was a good deal of hard drinking at Saturday-night dances. The favorite tipple of the most enthusiastic drinkers was raw South African brandy. After the dance the young couples helped one another into their cars and drove off erratically into the moonlit night, heading for the beach. The auto repair shops did a roaring trade, as also, after a really hectic weekend, did the hospitals and funeral parlors. Usually, however, a benign providence guided the merrymakers safely home and to bed, either their own or someone else's. So there was hardly ever a vacancy in the maternity homes. During the years we spent there, the town's main thoroughfare of a Saturday morning was never without its interesting quota of ruefulfaced, pregnant women, shopping, incongruously wearing beach sandals and thin cotton maternity frocks. But a few weeks after the event they would be back at the Saturday-night dance, with their husbands or with other people's husbands: there was really very little else to do.

The town had hard drinkers, but few drunks. In the muggy, semitropical heat the brandy oozed through the pores before it could destroy the liver. The hardest drinkers seemed to remain fresh of face, clear of eye, and steady of hand. In fact, their youthfulness was not only preserved but prolonged in alcohol. The nearest approach to a real drunk was a white-haired but straight-backed old rip of sixty-odd, who drank brandy before breakfast, wore open-neck shirts and tropical shorts, and took a swim in the sea every day. He had the complexion of a young girl and was seldom betrayed into even a momentary loss of dignity.

Only once in my presence did he let his guard slip. His usually rosy cheeks were pale, and his hand trembled ever so slightly. When I asked him if he was feeling unwell, he replied that he was recovering from a terrible experience. The night before, alone in his bedroom, he had seen out of the corner of his eye the handle of his wardrobe begin to turn. He stood there petrified as the wardrobe door slowly opened.

"What was it?" I asked. "A burglar?" For there was a good deal of Kaffir crime, and a favorite trick of the thieves was to hide in a wardrobe, creep out when everyone was asleep, and proceed to ransack the house.

"Worse than that," he said solemnly. "Out came a *polar bear*." And I realized he was recovering from a fit of d.t.'s.

Just before the end, he was reduced to drinking his brandy by levering the glass to his lips on the end of a handkerchief, which he pulled round the back of his neck with his other hand. He had suddenly got the shakes, which he never threw off. But he had had a good run for his money.

The town's other two hardest drinkers were one night driving home from a party when one of them accidentally touched the switch of the car's radio. Suddenly a voice began to speak softly to them, inside the car. Without a word, each opened his door and leaped out of the haunted automobile, which careered on without them until it ran into a lamppost. Neither was much hurt.

East London was one of several towns along the edge of the Indian Ocean. These scattered communities—East London's nearest neighbor was three hundred miles away—had all been carved out of low, thick, green, snake-infested bush. They were all built on the same pattern: clusters of white-walled, tin-roofed buildings between the green bush and the blue sea with its bright yellow beaches. Around them were enormous, six-thousand-acre farms. The farmers grazed sheep and grew maize, oranges, and pineapples. Most of the work was, of course, done by Negro laborers. The farmers were constantly on guard against their workers. The *Farmers' Weekly* advertised dogs for sale to farmers, the dogs being described as "real Kaffir-killers."

One day Jane found a starving, pot-bellied black child on our doorstep. She was incredulous when he begged for work; his arms and legs were match-stick thin and he looked about eight years old. Actually he was fourteen. If he had a name, we never discovered what it was; he had probably forgotten it himself. We called him "Piccanin," and put him to work in the kitchen. There was a shed in the garden which we said he could have for a room. Although Piccanin seemed to eat enormously, he put on no weight. One morning Jane went out into the garden very early. Out of Piccanin's shed burst no fewer than nine other little boys, all in an identical state of emaciation. Piccanin had been feeding and sheltering them. Such gangs of starving black children were common when there was famine in the Transkei, the great "native reserve" from which most of the Negro workers came.

Jane and I drove to the Transkei. A winding road led into a wilderness of softly rounded hills. This was the old original "Kaffirland," where the rags of civilization dropped away from the people. The old men wore only an enveloping red blanket, like a toga, and solemnly smoked long-stemmed Kaffir pipes. The proud-breasted women smeared their cheeks and foreheads with white clay, and walked like queens. On every hillside were patches of green cultivation, a quiltwork of tiny fields and plots, like the farms of medieval Europe. The people made their own pots and built their own huts, drawing crude but strong designs around doors and windows.

From the eastern side of the Kei River the Transkei stretched almost as far as Zululand. But you saw few young men there. With no railway lines and only a few bad roads, the Transkei was mainly a vast recruiting-ground for the farms, and for the Rand gold mines, one thousand miles away. The 1,500,000 Transkei Negroes could not grow enough to feed themselves and to pay their poll taxes and hut taxes too. The land, once fertile, was deeply eroded. Trade in the "native territory" was exclusively in the hands of white storekeepers, who also acted as recruiting agents for the mines. When a family got into debt, as was frequent, the able-bodied men were promptly signed up by the traders and packed off to the mines. The women and children were left. Periodically the maize crop failed, and then the women and children flocked into the surrounding "white" towns like East London, seeking work.

East London's 40,000 partly tame Kaffirs were a constant headache to the white citizens. As they did all the work, it was conceded that they were necessary. The problem was how to keep them out of sight when they were not needed.

This problem was at least partially solved by rigidly segregating the Negroes in an all-Negro township, the "location." Every white town had this Negro appendage, to which the Negroes were packed off after working-hours, and from which they emerged every sun-up to resume their tasks.

The chief amenity required by the location was a cemetery, for fifty per cent of the babies born there died before they were a year old. When the native cemetery was at last filled up, East London had to provide another. It would necessarily cost money, and there was a good deal of head-shaking over the onerous burdens placed by the Kaffirs on the white taxpayers. But after a stiff battle by the more liberal elements, land was acquired for the new Kaffir cemetery. When the first black corpse was carried to the graveyard, the ground was found to be so stony that dynamite had to be used to open the first grave.

An increasing number of Negroes were getting some sort of schooling, thanks mainly to missions. Some Negroes actually managed to struggle through to the higher grades and even, as an occasional freak, to university level. The whites found the "educated Kaffirs" very amusing. Much merriment was occasioned by the discovery, in an East London office, of a full-fledged Negro B.Sc. He was employed as the post "boy," and his main duty was sticking stamps on envelopes.

Another of East London's "educated Kaffirs" was Richard Godlo, an earnest young man who later became a member of the Natives' Representative Council. Godlo was regarded as a scream: he actually wrote letters to the local newspaper, complaining about the state of the houses in the location. An East Londoner confided to me: "You know, I once had tea with Godlo." He added hurriedly: "Of course, I only did it for a joke."

All Kaffir women were known to be immoral. Most of them had illegitimate children. The more respectable ones were employed as nannies. The black nannies spent their afternoons with their little white charges in parks where the swings and merry-go-rounds were all prominently marked: "For White Children Only." Meanwhile in the location their own children died like flies.

There was a very elaborate pretense that no white man would dream of even looking at a Kaffir girl (though Kaffir men were universally believed to lust continually after white women). One hot Sunday afternoon Jane and I, for want of something better to do, drove miles through the thick green bush, where the crimson aloes and tough cactus sprouted, to a village outside East London. The road danced and shimmered in a heat haze. The bushlands were utterly deserted. So was the village, or so it seemed. The little tin-roofed houses were shuttered and silent. The place had a brooding air. Dispirited, we turned the car to return by another route. Then a slight movement at the roadside drew our eyes. It was like one of those trick drawings for children, in which an apparently empty wood suddenly becomes filled with faces and figures: all you have to do is look for them. In the bushes on both sides of the road couples lay in a silent hot embrace: white man and Kaffir girl.

The still figures lying under the bushes paid no heed to us; we drove quickly back to town and never went there again. But when next we heard a white person become vehement about the strong physical distaste that "Europeans" instinctively and rightly felt for all Kaffirs, we looked at the talker with a new and calculating eye. And suddenly I read new meanings into sly hints that young men sometimes dropped about stealthy visits by night to the locations.

: 2 :

ALL THAT area around East London is known as "the Border." In 1820, British settlers had landed at Port Elizabeth. They had fought several wars with local native tribes. Finally the warlike Xosas had virtually committed suicide. A Xosa prophet arose who declared that a day of miracles was at hand. The people must destroy the crops and slay the cattle. When that was done, new crops and cattle would magically appear, and at the same time the white man would be driven into the sea. The Xosa people obeyed their prophet, but nothing happened, except that most of the tribe starved to death. This left the way clear for the British to commence a long feud with the Boers.

East London called itself "the Fighting Port." One reason appeared to be that it was still fighting the Boer War, which was concluded in 1902. Its inhabitants prided themselves on being British to the backbone. In 1910 the two British colonies and the two Boer republics that had fought the war came to-gether to form the Union of South Africa. There were to be no more Boers and no more Britons, only South Africans.

This made no difference to East London. Thirty years after union, the locally published wool report still began: "This year the Colony has had a good season. . . ." And the Boers were still the enemy. East London's chief bogeyman was Gen-eral James Barry Hertzog, South Africa's Boer Prime Minister. Hardly less disliked was South Africa's most famous man, Gen-eral Jan Christiaan Smuts. To East Londoners, Smuts was not the greatest man in South Africa; he was still the Boer guer-rilla leader who was fighting England. Pretoria, the capital of the Union, was regarded as simply the enemy capital.

To many East Londoners, the formation of the Union had not appeared a great triumph for political common sense. It had been a shameful betrayal of a great British victory. The British had beaten the Boers, and now the Boers were ruling the country, including the two former British colonies of the Cape and Natal. Only treachery could explain such a hideous outcome.

When Sir Patrick Duncan, an English-speaking South African who had been appointed Governor-General, visited East Lon-don, a prominent East Londoner was presented to him. Sir Patrick was, of course, the representative of the King in South Africa, but the patriotic East Londoner brushed this aside. Wagging a finger under the astonished Governor-General's nose, he fumed: "Duncan, you have sold out to the enemy!"

East London could not, single-handed, reverse the British decision to bury the hatchet and make peace with the Boers. What it did was to ignore, as far as possible, the whole sordid transaction. The Border put an invisible wall around itself. It had its own Iron Curtain. Boers who visited East London were made aware that, as far as the Fighting Port was concerned, the Boer War was still on. The Act of Union had made English and Afrikaans the two official languages of South Africa, with full equality between them. Anyone who spoke Afrikaans in East London had a thin time.

The Border prided itself on refusing to be fooled by glib Boer speeches. It was constantly on its guard against Boer plots to overthrow the British Empire. The whole of the rest of South Africa, except possibly "loyal" Natal, was regarded as writhing under the ruthless heel of a Boer oppressor. The country north of the Border, as far as Johannesburg, was deemed to be dangerous, enemy-held territory, full of wild Boers who would never think twice about cutting an Englishman's throat.

When Jane and I proposed to motor up to the Transvaal, our East London friends were filled with horror.

"You will have to drive through the Orange Free State," they warned us.

"It isn't very hilly, is it?" I asked innocently. "I understood it was quite flat." (For the trip, we had bought a small English car, which was not very good at climbing hills.)

"The Free State is Hertzog's territory," they said. They spoke his name like Romans referring nervously to Attila, the scourge of Empire. "They will know at once that you are *uitlanders*. It would be better to pass through by train. But if you must drive, you had better carry a gun."

There were moments, living in East London, when you had a queer feeling that time had slipped a cog. You expected to see redcoats marching down the main street with fife and drum, on their way to subdue the Boer rebels. It was like hearing people in the American South talk about Generals Lee and

Grant as if they were still alive and the outcome of the Civil War was still in doubt. Later we were to discover that this was not quite the phantasmagoria it seemed. A good many other South Africans, both Boer and British, were still fighting the Boer War. But East London carried this farther than any other place we ever lived in.

Colonel Cox was a craggy man with a carbuncled nose, who lived in a sprawling hilltop house overlooking the bay. The gallant colonel had a high English voice that whistled down his nose like drafts in a corridor. He had shrapnel in his left eye, and wore a monocle. The house was a museum of swords, muskets, battle flags, and mildewed books dealing with military campaigns. But his chief topic of conversation was the Great Boer Plot.

He regarded his fellow Englishmen in South Africa as dupes of the two Boers Smuts and Hertzog. "The Boers have never forgiven the English for destroying their republics," he trumpeted. "All this talk about union is eyewash. They'll turn the Union back into a republic, and the Boers will be top dog. The English will be told to get out. Smuts should have been hanged in '02."

"What you people don't realize," said our young Boer Nationalist friend, Piet van der Merwe, "is that Smuts didn't just make friends with the English; he sold out to them. He isn't a true Afrikaner, he's an Englishman. Whatever they may say, the English despise the Afrikaners. They want us all to become Englishmen, and we won't.

"Certainly I want South Africa to be a republic," said Piet. "What does the British royal family mean to me? This is *our* country. The English here still think of Britain as 'home.' They expect me to speak English, but they don't bother to learn my language, Afrikaans. Their idea of an Afrikaner is a half-witted poor white with nine starving children. Once, when my sister was ill, I rang up the hospital. I spoke in Afrikaans. I was told: 'If you want any help, ask for it in a civilized language.' One day soon we'll have our republic, and then the English will find that two can play at that game. And that will also be a day of reckoning for turncoats like Smuts."

: 3 :

THE BORDER regarded itself as the citadel of liberalism as well as the last truly British stronghold in South Africa. The old Cape tradition had been "liberal," as opposed to the Boer doctrine of "no equality between white and black in Church or State." The East London newspaper, the *Daily Dispatch*, when it was not uncovering Boer plots against the Empire, frequently published outspoken editorials advocating "equal rights for all civilized men irrespective of color." It argued that educated Negroes, like Richard Godlo, should one day be allowed a vote, just the same as a white man.

Most of the newspaper's readers were all for combating the Boers, but the paper's proposals for elevating Negroes roused violent opposition. The writers of such editorials were regarded as eccentric to the point of lunacy, but, on the whole, harmless, since no one could be expected to take such nonsense seriously.

The little main-street shopkeepers, who sat in the pink town hall as councilors, wanted everything to remain exactly as it was. Anything else they greatly feared, including even prosperity, since prosperity might bring about change.

When the country began to expand economically, there was a great rush of foreign firms to the coastal towns. British and American companies sought factory sites. But when they applied to East London, which had a respectable-sized port, the council not only turned them down, but wrote them rude letters into the bargain. It was pointed out that new factories would mean an influx of Kaffirs, and possibly of Boers as well. East London had as many Kaffirs as it wanted, and desired no Boers whatever. So the firms went elsewhere, mainly to Port Elizabeth, East London's nearest coastal rival, which obligingly began to rebuild and partly modernize its location to accommodate the Kaffirs who would come to work in the new factories, and which did not mind even an influx of Boers.

The people of East London moved like dusty wax figures in a bright sun-filled vacuum. Their minds became dulled to the color of putty. They even had no seasonal changes to stimulate them, for at the semitropical coast the birds do not sing, the flowers have no scent, and it is perpetual summer. They were condemned to live the lives of lotus-eaters, but at the heart of their languorous dream was fear—fear of the Kaffirs and fear of the Boers.

So the morning teas and the Saturday-night dances and the moonlit-beach petting parties went on. The young men who drank too much brandy became old-young men, acquiring respectability and dull wives, and committing secret, furtive adulteries. And the black babies went on dying in the location.

We were glad to be able to leave that town.

III

SOUTH AFRICA: KEEP IT WHITE

We had been some years in South Africa before Jane and I found time to visit Durban, the seaport and largest urban center of Natal. In the interim we had become acquainted with a good many other parts of South Africa, including that stronghold of the wild Boers, the Orange Free State, where, instead of having to carry a gun because we were obviously British, we were embarrassed by the overwhelming hospitality of simple and kindly folk who spoke Afrikaans but refused to accept any payment for the coffee they insisted that we drink on their farm stoeps, as their verandas are called.

We were still strangers to "British" Natal, which peered apprehensively over its jagged Dragon Mountain ramparts at the Boer Free State and the Transvaal. So we decided we must go there.

That summer of 1951, Durban's yellow beaches were crowded with vacationing whites sunning themselves a deep brown. The big hotels along the fringe of the blue Indian Ocean were doing a roaring trade. Zulu rickshaw boys, fantastic in feathers, beads, and huge horned headdresses, leaped and pranced along the promenade.

But the chief concern of the whites who were tanning themselves brown was, we found, to stay white. Durban's main thoroughfare, West Street, looked like London's Oxford Street, if Oxford Street suddenly ran headlong into Calcutta.

The streets behind the big hotels and away from the beach front swarmed with Indians. In Durban there were a quarter of

34

a million of them, outnumbering the whites as well as the Zulus. In Durban's big, airy town hall, harassed white officials were working on a plan to "keep Durban white."

"Racial zoning," said one of them, "is the answer. Some natural features are very effective barriers; for example, rivers, steep valleys, cliffs, hilltops." He coughed. "Green belts are no use; they simply become communal parks, thus encouraging contact." He shook his head. "Where there is *no* existing barrier between the zones we allocate to different races, we shall just have to create one." He illustrated. "Where only a road separates two groups, we'll have houses only on one side, drawing the boundary where the back yards of one race meet the front yards of the other race."

"Why?" I asked.

He blinked. "So that they don't share the same means of access to their houses."

"I see," I said.

"But race friction also occurs when one race travels through the living-area of another race. For example, here in Durban we have Negro and Indian pedestrians and cyclists going to their places of work through a white area. The whites have expressed considerable resentment and alarm." He sighed. "We did discontinue a colored bus service through that area, but the whites still aren't satisfied." He brightened. "Railroad travel, being more or less sealed off from the areas through which the railroad passes, is relatively unobjectionable.

"So, you see, what we're planning to do is to create rigid race zones and as far as possible prevent persons of different races having even to pass through other race zones." His brow furrowed. "There *is* one problem. Other towns round Durban are doing the same, but we can't be at all sure that an expanding Durban race zone—say Indian—may not in time come into contact with a white zone of some other town. And the devil of it is that we can't consult other local authorities."

"Why not?" I asked.

"My dear man, we must keep our plans strictly confidential; otherwise people would start speculating in land values! Zones

35

intended for white occupation are bound to go up in price; zones for Indians and Zulus are bound to depreciate."

I thought it over.

"What about the central areas?" I said. "How do you partition those? Indians own a lot of the stores."

He looked unhappy again. "People of all races mingle on the sidewalks," he admitted, "but it's very difficult to prevent without disrupting business altogether. And then again, *some* facilities are—well—communal. The law-courts, for instance. We can't very well keep Indians and Negroes out—especially Indian lawyers. It would scarcely be just." He shook his head. "You see, we have quite a problem."

: 2 :

DURBAN, IN FACT, had two problems. The other was monkeys. For years the little gray fellows had been encouraged to live in the thick woods that grew close to the town; they attracted tourists. As Durban grew, the monkeys became first a nuisance and then a menace. They stripped orchards, invaded houses, and leaped on schoolchildren in the playgrounds. Durban didn't know what to do about them, though many suggestions were put forward (one was to catch a monkey, shave off its fur, paint it red, white, and blue, and release it again to terrify its fellows back into the hills). Animal-lovers were up in arms against any plan to destroy the monkeys by shooting them or putting out poisoned bananas. So the monkeys went on ravaging the orchards and frightening the children.

But the Indian problem was much worse. Durban was originally built on sugar. The ebony Zulus were too wild and proud to work in the white man's plantations, so the planters imported "coolies" from India. Unfortunately the coolies refused to go back to India when they were no longer needed. They set up as lawyers and businessmen. And they multiplied.

"An Indian," said a white Durbanite wrathfully, "can live on the smell of an oil-rag." Although some of the Indians got rich,

36

the majority of them remained appallingly poor. Their hovels spread over the seafront flats and over the little green hills until Durban had some of the worst slums in the world. The whites disliked the rich ones even more than they abhorred the poor ones.

In Durban I had dinner with an Indian lawyer and his wife, who is a medical doctor. We sat on the stoep of their comfortable home (in the heart of a white area). A hedge separated the house from its neighbor. A woman came into the garden of the next-door house, nodded nervously to my host and hostess, and swiftly vanished indoors again.

Choudree laughed. "At first she wouldn't even speak to us. But then she got bolder. Though her husband doesn't approve, we are now quite good friends—more or less." He smiled wryly. "One evening she came up to the hedge and spoke to me.

" 'Mr. Choudree,' she said, 'some of my friends think I'm crazy.'

" 'Why?' I asked.

" 'They say I'm crazy to live right next door to a coolie. But you know what I tell them, Mr. Choudree?'

" 'No,' I said.

" 'I tell them,' she said," Choudree finished, chuckling, " 'if all the coolies were as nice as my coolie, the coolies wouldn't be half-bad; *that's* what I tell them.' "

He put down his cigar and rose. "Shall we go inside?"

I drove out of the city, past the sugar-cane fields and over a road that got progressively worse, to the hundred-acre farm of Manilal Gandhi, son of the late Mahatma. Here the Mahatma lived for years, fighting white South Africa's anti-Indian laws and writing about the doctrine of non-violence. His sixty-year-old son carries on the fight.

I found a small, meek man in an open-neck white shirt and slacks, planting tomatoes. He greeted me cheerfully and introduced me to his wife, Sushila, and his lovely daughter, Sita.

Manilal Gandhi had just concluded a long fast in protest

against anti-Indian laws and what he regarded as the South African attempt to place his people in new ghettos. But he would not at that time give his support to the Natal Indian Congress, which was organizing mass infringements of the *apartheid* regulations. Sipping a glass of honey and water, Gandhi said: "I don't believe in mass demonstrations, however 'non-violent.' I don't believe that true non-violence can be organized. It must be based on the individual, and it must come from the heart. Besides," he added frankly, "I believe the people behind the demonstrations are Communists."

Later that day Gandhi, an unobtrusive figure in a worn brown suit, humbly climbed the steps of the Durban municipal library (to which Indians are not admitted) and slipped into the reading-room. While a few whites stared in horror, he adjusted his spectacles and patiently read the files of the newspapers until an official touched him on the arm and asked him to leave. When he refused, his name and address were solemnly noted down, but no other action was taken. The same thing happened when he walked into the Durban railroad station and sat on a bench marked in large white letters: "For Europeans Only." A few white policemen watched him, with apparent amusement, but nobody interfered with him. Finally he walked out of the station, a rather lonely little figure.

In his large city office, a Durban businessman folded his hands on his desk and said flatly: "Oh, yes, you'll see a lot of Indians here. The first thing to remember about them is that though they look human, that doesn't mean we have to treat them as human beings. . . ."

: 3 :

THE NATAL Indian Congress was in a more militant than Gandhi-ist mood. Through an open window there were glimpses of a mosque against the blue sky, and washing hanging from peeling yellow balconies. The street outside was slummy and crowded with Indians. The hall itself was dingy, with broken

38

wooden benches. At the door, two Indians were distributing printed literature, and watching out for intrusive policemen. The literature at one and the same time appealed for "non-violence" and flamingly denounced the "Ghetto Acts" of the South African Government.

But the delegates to the Congress seemed more concerned with the alleged sins of global imperialism than with race laws in South Africa. Resolution after resolution dealt with "the war in Korea," "American imperialism," and "peace with the Soviet Union."

My friend Choudree shifted uneasily in his seat. Finally he rose and asked bluntly just what the war in Korea, American imperialism, and the Soviet Union had to do with the disabilities of colored folk in South Africa. He was listened to in a dead, not a respectful, silence. When he sat down, there was no applause. He got no seconder. The meeting went on discussing the evils of international capitalism. The delegates seemed well drilled.

"You see," said Manilal Gandhi in an undertone, "what sort of people these are." Manilal attended the proceedings throughout, but did not speak. When one or two personal followers begged him to, "What," he asked, "would be the use?"

During a recess two young men who had been the most violent trouncers of American imperialism approached me. They were handsome Indians, with well-oiled hair and aquiline features. Their eyes had flashed indignation when they spoke about American "brutalities" in Korea, but now they were exceedingly deferential. Was it true that I represented a great American news-magazine? It was; what could I do for them?

They looked at each other. Then one of them lowered his voice. "You can tell us: how is it possible for us to get visas? There is no freedom here. We wish to go to the United States."

But I was far more interested in a plump and not very prepossessing man who had started visibly as I entered the hall, and had been staring at me ever since. He wore gold-rimmed spectacles, and his brown skin was unhealthily pustuled. Yet he seemed to have more dignity than I remembered.

He shook me very warmly by the hand. "How glad I am to see you! It is a long time since we met. Tell me, what do you think of the Congress?"

"I don't know," I said dubiously. "There's rather a lot of— silly stuff, isn't there?"

"There always is," said Mr. Patel cheerfully. "But don't be deceived. Most of us are not Communists, believe me. But if the Communists are prepared to work hard— And, you know, we really are getting somewhere. This passive resistance is like a snowball: it keeps growing. We *must* have a mass movement, and a united front."

He grinned confidently at me. "You don't want to hear any more of those tiresome resolutions. Come with me and I'll tell you a story."

We left the dingy hall, and Patel plunged into a maze of mean streets. As we passed a particularly noisome slum, he jerked a thumb to where a broken outside staircase wound upwards; beside the stairs a door hung drunkenly on its hinges, revealing a water-closet. Mr. Patel walked in and used the water-closet. When he pulled the chain, it did not work.

"I live here," he said calmly as we resumed our walk. "I lost my job, you know. And I have been in prison." He seemed proud of it. "Probably I shall go there again, quite soon."

He marched me into an Indian café and ordered coffee. When he looked up at me, his brown eyes behind the gold-rimmed spectacles were twinkling. "It is different from the ship, eh?"

"You were going to tell me a story," I reminded him.

"Yes."

In 1949, two years before, the Durban Zulus poured out of their city slums and attacked the Indians in theirs. The battle began in the city streets and spread to the tin and wood shanties that sprawled over the little green hills on the city's outskirts.

"For a long time," said Mr. Patel, "some whites had been telling the Zulus that the Indians, not the whites, were their oppressors. The Zulus beat up Indians in the streets, and looted Indian stores. Many whites looked on approvingly. Only when the riot reached record proportions did the whites try to quell the Zulus. They did so with machine-guns. Over one hundred and fifty people were killed, including Indians who were tossed back into the burning ruins of their homes by Zulus brandishing assagais and screaming war songs."

Mr. Patel paused reflectively. "We Indians then and there decided that our only salvation lay in forming a united front with the Negroes. Otherwise, we believed, the whites would be encouraged to divert Negro unrest by permitting pogroms against Indians. That's why the Natal Indian Congress began to organize an Indian-Negro front, on the basis of mass resistance to race laws that affect Negroes and Indians alike. And that's why I joined it." He smiled at me rather slyly. "It is better to fight for freedom than to be slaughtered without a fight. If we don't do it now, we never will."

"Who told you that?" I asked suspiciously.

Mr. Patel laughed. "You did!"

"And you're the man who 'didn't want to give any trouble'!"

"Well," said Mr. Patel gently, "I am giving trouble now."

And he was. Shortly afterwards he led a procession of Indians and Negroes to a railroad station. There were two separate entrances, and the big notices were plain enough. One entrance was reserved strictly for "whites only"; the other was for "nonwhites"—Negroes (or "Kaffirs," as South Africans say) and Indians (or, as South Africans laughingly call them, "coolies").

Because this was no pathetic individual demonstration by a lone Manilal Gandhi, but "mass resistance," well organized, white policemen waited with rifles and revolvers to drive home the lesson of white supremacy and non-white apartness.

Mr. Patel walked firmly up to the white policemen. He looked them straight in the eye, probably as he did to me, years before, when he said: "You have not lived in Durban." To the policemen he said: "I am going to exercise my rights

41

as a human being and use this entrance to the station. I am aware that I shall be breaking the law, and I hope you will send me to prison."

Then he tried to walk past them, with his followers.

Being a passive, or non-violent, resister of white-supremacy laws takes more courage, I think, than being a white policeman carrying a rifle and having the Government's permission to use it against non-whites. The policemen, with one accord, closed in.

So, belatedly, I discovered the answer to the question I had asked Mr. Patel: "What goes on in Durban?"

IV

SOUTH AFRICA:
THE TOWN THAT DIED OF FRIGHT

At the end of 1952 I went back to East London, for I had a job to do. For some time we had been living in the Transvaal. I left Jane in our new home in Johannesburg and returned to East London alone.

The drums of black nationalism were throbbing wildly all over awakening Africa, and East London, after all, had not managed to escape change.

Though the town had grown somewhat, it looked the same. The air bus deposited me and my bag outside the railroad depot, near the top of the broad street that swept down to the holiday beach; I could see clusters of striped beach umbrellas, and bathers swimming in the surf. The old green-painted tearoom where you bought ices was still there.

The main street was also much the same. A few shops had changed hands or been altered, and there was a new department store. The town hall was no longer pink, but gray. But shoppers still walked under sidewalk awnings to protect them from the sun's glare, and there were still rueful-faced pregnant women, wearing beach sandals that showed their crimson toenails, and thin cotton maternity frocks.

The *Daily Dispatch*, where I had worked, was still in Caxton Street, and its front page was still solid advertisements, with the news tucked away on an inside page. The day's editorial lucidly argued the case for equal rights for all civilized men.

Yet the town had a frightened air, not easy to put a finger

43

on. People didn't like you to ask too many questions, and turned awkwardly away if you persisted.

A truckload of white police, armed with rifles and Sten guns, rattled along the street, and eyes watched it, half in gratitude and half in apprehension. A military plane, buzzing in the blue sky overhead, swooped down inquisitively near where the location still stood.

The Saturday-night dances were still being held, and I went the town's giddy social round with my old friend "Susan," the "society editress." Formidably equipped with pencil, notebook, and large horn-rimmed spectacles, she was swept, as she always had been, by a grateful management to her special table overlooking the dance floor, and as usual earnestly noted down the frock worn by Miss Smith and the names of Mrs. Jones's up-country guests. I marveled at her perseverance, but she went at it doggedly, for she had her column to fill, week by week, year after year.

The frocks had changed, but the faces had not, except that they looked a little older, a little more haggard. The bright, vacuous, bored expressions were the same. Too much brandy was still drunk.

It seemed to me, though, that there were fewer people than there used to be. I asked Susan.

"Oh, a lot of people don't like going out at night much now. They think it isn't safe. And the ones with children naturally can't go out."

"But haven't they all got servants?"

"Nobody trusts the servants any more. You simply can't tell whether your servant wasn't one of the murderers. You see," explained Susan, "they *all* come from the location."

The manager of the place sat down at our table.

"Have a brandy," he offered gloomily. "Very bad night tonight. Not half my usual people here. They're all staying at home in case there might be more trouble."

A couple stopped beside us. "We're off," said the man. "The girl *said* she'd phone if anything happened, but—you know,

44

you can't trust any Kaffir any more. My wife's frightened to leave the children."

We visited two more beach hotels and a night-club; everywhere the story was the same.

: 2 :

WHAT HAD happened was that the location, with its teeming, semi-savage Negro population, had spilled over into a murderous and bloody riot. The Negroes of the Cape and the other South African provinces had formed an African National Congress to voice their grievances. No other city produced more enthusiastic recruits than East London. Thousands were arrested, but the movement, instead of being crushed, grew. The Government prohibited the Negro leaders from attending or addressing meetings of their people, and told the white police to go ahead and shoot. But in East London the police gave the Negroes permission to hold a meeting, then changed their minds and ordered the meeting to disperse. In the ensuing riot two whites were murdered inside the location, an insurance salesman and a Dominican nun.

I had just come from Port Elizabeth, where there had also been a riot, followed by a one-day strike of almost all Negro workers. In his home in the Port Elizabeth location I had spoken to Dr. James Njongwe, Cape provincial leader of the African National Congress. Sitting with his head between his hands, Njongwe told me in a low, strained voice that he and the murdered nun (she was a fully qualified medical doctor) had attended the same classes at the Witwatersrand University in Johannesburg. He was horrified by the savagery displayed by his own people.

Many of the leaders of the African National Congress were Negro doctors. They had held dying black babies in their arms and watched the faint spark of life go out, and knew from personal experience what conditions in the locations were like.

45

They were for the most part reasonable men, willing to act as a bridge between white and black.

Njongwe was far better educated than the majority of his white masters. But, as a Kaffir, he had no political voice, and was compelled to live amid the squalor of the segregated location.

We sat in the living-room of his house, surrounded by the shacks of the less well-to-do Negroes who were his patients. There was a big combination radio-phonograph and a large piano. Njongwe could afford such luxuries; all he lacked was freedom. He wore a brown dressing-gown over his chocolate-striped pajamas, and with his broad shoulders he looked like a handsome prize-fighter. Nervously he smoked cigarettes and talked in his deep, earnest voice.

Did he believe a peaceful solution to the race problem in Africa could still be found? Njongwe nodded emphatically. "*Any* problem can be solved peacefully, if only men of good-will agree to get around a table and discuss it frankly." What did he want for his people? Chiefly, an easing of the color-bar, so that Negroes no longer had to carry passes and were no longer harried day and night by white policemen; more education and freer economic opportunities; for the educated, who were able to pass a "civilization test," a free and equal vote.

I had just come from the office of a white police chief who had defended the police shootings by declaring: "It's them or us now, all over Africa." And I had lunched with a white city councilor who, when I told him I proposed to visit Njongwe and suggested that he come along, had admitted he had never even set foot inside the location, and was horrified at the very idea of meeting and talking on more or less equal terms with a Kaffir.

As we spoke, Njongwe and I, his little four-year-old son entered the room. With a passionate gesture, Njongwe lifted the child onto his knee and caressed him. He was a chubby little boy, with large, intelligent brown eyes. "What chance do you think *he* has?" asked Njongwe, looking at me over the child's head.

But East London was much worse than Port Elizabeth.

What had actually happened on the night of the riot? Everywhere I went, I seemed to run into a brick wall. When I spoke to old friends, their eyes became blank. If I went on asking questions, they became sullen. If a solitary Kaffir loitered a moment too long outside a white home, the watching whites rang up the police. Men and women were going about armed.

The sprawling farmlands surrounding East London were in a state of panic. In drowsy Grahamstown, with its schools and its cathedral, they had put machine-gun nests over the city gates. Heavily armed police patrolled Kingwilliamstown. The white farmers had banded themselves together for mutual protection.

I drove twenty-five miles out of East London to Macleantown, on the fringe of the Transkei. The East London police chief had received a frantic telephone call for help; he was told that the Kaffirs were threatening to murder all the whites. On the way, we passed native women walking along the road, balancing pots on their heads—the most graceful sight in Africa. Negro men were at work in the fields. Everything seemed peaceful. But some of the white farmers had locked themselves with their wives and children in a church hall.

As we drove back to East London, the police chief said: "We've had at least a score of these false alarms in the past forty-eight hours. I daren't ignore them, but"—he rubbed his red-rimmed eyes—"it would be nice to get some sleep for a change." I felt sorry for him, but not for the zealous young Afrikaner policemen who followed us in a troop-carrier, their fingers obviously itching for their triggers, and their eyes lusting for a Kaffir between the sights of their rifles. Nor could I feel sorry for the farmers, who no longer felt safe even when guarded by the fierce dogs they had trained to be "Kaffir-killers."

I was still trying to find out what had really happened on the night of the riot, when two whites had been murdered by a Negro mob, and, according to the official figure of casualties, the police in the course of their duties had shot seven Negroes.

47

City councilors told me they had been "sworn to secrecy." The Mayor, asked if the official casualty figures were correct, blanked his eyes (he was an honest man) and replied slowly: "I don't know." The police themselves, though otherwise amiable, were obviously under strict instructions to say nothing. The superintendent of the hospital, where some of the Negro casualties had been treated, supported the police figure—but firmly declined to produce his case records. Even the reporters on my old paper were not talking.

Gradually, after much hard digging, involving furtive interviews with Red Cross officials, less inhibited doctors, and the undertaker who carried out Negro burials, I was able to piece bits of the story together. It was a remarkable one.

The shooting began at half past four in the afternoon (a Sunday), when a Negro crowd of six thousand refused to obey the police order to disperse within five minutes. The Negro meeting was held in an open space surrounded by bushes, on the edge of the location. On the other side of the road, a few yards away, were white-occupied bungalows. When the shooting began, the families in the bungalows left their homes and fled into the town.

The police, armed with rifles and Sten guns, drove the Negroes back through the bushes into the location. It was about this time, amid the general confusion, that the white insurance agent was trapped and murdered inside the location. A few yards from where he died, and not much more than a hundred yards from the location police station, manned by whites, another Negro mob held up the automobile in which the Dominican nun, Sister Aidan, was traveling with baskets of food for Negro sick. The white-coifed nun was not afraid. She had been visiting the location daily for over four years. When the mob stopped her car, she got out and confronted them. A moment later they had cut her throat. Her mutilated body was tossed back into the car, which was set on fire. Later the charred body was taken from the car again and parts of it hacked off, and eaten, while the mob screamed "Africa!"—the slogan that the

African National Congress had popularized with their followers.

After the murders the police threw an armed cordon round the location, so that no one could enter or leave. They also put armed guards round the hospital, and newspaper reporters and photographers were warned off. What happened after that will probably remain a matter for conjecture only. The white townspeople (not a single man, woman, or child believed for a moment in the "official" casualty figures) heard shooting going on in the location until well after midnight. A visitor to the location the next day said afterwards that the paper-thin walls of the tin shanties were riddled with bullet-holes. It is known that at least two elderly Negroes were shot dead as they lay in bed. None of the forty thousand Negroes in the location had firearms.

Nobody, not even the police themselves, knows how many Negroes were killed or wounded that night. For the Negroes, after the police had gone, buried their own dead and tended their own wounded. A visitor to the location cemetery counted many fresh-dug graves the day after the shooting. Other corpses were hurried off into the surrounding bush, to be buried in secret.

The seven "official" corpses had to be buried more publicly. Three days after the shooting, the funerals of four of them were held. The police warned that they could not take the responsibility of allowing a party of whites to enter the location, as this might start another riot; but they agreed to take a number of white reporters to the graveside in a troop-carrier.

Arthur Mapleson, of the London *Daily Express*, and I sat side by side in the steel-lined, wire-meshed troop-carrier as it lurched and nosed its way through the maze of bullet-pocked tin shanties. We were flanked by young, fresh-faced Afrikaner policemen—farmers' sons in blue uniforms—clutching rifles. One had a Sten gun. We passed the spot where the Dominican nun's charred body had been taken from her blazing car and further mutilated. The inhabitants of the location watched the troop-carrier, their black faces stony and expressionless. But a little half-naked boy, seeing the armed policemen through the strong wire mesh, solemnly pointed a finger. He made the motions of firing a gun and said loudly: "Bang, bang." He was about the same age as Njongwe's son.

The cemetery was in a hollow at the farther end of the location. Beyond it was a steep bluff, thick with green bush. The mourners had already arrived, and the graves were already dug. The coffins lay on the fresh-turned earth, waiting to be lowered.

The troop-carrier and the rifles were unnecessary, after all. The black mourners paid no attention to us whatever. They behaved as if they were alone with their dead. Mostly they were women, wearing long, somber dresses and the black *doek* or turban of the Bantu. There were a few Negro men, in their rough working-clothes.

The young white policemen came out of the troop-carrier with a great clatter of boots and rifles and squatted on the grass, a few yards from the Negroes. Plainly they did not relish being ignored, after all the trouble they had been put to to come here. In Port Elizabeth I had heard a police officer grumble because there had not been more shooting—"we were ready for a real battle"—and these police were evidently of the same mind. They talked in loud, rough voices and watched the Negroes irritably. The funeral service started, and the women began singing hymns. Some of them wept. In elaborate pantomime one of the young policemen mockingly wailed his grief. His companions roared with laughter. Still the mourners paid no attention. Often I had seen white people act as if black people near them were totally invisible. Now the boot was on the other foot.

When the service was over, and the earth shoveled in on top of the coffins, a slim, well-dressed Negro walked slowly away toward his automobile. He was Dr. Robert Ross Mahlangane, one of the local leaders of the African National Congress and, like many of them, a medical man. "Black pig!" grunted one of the policemen as he passed. Dr. Mahlangane gave no sign that he had even noticed the policemen.

I visited Richard Godlo in his cramped little house in a slum quarter where Indian, half-caste, and Negro children played in the gutters. Godlo was one of the few East London Negroes (Mahlangane was another, and lived close by) not compelled by law to live in the location. The tiny hallway was dark and smelled of cooking. There were crude religious pictures on the walls. Ten years before, Godlo had been a passionate crusader for his people; he was regarded suspiciously by the whites as an "agitator." But the organized movement for Negro freedom, under fiercer leaders, had left Godlo behind. He had become plumper and fuller in the face, but his eyes were sad. With a melancholy earnestness he assured me he was "out of politics" now. He did not want to talk about the shooting in the location. He felt that the African National Congress had got into "wrong hands." He was a very unhappy and perplexed man, and I did not care to press him. When he thanked me, too volubly, for coming to see him, I was reminded of Mr. Patel.

East London, it seemed to me, had put down its local black insurrection—for the time being. But in the process it had scared itself to death. Bathers still plunged in the surf or lay on the golden beach under gaily striped sun umbrellas; but the town would henceforth live in the atmosphere of hate and revenge.

The night before I left, I went back to the location. Overlooking the dark huddle of tin shanties, the police station was dazzlingly lit by powerful searchlights, so that it would be impossible for anyone to approach unobserved. It looked like a fort in hostile territory—as in fact it was. A troop-carrier, empty, was pulled up in front of it; the men who had come out of it were having hot coffee in one of the offices, their rifles stacked beside them. Somewhere in the maze of shanties below, a fire was burning hotly, waxing and waning like a beacon. From the huddled huts of the location came shouts, screams, and drunken yells.

Someone had set fire to a hut, but the police were not unduly perturbed. "Pity the buggers didn't burn the whole place down and save us the bother," said one. "Trouble?" said another,

51

surprised. "Oh, no: just the usual drunks. There'll be a few stabbings and a bit of arson, but that's usual. The rioting is over."

The police still stood guard with their rifles, in case the Kaffirs should try to come out of their ghetto. Otherwise the location was back to normal. But the white townsfolk would always be afraid of that "next time." You couldn't trust the Kaffirs any longer—if anyone had ever been foolish enough to trust them at any time.

I returned to my hotel on foot, through the silent, deserted streets of the white town. It still smelled of bats and overripe, decaying fig trees. It was like a town of the dead. Perhaps it had already died, without being aware of it.

South Africa was changing; Africa was changing. In the morning, as the little Lodestar lifted up into the hot blue sky from its green air-strip, the country unrolled below. There were the plowed fields and scattered homesteads of the frightened farmers. Tanks and armored cars now patrolled the lonely ribbons of highway that linked all these little white communities along this coast, from Durban to Cape Town. There was the Indian Ocean, vast and blue. The political leader of the whites in South Africa was already rumbling that over that ocean might one day come the ships of Mother India to destroy *apartheid* and end white supremacy. The 300,000 Indians of Natal, with Mother India's approval, had already pledged support and provided active leadership for South Africa's awakening and resentful 9,000,000 Bantu. Where this vast coastline curved north, but still rested on the Indian Ocean, the Indians had a firm foothold on African soil, in East Africa. To the north, also, were many more millions of Negroes; and the drums of black nationalism were throbbing in the Rhodesias, in West Africa, and in Kenya. Above all, in Kenya, where fanatical Mau Mau terrorists had turned the whole Kikuyu tribe, 1,000,000 strong, against Kenya's 40,000 whites, and were pledged to drive the white man into the sea.

I had seen the beginning of a deadly struggle, and, though it would assuredly be long and tragic, I might live to see the end, whichever way it turned out. Yet only a little while before, any white man in Africa would have confidently laid a bet that not for at least a century would the black millions begin to think of turning against their white masters. As elsewhere in the world, events in Africa were speeding up.

The Lodestar passed Grahamstown on the right, with its white machine-gun nests, and turned its nose toward Port Elizabeth, where I would change planes for Johannesburg, with its gold mines and its teeming Negro shantytowns. They were tough and ruthless in Johannesburg, not soft and afraid as they were in East London. Young Afrikaner policemen had come from the Transvaal to protect East London against the Kaffirs East London had vainly hoped to ignore. What bloody sunrises might Africa yet see?

V

SOUTH AFRICA: PENNIES FROM HELL

I FIRST SAW Johannesburg in the company of a financier, which is as it should be. It was the roaring postwar year of 1946.

Far below, a tiny round swimming-pool gleamed up at us from someone's large garden, like a blue eye. There were fields and roads and the scattered red roofs of dolls' houses, clustering more thickly as we flew on toward a smudge of smoke and a vague skeletal tracing of gaunt concrete buildings etched on the horizon. My bluff companion pointed with a proprietorial air.

"Johannesburg," he said.

The city grew and expanded and the buildings took the definite shape of apartment houses and office blocks. Astoundingly rising in their midst, boldly shouldering them and peering down streets where toy trams and buses ran, were bright yellow mounds, pyramid-shaped.

"Mine-dumps," said my new acquaintance.

We flew over Johannesburg, over the concrete buildings and the yellow mine-dumps, and came to a small ridge of hills. Down over these hills sprawled a grotesque huddle of mud and tin huts, crammed together, shapeless, seemingly endless.

"A Negro shantytown," said my informant.

We flew on over it quickly, and the ridge of hills closed in behind us, shutting the city itself out of sight, for we were coming down to land. There was nothing in sight now but vast plains, a distant river, and directly beneath us the familiar pattern of an air terminal, with its control tower and runways.

"Down there," said my financial friend, indicating the empty

54

plains, "they're mining gold. You can't see anything, of course, but the mines run right under the city and all the way out here. Deep under that grass and soil, there are shafts and tunnels and cross-cuttings. And they go very deep indeed. Johannesburg is almost 6,000 feet above sea-level; the deepest mines go down more than 8,000 feet."

I knew he knew what he was talking about, for he had a well-manicured finger deep inside the gold pie and had pulled out many a plum. At that time he was chairman of several dozen different sorts of companies, all built on gold. He sat at the apex of a pyramid of holding trusts whose affairs were so intermeshed that millions of pounds ran smoothly between them, like water rushing through a complexity of channels to an appointed destination, which happened to be his bank balance. He had built the channels himself, so he must know.

The illuminated panel flashed a warning to stop smoking and fasten seat-belts. My companion regretfully dropped his cigar into the built-in ashtray and slid it out of sight into the arm of the seat. He was not much more than forty, and had a round, merry face and a strand of black hair plastered over one eye. He did not look at all like a millionaire. He was dressed sloppily and his tie insisted on disappearing under one wing of his shirt-collar. But he was the genuine article, all right. You knew that by the deferential air of the tall young secretary who sat in the seat behind him hugging a brief-case, by the royal manner in which he was swept through the formalities at the airport, and by the large black limousine with cap-touching chauffeur which awaited him.

He insisted on giving me a lift into town, and on the way he talked.

"My father knew this place when it had only one street and a row of wooden shanties," he chuckled. "No sidewalks; one chemist's shop; one doctor; but fourteen liquor saloons. Sammy Marks used to drop round to our place; he started life as a secondhand-clothes dealer, ended a millionaire and a mining magnate. So did Barney Barnato, who arrived in this country a barefooted boy, with a box of cigars and no money at all. Abe

Bailey won sixty-four thousand pounds by backing a racehorse called Lovematch, and ended by buying up half the Rand. And it's still going on: look at me!"

We swept up a broad highway past scarred mine-dumps with harsh yellow grit swirling off their tops, past clanking minehead machinery, and burly Negro miners wearing tin helmets and sleeveless undershirts who poured through a huge wooden gate. The road became lined with cheapjack stores, white miners' ugly brick houses, secondhand-auto dealers. We passed billboards, one showing a broad-shouldered man quaffing beer and bearing the legend: "The Beer That Built the Men Who Built the Rand!"

"Don't you believe it!" roared my millionaire, thumping the back of the seat in front of him. "We Jews built the Rand."

In broad Commissioner Street the traffic flowed thick and slow as molasses between the massive buildings, which showed only a slice of blue African sky. "Sixty years ago you could have bought any of these building sites for a couple of oxen," he said, snapping his fingers jubilantly.

Before he dropped me at my hotel, he showered me with cards of introduction, scribbling his name on each. "Go anywhere—ask them to show you anything—come and see me!" he cried.

The big car swept him away.

: 2 :

JOHANNESBURG WAS in the middle of a gold boom. It was a city in fever. It was not the first fever, and it would not be the last. If there had been no gold, there would have been no city, for only madmen, I thought in those first days, would otherwise have chosen such a site.

In the brief spring and fall, there were golden windless days of blue skies, when the air had the quality of champagne. Then it was good to be alive, and the people walked about their mountaintop city like gods. But the climate was treacherous, with temperatures soaring and slumping like bucket-shop shares, drawing a fantastic fever-chart for Johannesburgers, who might wake to a frost-bitten morning only to be plunged before noon into scorching heat, like lobsters tossed into boiling water.

In the midwinter month of July, icy winds sometimes howled across the bare stony plateau and beat against the houses exposed on the high ridges, ripping off roofs and hurtling them a block away. People longed for summer's forgotten warmth, or fled to the golden beaches of Durban, four hundred miles away.

But in the summer months, tension mounted in the dry and dusty heat, until you gasped for air. Then the brassy sky filled with black thunderclouds, and forked lightning savagely shattered the ironstone *kopjes* (hills). Torrential rain deluged the town, flooding roads and sweeping away bridges, but bringing relief. A Johannesburg summer thunderstorm is a thing to see. The lightning played savagely about the buildings, and the sky was a vast turbulent ocean of scudding clouds, while the thunder crashed like artillery along the ridges. To add to those dangers and discomforts, the thick gritty particles constantly blown off the hard yellow dunes of the encircling and encroaching mine-dumps irritated the throat and stung the eye.

"Built on gold," said my friend Ernest Shirley cynically, "and dedicated to delirium."

Sixty years before, when news of the first gold strike reached Kimberley, men abandoned the diamond diggings to join in the race to the Rand, and fought savagely for wealth on the barren plateau. They arrived in rocking stagecoaches, pulled by exhausted, foam-flecked horses, to find a canvas town already growing, and busy carpenters knocking together wooden booths to serve as shops. One rugged pioneer left his ox-wagon in the great empty space that was the town's first rough market square. When he returned, a few days later, he had to take the wagon to pieces to shift it, for it was closely hemmed in by a forest of newly built shacks.

The city grew like a lusty giant, until it found its modern shape: tumbledown iron-roofed shacks still existing in the shadow of concrete skyscrapers, like weeds lodged in the crevices of tall cliffs; broad boulevards and choked alleys—unplanned, chaotic, but immensely rich.

Fine shops rubbed shoulders with old-clothes dealers' stores. You turned a fashionable corner and found yourself in a noisome slum. And the people were as motley. There were Englishmen, Boers, Jews, Greeks. The muddy tide of immigration from half the countries of Europe mingled on the narrow, crowded sidewalks with turbaned Hindus, fez-wearing Moslems, slant-eyed Chinese, and blanket-wearing Kaffirs straight from the native villages, called *kraals*.

With Shirley I wandered about the streets, trying to grasp the city's meaning. The Rand Club, dark with oak and heavy with the smell of rich food and expensive cigars, had a dull somnolence. Here the millionaires had huddled, white-faced, while rifles cracked in the streets during the great mine strike that almost became a Red revolution in 1922. But order had been restored, and the Rand Club had recovered its ponderous dignity. Its elderly inmates swam like slow, large-gilled fish in a tropical twilight, and conversations were conducted in discreet whispers. But in near-by Hollard Street the brownstone stock-exchange building rocked to the trampling feet of exuberant brokers as if teen-agers were enjoying a jam-session, and the interior was a marbled maelstrom of shouting, red-faced men. Even stenographers and office boys were buying gold stock and dreaming of wearing mink coats and driving Cadillacs. Every afternoon, at every street corner, newspapers were snatched from the newsboys by men and women who conjured paper fortunes for themselves out of scribbled figures hurriedly penciled in the margin beside the stock price quotations. In the crowded hotels and night-clubs, waiters collected five-pound tips for serving two-shilling drinks, and company promoters threw lavish dinner parties. In booming Johannesburg every night was Saturday night.

Once we climbed to the top of the newest building, which had a glass-enclosed penthouse dizzily overlooking the sprawl of the city. While we were admiring the view, the floor seemed to tilt. A plate crashed in fragments, and the windows chattered like teeth.

"What is it?" I asked, grasping a chair for support. "An earthquake?"

"Only a tremor," said Ernie carelessly. "In Johannesburg you become used to them."

Miles away, and half a mile under the city, there had been a rock-burst in a gold mine. Tons of rock had suddenly collapsed, entombing a score of men. The shock was felt all along the Reef (as Johannesburgers familiarly call the Witwatersrand), and set the seismograph needles swinging in the Johannesburg observatory. But, as Ernie said, in Johannesburg you became accustomed to these "tremors." After experiencing a few of them, I ceased to think in terms of earthquakes, and, like everyone else in the Golden City, scarcely paid any heed to them. They were simply part of the atmosphere of the place, like the weird storms, the gritty dust you breathed, and the violent changes of temperature.

Because of the boom, Johannesburg's skyline fluctuated like a line drawn by a drunken man. It changed almost from day to day as buildings were feverishly pulled down and bigger ones went up in their place. Building contractors were hurriedly throwing up new office blocks, new cinemas, and new piles of luxury apartment houses, which clotted like cream on the already overbuilt Hillbrow ridge. Finally, for sheer lack of breathing-space, blocks of apartment houses began to rise far out of town, in the middle of astonished green fields. It had become fashionable to try to get away from it all, even if this meant running two motor-cars instead of one and spending hours in a solid queue of automobiles blocking one of the unplanned city's few main arteries. People were also building country cottages (with swimming-pools and tennis-courts), villas, roadhouses, new garages, in every fast-growing suburb.

My friend the financier—at that time the newest star in the fast-revolving, dizzily dissolving financial galaxy—built himself a marble mansion modeled on the Parthenon, and posed for his picture between two of the pillars, smoking a cigar and holding a cocktail glass.

Underneath it all, despite its city hall and symphony orchestra, its eight hundred beautiful parks ablaze with flowers and elegant with artificial lakes, Johannesburg remained a tough mining-camp. It had its outcasts and castoffs. In the parks the white hoboes sprawled under the scented, white-waxen flowers of the frangipani trees, passing bottles of cheap wine from hand to hand. Drunks waltzed through the center of town, monopolized the public benches in an alcoholic stupor, or lay stretched out on the sidewalks with their heads pillowed in the gutter. These "poor whites" were of both sexes and all ages. But they all had the same tight glaze over cheeks and eyeballs: they were pickled in wine. Banded together in "sherry gangs," they roamed the city streets, often assaulting passers-by. Many a man who had paused too long in a city saloon on his way home from work was trailed by a "sherry gang." He would be found next morning in an alley, stark naked, stripped of both money and every stitch of clothes, and unconscious from a severe kicking by heavy, malignant boots.

Ernie Shirley and I visited the Mei-Mei bazaar, in the heart of the city, a stone's throw from one of the great new concrete apartment houses. We passed through a guarded gate back into primitive Africa. The black medicine men had their stores here: wooden booths over whose doors hung bunches of reptiles' skins, birds' claws and feathers, dried snakeskins, mammalian skeletons. Ranged in neat rows on shelves inside were bottles of "lions' fat," herbs used for making medicine, and powdered love potions. In one of the dark little booths, a very fat white man lay stretched full-length on the floor. His eyes were closed and he was breathing heavily, as if he were drugged. Squatting beside him was a skinny Negro medicine man, dressed in mangy monkey-furs and wearing a monkey-fur cap. He took a pinch of brownish powder in the palm of his hand, mixed it with some fat, and smeared the fat white man's nostrils. The fat man did not stir.

The Mei-Mei medicine men, Ernie said, were visited by whites as well as blacks. The Negroes bought herbs that were supposed to cure their ailments, love potions to regain the affections of their spouses, charms to ward off ill luck, and poison for the destruction of their enemies. The whites who visited the medicine men superstitiously sought Negro cures for cancer and other diseases—and sometimes more sinister Negro aid. There was a considerable belief in the powers of black witchcraft among the "poor whites."

Elsewhere in the Mei-Mei bazaar Negro craftsmen were busily making spears and shields. Tall, powerful Zulus, copperskinned Basutos, and bangle-jangling Transvaal tribesmen mingled in the crowd that choked the bazaar's narrow lanes. All this was within a block or two of Eloff and Commissioner streets, where jewelers' windows blazed with diamonds, and white crowds filled the tea lounges and listened to string orchestras genteelly playing musical-comedy selections.

As business boomed, the city sucked in fresh supplies of indispensable black labor for its growing factories. The Negroes came from as far afield as the Rhodesias and Nyasaland. They swam crocodile-infested rivers and walked hundreds of miles through lion-infested bush to reach the fabulous City of Gold.

Eagerly they crowded into the growing metropolis, trampling underfoot the "pass laws" that were meant to keep their urban numbers manageable. They spilled out of the already crammed locations into new raw shantytowns and squatters' camps, ringing the Golden City like a black rash. Ernie and I visited a squatters' camp, where the Negroes had built rude shelters, made of gunny-sacks stretched over wooden poles. They even lived in "houses" made of cardboard, and in tar-barrels. Women squatted in the thick dust, suckling brown-eyed infants. Everywhere there were great heaps of stinking refuse, swarming with bloated flies. The camp was run by a one-eyed "boss," who deeply distrusted all whites.

We spoke to a tall, handsome white clergyman who had built a church of gunny-sacks in the midst of the squalor and was trying to bring some elements of decency back into the

61

lives of these uprooted people. He told us that babies died faster than they were being born, but that more people were always crowding into the camp. By allowing these squatter camps with their thousands of inhabitants to grow up on its fringes, he said, Johannesburg with all its wealth was risking an epidemic that would be worse than London's Great Plague. "Disease," he added pointedly, "knows no color-bar." But he was disliked by the Negro bosses who ran the camp, and finally his church of sacks was burned down by an inflamed mob and he was forced to leave. Subsequently, he was hauled into court and charged with living in a "native area" without official permission. He was the Reverend Michael Scott.

In the shanties and the camps Negro gang-leaders rose to power, organizing crime on a bigger scale than had yet been known even in Africa's little Chicago, which was what whites who did not live there called Johannesburg. The material ready to the gang-leaders' hands was the Negro kids for whom there were no schools, and who became the new generation of knife-wielding, drug-sodden *tsotsis* (young Negro toughs, black gangsters).

But in the locations, camps, and shantytowns every night was Saturday night too. Fat black *skokiaan* (bootleg) queens rolled out the barrels of illicitly-brewed Kaffir beer, spiked with carbide and methylated spirits, and sometimes more nightmarish ingredients. White police raiding a location beer party upended a barrel to spill its contents on the ground. Out fell a freshly severed human foot. "Putting a kick in the drink," quipped a Johannesburg newspaper in chronicling the incident. In the brawling locations, murders averaged three and one half a day. No one was ever likely to be able to trace the deceased owner of the foot or to discover in what circumstances he had been deprived of it. But everyone knew that the old tribal witch doctors still plied their grisly trade in those human warrens. Part of their ritual demanded human flesh, preferably stripped from the victim while he was still alive. To consume or taste such flesh conferred big magic. Some of the mysterious bottles on the medicine men's shelves in the Mei-Mei bazaar contained more than "lions' fat."

While the locations, shantytowns, and squatters' camps swarmed with Negroes who found jobs in shops and factories, or simply lived a life of crime, there were another 300,000 Negroes who worked in the gold mines. But these Negroes were housed in segregated mine compounds. The all-male labor force was strictly controlled, and provided with organized recreation. The Negroes in their turn provided recreation for white visitors to the mines.

One Sunday we visited a gold mine near the city to see a "tribal dance." With other white rubbernecks, we took our places in a concrete grandstand, sitting on matting made of coir, the elastic fiber from coconut husks, looking down on a sunlit arena. Into the arena there presently shuffled a line of Negroes. Workers in the mine, they had put off their tin helmets and undershirts and wore beads, bangles, and skins; some of them carried blunted spears. The musicians squatted on the hard-baked ground, with tall cylindrical drums, and big wooden "Kaffir pianos," which were a sort of giant xylophone. They slapped the drums and beat on the "pianos," creating a wild, tom-tom rhythm. The dancers shuffled, swayed, and jerked until the sweat was streaming down their faces and naked bodies. Eager whites moved down from the grandstand and walked about between the lines of dancers, with whirring cine-cameras. A good time was had by all.

But suddenly, in the middle of the gold boom, there was unrest in the compounds. "Communists" had furtively organized a trade union of tribal miners. This must have presented some difficulty, for there was a law against more than twenty persons assembling together on "gold-bearing property." The law was used to prevent Negro meetings. Nevertheless the union got itself organized, and claimed to have thousands of members among the miners. The union demanded more pay for the Negroes. The mine-owners refused to recognize the existence of the union. But the Negroes went on strike just the same. In the past the Rand's 30,000 white miners had often struck, and had usually succeeded in getting their demands met, for their union was both recognized and powerful. But for the Negroes to adopt the same methods was unprecedented.

With several hundred thousand tribesmen suddenly idle and ripe for mischief on its doorstep, Johannesburg was almost in a panic. There were rumors that the striking black miners would force their way out of the compounds and march on the city, to begin an orgy of looting and raping. Heavily armed white police drove out to the compounds in army trucks to keep order. At one compound the Negroes tried to get out through the great wooden gate. The police fired on them and drove them back.

After a few days of tension, it was announced that the strike was over and the Negroes were underground again, digging for gold. Few inquired just how the strike had been broken; few cared. The Rand Club heaved a sigh of relief. Johannesburg resumed its gambling in gold stocks. The Negroes went on digging gold.

: 3 :

IN SOUTH AFRICA, financial wizards who make millions in paper come and go, but the really great "Randlords" are as aloof as Olympians from the mere stock-exchange strife.

Every morning a Rolls-Royce glided through the streets of Johannesburg, borne like a burnished black barge on a stream of lesser traffic. Promptly at half past eight it stopped outside a heavily Byzantine-looking building. Up the broad flight of steps, between the two fountains with water tinkling into their great stone basins, marched a spry little gray-haired man who passed through massive bronze doors into the building's cathedral-like interior. Sir Ernest Oppenheimer had begun another day.

The Oppenheimer fortune was built on diamonds, gold, copper, and coal. The Oppenheimers' Anglo-American Corpo-

64

ration controls enterprises worth about $3,000,000,000. These enterprises include six gold mines and four copper mines. The gold mines and the copper mines earn about $70,000,000 a year. But the Oppenheimers also operate diamond mines, which earn about $55,000,000 a year. Lest the price of diamonds should fall, the Anglo-American Corporation keeps a hedge-fund of $180,000,000.

In 1951 Sir Ernest Oppenheimer gave up a number of his chairmanships and directorships: in the President Brand Mining Company, the President Steyn Mining Company, Rand Selections, South African Land & Exploration, Welkom Mines, Brakpan Mines, Daggafontein Mines, Springs Mines, Libanon Gold-mining Company, Blyvooruitzicht Gold-mining Company, St. Helena Gold Mines Ltd., Spaarwater Gold-mining Company, Rand Leases, African Metals, the Vanderbijl Engineering Corporation, and the Union Lime Company. He remained associated, however, either as chairman or as director, with Anglo-American Corporation, De Beers, African Explosives & Chemicals, Anglo-American Investment Trust, Rhodesian Anglo-American, Nchanga Consolidated Copper Mines, Industrial Diamond Distributors, the Diamond Corporation, Consolidated Diamond Mines of South-West Africa, Premier Diamond Mining Company, the Diamond Trading Company, Orange Free State Investment Trust, West Rand Investment Trust, Hambros Bank, Barclays Bank, the British South Africa Company, West Springs Ltd., Companhia de Diamante de Angola, and Western Ultra-Deep Levels. His son Harry was at this time himself a director of forty-five gold-mining, diamond, coal, land, industrial, and finance companies.

The size and complexity of the Oppenheimers' Anglo-American Corporation indicate the concentration of financial power that exists in Johannesburg; for, though now the largest, the corporation is only one of six similar gold-plated trusts based on the Rand. The Oppenheimer pyramid itself consists of seven sub-trusts, controlling diamonds, gold, copper, coal, and real estate, steel and engineering plants, chemical works, finance and food companies. But there is a considerable degree of reciprocity between the Oppenheimer enterprises, held together by the Anglo-American Corporation, and the other five big trusts on the Rand. They hold stock in one another's properties, and it is remarkably difficult to determine precisely where one's sphere of influence really ends and another's begins. So far as gold-mining is concerned, the six big trusts work together through a Chamber of Mines and a Gold Producers' Committee. The committee effectively controls the supply of Negro labor to the gold mines, drawn from all over Africa and funneled to the Rand through a Recruiting Corporation. It also operates the world's largest gold refinery.

This concentration of financial power is not confined in its operations to the continent of Africa: its enterprises encircle the globe. The men of the Rand have interests in tin, oil, rubber, and other raw materials in a score of countries from South America to the Far East. The concentration of power has been achieved in the relatively short space of about sixty years. When the great diamond discoveries were made in South Africa in the 1860's, they quickly led to the formation of over one thousand competing companies. Within a few years nearly all of these had been welded into a single empire by Cecil Rhodes. Similar swift amalgamation followed the discovery of gold on the Rand.

What does it feel like to be a Randlord, possessing great wealth and considerable power in a still half-raw metropolis that is the financial capital of what, until quite recently, was "the Dark Continent"? The simple answer is that nobody save a Randlord knows. But a striking and swift psychological change has occurred to match the swift concentration of power in a few hands. The original Randlords of the late nineteenth century were with few exceptions get-rich-quick schemers and financial buccaneers. Onto a London music-hall stage in the 1890's strode a comedian whose fingers sparkled with diamonds. He produced a large cigar and airily lit it with a five-pound note. He was caricaturing the new South African millionaires, who drank champagne by the case and ate off solid-gold plate. The collective name for them was "Hoggenheimer," the diamond-encrusted, cigar-puffing Jew who manipulated the stock market and lashed his niggers.

Today's Randlords are ultra-conservative and publicity-shy. They do not lead ostentatious lives. But the unseen power of the Gold Producers' Committee in Johannesburg has been compared with that of the Politbureau in Moscow or the College of Cardinals in Rome. They are austere men who know to within a fraction of a pennyweight how much gold a ton of ore will yield. Immensely rich, they make no parade of their wealth. They show emotion only when someone suggests that these are pennyweights from hell, not pennies from heaven. When the Government of a British African territory north of the Limpopo River proposed to check the flow of black labor to the Rand mines on the ground that the steady drain was disrupting the Negroes' tribal life and putting nothing constructive in its place, a spokesman of the Chamber of Mines heatedly attacked this "interference with the freedom of labor to sell itself in the best market." The Negroes recruited by the mines' efficient labor-procuring agencies earn about forty-five cents a day in cash.

The Oppenheimers own and occupy a sprawling many-acred estate in the Johannesburg millionaires' suburb of Parktown, where land is worth up to $15,000 an acre. But, despite a personal collection of diamonds valued at $750,000, such treasures as the diamond-crusted gold snuffbox of the Emperor Franz Josef, a number of valuable paintings, and a remarkable library of first editions, the Oppenheimers live simply. They are easier to talk to than most Randlords.

I drove through open gates, swept up a gravel drive, alighted from the car, and pressed the front-door bell. I was shown into a room whose windows opened on a terrace overlooking a wooded slope. Armchairs and divans were scattered about. Framed photographs of Oppenheimer grandchildren stood on a piano. Over the fireplace hung a Renoir.

A small gray-haired man in a plain gray suit slipped unobtrusively into the room. He spoke with a perceptible German accent, and his hazel eyes were quietly amused.

67

When in a private house you are shown a chandeliered reception room sufficiently regal for kings to hold audiences in, you politely express admiration. From the trim little man in whose soft white hands, smelling faintly of cologne, there reposed so much power, my politeness evoked a flickering grin.

"Rather amusing, I think," he said.

It was not the phrase I would have chosen. But a particularly choice blue diamond in his private collection was also "amusing." So was the Renoir; so were the first editions.

He looked at me, ducked his head, and made a quick, amused gesture with his soft hands. "Now sit down, make yourself comfortable, and have a whisky and soda," he commanded.

As he sipped his, his mild eyes studied me quizzically, and I felt that he was thinking I was "amusing" too. In short, he was quietly laughing at me. He seemed to regard his wealth and power as something slightly preposterous, and the world and people as chiefly a source of gentle fun.

Sir Ernest Oppenheimer was born on May 22, 1880, in Friedberg, a little German town near Frankfurt; he was the fourth son of a German Jew who owned a tobacconist's shop. Two older brothers, Bernard and Louis, went into the diamond business, worked for a time in Kimberley in the days when Cecil Rhodes was creating De Beers, the great diamond-mining company based on the Kimberley mines, and then joined the London diamond firm of Anton Dunkelsbuhler & Co. Ernest joined the firm in 1896.

"My path," he told me gently, "was made smooth. My parents, and my brothers, doted on me." By the time he joined them in business, both Louis and Bernard were already wealthy men. In 1902, the year Cecil Rhodes died, he was sent to Kimberley to study diamond-mining. Kimberley, the scene of the early diamond rushes, of rough bearded miners living in tents, drinking brandy out of the bottle, and cursing the Kaffirs, had begun to lose its Bret Harte overtones. There were churches, and the men wore top-hats.

A new mine had just been discovered, three hundred miles from Kimberley, and near Pretoria. But the men of Kimberley apparently found it impossible to conceive that diamond discoveries made outside their area could amount to much. Oppenheimer persuaded his brothers to believe otherwise, and Dunkelsbuhler & Co. acquired shares in the new mine, which were subsequently sold at a handsome profit to De Beers. "That," he told me, "was the first real money I ever made." The mine later yielded the Cullinan Diamond, which became part of the royal crown and scepter of Britain.

For his part in the Premier Mine transaction, Oppenheimer incurred the enmity of powerful De Beers directors. They felt he had outwitted them. The feud did not end until 1929, when Oppenheimer became a director of De Beers himself. The purchase of shares in the Premier Mine near Pretoria was his first big coup. His second was when he persuaded Dunkelsbuhler to invest money in the gold mines on the East Rand. Over a million dollars were required. To raise this sum, the Anglo-American Corporation was formed. Among the original investors were J. Pierpont Morgan and Herbert Hoover. The East Rand mines proved to be highly profitable. With his share of the profits, Oppenheimer bought out German diamond-producers in South-West Africa. By acquiring those remote diamond fields, which proved exceptionally rich, he put himself in a position to buy his way into the citadel of De Beers. By 1926 he had quietly acquired fifty per cent of De Beers shares. The next step was to buy control of the Northern Rhodesia copper belt.

In the late twenties and early thirties, new diamond discoveries threatened to depress the price of diamonds below the profit-making level. The South African Government threw open large tracts of diamond-bearing land to "poor whites." De Beers was compelled to buy up the large quantities of diamonds thus produced, in order to keep them off the world market. Oppenheimer, who had been appointed chairman of De Beers, formed a Diamond Corporation for this purpose. The Diamond Corporation acquired 36,000,000 dollars' worth of diamonds that it did not dare try to dispose of. The severe attack of indigestion it incurred did not begin to pass off until 1937.

Sir Ernest Oppenheimer sipped his whisky and soda. "These were my years of struggle," he said, like a historian surveying a grim era.

Until then, he confessed, he had been regarded by many as a flippant fellow. He owned racehorses, gave large parties, and was suspected of tossing a coin to decide whether he would attend a board meeting or go fishing. Then he applied himself solely to business, worked a sixteen-hour day six days a week, and acquired the knack of being able to quote complicated figures accurately for several hours, without recourse to notes.

His personal life also took unexpected turns at this time. His nephew, Sir Michael Oppenheimer, son of his brother Bernard, was killed in a flying accident in Johannesburg. A few months later Sir Ernest's wife died. A year later his son Frank was drowned at Madeira. Two months afterwards Sir Ernest married his deceased nephew's widow. By this marriage, she remained Lady Oppenheimer; he acquired an eleven-year-old stepson who was also his great-nephew; and Harry Oppenheimer, Sir Ernest's own son, acquired a stepmother who had previously been his cousin's wife.

The recovery of the diamond market, combined with the growing prosperity of Anglo-American Corporation's East Rand gold properties, put the Oppenheimers in an especially advantageous position. The East Rand mines were yielding fifty-one per cent of South Africa's total gold production, which at that time, in the mid-thirties, was valued at $200,000,000 a year. Copper and coal were also making large profits.

Oppenheimer turned his restless attention to the possibility of finding a new Rand in the Orange Free State. Another Randlord, Sammy Marks, had established among other enterprises a landholding company that held mining options over thousands of corn-waving acres in the Orange Free State. A favorite remark of Sammy Marks was: "Second-hand clothes don't fit well; I know, for I began my career as a dealer in second-hand clothes." But a large part of Oppenheimer's career had been devoted to buying up second-hand clothes, then going through the pockets and finding unexpected fortunes. He had realized the value of the Premier Mine before De Beers. The South-West African diamond fields produced riches for him that had eluded their original German owners. The same applied to the East Rand mines. Now he acquired from Marks's heirs the Orange Free State mining options. A borehole sunk on the farm *Geduld*, which means "Patience," yielded colossal values, which ensured the establishment of thirteen new gold mines over an area twenty-eight miles long and seven miles wide. Oppenheimer's holdings in the new area, added to Anglo-American Corporation's many other enterprises, made him the most powerful of the Randlords.

And the lord of diamonds, gold, copper, and coal might in the atomic age also be the lord of uranium. During the Second World War, South Africa's Prime Minister, Jan Christiaan Smuts, made acquainted with the outline of the Manhattan Project by his friend Winston Churchill, with the approval of Franklin Roosevelt, gave secret instructions that the uranium content of the Rand gold mines should be ascertained. The mines were found to be rich in uranium, and the new Free State goldfields are no less rich. South Africa is expected to become a leading uranium-producer, and the Oppenheimer empire will play a large part in this development.

On my way home after saying good-by to the courteous little man, I drove past the dark-gray bulk of the Witwatersrand University. And I remembered how I had once talked there with Professor Herbert Frankel, South Africa's leading economist, and what he had said to me. "This country," said Frankel, "has a system of an open society and a closed society. The superstructure is at times as brilliant as Hollywood. But the foundations are those of slavery, serfdom, ignorance, rigidity; of laws against the rights to till or own land; against movement; against rights to education, work, and immigration."

Johannesburg is built on a series of ridges, and the gray university stands on one of them. From there you can see the city spread out around you: the tall concrete buildings of the midtown section; the looming masses of the intruding mine-dumps; the streets and houses that stretch away, until white Johannesburg abruptly becomes black Johannesburg, with its sprawling overcrowded locations, shantytowns, and disease-ridden squatter camps. It was night, and the city flared garishly. Green and crimson neon signs snapped on and off. Lights gleamed in the apartment houses crowded on the Hillbrow ridge. Far off, lights gleamed also on a minehead, where great cages raised and lowered sweating black men, faster than Manhattan's swiftest elevators, to and from depths exceeding a mile. Down there, in the bowels of the earth, lay the secret source of the city's crude strength, the yellow metal that had created this fevered patch of shifting lights on the empty veld. And now to gold would be added uranium, a yellow mud that might be used to make atomic bombs, which might devastate other cities, far away.

Johannesburg sprawled and spawned around me, restless, unsleeping, built of concrete, its million lights flashing under the white African stars, an alien ferment in the heart of Africa: race melting-pot, city of yellow metal and yellow mud, of white *baas* and black Kaffir.

In whose hands, I wondered, lay the power.

VI

SOUTH AFRICA: THE CITY AND THE TIGER

THE *tsotsi* ran down the middle of the Johannesburg street. His head was thrown back, his thin chest heaved, and he furiously pumped his pipe-stem arms. His wide-brimmed hat had fallen off, and he wore no jacket. On his gay-colored shirt, between his gaunt shoulder-blades, a sweat patch spread. Two white policemen pounded after him, blowing whistles and drawing their revolvers.

The crowd of Negroes on the sidewalk shouted: *"Hamba!"* which means "Go!" cheering the *tsotsi* on. But a white traffic cop stepped out from between two parked cars, and thrust a fat calf encased in black leather between the *tsotsi's* legs, tripping him. He fell heavily, and the two panting white cops as well as the traffic cop piled on him and hauled him to his feet. He wriggled like a black fish as they tried to put handcuffs on him.

The policemen were suddenly aware of being surrounded by a black crowd. Three white men stood with their black captive in the middle of the sunlit street, encircled by the hostile black faces. Sensing their irresolution and the crowd's partisanship, the *tsotsi* suddenly wriggled free and dived into the crowd, which absorbed him. The three whites started to go after him, and the crowd closed in.

A fat Indian shopkeeper who had been watching went swiftly indoors.

That night there was fighting in several parts of the city. Negroes collected stones and threw them through the windows

73

of streetcars reserved for whites. They also smashed and looted Indian stores. The white police, armed with rifles, chased from one storm-center to another in trucks. There was a good deal of shooting.

All this happened in Johannesburg in 1949 because the white policemen tried to arrest the *tsotsi*. A *tsotsi* is a young detribalized Negro who has grown up in the city slums and has become a gangster. The *tsotsis* of Johannesburg wear wide-brimmed soft hats, pulled low over their watchful eyes, bright-colored shirts, and flaming ties. On their thin wrists they wear large silver watches that don't run. They smoke *dagga*, which is the same as marijuana, and they can handle a knife with deadly effect.

The particular *tsotsi* whom the black crowd helped rescue from the white policemen was being pursued because he had just stabbed a young Negro girl to death. But the crowd did not pause to find this out. They went to his aid, with no questions asked, because he was black and the police were white.

In the gaunt barracks of the Johannesburg police headquarters, in Marshall Square, with its dirty stone corridors and broken-paned windows, a white detective talked to me about black crime. "It's growing," he said prophetically, "and it will get worse. Walk down any alley and you'll be lucky if you come out without a knife in your back.

"Of course," he said, smiling thinly, "nobody cares what happens in the locations—except the poor bloody police who have to go in there, and the poor bloody law-abiding Kaffirs who get beaten and raped and murdered every night by the *tsotsi* gangs. But will the blacks stay forever in their 'locations'? When they start to come out, at night, with knives, they'll go for the fine white houses with the swimming-pools and the tennis-courts. You'll see."

The townward stampede of uprooted Negroes was fast producing chaos. I visited the Johannesburg pass office, which was supposed to control the influx. Bewildered Negroes queued up around the grimy building and stood four deep in dingy corridors, waiting to be issued passes allowing them to live and work in the city. Sometimes they got them, and sometimes they landed in jail for not already having them.

My second visit to the pass office was on personal business. I'd hired a "boy" who was seeking work and sent him to the pass office to have his papers put in order. He waited in the queue every day for a week. On the eighth day he went off to the pass office again and did not return. So I went to see what had happened to him.

A dispirited official consulted a tattered book, then called in another official. They pored over the book, muttering names. None of them was the name of my man.

One of the officials had an idea. "Could it," he asked the other official, "be the one that escaped yesterday?"

The other official brightened for a moment, then shook his head. "No, we got him back, but he had a different name."

"Do you keep these people locked up here?" I asked, surprised.

They looked at me in silent pity. "If their papers aren't in order, we hold them for the police."

Somewhere in the dingy building, I thought, there must be detention cells; my man might be in one of them now, but it did not look as if I should ever find out.

The first official bent over the book again and stabbed at a name with his finger.

"Did you say 'Joseph Dhlamini'?"

"That," I said, "is what I've been saying for the past half-hour."

"Ah," said the first official. He closed the book and looked at his friend in triumph. "That's the one."

"That's the one," said the second official.

"Well," I said, "what *happened* to him?"

"Man," said the second official, beaming broadly, "there's been a mistake." He laughed. "We sent him off this morning in a truck to Louis Trichardt. We thought he was a prohibited immigrant!"

I recovered my servant two days later, somewhat the worse for wear. But this time he got his pass.

Johannesburg's black crime wave mounted, just as my friend the detective had prophesied. He rang me up one evening. "How would you like to see a war?"

"Where," I asked suspiciously, "is it?"

"Western Townships," he said cheerily. "Bloody murder going on. With bayonets."

In the Western Townships area, Negroes, half-castes, and poor whites lived cheek by jowl, in a maze of dirty streets and back alleys cut across by streetcar and railroad tracks. My friend picked me up and explained the position as he drove.

"There's a gang of Basutos who call themselves 'the Russians.' They've been terrorizing one of the other Negro sections. This morning two of the Basuto leaders got out of a train at the Newclare station. A rival gang had prepared a reception party. One Basuto was knifed as he stepped off the train; the other had his head split open on the platform. Brains all over the place. Now, tonight, the Basutos are threatening to take their revenge."

The two warring territories were divided by the railroad track, which was crossed by a bridge. The bridge was guarded by white policemen, armed with rifles. We stood on the bridge in the thick dusk. On either side of the tracks the huddled hovels were unlighted. But periodically, out of the darkness, came a wild, bloodcurdling yell. "They're working themselves up," said my detective friend philosophically. The uniformed policemen said nothing, but hitched their rifles higher. Under their helmets their faces were expressionless.

The first wave of invaders were "the Russians," but they did not try to storm across the bridge, guarded by the policemen. Under cover of the darkness, they slipped down the steep embankment and ran across the tracks. Their opponents were waiting for them, and before the police knew what was happening, a pitched battle was in progress.

Thrown back, "the Russians" tried to cross into their own territory again, this time over the guarded bridge. They were huge men, wrapped in gaudy-patterned blankets, and under their blankets they clutched a fearsome miscellany of weapons

—butchers' knives, iron bars, spears, rusty bayonets, axes, and knobkerries (short clubs with a knobbed end, used as missiles). When they saw the police, they began dropping their weapons, and the police contented themselves with disarming them, cuffing them, and chasing them across the bridge into their own area.

Presently another horde of angry Negroes, also armed, charged onto the bridge in pursuit of the fleeing "Russians." They, too, stopped when they saw the police, who calmly formed a line across the bridge and significantly lifted their rifles. The job of the police evidently was to prevent the two sides from clashing, but not to arrest anybody. The second batch of Negroes sullenly retreated, and quiet descended on the scene.

But later that night, after the police had withdrawn, the "Russians" came back in force and drove the rival Negroes from their homes, which they triumphantly occupied. The dispossessed Negroes built temporary shacks for themselves on an open square, and appealed to the authorities to eject the "Russians."

"What will happen now?" I asked my detective friend.

"Nothing," he said calmly. "The war is over and the 'Russians' have won."

Months later, the "Russians" were still occupying the displaced Negroes' homes, and the displaced Negroes were still camping disconsolately on the square.

All this happened within three miles of Johannesburg's palm-tree-flanked city hall, with its marble staircases and crimson carpets, in the center of the city.

As black crime increased, tension and fear stalked the city streets and crept like a dark tide over the suburbs. People preferred not to walk about at night; and when they went to bed they kept revolvers under their pillows. They put steel bars over their windows, and bought great Danes. For a large and growing city, Johannesburg after dark presented an odd spectacle: miles of well-lit streets, stretching away on every side, lined with carefully shuttered shops and stores, and all deserted save for the Negro night watchmen huddled in the doorways with knobkerries over their knees. It was as if, each night, the city's white population vanished into thin air. Even during the daytime the streetcars for whites, whose routes passed colored areas, were protected with stout wire mesh against frequent stone-throwing. After dark, outside of a small central area occupied by cinemas and restaurants, there were no whites to be seen.

The Great Gold Reef extends for one hundred miles east and west of Johannesburg. All along the Reef are satellite mining towns, from Krugersdorp and Roodepoort in the west to Germiston and Springs in the east. Each little mining town has its own location for its Negroes. Some of these locations were fenced in and guarded like internment camps. But the Reef towns, too, were deserts of well-lit, empty streets after dark. At night the whole Reef glowed and glittered, but there were few people abroad. It was like an abandoned fair.

"What's the use of having a garden if the price you pay for it is having to sleep with a loaded revolver under your pillow?"

The man who asked the question owned a large house in one of Johannesburg's pleasant suburbs. The house overlooked trim lawns, their privacy opulently ensured by a mile of encircling hedge. But the black tide of the shantytowns had lapped closer, and there were frequent housebreakings in the neighborhood.

The incident of the garden "boy" was the last straw. Hailed as a docile treasure, this man's garden "boy" had dramatically turned out to be a main prop of the African National Congress, a fiery talker at location meetings, where unsmiling black faces were willingly upturned to him when he denounced the white *baas*. The police had come and taken him away, but he still left uneasiness behind in that hitherto tranquil white home where, if my friend's wife dropped a knitting needle, she rang a little silver bell and a servant came to pick it up for her.

"We're moving into an apartment," said my friend. "It won't be half as comfortable, but it will be a lot safer."

Of all Johannesburg's half a million black folk, the "flat-boys" were considered the luckiest and the most reliable. In the safe heart of the city, up on the Hillbrow ridge, the "flat-boys" went smiling about their work in their blue canvas uniforms, their big bare feet slapping on the teak floors they kept so highly polished. "They are the 'raw' ones straight from the kraals," my friend explained. "The agitators can't get at them, because they don't live in the locations, but have their own quarters, up on the roofs of the apartment houses."

He seemed to think it was just like having your own compound, as if you were a gold mine.

I wondered if he or any other white person knew what really went on inside the kinky head of a "flat-boy." One Johannesburg lady who tried to find out got a disconcerting answer.

Her devoted "flat-boy" was down on his bare knees polishing the floor. All she could see was the top of that kinky black head. His name was Joseph, she knew. It suddenly occurred to her that that was all she knew about him. In her hand was the morning newspaper, and in the paper was the lurid report of a particularly atrocious murder, of a white woman "by natives." She looked speculatively at Joseph's bent, submissive woolly head. The thought that had occurred to her, she knew, was utterly foolish. "Why," as she said later, "I've often left the children alone with Joseph. He *adores* them!" But the thought nevertheless simply wouldn't be suppressed. And, acting on crazy impulse, she broke one of the unwritten laws regulating the relations between white and black in the black man's continent: she addressed a black person as a human being instead of as an animated scrubbing-brush and asked a personal question.

"Joseph," she blurted out, "you would never harm *me*, would you? Or the children? Or any of us? I mean," she floundered on as Joseph raised his kinky head and gazed at her, apparently uncomprehending, with his big brown eyes, so like a faithful hound's, "I mean—I know you black people aren't always treated right—and there's a lot of bad feeling between white folk and black—but you would never—?"

She stopped, in utter confusion.

79

Joseph wasn't confused. He grinned. Then he said: "No, missus. When time comes, I go next-door flat, kill that missus. Next-door 'flat-boy,' he come here, kill *you*."

And he went on with his polishing.

: 4 :

LIKE EVERYONE else who lived in Johannesburg, Jane and I in our years there slowly changed in our attitude to the city. We became Johannesburgers and found ourselves defending the place, almost jealously, against critics.

Johannesburg is the largest white (as well as the largest Negro) city in Africa south of the deserts. Most whites in Africa live in small communities; most Negroes still live in tiny villages. I have met white men who regarded Johannesburg with an almost superstitious fear. It gave them claustrophobia, stunned them with its glamor, horrified them by its sheer mass. One Rhodesian admitted to me that on his first visit (which was also his last) he drove, sweating, with his family through a nightmare of traffic, holed up thankfully in a hotel for the night, and left next morning at sunrise, when the streets were still empty. Whites elsewhere in Africa, including the Union itself, regard Johannesburg as Midwesterners who have never been there regard New York.

Nevertheless, there came a time when we would have lived nowhere else in Africa. Cape Town is more genteel: it is to Johannesburg what Boston is to New York. Durban has its golden beaches. Bulawayo and Salisbury are pretty towns. Nairobi is trim. But Johannesburg is alive. It crackles with energy, conquers by sheer, brute strength. It is raw, rugged, brutal, sophisticated, immensely rich, appallingly poor, all at the same time. It is like a clenched fist raised to strike, a black cloud presaging doom. And then, one fall day when the air is like champagne, or one spring morning when green buds are bursting on the trees, or one velvet evening when the noise of the traffic is stilled and two Negroes pass by, softly plucking at

80

guitars while their warm Negro laughter fills the air, you discover that the city is beautiful, and may even have, tucked away somewhere, a heart. And after that you never quite shake off its spell. "It's like living with a tiger," said Ernie Shirley. "Dangerous, but attractive."

There came a time, at the height of the boom, when there was an uneasiness in the air, like the tightening tension that precedes a Johannesburg thunderstorm. One day I went to see my friend the financier. He had scribbled me a list of shares I ought to buy if I wanted to be in on a good thing, but I had never got around to it. I noticed, however, that the shares he mentioned had indeed gone up, to the figure he had predicted. And then, mysteriously, they had slumped. It seemed that I had missed my chance.

I had seen him on several occasions, an untidy, rotund little man, always talking and gesturing and being whisked away to somewhere else by anxious secretaries. Once I glimpsed him at a large dinner party, looking curiously unreal in formal evening dress. On another occasion I saw him open one of his own new factories, accompanied by a Cabinet Minister. That time he had a smut on the side of his nose, and needed a haircut, but seemed to be thoroughly enjoying himself. But there was a blunt Yorkshireman there who listened to him with a doubting smile. When he had finished expounding something to the Cabinet Minister, I heard the Yorkshireman mutter sardonically: "Don't meddle with real things like machinery, Herbert, my lad: stick to your paper shares—so long as you're sure *they* won't let you down."

He had his headquarters at the top of a large building that bore the name of his biggest company. Outside large double doors of frosted glass and chromium, a man in uniform wrote your name in a book and spoke into a telephone before letting you through. Beyond the double doors was a suite of offices.

There seemed to be a good deal of confusion. A fat man smoking a cigar was trying to pacify two women with metallic-looking blond hair who were arguing furiously. Another man was looking gloomily out of the window, with his hands behind his back. A third man, very red-eyed as if he had not had any sleep for a long time, was reading a typed sheet covered with figures. I noticed that his hands were shaking.

Nobody paid any attention to me, until a door burst open and my financier thrust himself into the room. He stopped short, staring at me, and I was dismayed by the change in his appearance. It wasn't that he was untidy, he was always that; but his features, which I remembered to be round and merry, seemed to have run like tallow, and his cheeks were the same color. He had shrunk. He passed a hand through his tangled black hair as we stared at each other; and then he recognized me and advanced with a laugh that was too loud.

"My dear chap, it's you, at last!" He grinned like a rueful but still plucky shark. "Only you're a bit late."

The two women had stopped quarreling to gape. The fat man snatched at his cigar and opened his mouth to say something. The red-eyed man started up. Only the man with his back to the room went on looking somberly out of the window.

He ignored them all and with an arm round my shoulders began to walk back into his inner office.

The fat man, in an injured voice, began: "Now, look here, old chap, I've been waiting for—"

"Herbie!" squealed one of the women. "Herbie!"

He turned round and looked at them, as if seeing them for the first time. The red-eyed man holding the typed sheet of figures he ignored. But to the others he said, coldly: "Shut up!"

Then we were in his own room, with the door closed on them. It was a large, richly furnished office, with two walnut desks, a thick carpet, and a glass-fronted bookcase. He strode up and down the carpet between the desks, on which stood several telephones. He looked absurdly like a trapped Napoleon, except that the knot of his tie had vanished under a wing of his collar, and his hair was savagely rumpled. It was the tie of a famous English public school; his father, the old German Jew who had emigrated to South Africa, had had his son educated in England.

"Bloodsuckers!" he said, smashing a fist on one of the desks as he passed it. "Leeches! Bloody parasites!" He turned to me and forced a pale grin. "They're out for what they can get, old man. Always have been. But now it's salvage they want. They think there may be something in the wreck for them, even now."

I stared at him, uncomprehending.

"Everything's going smash," he said. He seemed to be enjoying himself in an ugly sort of way. "No more mink coats for Mae. No more pretty diamonds for Peg. That fat chap—"

"Yes?" I said.

"My cousin," he sneered. "We called him Useless Lucius. Never did a day's work in his life. He's been getting credit on the strength of my name. Now he wonders how he's going to meet his bills. No more hot tips from good old Herb, eh?" He looked at me and asked sharply: "Those shares I told you to buy. Did you buy them?"

"No," I said meekly, "I forgot."

"More fool you," he said. "You could have made a pile. I did. No use now, though." He rubbed his eyes, and the gesture seemed to remind him of something. "One of the fellows out there is the manager of my new factory. I took him away from a good position, offered him double salary. Now he'll be out of a job, unless they keep him on. I feel sorry for *him*. The other chap," he said casually, "is a detective."

He took a bottle and glasses out of a desk drawer. "Have a drink?"

"No, thanks," I said.

"Then you don't mind if I do." He poured whisky with one hand and flipped open a box of cigars with the other. His hands were remarkably steady. He lit his cigar with a flourish and raised his glass. "Well, here's to crime!"

"What did you do?" I asked curiously.

"They'll say I stole a million or two. I didn't. All I did was to borrow—a temporary loan, from one of my own companies." He scowled. "I offered to make good the money," he shouted. "I had it, too. My check was good. But they wouldn't take it. Oh, no. I'd broken the Companies Act—or some damned

83

thing. Who ever heard such rot? It's done every day, they all do it." He mentioned powerful names. "But it was a frame-up, you see: they wanted to smash me. Little Herbie had got too big for his boots. And they've succeeded, damn them!"

Later I read in the evening papers that he had been arrested. The trial was a big affair, but only a skilled accountant could have followed the evidence in detail. Breath-taking sums were mentioned, mountains of ledgers produced and compared. The affairs of over a score of companies were involved. Somehow the pyramid had collapsed and the crisscrossing channels that irrigated it with money had sprung a leak. In the dock he was confident at first, but then he began to quarrel with his lawyers and insisted on writing out long statements and trying to read them to the judge. He also wrote a remarkable series of letters to every member of the Cabinet, identifying his enterprises with the prosperity of the country and warning of national calamities unless he were set free. But it seemed he was not, after all, quite so important as that. The judge found him guilty of "embezzlement on a gigantic scale," and sent him to prison for a number of years. But there were no national calamities, and the great gold boom went on.

VII

SOUTH AFRICA: BOER MOSES

ONE RED-HOT afternoon in 1948, when the flat-topped *kopjes* were casting sharp shadows and the cornstalks were nodding drowsily on the sun-baked plains, a train toiled across the high plateau of the Transvaal and halted at the Potchefstroom railroad station. Onto the cindery platform stepped a fat old man who looked as if he were smelling a bad egg. Despite the heat, he wore a heavy dark suit, and a high, old-fashioned collar constricted his thick neck. He carried his hat in his hand, and the fierce sun beat on a large bald head covered with brown freckles. Respectfully awaiting him were a number of bearded Boer farmers, and Boer professors from Potchefstroom University College. A small band struck up a patriotic Boer air. One of the professors advanced and surprisingly mantled the distinguished visitor in the ample folds of a *vierkleur*, the old Boer republican flag. The elderly gentleman smiled for the first time. "South Africa," he declared in his strong preacher's voice, "is again ours!" The crowd cheered.

Dr. Daniel Francois Malan, the Boers' Moses, wandered for fifteen years in the political wilderness looking for the road to Canaan before at the age of seventy-three he defeated General Jan Christiaan Smuts, who was seventy-five.

If his victory surprised even himself, as is probable, Dangerous Dan Malan concealed the fact well. But for most Englishmen in South Africa the defeat of Smuts and the victory of

85

Malan came like a staggering reversal of the order of nature. They simply could not believe it had happened. It was like the end of the world—as for them, in a sense, it was.

"Damn it!" said a dazed Englishman. *"Malan wanted Hitler to win the war!"*

English South Africans assured themselves that the new Boer ascendancy couldn't possibly last, and waited for the Malan government to collapse.

But I had watched the Boer nation being won over to Malan by well-tried methods. Malan's Nationalists stayed home and studied Nazism while Smuts's armies were away helping to fight the *Führer*. Malan's victory over Smuts was the culmination of a Boer emotional orgy which combined the clamor and glitter of a three-ring circus with the fine frenzy of a religious revival. The Nationalists grew beards to demonstrate Boer virility. At their huge open-air campfire meetings, they ate basinfuls of mutton chops, consumed yards of thick sausage, lustily bawled hymns, and beat up political dissenters with knuckledusters. They unfurled republican flags, at the sight of which all present wept copiously and recalled atrocities inflicted by the British on Boer women and children in concentration camps during the Boer War. They swore mighty oaths, and sang patriotic songs. In lumbering ox-wagons they trekked hundreds of miles up and down South Africa, and prayed earnestly to God to be relieved of the yoke placed on their necks by the English. Boer children, wearing Boer uniforms, marched in endless processions, and vowed to be undyingly faithful to the *volk*, crying: *"Hou koers!"*—"Hold steadfast!"

Dr. Malan was the *Volksleier*, or Boer *Führer*. A paunchy and pugnacious old man, he had no doubt at all that he was chosen by God to lead the Boer *volk* to freedom. At a tumultuous Nationalist rally I heard him declare unsmilingly: "There are only two opinions: the wrong one, and mine." Everybody cheered.

When Malan beat Smuts, the English South Africans not unnaturally shivered in their shoes. They felt that the day of wrath was at hand. It was anticipated that Dangerous Dan would proceed to make his Boer folk a *Herrenvolk* in a republic run by the Nazi-style storm-troopers of the Nationalist Party.

Malan loved to make long speeches. His orations seldom lasted less than two hours. I heard him speak to his Boers at the Voortrekker Monument near Pretoria. He lengthily traced the political history of South Africa from the year 1838 onwards, giving an almost day-by-day account. The monument had been built to commemorate the Boers' victory at the Battle of Blood River over the Zulu chief Dingaan, who had previously massacred a small party of Boers after promising them safe passage. Listening to Malan harangue, an irreverent South African whispered to me behind his hand: "Dingaan at least was briefer; he just said: 'Kill the white wizards.' "

The man who had defeated Smuts was the antithesis of Smuts. Even in his middle seventies Smuts walked lithely. He often donned a bush-shirt and shorts and went scrambling up the steep slope of Table Mountain like a schoolboy. Malan, two years younger, walked heavily on his two flat feet, and took as little exercise as possible. Smuts crackled with life, but Malan was as ponderous as an overweight owl.

South Africans told this story about Smuts and Malan:

Smuts and Malan were having an argument about whether the Jew or the Afrikaner was the shrewder businessman. Smuts said the Jews were shrewder, Malan said the Afrikaners were. Smuts proposed an experiment to decide who was right.

Smuts and Malan first visited an Afrikaner store. Smuts asked to see some teacups. When the trader produced some, Smuts said he had to have left-handled teacups. The Afrikaner storekeeper apologized for not having any.

Smuts and Malan then visited a Jewish store, where Smuts asked to see teacups, the Jew produced some, and Smuts explained that he wanted left-handled teacups. The Jewish trader beamed, whisked the teacups away, and brought them back again turned round, so that the handles were on the left side. Smuts bought them.

On leaving the shop, Smuts said to Malan: "You see?"

Malan shook his head. "It doesn't prove anything," he

argued. "It was a pure coincidence that the Jew happened to have left-handled teacups in stock."

Politically astute, Malan was also excessively absent-minded. When a South African cricket team was about to sail for England, somebody thought it would be a good idea for the Prime Minister to shake them by the hand before they embarked. The members of the team were brought to the House of Assembly in Cape Town, and Malan came out to greet them. He shook hands all round, but disconcertingly said he hoped they had enjoyed their visit to South Africa. He had mistaken them for an English cricket team returning to England.

Nevertheless the apparently slow-witted Malan beat Smuts politically. By doing so, he became the most influential man in Africa. And the English trembled for their future.

There was certainly no doubt about Malan's almost Svengali-like influence over his own supporters. One of the very few Afrikaners who did not fall under the old man's spell told me: "If Malan got up tomorrow and praised the British Empire instead of denouncing it, the Boers would instantly say he had been inspired by God and would start waving Union Jacks." There seemed, however, to be no immediate danger of this happening. When Malan visited Holland, he was asked by a Dutch journalist why, during the Second World War, he had sympathized with Hitler. Malan indignantly denied it, but added revealingly: "We were not pro-German, only anti-English."

As Prime Minister, Malan took over from Smuts an official residence in Cape Town: the sprawling, white-gabled mansion called *Groote Schuur*, the Big Barn, which had belonged to Cecil Rhodes. He also acquired another official residence in Pretoria, and a third in Natal.

His Nationalist ministers and their wives drove around in shiny Cadillacs and Packards. Malan nevertheless continued to denounce pomp and the evils of great wealth.

Malan's second wife, Maria, was thirty years her husband's junior. She was a lively, handsome woman with Irish as well as Boer blood, and had been a Nationalist Party organizer. Malan married her after the death of his first wife, by whom he had two sons. He and Maria adopted a German war orphan, a little girl whom they called *Marietjie*, or little Maria.

Malan did not like to give newspaper interviews, save in the form of lengthy written answers to questions he himself had helped to frame, like messages handed down from Mount Sinai.

He also disliked being photographed. At official garden parties he sat in the brilliant South African sunshine, wearing a silk top-hat, formal black cutaway coat and striped trousers, glaring disapprovingly at photographers, and looking as if he had been stuffed.

The best pictures ever taken of him were by my friend David Douglas Duncan, of *Life*. Malan was taking part in a tree-planting ceremony on the slope of Table Mountain. Dave sat down beside him and proceeded to take pictures. Malan took his wife's hand in his, and Dave raised his camera. Malan at once released his wife's hand and frowned majestically.

"Hold her hand!" Dave insisted, and Malan sheepishly obeyed.

When a burly plain-clothes detective who was the Prime Minister's bodyguard tried to shoo Dave away, Malan motioned the detective aside.

The Boers, normally an austere and God-fearing people, have a weakness for fancy costume. During the Second World War a Boer who shared Malan's antipathy for British imperialism and who wanted Germany to win the war embarked on a bold career of sabotage. He and his followers tried to blow up troop trains, though generally they only succeeded in blowing up themselves. Some Boer policemen were so struck with admiration of this band that they let the leader slip through their fingers after they had surrounded his hiding-place. He had taken refuge in a sympathizer's house. When the policemen arrived, he asked them, as a favor, to let him have a bath before they took him away. The police obligingly retired, and he escaped out of the bathroom window.

Finally, after boasting that he would never be taken alive, he was captured on Christmas Eve, on his way to Pretoria. To the amazement of all, he was wearing a paper cap and a false nose. He explained that he had been attending a children's party. A court was uncharitable enough to find him guilty of treason, but he was, of course, released as soon as Malan came to power.

Malan's followers dressed themselves up in old Voortrekker costumes. The men wore beards and powder-horns, and the women wore long skirts and poke-bonnets. When South Africa celebrated the tercentenary of Jan van Riebeeck, the first Governor of the Cape, the wives of the Cabinet ministers, including Mrs. Malan, wore period costumes and posed as governors' wives of the seventeenth century. Mrs. Malan wore a velvet skullcap and a dress of rich black brocade and old gold. The ladies performed stately minuets before a large and admiring crowd. Even when the pageant was over, the ladies showed a marked reluctance to put off their colorful costumes; they continued to wear them for some days, to the bewilderment of tourists coming off the ships at Cape Town. The tourists said it gave them an eerie feeling to turn a corner and see a lady in seventeenth-century attire advancing toward them.

Mrs. Malan caused quite a stir by wearing her period costume to a Governor-General's formal garden party. Then she regretfully put it away. But when she visited London in 1953 to attend Queen Elizabeth's coronation, she took her seventeenth-century costume with her. Unfortunately, no opportunity arose of wearing it; she wore a mantilla instead. Dr. Malan wore his silk top-hat and sponge-bag trousers.

A number of Boer republicans were aghast that, after five years of Malan's rule, there was still no sign of a republic, and Malan had gone to the English Queen's coronation. Some of them also muttered against the ostentation of several of Malan's ministers and their smartly dressed wives, who now did not hesitate to appear in public wearing make-up. It was said that they were no better than the wealthy and sinful British whom they had condemned so loudly in the past. But nobody dared criticize Malan openly. The road to Canaan might seem devious, but Moses knew best.

: 2 :

DANIE MALAN and Jannie Smuts were born in the fruitful Cape, on neighboring farms. Their parents were friends. They attended the same Sunday school. When Smuts went to Stellenbosch University, Malan followed him shortly after. The first person to greet Malan was Smuts. "Danie!" he cried in welcome, and the two went off, arm in arm. They were a contrasting pair, for Smuts was tall and thin, Malan squat and podgy. Smuts was a brilliant scholar, Malan a plodder. Between such men, hero-worship will always alternate with envy, and half-conscious patronage breed distrust. They were to oppose each other all their long lives.

Smuts, the thin, eager flame, went on to Oxford University, where he studied poetry and law, and wrote a thesis on Walt Whitman. He returned to South Africa to come under the spell of Cecil Rhodes, broke with him, and emigrated from the British Cape to the Boer Transvaal, where he quickly became President Paul Kruger's right-hand man. In Kruger's capital, Pretoria, he learned to hate the British. He fought them in the Boer War and achieved world fame as a guerrilla fighter, raiding on horseback all over war-ravaged South Africa at the head of a ragged, gallant band, with Kant's *Critique of Pure Reason* in his knapsack for light reading. Finally he made peace with his enemies, who became his friends.

Malan, the sober plodder in plain black, went to Holland to study theology and wrote a thesis on Bishop Berkeley. He returned to the British Cape to be a minister of the Dutch Reformed church. He took no part in the war that was consuming his country like a veld fire. But when peace was concluded, he denounced Smuts as a traitor who had sold out the Boers, and inveighed from his pulpit against the conquering British.

Smuts took South Africa into the First World War, on Britain's side, putting on a uniform again to fight in German East Africa. He became a member of Lloyd George's Imperial

91

War Cabinet, and ended the war as Prime Minister of South Africa, one of the architects of the League of Nations, and one of the most famous men in the British Empire.

Malan denounced South Africa's participation in the war, sympathized with Germany, and called Smuts a "renegade" and "a handyman of Empire."

In South Africa, political hatreds run strong, narrow, deep, and bitter. Politics divide families, setting brother against brother, and father against son. Between the followers of Malan and the followers of Smuts this sort of hatred crackled and spluttered through long years.

Yet between the two leaders there remained, all through these acrid years, a strange bond that no political differences could break. When Smuts was in power and Malan in opposition to him, they snarled and sniped, two aging men who could become white with passion at the very mention of the other's name. When Smuts was defeated and Malan at last made Prime Minister, the snarling and the sniping continued, and was indeed intensified, for Smuts in defeat was bitter, and Malan in power was inexorable.

But one day Prime Minister Malan was seated on a platform at a triumphant Nationalist Party congress, where the *vierkleur* waved and the regimented Boer Nationalist youth stood stiffly and proudly at attention. All that Malan had fought for was coming to pass, and the different dream that Smuts had cherished seemed in ruins. They handed Malan a message, passed up to the platform by eager hands over jubilant heads. The message said that Smuts, the great, broken foe, was dead. And Malan said: "Jannie." He bowed his head, and put his face in his hands, and wept like a child.

Despite these tears, the Nationalists made the most of Malan's victory. Top-ranking soldiers who had served under Smuts were demoted or removed and their places in the army filled with subordinates who had faithfully served the party. Men who during the war had been sent to prison for high treason were immediately set free. There were large-scale "purges" in the public service, and before "grievance commissions" good Nationalists laid charges against "Smuts men."

Old scores were raked up and old feuds settled. New laws were passed to purge the trade unions of "Communists," and Nationalist ministers awarded themselves increasing powers over persons and property. By special legislation steamrollered through Parliament, the courts were prohibited from interfering. When the Supreme Court of South Africa sought to protect the Constitution against such infringements, the Nationalists proposed to set up a "High Court of Parliament," consisting of Nationalist M.P.'s, to override the Supreme Court, whose black-robed judges were derided as "the six old men in Bloemfontein."

The chief glory of Nationalist rule was *apartheid*, though it occasionally had odd results. South Africa had always had race segregation, but under Smuts Negroes had used the same doorways, staircases, and counters in public buildings as whites. This was now stopped. Railroad stations and post offices were partitioned to ensure that white and black never mingled.

One evening I walked up to the telegraph counter of the central post office in Johannesburg to hand in a cablegram. The counter was five feet long, and I took my place opposite the solitary clerk. To my surprise, he motioned me curtly to the other end. "Look at the new notices," he commanded.

The counter was now divided into two two-and-one-half-foot lengths. Over one half a notice proclaimed "Europeans Only." The other half had a notice saying "Non-Europeans Only." The division was marked by a swing gate.

Meekly I passed through the gate into the white section. The clerk sternly kept in step with me on his side of the counter and then accepted my cable.

I was the only customer.

"It seems," I ventured with a nervous laugh, "a bit unnecessary when there are only the two of us here."

He frowned at me. "So you don't like our *apartheid* laws!"

"No, no! Only, in the circumstances—"

93

"The law," he thundered, "is there to be obeyed." He added fervently: "*Apartheid* is the only way to save our white civilization."

I crept away abashed.

Two weeks later I entered the post office at the same hour with another cablegram. Remembering my lesson, I carefully approached the white section of the counter, though the clerk happened again to be at the half for non-whites. To my surprise, he snapped: "Come over here, can't you?"

"No," I said, "I can't."

"Why not?"

"Because of *apartheid*." I pointed to the notices.

"Look," he pleaded, "I'm *busy*. I'm *tired* of walking up and down from one half of the counter to the other."

"Sorry," I said regretfully, "but the law is the law. Don't you like our *apartheid* laws?"

"*Apartheid*," he said firmly, "doesn't begin until half past five. Until then you can be served at *any* part of the counter."

"Sorry," I said again, glancing at my watch. "You see, it's now five thirty-five, so *apartheid* is in force."

Wearily he picked up his pencil and walked across to my half of the counter. "Sometimes," he confessed, glancing over his shoulder to make sure nobody was listening, "I think this *apartheid* is just *silly*."

"Don't forget we've got to save white civilization," I said.

: 3 :

MOSES HATED the golden calf. Malan, the Boer Moses, hated it so much that in his youth he even had an ideological flirtation with another prophet, Karl Marx. When he was a preacher in Graaff-Reinet, a small wool-growing town in the Cape Province, he agreed to address the local literary society. They feared he might deliver a lecture on temperance, for he was an eloquent thunderer against the evils of strong drink and had made himself highly unpopular in his previous parish, which was the

94

center of a winegrowing area. But when the thickset, black-clothed young clergyman got up to speak, he astounded them by sternly expounding the doctrines of Marxist Socialism. He had the speech printed in a pamphlet, from which, years later, his enemies gleefully quoted.

To Malan, "capitalism" was evil because, in South Africa, most of the capitalists were either British or Jewish, and many of the white proletariat were Boers.

"Capitalism," as practiced in South Africa, had brought other evils on the Boer *volk*. In Graaff-Reinet he visited a poor quarter of the town. What he saw there filled him with a horror that never left him. In the slum streets, white children—Boer children—were playing, unperturbed, with colored children. Thus was planted in his mind the seed of what became the doctrine of *apartheid*, the compulsory separation of white and colored in all spheres of life—unless the white was *baas* and the colored was servant, a relationship to which he had no objection. The Boers had *always* had colored servants.

When in 1939 Smuts for the second time took South Africa into a war at Britain's side, Malan was joined by other Boers. All through the war years, while Smuts sent South African troops into Abyssinia and the Western Desert and accepted a British field-marshal's baton, the strength of Malan's party grew. Many Boers longed secretly or openly for a German victory. Smuts, busy with the problems of the war, his mind ranging over the whole world (he was already thinking in terms of a new League of Nations that would not easily fall apart as the old one had done), too lightly disregarded the hostile muttering of the Boers in the small scattered *dorps* on the *platteland*. That he should help to win a world war but lose South Africa seemed to him inconceivable.

Smuts had largely left domestic issues to be handled by his deputy and chosen successor, Jan Hofmeyr, a small, chunky Boer with a big head full of ideals. Hofmeyr's plan for postwar South Africa was as an industrialized, twentieth-century state, in which there would not be much of a place for the old Boer way of life on sprawling farms plentifully supplied with cheap

95

Kaffir labor. Hofmeyr wanted the Negroes in the towns, as workers in the new factories.

Malan denounced this plan. The farmers would be deprived of Kaffirs. Boers driven off the land into the towns would find themselves competing with Kaffirs for low wages. The towns, filled with Kaffirs, would become breeding-grounds for Communism.

Worst of all, the "economic integration" of whites and blacks which Hofmeyr preached would inevitably produce race mixing at the lowest level. It would be Graaff-Reinet all over again, with Boer children living in slums and playing with colored children as equals. The proud Boer nation would lose its racial purity, and the Boers as a separate people would vanish in a coffee-colored mass. Only the capitalists, the British and the Jews, would gain from this state of affairs.

Above all else, Malan and his followers disliked British imperialism. The British Empire had swallowed up the old Boer republics. In 1910 a new Union of South Africa was formed. There were to be no more Boers and Britons, only South Africans. Most of the Englishmen in the Union were prepared to become South Africans, but most of the Boers were not. They wanted the Boer nation to continue, and they still hoped one day to reverse the defeat suffered in the Boer War. Then the English could remain in South Africa by becoming Boers or they could get out. In order to become a Boer, an Englishman must speak the Boer's language, Afrikaans, and must adopt the Boer way of life. He must sing *Die Stem van Suid Afrika* instead of *God Save the King*, and must salute the republican flag, the *vierkleur*, instead of the Union Jack.

"A Frenchman or a German who decides to become an American," a Nationalist explained, "is accepted provided he really becomes an American, and ceases to be a Frenchman or a German. Why should an Englishman in South Africa be treated differently?"

The English could not accept this argument. They were prepared to become South Africans if the Boers were prepared to do the same. They could no more become Boers than a Frenchman could become a German. Malan, by preaching the continued existence and eventual triumph of the Boer nation, made it impossible for a new, "South African" nation to arise. But he mightily inflamed the nationalism of the Boers, who clung tenaciously to their Boerhood.

Malan rallied his Boers round the standard of *apartheid*. He passed laws against "mixed" marriages. At the same time he gave assurances to the *platteland* Boers that their farms would never lack Kaffir labor.

He promised that the Nationalists would wage war on the capitalists and the Jews, humble the British, take the trade unions out of the hands of "Communists," clean up the Kaffir-choked towns, and avenge all Boers who during the war had been put in internment camps by Smuts for not being sufficiently "loyal" to the British Empire. The Boers were the Israelites who had been too long wandering in the wilderness, and their political opponents were the Philistines and Egyptians. Malan promised to smite them. In a hotly contested election—tough young Nationalists howled like famished wolves on the kill when it was announced that old warrior Smuts had lost not only the election but his own seat in Parliament as well—the Nationalists were swept to power and Malan could tell his Boers: "South Africa is again ours."

VIII

SOUTH AFRICA:
THE NEW BOER WAR

THE VOORTREKKER MONUMENT seemed to me to be a suitable place to visit before calling on some of South Africa's new Boer rulers. This monument which the Boers built for ancestor-worship squats heavily on a hill near Pretoria. Square and lumpish, with little exterior elegance, it stands for strength, tenacity, endurance. There is an encircling wall crudely decorated with ox-wagons, and the broad steps leading up to the entrance are flanked by rough-hewn heads of stern, bearded men who look out over the country they conquered. This is the monument of the Voortrekkers, the Boers who carved out the veld republics.

The monument crouches on its *kopje* with a brooding air, and, from a distance, looks disconcertingly like a very large public lavatory. But inside there is a lofty marble hall, with marble friezes round the towering walls. In the center of the marble floor is an orifice like a well. Visitors tiptoe across the vast expanse of echoing marble and look down the well on an immense sarcophagus that rests in its cold stone vault. High above their heads is the monument's great domed roof, which has a hole in it; and the place is so designed that once a year, on Dingaan's Day, December 16, a shaft of sunlight strikes the silent sarcophagus like a glittering lance. And the Boers pray for their ancestors.

On December 16, 1838, at the Battle of Blood River, the Boers defeated the Zulu regiments, and broke the power of the great Zulu tyrant, Dingaan, who had murdered a party of Voortrekkers a few weeks before. This murder, and others, are depicted in marble in the friezes round the walls of the Voortrekker Monument. The friezes show blood-lusting Negroes massacring whites. On certain days parties of Negro schoolchildren are allowed to visit the monument so that they can see what sort of people *their* ancestors were.

Lying in a green bowl of *veld* rimmed with blue *kopjes*, Pretoria was heavy with the scent of purple-flowered jacaranda trees, whose rich petals drifted down in showers to carpet the streets. On a hill dominating the town, the Union buildings etched a gracious silhouette against the burning blue sky: long, low buildings, with twin clock-towers that sonorously chimed the passing hours, and a vast frontage of balustraded stone terraces and steeply falling gardens massed with flowers. Under the clock-towers, amid a maze of broad corridors and winding staircases, the Cabinet ministers and their secretaries conducted the political business of the vast country that was ruled from here.

The most important politician in South Africa after the Prime Minister, Dr. Malan, was a short, burly, blue-eyed man with crisp, upstanding black hair, Johannes Gerhardus Strydom. Looking like Yugoslavia's Marshal Tito, neatly encased in a dark-blue suit that stretched tight across his broad shoulders, he was too restless to sit still. He hopped up from behind his big desk, strode the carpet, and threw himself into another chair, swinging his legs.

"Of course we want to make South Africa a republic," said Strydom briskly, "and we shall do so."

I asked him about the feelings of the English in South Africa, who violently oppose any idea of a republic. He laughed.

"The English talk a lot," he said, "but they never do anything. We have already taken them far along the road to a republic. We have our own flag and our own national anthem. Each time we took a step forward," Strydom explained with cheerful cynicism, "the English kicked up a great fuss. We simply waited for the fuss to die down, and then we took another step. Now it's too late for the English to do anything about it. They've already conceded too much. A republic is inevitable and the English know it."

Strydom radiated brisk self-confidence. He seemed like a man who knew where he was going. His political opponents regarded him as the most dangerous man in South Africa.

Hans Strydom was born in 1893, in what was then British Cape Colony. Like Malan and Smuts, he was educated at Stellenbosch. He became an ostrich-farmer in 1912, when ostrich feathers were literally worth their weight in gold. But two years later the fabulous industry collapsed. Strydom cut his losses and took a job as a civil servant. He studied law at Pretoria and became a country attorney. But his chief interest was politics. He entered Parliament in 1929, as a Nationalist. His constituency was the Waterberg, a vast arid tract of land occupied by hard-bitten Boer farmers in the northern Transvaal. He became known as "the Lion of the Waterberg."

Strydom married the South African actress Marda Vanne. The marriage did not last long. Miss Vanne has been reported as saying that a monotonous diet of prayer meetings and politics had a disastrously slimming effect on wedded bliss. In 1931 Strydom married again, this time choosing as his bride a clergyman's daughter.

Strydom is an energetic political speaker, to put it mildly. "He gets as much exercise from a forty-minute speech," said one student of his platform manner, "as most people do from a strenuous game of squash." A born barnstormer, he whirls his arms, shakes his fists, and makes full use of a healthy pair of lungs. The political message he has consistently preached is pungently unambiguous. In South Africa, the white man must always be *baas*. That is one reason, among others, why Strydom is determined to take South Africa out of the British Commonwealth. "The British Empire," he says crisply, "has as one of its cornerstones equal rights for everyone, irrespective of color or smell." According to Strydom, the Empire's other cornerstone is Jewry. "The detestable British-Jewish liberal democratic system," he once told a meeting of Boers, "is a crime against the *volk*."

When Hitler's Germany failed after all to win the war, a number of Boer Nationalists discreetly retired from the dangerously exposed position they had occupied as apparent Hitler-worshippers. Not Strydom. Assuming the unpopular role of Hitler's last defender, he argued that by foolishly crushing Hitler, Britain, France, the United States, and Field-Marshal Smuts of South Africa had pulled Stalin's chestnuts out of the fire for him.

By 1935 Strydom had become the leader of the Nationalists in the Transvaal and effective boss of the Nationalist political machine there. The Nationalist Party is organized on a federal basis, but the Transvaal, which has the gold mines and most of the country's industries, is the wealthiest and most populous of the four provinces. When the Nationalists came to power, Strydom's control of the party machine in the Transvaal automatically made him potentially the most powerful politician in South Africa. The Cape Nationalists, of whom Malan was of course the most prominent, and who had formerly led the party, faced the prospect of having to take a back seat. But when Malan formed his Cabinet, Strydom got only the modest position of Minister of Lands. This was probably by choice. Still in his fifties, he could afford to wait. His Transvaal supporters had no hesitation in acclaiming him as Malan's successor, destined in time to be "first President of the Republic."

Strydom is an intensely ambitious man. He would like to be first president of the republic. But his whirlwind performances on public platforms may be misleading. "On the stage, he behaves like a dancing dervish in a fanatical frenzy," said a South African who knows him well, "but off stage he cools down immediately. It's all part of the act." In private conversation Strydom gives an impression of bold and confident purpose, but not of fanaticism. He has a distinct sense of humor, which the true fanatic traditionally lacks. With his stocky build, fresh complexion, and piercing eyes, he looks like a sailor and has the temperament of a fighting Irishman.

: 2 :

IN ANOTHER corner of the Union buildings a man who looked like a university professor spoke with burning sincerity about his favorite dream, or nightmare, *apartheid*. At first he spoke mildly, discussing the subject almost academically; but after a while he raised his voice, and was soon thumping the table.

"What," he demanded angrily, "would the United States do if four fifths of its population were Negroes and not whites? What, in fact, did the American colonists do to the red Indians? They exterminated them. But when we South Africans merely propose to segregate our natives, in order to defend our white civilized values, we are wickedly maligned. South Africa," he shouted, with real tears in his eyes, "has been unjustly accused at the bar of so-called world opinion, which demands that we should commit race suicide! South Africa will never do that! We would rather die!"

He groped for a handkerchief and wiped his eyes. It was an embarrassing moment. Then, astonishingly, the professor took charge again. "You must excuse me if I seem emotional," he said mildly, "but, you understand, to us this is a matter of life or death."

Dr. Hendrik Frensch Verwoerd is a highly cultured man. His appearance does not belie him: he was once a university professor. Born in 1901 in Holland, he arrived in South Africa when he was two years old and was educated at Cape Town, Bulawayo, Brandfort, and the University of Stellenbosch. Then he went overseas and studied at the universities of Hamburg, Leipzig, and Berlin.

For eight years, from 1928 to 1936, he taught applied psychology and sociology at Stellenbosch University. Like Malan and other Boer Nationalists, he was much perturbed by South Africa's "poor white" problem. Most of the poor whites were Boers, and in the late twenties and early thirties it was scarcely an exaggeration to say that most Boers were poor whites. Verwoerd helped organize a "model village" housing scheme for the rehabilitation of poverty-stricken Boers; he also organized a congress to discuss the entire poor-white problem.

In 1937 he quit his professorship at Stellenbosch and accepted the job of editor of a Boer Nationalist newspaper, the *Transvaler*, which is published in Johannesburg. Malan had edited the Boer paper in Cape Town, the *Burger*, which had some hard things to say about the English; but in comparison with the *Transvaler*, as edited by Verwoerd, the *Burger* was liberally pro-British.

Just before he became editor of the *Transvaler*, Verwoerd, with a number of other Stellenbosch professors, had strongly opposed the admission to South Africa of Jewish refugees fleeing from the Nazi terror in Germany. When South Africa decided to join the war against Hitler, the *Transvaler* awarded its sympathy to the *Führer*: in an interesting court case, a judge declared that Verwoerd had made his paper "a tool of the Nazis in South Africa." No official action was taken against it, but the paper was understandably unpopular with South African soldiers who were fighting the *Führer's* armies. In 1941 two masked men waylaid Verwoerd outside his Johannesburg home. One carried a revolver and the other a sawed-off shotgun. Verwoerd, who certainly does not lack courage, told them to go ahead and shoot. They let him go.

Tall—over six feet three inches—and strongly built, Verwoerd, with his shock of gray hair, slight stoop, and normally mild manner, looks, as I have said, every inch the professor. His political opponents say that his mildness is deceptive and that under it lurks the steely strength of the fanatic. "Strydom sometimes behaves like a fanatic, but Verwoerd is one," said a candid critic. "He is the more dangerous of the two because his sincerity is unquestionable. Strydom can be cheerfully cynical; Verwoerd is never cynical and seldom cheerful. He is the sort of man who would put a heretic on the rack and then, with the tears streaming down his cheeks, would torture the heretic's body for the salvation of his soul." In Verwoerd's eyes, a heretic is a person who does not believe in *apartheid*.

Verwoerd has described himself as "an extremist Afrikaner," and has admitted that he is a member of the Broederbond, the Boer secret society that Englishmen in South Africa believe to be as powerful politically as the Chamber of Mines is economically. The Broederbond's goal is said to be the setting up of a South African republic in which the Boers would be top dogs and the English crushed underfoot.

Despite his late entry into politics—he was given a seat in the Senate only in 1948, after he had failed to be elected to the House of Assembly—Verwoerd is a powerful man in the Nationalist Party. He is the party's deputy chairman on the Witwatersrand, and one of the three Transvaal members on the party's federal council, the other two being Strydom and Labour Minister Ben Schoeman.

After the Nationalists came to power, Verwoerd quit his editorship of the *Transvaler* to become Malan's Minister of Native Affairs. In this key post he was able to start translating his *apartheid* theories into practice. He visited the reserves, areas set aside for Negroes, talking to tribesmen, and also toured the Rand mine compounds and shantytowns, striding through dust, filth, and flies and inspecting the huddles of tin huts. He probed into Negro alleys that had seldom been visited by a white man, far less a Cabinet Minister, and toured the dismal squatters' camps. What he saw made him more convinced than ever that *apartheid* was the only solution. Despite strenuous Negro and Indian opposition to it, he also believed that *apartheid* was in their best interests as well as in the interests of the whites.

"The native," Verwoerd has said, "has his own racial pride and would also welcome *apartheid*. He must have an opportunity to develop. But he must not be an imitator of the white man. We would sincerely like to have the non-Europeans as allies rather than have racial strife."

To achieve this ideal, Verwoerd outlined a plan to develop the native reserves to the point where they could become "self-contained." The Negroes would live there, and the whites would occupy the rest of the country. Other "non-Europeans," like the Indians, would also have their "own areas."

Like other professors, Verwoerd found that plans drawn up
in the study do not always work out smoothly when applied in
the real world outside. He was compelled to give the assurance
that "industry and commerce need have no nightmares: they
will still have their negro labor." How this was to be reconciled
with *apartheid* he did not go on to explain.

: 3 :

ONE BOER Nationalist occupying a ministerial office in the
Union buildings who seemed untroubled by doubts was the
powerful Minister of Justice, Charles Robert Swart, or, as
friends and admirers called him, "Blackie" Swart, who in private life is an extremely genial man. Swart was born in 1894
and so was only five when the Boer War began. Nevertheless,
he never tires of discussing that conflict and describing the
atrocities committed by the British against the Boers. An un-
usually tall man—well over six feet—he has had an extraordi-
narily varied career. He was in rapid succession a schoolteacher,
a school inspector, legal adviser to a town council, and a lecturer in agriculture. Then he visited the United States, studied
journalism at Columbia University, acted in a Hollywood film
(as a giant), and was a newspaper reporter in New York and
Washington.

Before this he had been organizer of the Nationalist Party
in the Orange Free State, and acted for a time as private secretary to the Nationalist leader General Hertzog. He returned to
South Africa and entered Parliament before he was thirty. His
political career owed much to Hertzog, but in 1940 Hertzog
accused him of "reprehensible and undermining activities."
Swart won the ensuing fight, and replaced the aging Hertzog as
leader of the Nationalist Party in the Orange Free State. This
put him, in form at any rate, on a level with men like Strydom,
and even Malan himself, in the inner councils of the party.

In 1940, the year of his triumph over Hertzog, Swart came
out in support of the Ossewa-Brandwag, an openly fascist and

semimilitary Boer organization. "The O.B.," said Swart, "will eradicate all traitors." He branded Britain as the "robber of Boer freedom," and called Smuts one of the "accursed 'loyal Dutch.'" He also talked about the coming "New Order," which would give the English in South Africa short shrift. He stopped talking about the "New Order" when it became clear that Germany was not going to win the war.

When the Nationalists came to power, in 1948, Swart discovered two new enemies: Negroes and Communists. The latter were to be dealt with under a Suppression Act, which gave Swart far-reaching powers: he could "name" anybody he pleased as a Communist, and subject the victim to various penalties, such as ejecting him from his job. The person thus "named" could not go to court and have the matter argued out, since Swart need not produce any evidence whatever that his victim was in fact a Communist. Swart's unsupported word was sufficient. This proved a very handy weapon against obstructionist trade-union officials and other critics of the Nationalist Government.

As for the Negroes, who were becoming politically restive, Swart shook a cat-o'-nine-tails at them and declared: "Violence will be met with violence, and physical assault by thrashings." He encouraged the police to shoot to kill if Negro crowds threatened them. He also extended the thrashing treatment to Negroes and Indians who defied *apartheid* laws.

Swart's activities made him somewhat less than popular with a good many South Africans. He reorganized the police force, virtually creating a force within the force. It was called the "Special Branch." The former Special Branch had consisted of a few detectives mainly engaged in warring against illicit diamond-buying, a well-known South African pastime. Swart's Special Branch was somewhat different. It consisted of hard-faced men with their hands stuck deep in the pockets of raincoats with the collars turned up. They attended all meetings of Swart's political opponents and, in offices sealed off from the public gaze, busily compiled confidential dossiers on citizens who had incurred Swart's displeasure. With a fine contempt for normal police procedure, they reported direct to the Minister, bypassing officers who were nominally their superiors in rank. Some of these officers were indignant when they discovered that they were being reported on, too.

"Mr. Swart's Special Branch," bitterly commented the Johannesburg *Star*, a leading English newspaper, "is the nearest approach to the NKVD this side the Iron Curtain."

: 4 :

As a smeller-out of hideous plots against the *volk*, Swart was outrivaled only by Eric Hendrik Louw, who for a while represented the Malan government at the United Nations. Louw has had a wide experience of international affairs, and has a poor opinion of the way other people conduct them. As long ago as 1926, on a visit to the United States, he severely admonished New York and Washington newspapermen for their ignorance about South Africa, and darkly referred to "unscrupulous correspondents." At that time he was South Africa's Trade Commissioner in Canada, having been appointed to the post by General Hertzog. Later he was made South African High Commissioner in London. The High Commissionership is a job that calls chiefly for tact. What Louw wanted—and said so—was higher diplomatic status which would entitle him to inform the British Government where it was going wrong in the conduct of foreign affairs. General Hertzog shifted him first to Washington, then to Rome, finally to Paris. Hertzog was a strong supporter of the League of Nations: Louw cheerfully told Frenchmen that the League was a "miserable failure." General Hertzog brought him home again.

Back on the veld, Louw discovered the Jews. They were, he said, plotting to "flood South Africa" and overwhelm the Boer *volk*. They were also stealing all the cement, thus making it impossible for Boers to build homes. The Jews kept him happily occupied for a considerable time.

But when Malan came to power, Louw was chosen to speak

for the new South Africa at the United Nations. The U.N., he soon found, was if anything worse than the old League. For one thing, it was filled with foreigners.

"I am glad," he was reported to have told a Nationalist Party gathering, "to be back after three months of mixing with Siamese, Indians, Russians, and God knows what." He allowed eleven months to pass before explaining that he had not said this at all, and that the words had been put into his mouth by unscrupulous reporters. "What I did," he said, "was to express pleasure at being back in South Africa among my own people. As a matter of interest, I referred to the diversity of races at the United Nations Assembly."

It was just another example of how Louw is constantly and maliciously being misrepresented in the newspapers, both in South Africa and overseas. His feud with the press has lasted for many years, and he has virtually bales of news clippings to prove it. He carries them around with him, and produces them on public platforms, quoting from them and glaring at the reporters present, whom he challenges to misreport him this time if they dare. Unfortunately, they nearly always do. Curiously, the people at the meetings nearly always agree with the reporters' version of what Louw said, not with Louw's version. An irascible man with a rasping voice, he has been compared by unfriendly audiences to the late Dr. Goebbels, whom physically he somewhat resembles.

: 5 :

A MUCH smoother character is Dr. Theophilus Ebenhaezer Donges, Malan's Minister of the Interior. A highly successful barrister, Donges did not enter Parliament until 1941, when he was forty-three; but he had been assistant editor of Malan's old newspaper, the *Burger*, and was already highly respected in Nationalist Party circles. His father was a Dutch Reformed Church minister, but Theophilus studied at London University, was called to the Middle Temple, and became almost more English than the English. A bland pipe-smoker, he played cricket and familiarly quoted Lewis Carroll and other peculiarly English writers. When Dr. and Mrs. Donges were received at Buckingham Palace in 1951—they took with them to London a "basic wardrobe" of four suits, four cocktail dresses, and four evening gowns—Mrs. Donges told reporters: "I was so enthralled by the Queen's personality that I cannot even tell you what she was wearing."

Despite these English influences, Dr. Donges has been since 1933 a deacon of the Dutch Reformed Church, which is not notorious for its love of the English or of English ways. More important, he was for many years vice-chairman of the Broederbond.

Broederbonder Donges directed the activities of the Boer Nationalists' Culture Front, including the Christian National Education Institute, which fought for separate schools for English and Boer children, and attacked all "anti-national" manifestations in education, including "liberalism" in race relations and hints that the theory of evolution might have a better scientific basis than the teaching of the Book of Genesis. Donges was also a director of the *Federale Volksbeleggings* (Federal People's Investments), a key institution in the intricate machinery of the *Reddingsdaadbond* (Savings Movement League), an organization that sought to unite all Boer businessmen on a "national" basis.

As Malan's Minister of the Interior, Dr. Donges set about the task of legalizing the revolutionary changes that the Nationalists had promised to introduce. British immigrants were told that they would have to wait five years to become South African citizens, instead of the former two years. They would also have to satisfy Dr. Donges of their eligibility on other grounds. (South Africans are automatically recognized as British subjects.) Dr. Donges also claimed the right to seize any South African's passport at any time without giving any reason. But Donges ran into trouble over *apartheid*. When he tried to take the country's one million half-castes off the ordinary voters' roll, the Supreme Court ruled this unconstitutional. Dr. Donges tried to set up a "High Court of Parliament," consisting of Nationalists, to overrule the Supreme Court. The Supreme Court ruled this unconstitutional too. As a result Dr. Donges's prestige suffered. Nationalists began to ask themselves if he was quite so brilliant, after all. Until then he had been regarded as having more brains than any other man in the Cabinet. In fact, he was already fighting a losing battle with Strydom, who controlled the Transvaal political machine. Donges belonged to the once all-powerful but now overshadowed camp of the old Cape Nationalists. At one time he had been thought the man most likely to succeed Malan. As Strydom's star rose, Donges's faded.

: 6 :

THESE WERE some of the men who sat in big offices in the Union Buildings in Pretoria. Malan had brought them there, but Malan was old. Who would be the new Boer Moses?

On a previous occasion, I had visited the Union Buildings, to see Field-Marshal Smuts. The old man had just returned from San Francisco, where he had helped lay the foundations of the United Nations, whose Charter he had also helped to write. A tall, spare figure, with thin white hair well brushed, a small white beard attached to an aggressive chin, and burning blue eyes, he looked like a wispy prophet. He stood erect, one veined hand on the small of his back, the other clenched and resting on a chair. He spoke about the new world he hoped to see emerge from the shadows and wreckage of war, and the part South Africa should play in it. He was not, as his Boer opponents alleged, a "negrophile." He was not even a "liberal." He was highly distrustful of the racially mixed United Nations' race idealism. He did not believe that all men had been created equal—or even all races.

"South Africa is being criticized," he said in his quick, slightly lisping English. "They say we treat the natives harshly. And it is true that, sometimes, our young white South Africans act brusquely towards the native folk. They feel the natives are their inferiors. They are right.

"But we have to work with those people in the United Nations. South Africa cannot stand alone. This is a twentieth-century world: the world, they say, of the Common Man." He smiled somewhat skeptically, looking, with his white goatee, like a thin Spanish grandee.

"What is our policy to be, here in South Africa, with its many races, and the white man in a minority? We cannot solve the problems of our grandchildren for them. We shall be all dead, and the problems may have changed. The thing must work itself out gradually. Meanwhile, we can be just. When we see a thing is wrong, we must simply try to put it right, without fretting over what the consequences may be in a hundred years' time. If a negro child is hungry, we must feed it; if it is naked, we must clothe it; if it lacks schooling, we must educate it. We are all here to stay in South Africa: Boer and British, black and white. We must learn to live with one another, to understand one another, to act as Christians towards one another. There is no other way for us."

But the new men who had taken over the Union Buildings and who ruled South Africa had different ideas.

IX

SOUTH AFRICA: "I DECLARE THIS PRISON OPEN"

THE NATIONALIST PARTY got most of its support from the *platteland*: the Boer farmers who lived on the great flat plains of the Orange Free State, the green hills, with their vineyards, of the Cape, and the high corn-growing plateau of the Transvaal. They were descendants of the bearded Voortrekkers who had broken the power of the tribes, marched inland to escape hated British rule, and carved huge ten-thousand-acre farms out of the veld. The farmers were God-fearing men who loved the land and deeply distrusted the people who lived in cities.

Many misfortunes had befallen them. Because they grew corn year after year, their soil began to blow away. On the great ranches of the Karroo, sheep nibbled down to the grass roots and created desert. Sandstorms became more frequent, until over thousands of square miles of the Orange Free State and the Cape the wind raised dust-devils from the parched, crumbling earth, and pilots flying the big sleek passenger planes between Johannesburg and Cape Town reported "visibility nil" at ten thousand feet. All over the vast Union, and extending deep into South-West Africa, the deserts were on the march, the land becoming waterless and treeless, the soil structure collapsing. South Africa, once a producer of seventy-two million bushels of corn a year, found itself in some years producing only thirty million bushels—not enough to feed its people and its cattle. The very plows that were imported brought death to thin, phosphate-deficient soils, under burning African skies.

Three encroaching deserts pointed their daggers at South Africa's corn-growing heart: the Kalahari, the Namib, and the Karroo, which within living memory had not been a desert at all.

Over the flat, horizonless Orange Free State, in the years of drought, the sky that was a cloudless blue by day turned at dusk to a splendid crimson, a deceptively beautiful sunset created by the shifting curtains of dust that once had been firm red soil. The rivers, when they were not dried up, were blood-red with the thousands of tons of lost soil that washed away into the oceans. An expert calculated that the South African soil thus fed into the sea would each year fill enough railroad trucks to circle the earth three and one-half times. Year by year the desert sands crept eastward, until the stony waste touched Bloemfontein, the capital city of the Orange Free State, which when the Voortrekkers built it, in 1846, had been a place so pleasant that they named it Flowering Spring. The advancing desert replaced flowers with the *bitterbos*, the bitter shrub. A Government commission reported "appalling denudation, impoverishment and weed infestation," and declared: "Unless the deterioration is arrested, our prairies are doomed."

The doom was coming quickly. Over these open prairies, only a short time before the arrival of the Voortrekkers, vast herds of antelope had grazed. Now, during the increasingly frequent and increasingly prolonged droughts, the dying sheep and cattle trampled the mud round the drying waterholes. Each year of drought thousands of farmers watched their soil die. The once fertile land cracked into gullies that became ravines. On many a homestead, the impoverished farmer listlessly watched his Kaffirs trek away, and saw his family reduced to living on porridge, bread, and bitter black coffee. The red dust of erosion floated in the coffee-cups even as they raised them to their lips.

Finally, from many farms the owners themselves trekked off, following their Kaffirs toward the towns in search of work. Often the only sort of work they could find was work that the Kaffirs could do as well, and do far cheaper.

So there grew a great bitterness in the heart of the Boer

113

volk, and this was usually directed against the people who lived in the towns and who did not understand what it meant to a man who had owned land to lose it in this fashion.

By the time Malan came to power, though erosion was still rife, the great poor-white problem had been at least partially solved. Many poor whites—at one time estimated at one third of South Africa's total white population—had been more or less successfully absorbed in new urban industries. Their wages were low, they still resented and feared the Kaffirs, and they voted solidly for the Nationalist Party; but they were no longer uprooted people moving drearily from job to job. The farmers who had managed to remain on the land were more prosperous than they had been for years, for food prices were high and land values were steadily rising again.

What the farmers now complained of was a great shortage of labor.

: 2 :

I ARRIVED in a dusty Free State dorp as dusk was falling, one evening in 1952. At this hour the single main street was broad and deserted, but farmers' cars, Chevrolets and big Buicks, were parked outside the one hotel. Their owners sat on the hotel stoep, drinking beer and discussing their troubles.

"I can't keep a Kaffir on my place," said one of them angrily. He was an enormous man, with arms like a blacksmith's and he sweated as he sat in his shirtsleeves drinking beer. "The minute you look the other way, the young ones are off to the towns. I told my oldest 'boy' if any more of his sons ran off, he'd have to leave too, though he's been with me twenty years, for I wasn't going to be left with the old men and the women to feed while the young men deserted."

"What did he say?" mildly inquired a thin, gray-haired man.

"Oh, he was scared. It wouldn't be much fun for him and his old wife to be turned off my land at their age. If a Kaffir could go pale, he would have, I can tell you. I could almost hear his teeth chattering.

" 'Yes, *baas*,' he said, nodding and shaking like the old fool he is. 'No, *baas*. I'll see they don't run away, *baas*. I'll talk to them, *baas*.' "

The big man laughed coarsely.

" 'You damned lying Kaffir,' I said, 'I bet you help them to desert.'

" 'No, *baas*!' he howled. 'I try to stop them, *baas*.'

" 'Why the hell do they do it, then?' "

"Ah!" said the gray-haired man, showing interest and some amusement. "Did he tell you?"

The big man scowled. "He had the nerve to tell me to my face that they liked working in the towns better.

" 'The young people are changing, *baas*,' he said. 'They don't like the old ways any more. It's not like the old days, when I was your biggest, strongest worker.'

" 'You knew you'd get a boot up your backside or a good sjamboking if you didn't work,' I told him.

" 'Yes, *baas*,' he said, pretending to look pleased about it.

" 'That's what your sons will get if they try to desert,' I said.

" 'They know that, *baas*,' he said. 'But times have changed. They say they can earn more money in the towns. And maybe their children can even go to schools. So they say, why should they work for you for a few shillings a month and a handful of mealies, when there are jobs in the big factories?' "

The big man snorted. "That's what things are coming to, when one of your own Kaffirs can turn round and talk to you like that!"

"Why don't you build them a school?" asked the gray-haired man.

The mountainous man shifted his bulk and stared as if he couldn't believe his ears; he had small hazel eyes, in a rather stupid moon-face.

"Well, by God, Viljoen, if I didn't think you were joking—"

"But I'm not joking," said the gray-haired man patiently. "I

115

think too many Kaffirs are going to the towns; and most of them would be better off here on the land. I've seen the shanty-towns of Johannesburg. But your old 'boy' was right, times are changing. The Kaffirs are human, they want their children to get some of the advantages they didn't. A school would make them more contented. You can get a grant, you know; and the church would help—"

"And turn them into damned agitators!" bawled the fat man, in a rage. "Why, you know as well as I do that the educated Kaffirs are the worst of the lot!" He glared round the circle of faces. "Not one of my 'boys' can read. If I found one of them doing it, I'd kick him off the farm!"

"I thought you wanted to keep Kaffirs on your farm, not force them off," said the gray-haired man, amused.

"When a 'boy' of mine deserts, I send for the police," said a red-faced man with a reedy voice. "It's their job to bring de-serters back. That's what we pay taxes for, isn't it?"

"You can hold the parents responsible if the young ones run off," said another farmer. "They owe a duty to their *baas* to keep their sons at home for farm work. You can stop their pay."

"Christ!" said the fat man, disgusted, "I'd make a fortune out of that, wouldn't I? I pay them ten shillings a month!"

The other farmers laughed.

Afterwards, when we were alone, Viljoen said: "Don't pay too much attention to that talk. A *good* farmer *never* lacks labor. The Kaffirs get to know who are good farmers and who aren't. They'd much rather stay on the land than move to the towns, provided they get anything like fair treatment."

"What's your labor situation?" I asked.

He laughed. "I'm not boasting, but when any 'boy' of mine is thinking of leaving, there are ten queuing up at the farm-gate to take his place before he's made up his mind! I don't pay higher wages than anyone else, but I do try to be just, and to look after my labor. And the 'boys' know it." He grinned. "And *I'm* building a school for their kids, on my land."

But Viljoen was in a minority.

116

The plan the farmers worked out to solve the labor shortage, in co-operation with the Nationalist Government, had nothing to do with schools.

I went down to Kroonstad, which is in the heart of a rich corn-growing area of the Orange Free State. The blue sky was pricked by church steeples, and the little town had a fat and prosperous look. I was directed to the homestead of the district's leading farmer, a ruddy-cheeked and cheerful man who owned thousands of rich acres and was reputed to earn over one hundred thousand dollars a year. He greeted me cordially.

"You've come to look at our new project," he said enthusiastically. "This is a big day for us, I can tell you! Of course, ours isn't the first farm jail in the country, but it's the first in the Free State. It's a great honor that the Minister should be coming in person to open it."

"How exactly does the scheme work?" I asked.

He settled himself comfortably in his chair.

"Well, it's like this. First of all, we farmers clubbed together to provide the money. We managed to raise quite a few thousands. Then we approached the Government with our proposal." He coughed modestly. "It so happens that my uncle is the Director of Prisons. We didn't have any difficulty."

"And the proposal?" I asked.

"We said we'd build this jail if the Government would supply the convicts. Then we draw on the jail for convict labor, and pay the Government one shilling ninepence a head per day for the labor we use. Of course, the Government feeds them."

I made a rapid calculation.

"Would you say this convict labor is cheaper than free labor?"

"Well," he hesitated, "since we don't have to feed, clothe, or house them—"

"I can see," I said, "that the scheme has definite advantages."

"For the Kaffirs too," he said quickly. "In ordinary jails they're cooped up. A Kaffir hates that. But out here they get

117

fresh country air and a chance to show what they're made of. A farmer might offer one of them a regular job, after he was free, if he turned out to be a good, hard-working 'boy.' And, above all, they're back on the land, where they belong! To my mind," he went on proudly, "we're doing a great national service with this scheme. The country needs more food production, and this is one way to achieve it."

"Some people," I said cautiously, "have attacked the scheme as undemocratic."

"Townsmen," he said contemptuously. "And that's just where they're wrong. The scheme is thoroughly democratic."

He leaned forward.

"I can prove it, in one sentence. We laid it down at the very beginning that even the richest farmer will get no more Kaffirs from the prison than a poor farmer. Share and share alike, and no unfair advantages!"

"One more question," I said. "Don't your womenfolk feel a bit nervous that you should be employing criminals on the farms? Of course, I realize they'll be well guarded, but—"

He laughed heartily. "But these Kaffirs aren't criminals! No, no, we thought of that too." He shook his head emphatically. "We wouldn't dream of employing *tsotsis* and housebreakers and the other Kaffir riffraff from the towns! You're quite right, our wives would be terrified out of their wits."

"But," I said, bewildered, "I understood these convicts are men who are serving ten-year sentences—"

He enlightened me. "Yes, of course they are. But they're not criminals. Not *really* criminals, if you follow me."

"I don't think I do."

"These convicts," he said triumphantly, "are all from Zulu-land, not from the towns. They were sent to prison for taking part in tribal fights. Oh, they killed people, and the law called it murder. But it's just a part of their age-old customs. They're fine, upstanding, unspoiled chaps—not criminals at all!" He rose. "Now I'll take you out and show you the jail."

118

: 3 :

THE FLAT countryside and the tall blue-gum trees lining the
road recalled a Dutch painting. We drove to the jail in my
host's new powder-blue Dodge. Off the road, to the right, half
concealed by the trees, were low white buildings surrounded by
a high wall. This was the prison. It looked pleasant enough.
The prison superintendent, a thin-necked man with spectacles
and a mild air, had a cottage in the grounds. When we drove
up he was watching a number of Negro convicts planting
flowering shrubs in front of his cottage. They wore red jerseys
and white shorts. A Negro guard in a black uniform carried, not
a rifle, but an assagai, a short spear. He looked sleepy. The convicts dug holes, lifted the shrubs into place, carefully smoothed
the disturbed earth, and wheeled barrows to and fro. They were
barefooted, broad-faced men with amiable expressions. They
stank a little as they sweated in the hot sun.

The superintendent opened a locked door, set in the high
wall, and we entered the prison. There was a stone courtyard,
with a steel gate beyond which was a larger, inner courtyard,
into which we passed. More convicts were being exercised in
the yard, marching round or standing stiffly in rows. The cells
were large and bare, with strips of coir matting on the stone
floors, for bedding. Once the farm jail was officially opened, the
convicts selected as laborers by the farmers who had built the
prison would spend most of their time out in the fields, but
would be locked up in the jail each night.

When we emerged after inspecting the convicts and the cells,
a number of motor-cars had arrived and were neatly parked
beside the prison wall. The farmers were arriving for the opening ceremony, which was to be performed by the Minister of
Justice, Charles Swart. The farmers had brought their wives
and children with them. All were wearing their Sunday best and
seemed pleasantly excited. The men wore broad-brimmed hats
and new suits. They moved stiffly in their fresh-laundered

119

shirts, and fingered their ties. Their wives wore summer dresses, and hats decorated with artificial flowers. The little boys wore hats like their fathers', and were uncomfortable in well-pressed pants. The little girls' carefully braided yellow hair gleamed in the sunlight.

In front of the prison, long tables had been set out. They were adorned with flowers. Behind the tables were chairs for the principal guests. The farmers, with their wives and children, would occupy benches facing the long tables. Meanwhile, waiting for the Minister, they strolled about, talking in low voices and glancing up at the high prison wall. The children looked subdued, as if they were at Sunday school.

The Minister arrived in a large black limousine. Very tall, with a long, thin neck and thick gray hair, he wore a dark-blue suit; with his thin mouth, sharp nose, and spectacles, he looked like a younger De Valera. Carrying his hat carefully in his hand, he went about, shaking hands with the farmers and their wives and talking to them in Afrikaans. Like a good politician, he knew the names of them all and pretended to recognize them as old friends.

Everyone sat down, Swart and the leading farmers with their backs to the prison wall, and the others facing them. My friend, who sat beside the Minister, got up and made a speech of welcome, in which he explained how the prison had come to be built, and how it would benefit not only the farmers, but the whole country. There were other gracious speeches. Then Swart rose to speak.

He praised the farmers for their enterprise and said the Government welcomed this fresh approach to a vexed problem. Everyone knew that the farmers were short of labor. Meanwhile the prisons were overcrowded with Kaffirs who had forsaken the good life on the land to become criminals in the towns. The inmates of the new farm jails were not criminals in that sense at all. But if there were no farm jails, the Government would be compelled to lock them up with real criminals, from the towns, which would be very bad for them. The farm jails were actually saving those men from sordid criminal contacts, and restoring them to the land, where they belonged. Thus the convicts would benefit as well as the farmers. He personally hoped there would be many more farm jails throughout the country before long. Some people had criticized the scheme as encouraging the manufacture of criminals, since the more convicts there were, the more labor the farmers would get. But this was mischievous nonsense. Other critics said that prison labor should not be hired out to private persons; but this had always been done in South Africa, with nothing but benefit to all concerned. He would just like to give the farmers one word of friendly advice. The convicts, after all, had been sentenced to prison for breaking the law. The farmers must not mollycoddle them, but must make them work hard. There should be no nonsense about that.

The farmers and their wives applauded loudly, with many a "*Hoor, hoor!*" ("Hear! Hear!")

On the wall of the prison, beside the prison door, there hung a white cloth. It looked like a large table napkin improvised for its present purpose. Swart advanced toward it and pulled it aside, revealing a marble tablet set in the prison wall. The tablet commemorated the official opening of the farm jail by the Minister, and paid tribute to the farmers who had contributed the money to build the prison.

"I have much pleasure," said Swart, "in declaring this prison now open." Everyone clapped his hands again.

Toward the end of Swart's speech a number of farmers' wives had got up and tiptoed away, toward the prison superintendent's cottage. They now emerged triumphantly, bearing trays of teacups and plates of scones and cakes. They set them down on the long tables, amid the flowers, and began passing the cups and plates around. Swart sipped his tea and ate a scone with every appearance of enjoyment. The children, who had been fidgeting in their new clothes, brightened up and began to run round the prison wall, chasing one another with shrieks of laughter. Everyone was relaxed and good-humored. They might have been attending the opening of a new church hall.

X

SOUTH AFRICA: MEN AGAINST MALAN

ON THE broad steps of the Johannesburg city hall, flanked by palm trees, I had watched many a political scuffle. During the Second World War the tough storm-troops of the Ossewa-Brandwag, the Nazi-minded Boer organization, fought street battles here with Smuts's soldiers, with bricks and bottles flying through the air. After Smuts's political defeat in 1948, Nationalists and Smuts men brawled here again.

One night in 1951 I saw Smuts's ex-soldiers march once more. All over the city they formed well-drilled platoons and marched toward the city hall, singing old army songs and carrying smoking torches. They had not come to fight, but to listen to the first man in South Africa to offer a serious challenge to the triumphant Nationalists. It was a piquant situation, for Dr. Malan's new opponent was himself a Malan.

In front of the city hall the crowd massed in the flickering light of five thousand flaring torches. A lean man with reddish hair and a keen young face stood up on the steps to address them, and the crowd roared: "Sailor!" He wore a sheepskin jacket, such as the R.A.F. boys wore in the Battle of Britain, and a row of ribbons and war medals. He might have stepped out of one of John Buchan's adventure novels.

Adolphus Gysbert Malan was born on a farm in the Cape Province. He is a distant cousin of Prime Minister Malan. He was called "Sailor" because he had been trained for the navy and spent years at sea. When he went to England and joined

122

the Royal Air Force, the name stuck. A born pilot, he graduated bloodily at Biggins Hill, and shot down so many of Göring's planes that, violently protesting, he was dispatched to America to be paraded as a typical British hero. He married an English girl and when the war was over took her back to South Africa with him. He knew no trade except fighting, and for a while life threatened to be dull. Then he made what seemed to him a momentous discovery: the war against Nazism was still on, and it was being fought in South Africa.

Standing up on the city-hall steps before the Johannesburg crowd, all war veterans like himself, Sailor Malan for the first time in public expounded his simple philosophy. "You chaps fought the Nazis and licked them. That should have been the end of it. But while you were knocking the hell out of Rommel up there in the desert, some people down here in South Africa were trying to stab you in the back. They went around heiling Hitler and calling you 'Smuts's bloody khaki-boys.' Now they're running our country, and where does that get us? They say now they're not Nazis any more, but the leopard doesn't change its spots. If you let them get away with it, they'll cheat you of your victory. You fought for democracy, but they don't like democracy. Well, are you going to let them get away with it?"

The crowd roared: "No!"

That was the start of the Torch Commando, whose numbers grew in a very short time to almost a quarter of a million, causing Dr. Malan to declare solemnly that this proved they were all Communists.

One bright May morning I boarded a Skymaster and flew from Johannesburg to Cape Town. Encouraged by the success of its parades on the Rand, the Torch Commando had decided to stage a monster procession in South Africa's mother city, and to present a petition to Parliament demanding that the Nationalist Government bow to the will of the people and re-sign forthwith.

That night I motored to the little town of Somerset West, some thirty miles from Cape Town, where Sailor Malan had established his headquarters on the eve of the great march. I found him walking briskly up and down in front of his hotel, smoking a pipe, a lithe, slight, sunburned man, with forthright views that he was only too eager to impart to whoever cared to listen, provided they agreed with him. He hauled me into the hotel bar and ordered me a brandy, then immediately began to explain what the Torch Commando hoped to achieve, and how. The bar was deserted save for us and the barman, polishing glasses. After a few sentences Sailor broke off, eyed the barman suspiciously, and marched me outside again. "I bet that fellow's a Nationalist spy," he said.

We adjourned to his room in the hotel, and he strode up and down, lighting his pipe and letting it go out again, and pouring forth his soul.

In the R.A.F. his motto had been: "Shoot 'em down in flames," and he still stuck to it stoutly. "Get them out," he said. "That's all we have to do. Get the so-and-so's out." He used a naughty word.

"But how?" I asked.

He did not give a direct answer, but he looked at me darkly. "If they get really tough," he said, "we go underground."

It did not seem to me that thousands of people marching with flaming torches was undercover work, but I did not like to say so. No doubt he had worked out different methods for meeting different situations.

"Tell me," I said, "can other people besides whites join the Torch Commando?"

He looked at me incredulously. "Any ex-soldier can join. It's an ex-soldiers' organization. D'you think we've forgotten the work of the Cape Coloured Corps, and the Indian and Negro stretcher-bearers, while these so-and-so's were trying to stab Smuts in the back, here in the Union? We all fought for democracy, my lad, and we're all going to get it!"

All next day Cape Town prepared for the peaceful invasion of the Torch Commando. When the Commando finally marched in, it was the gaudiest spectacle the city had ever seen. The line of waving torches seemed endless; the long procession took two hours to pass a given spot. Whites marched shoulder to shoulder with coloreds. The colored ex-soldiers bore themselves proudly; Englishmen slapped one another on the back and prophesied the speedy downfall of the Nationalists, whom they loathed.

Sailor Malan rode in a slow-moving jeep, wearing his old sheepskin jacket, and his medals glittering in the light of the torches.

In a great open space near Cape Town's foreshore and under the lee of the city's grim seventeenth-century castle, he spoke to his followers amid a sea of tossing torches. He did not say anything that he had not already said in Johannesburg and elsewhere, but the crowd cheered themselves hoarse. Then he asked them to disperse peacefully and announced that he would now go to the House of Assembly and present the Commando's petition to Parliament. The crowd, however, decided to follow. A police cordon had been thrown round the House of Assembly. The police let Malan and a few followers through, then closed their ranks. A colored man poked his torch at a policeman, and a few others decided that this was a lot more fun than listening to speeches. The police were ordered to make a baton charge. Shortly afterwards, free fights were in progress. The fighting spread rapidly to adjoining streets, and soon white policemen were pursuing colored people and wielding their batons with accustomed vigor against colored skulls.

The Torch Commando's great parade ended in a first-class riot.

The Cape Town riot had an unforeseen and distinctly chastening effect on the Commando. "This," said the Nationalists, "is what comes of allowing coloreds to march arm-in-arm with whites through the streets." An astonishingly large number of Torchmen, who had enthusiastically pledged themselves to fight for democracy, seemed to think so too.

When the Commando held its first national congress in Johannesburg, the meeting was private. "One section of the press is hostile," said Sailor, taking a leaf from the other Malan's book, "and would distort our words." He seemed much less confident and more ill at ease than when I had seen him last. At my last glimpse of him, in Cape Town, before the riot began, his hand was being wrung by tearfully grateful and slightly tipsy colored ex-soldiers. The one definite thing to emerge from the Commando's first national congress was that only whites would henceforth be eligible for membership.

When Sailor Malan returned to South Africa, he was befriended by Harry Oppenheimer, Sir Ernest Oppenheimer's son and heir. Harry, only a couple of years older than Sailor, was an ex-soldier himself. He had fought in Libya with Smuts's "desert rats," who wore black berets and crept under cover of night as near as was not totally suicidal to Rommel's lines, to establish listening-posts. Now returned to civilian life, Harry was a director of forty-five opulent Oppenheimer companies, and was manifestly destined to take over the tiller of the Oppenheimer empire. He found a job for Sailor in Kimberley, where the diamonds are sorted.

Harry was a member of the United Party, which opposed the Nationalists. Harry was as much at home in the perplexing world of politics as Sailor had been in the cockpit of a Spitfire. "When it comes to politics," said Sailor fervently, "I never make a decision without first consulting Harry."

Harry's influence on the Torch Commando would certainly appear to have been far from negligible. "Torch" meetings were held in a board-room in the Johannesburg headquarters of the Anglo-American Corporation, and energetic young members of the Anglo-American staff began to play a prominent part in directing the policies and planning the campaigns of the Commando.

In the course of its somewhat tortuous evolution, the Commando acquired other strange new allies.

At Wakkerstroom, a Nationalist stronghold near Johannesburg, I rubbed my eyes when I saw Sailor Malan sharing a platform with a golden-bearded Boer, J. D. Jerling, who had been a commandant of the Ossewa-Brandwag. After Hitler's defeat, Jerling had seen the light and joined the United Party. It now seemed to him quite natural that he should join the Torch Commando too.

Wakkerstroom was a typical Transvaal dorp, surrounded by bare brown hills. The United Party was contesting a by-election there. All day, dusty motor-cars rolled up to the polling-booths. Bearded, gnarled Boer farmers alighted from them, wearing Nationalist Party rosettes. The Torch Commando men arrived on motorcycles, wearing leather jackets and gauntlets. They drove briskly up and down the little town's one street, their cycles' exhausts making an ear-splitting din. The farmers regarded them without favor, and went on voting stolidly Nationalist. The Commando men slapped their gauntlets defiantly against their thighs, and drank rather more beer than was good for them. The United Party lost the by-election.

The Nationalists wanted to take half-castes off the common voters' roll. Sailor Malan opposed this, but at the same time strenuously denied that half-castes were eligible for membership in his Torch Commando, though many half-castes were war veterans. A Torchman confidentially explained to a Boer farmer why the Torch opposed the removal of the half-castes' voting rights. "The half-castes," he argued, "dislike the Negroes just as much as you and I do."

Down in Natal, which is the most "British" part of South Africa, the Commando still retained its glamour. There was talk of Natal seceding from the Union, to show what the British thought of the country's Boer Government. The Torch Commando briskly took charge of the secession band-wagon, and a monster torch parade on familiar lines was held in Durban.

Among the spectators was Manilal Gandhi. "Outside the city hall," he told me dryly, "a Torchman with a handlebar mustache glimpsed another Torchman with a handlebar mustache. Bellowing delighted recognition, he propelled himself through the crowd like a Channel swimmer intent on reaching the farther shore. The two mustaches met and muscularly shook hands. 'I say, old boy,' bawled one Torchman to the other Torchman, 'isn't this *fun!*' "

Dr. Malan hastened to Durban and bluntly asked the English: "How will you get rid of the Indians without me to help you?" Durban, and English Natal, had no answer. The Torch guttered.

: 2 :

THE DECLINE of the Torch coincided with the growth of an Indian and Negro "passive resistance" campaign, which borrowed freely from the teaching of Mahatma Gandhi even though it accepted some of its leaders from the ranks of the Communists. The Indian and Negro politicians formed a "united front." In Johannesburg the leaders were Yusuf Cachalia, a handsome young Indian, and Walter Max Sisulu, a tough little Basuto who wore as a sort of uniform a brown beret and corduroy trousers. All over South Africa their followers challenged the police to arrest them, and went to prison singing songs and shouting: "Africa!"

One night in Johannesburg I watched white police swoop on the headquarters of the passive resisters. They surrounded the building and waited with their rifles at the ready. The resisters trooped peacefully downstairs, led by Yusuf Cachalia, who walked up to the policeman in charge and asked him what he wanted.

"Line your men up against that wall!" snapped the policeman.

Cachalia, a tall and graceful young man with airy defiance in every gesture of his slim brown wrists, looked at the policemen who blocked both ends of the street, clutching their rifles.

"Are you going to shoot us now," he drawled, "or will you wait until later?"

The resisters obediently lined themselves up against the wall, but there was some delay in bringing up patrol wagons to remove them to prison. While they waited, they sang sad, soft songs in the dusk. The songs gradually changed to a more cheerful tempo, until they were shuffling their feet and performing little jazz steps. When the patrol wagons arrived, they got

128

into them still singing, and crying: "Africa!" The police looked somewhat foolish.

In the weeks that followed, thousands of Negroes and scores of Indians were arrested in many parts of the country. Then a few white "liberals" joined the campaign, led by Patrick Duncan, the son of a former Governor-General of South Africa. At Duncan's side was Manilal Gandhi, son of another famous father.

Duncan, still recovering from a motor accident, arrived in Johannesburg on crutches. He was thirty-four years old, and had frank blue eyes and considerable charm. With him was his pretty young wife, Cynthia, daughter of Sir Patrick Ashley-Cooper, a director of the Bank of England. Duncan had thrown up his job as a British colonial officer in Basutoland to join the Negroes' campaign. Before serving in Basutoland he had been private secretary to Sir Evelyn Baring, when Baring was the British High Commissioner in Pretoria. "I was a very bad secretary," he told me ruefully. "Once I lost Baring's sword just before he was to appear in full ceremonial dress before the King and Queen."

Duncan was a devout Christian. The South African leaders of the Anglican Church, to which he and his wife belonged, had already championed the Negroes' cause. "There are circumstances," declared the archbishop of Cape Town, the Most Reverend Dr. Geoffrey Clayton, "in which it is a man's duty as a Christian to refuse to obey a particular law; certainly there is in the teaching of the Church no obligation on a man as a Christian to obey unjust laws." The bishop of Pretoria, the Right Reverend Robert Selby Taylor, announced: "In my judgment, there are occasions when the laws of the State become so onerous that a Christian is compelled to obey the voice of God, expressed through his own conscience, rather than the laws of man."

With his injured leg stretched out on a chair, and his crutches propped up behind him, Duncan said thoughtfully: "I decided that deeds count for more than words." He was no Communist, he added. "I fully believe that Communism is a worse menace to the free world than anything else, including the race policies of the present South African Government." But, though there were Communists in both the Indian and the African congresses, "the two congresses have not spoken a single word of hatred against whites, as whites." Only if some whites supported the aspirations of the Negroes and Indians could a bloody race clash be avoided. "I look forward," said Duncan firmly, "to the African National Congress and its ally, the South African Indian Congress, becoming great, responsible political organizations." He added that as a Christian he had the most profound admiration for Gandhi.

Cynthia Duncan said quietly: "I feel like a soldier's wife. I wish it were any other man than my husband doing this. But I know he has to do it."

Manilal Gandhi had long hesitated to take part in the passive-resistance movement. He distrusted Communist influence. But when he heard that Duncan was joining the movement, he decided to go along with it.

Duncan and Gandhi planned to visit a location near Johannesburg and to address the people. To enter a location they needed a pass, but as they had no intention of asking for one, they knew they would be arrested. This was just what they wanted, but they feared the police would arrest them before they had made their gesture. Elaborate precautions were taken to throw the police off the scent.

Police cars with spluttering radios sought the pair frantically. So did excited newspaper reporters. Hoping for a lead, the baffled police followed the reporters' cars. A long line of cars spent some time, twisting and turning, round the glittering yellow mine-dumps of the Rand, until someone realized that everyone was simply following everyone else. Meanwhile Duncan and Gandhi safely reached their destination.

I watched them march through the dusty streets of the segregated township, past tin shacks, deep potholes, dustbins crammed with refuse, open drains, and broken-down privies. Duncan hobbled briskly on his crutches. He was bareheaded, and his green tie flapped in the breeze. Manilal Gandhi, a little out of breath, trotted by his side. Mangy curs yapped at their heels, and ragged Negro children, wide-eyed and with their wondering hands clapped over their mouths, watched their progress. They were soon surrounded by a cheering crowd, many of whom wore the green, gold, and black armband of the African National Congress. The crowd gave the Congress salute, an outheld fist with the thumb turned up, and yelled: "Africa!"

In the heart of the township slum, Duncan halted and raised himself on his crutches. Speaking in Sesutu, a Negro dialect, he said: "The road before us is long and hard, but we must tread it in peace, and with nothing but love in our hearts for all who live in this land." He raised a hand and returned the Congress salute, saying vigorously: "Africa!" Then he turned to a Negro bystander and asked quietly: "Please show us the way out."

The crowd followed the pair back to their car, where Cynthia awaited them. Before they reached it, the perspiring police arrived. A police officer ostentatiously buckled on his revolver holster, then told Duncan and Gandhi: "You are under arrest." Gandhi bowed slightly. Duncan smiled. As they were driven away in a police car, the Negroes raised their fists and shouted: "Africa!" Duncan waved to them.

Left behind, Cynthia sighed to me: "Oh, dear, I forgot to give him a toothbrush." Next day she visited her husband in prison and handed over his toothbrush, a volume of Bacon's essays, and an Afrikaans Bible.

Most whites in South Africa thought that Gandhi, and "renegades" like Duncan should be hanged, or deported.

: 3 :

THERE IS nothing lowbrow about South African politicians. The top-rankers are tireless dialecticians and several of them have had dignified doctorates conferred on them by applauding universities. Dr. Malan studied mathematics as well as theology.

The late Jan Smuts was a philosopher as well as a politician. He was also a soldier, a botanist, a biologist, and a physicist. He kept up a brisk correspondence with such intellectual lights as Einstein, Niels Bohr, and Max Planck. His right-hand man, Jan Hofmeyr, was principal of the Witwatersrand University before he was thirty.

Smuts led the South African Party. He was opposed by Hertzog, who led the Nationalist Party. Then Smuts and Hertzog fused their parties in the United South African National Party. Malan then formed his Purified Nationalist Party. Later, Hertzog broke with Smuts and joined Malan. The new grouping was called the Purified Reunited Nationalist Party. But after a short while Hertzog deserted Malan, who promptly rechristened his party the Repurified Reunited Nationalist Party. Smuts continued to call his party the United South African National Party.

Most white South Africans found a political home in one or other of the two parties. But the four fifths of the country's population who were non-white could not belong to either, since membership was confined to whites. Moreover, on the "color issue" there was little discernible difference in principle between the two white parties. Both believed that the white man must be boss. The furious disputes between them were confined to other matters. The disputes were conducted with great dialectical skill, but resembled debates between medieval scholars over the number of angels who could dance on the point of a needle.

Jan Smuts was a first-rate politician. He could talk for hours on any subject and at the end leave his hearers with the impression that they had listened to something very profound whereas in fact he had said nothing whatever. When he died he was hailed as statesman, warrior, philosopher, and scientist. Subsequent workers in those fields have made the melancholy discovery that he did not contribute anything new, or, if he did, it was generally wrong.

Smuts nevertheless was a great man. He could grasp other

men's ideas and sweep them unblushingly into the broad stream of his own discourse. He was on intimate terms with other great men, who after intellectual contact with him came away bubbling over with new ideas, which they thought he had expressed. In fact, the ideas were their own, but they might never have conceived them if Smuts had not stimulated them. "A talk with Smuts," said one man who knew him well, "is like having an electric massage."

The South African Parliament meets in Cape Town for a few months a year. But the seat of government is Pretoria. Every year the Cabinet ministers, their wives, their secretaries, their secretaries' wives, and many of the civil servants and *their* wives travel the thousand miles from Pretoria to Cape Town for the session. Every year also, they move back again. This costly migration has become as integral a part of South African life as Dingaan's Day, poor whites, *boerewors* (sausage meat, a favorite Boer dish), and the Durban July Handicap. "South Africa," said a wit, "has two flags, three capitals, four provinces, and five races; its motto is 'Unity is Strength.'"

When he was working in Pretoria, Smuts lived in a ramshackle bungalow at a place called Irene. Distinguished guests were frequent, but slept in trundle beds and liked it. Meals were informal, and often out of cans.

Up at dawn, Smuts would set off across the veld to collect specimens of new grasses. When in Cape Town, he occupied the Prime Minister's grand official residence, but frequently sneaked out to scramble up the side of Table Mountain. On trips abroad, he bounced into New York or London in midwinter wearing an open-neck bush-shirt.

Smuts's political policy was simple; he just did not have one. At no time did he ever invent or propound a clear-cut solution of the country's pressing color problem, or of the real rift between Briton and Boer. But this lack was concealed by the silver quality of his eloquence, and by his Olympian attitude to all mundane issues. "When you ask Smuts if black men should have the vote," said a baffled interviewer, "he talks intelligently and entertainingly about the probable future of *Homo sapiens* in the atomic age." Smuts had a Wellsian brain, which dismissed troublesome details, especially the ones nearest home.

After Smuts died, the United Party was led by a young lawyer, Jacob Gideon Nel Strauss. To him Smuts bequeathed his politician's black velvet-lined magic cabinet, his mirrors, and his conjuror's stick. Unfortunately, Strauss was no magician. He could wear Smuts's hat, but could produce no rabbits from it. With Smuts gone, the United Party's lack of even a political philosophy became painfully evident. "Trying to discover what the United Party's policy is," said a candid critic, "is like having a wrestling match in a hammock."

Strauss did his best. Despite disastrously boyish good looks, he contrived to add twenty years to his age. He wore horn-rimmed spectacles, and addressed astonished members of the party who were older than himself as "my boy." Smuts had suffered from sciatica; Strauss addressed meetings with one hand clutching the small of his back. Like Smuts, he developed an attractive slight lisp, and seriously considered the idea of growing a small tufted beard.

The Nationalists were crafty and seasoned campaigners. They rudely called their new opponent "little Straussie," and baited political traps with questions of the order of "Have you stopped beating your wife—yes or no?" Thus when Strauss opposed *apartheid*, they asked him if he wanted white girls to marry Kaffirs. When Strauss indignantly denied it, they asked him why in that case he opposed *apartheid*.

In all those encounters, Strauss invariably led with his chin, afterwards picking himself up dizzily from the canvas to ask who had struck him. One political commentator regretfully reported: "It is like watching a boxing match between a master of ringcraft and an actor playing the role of a world champion. Unfortunately for Mr. Strauss, the fight is real." Another said it was like watching a Methodist minister of impeccable morals march into a dockside saloon to tell the inmates what he thought of their drinking habits. Every time that the swing doors opened and a disheveled figure came flying out, it was the Methodist minister.

Within a few years of Smuts's death, the United Party, which had stood for so long between Malan and power, was not only crumbling at the edges but only half-heartedly opposing measures aimed at its own eventual extinction.

A tougher nut to crack than Strauss was Emil Solomon Sachs, the bespectacled secretary of the Garment Workers' Union and a militant apostle of working-class unity. For years before Malan's victory Solly Sachs was a thorn in the Nationalists' side. For this there were two reasons. He organized his garment workers, and succeeded in raising their wages, without bothering about who was white and who was colored. This ran directly counter to everything the Nationalists were fighting for, and what made it worse in their eyes was that it worked. Instead of white Afrikaner girls shuddering at the very thought of associating with colored girls, they struck in sympathy with them. The second reason was that Solly for a long time made money out of Nationalist attacks on him. He was South Africa's most successful suer, and was repeatedly awarded damages for defamation arising out of scurrilous statements in Nationalist publications.

Loathed by the Nationalists, Solly was not exactly beloved by the Communists. In 1931 he was expelled from the Communist Party for lacking revolutionary fervor and for reformist deviations. In plain language, Solly believed in improving working-conditions by bargaining with employers, not by wrecking factories. On broader issues, he declared that what South Africa needed was not Socialism but more capitalism to replace current feudalism, adding: "Not Lenin, but Lincoln." The Communists were naturally incensed by those bourgeois sentiments.

Nevertheless, when the Nationalists came to power, Solly was "named" as a Communist under the interesting new law that gave the Government power to call any person a Communist without giving him the right to challenge the verdict in a court of law. Then, having been officially dubbed a Communist, Sachs was expelled from his post of secretary of the Garment Workers' Union, which meant that he was deprived of his only means of livelihood. Finally, he was arrested for addressing a meeting of his trade union in defiance of a Government order not to do so. After that, Solly prudently left South Africa.

In the course of his war against the United Party, Dr. Malan declared: "A vote for Strauss is a vote for Sachs." This seemed rather unfair to Strauss, whose only complaint against the Nationalists' onslaughts on the toiling masses, as distinct from their onslaughts on the middle-class English, was that the Nationalists were antagonizing "a hitherto docile labor force."

: 4 :

"WE ARE fighting another Blood River battle for white civilization," cried the speaker fervently. "This time we fight against the black hordes of the whole of Africa, supported by white liberals and Indians." In the audience, even Boer children wept with emotion.

Stumping the country, Dr. Malan's Finance Minister, Nicholas Havenga, declared: "The United Party and the United Nations are demanding equal rights for white and black! What is your answer?"

In scores of dusty dorps throughout the land I heard other Nationalist speakers hammer home the simple lesson. Meetings often began at ten o'clock in the morning and went on until four in the afternoon. The Boer *volk* take their politics seriously.

After five years of Nationalist rule, South Africans were being asked to vote for or against Malan. A vote for Strauss, they were told, was a vote for Communism, for white-black equality, for the hated United Nations, for British imperialism, for "Hoggenheimer," for Yankee domination.

Strauss retorted: "The Nationalists are digging the white man's grave in South Africa. They are creating *apartheid* not

136

only between white and black, but between South Africa and the rest of the world."

On polling day, from the Rand to Table Mountain and from Durban to Windhoek there were half-mile-long queues standing four deep outside the polling stations. Uniformed nurses wheeled patients from the hospitals on stretchers to cast their votes. Some early voters rushed to the polls in pajamas and dressing-gowns.

Thanks partly to an electoral system that made a Boer farmer's vote worth the votes of two townsmen, Malan, though he polled fewer votes than Strauss, got far more seats. Still opposing Malan were a million English-speaking South Africans and almost half a million Afrikaners. He was also opposed by ten million Negroes, Indians, and half-castes, the vast majority of whom had no vote. Nevertheless Malan won the election hands-down.

In Pretoria I watched the old man laboriously mount a platform, nervously grasping his wife's arm. Nearly seventy-nine, he walked with difficulty. But his color was good, and he looked cheerful. He had good reason. On this, his second triumphal election procession from Cape Town, he had passed through a thousand miles of solidly Nationalist territory. At every whistle-stop he was greeted by cheering mobs waving Boer flags.

In Pretoria's floodlit Church Square twelve thousand Afrikaners fervently sang hymns. Attentively at the old man's side stood Hans Strydom, not yet sixty and hopeful of the succession.

I watched Malan's ministers drive away from their triumph in their shiny black Cadillacs and Packards, accompanied by their well-groomed wives. In five years the new Boer rulers had come a long way, from being country-town attorneys, university professors, and unsuccessful farmers to become the masters of the richest part of Africa. I did not think power was likely to soften them. South Africa would become an increasingly difficult place for a reporter who sought to state the facts as he saw them. I had seen a growing hostility toward a free press, and a mounting hysteria against "foreign criticism." I had also seen free speech emasculated, political rights curtailed, the courts of law silenced or sidetracked, trade unions shackled, freedom of movement suspended, the means of livelihood of opponents of the Government destroyed or threatened, and a vast growth of government by decree, rubber-stamp, and, where necessary, jackboot and "special" police. The Nationalists demanded freedom for themselves, but progressively denied it to anyone else.

"What will happen now?" I asked an Afrikaner friend who did not support Malan.

"South Africa is on the road to a one-party state," he said, "and the screw of *apartheid* will be turned ever tighter on the ten million people who weren't lucky enough to be born white."

"And the English?"

He shrugged.

Half a century after the British military victory over the republics of the Boers, the last remaining British stronghold in South Africa was Natal. Among Natal's lush green hills, the English with their Zulu and Indian labor grew sugar, and lived in white-pillared mansions with white poinsettias growing round their doors. In Natal, English was spoken, Afrikaans almost never.

"Now," said Strydom after the second Nationalist victory, "we must eliminate British imperialism from Natal."

Seventy-seven-year-old Senator Heaton Nicholls of Natal retorted: "The Union of South Africa has proved a complete failure. The time has come to end the sordid marriage between Boer and Briton."

The *Cape Argus* drew a line across the page of South African history from the time of the creation of the Union of South Africa in 1910 to the second and greater Malan victory in 1953 and declared: "The brutal reality is that we are two nations."

The Nationalists had urged *apartheid* between white and black. Now some English South Africans were prophesying *apartheid* between white and white.

Meanwhile the black men and the brown men looked on, and thought their own thoughts.

XI

BECHUANALAND: THE ALIEN CORN

THE TRAIN, scarcely moving, seemed to be suspended in a hot purgatory, with Johannesburg far behind and Palapye, in Bechuanaland, unattainably far ahead. Dust thickened on the green leather seats, lay uneasily on the window ledges, and coated the jogging glass with a red film. The leather seats were hot to the touch.

We struggled along the corridor to the diner and drank flat, warm beer. Through the dust-coated windows, all we could see was the Kalahari Desert, a vast flat plain of sun-baked rocks and stunted bushes under a flat blue sky. The desert is a great triangular-shaped wedge that splits Malan's "greater South Africa," being thrust between the Transvaal and South-West Africa. Passing through the Khamas'[1] country, the train skirted the fringe of the Kalahari, trailing dirty smoke along its edge. The interior of the Kalahari has scarcely been explored.

One man with us, T. C. Robertson, said: "A British expedition traveled for five weeks across the Kalahari. They crossed 2,600 miles and never saw water. One day they came on a small party of Bushmen, trudging on foot in pursuit of one lonely cloud. The little men carried bows and poisoned arrows. A wrinkled little Bushwoman was laden with empty ostrich shells.

"'We follow the cloud,' explained the Bushman chief. 'When it rains, she will fill her shells with water.' The Bushmen said they had been following the cloud for weeks. Meanwhile

[1] The Khamas are the traditional native rulers of Bechuanaland; hence Tshekedi Khama, Seretse Khama. Khama is the royal family name.

139

they lived by hunting game. The rainless desert contains great herds of game, and a Bushman can outrun a deer. But no one, not even the Bushmen, knows how the animals live without water; and nobody knows how the Bushmen survive either.

"The Bushwoman was a rain wizard and a great sorceress. The expedition were carrying twelve tons of water, and they gave the Bushmen a three-gallon tin. They handed it to the Bushwoman. She drank a gallon and a half, without stopping. Then she paused, and drank the other gallon and a half. The others got none.

"The Bushmen made the British party a present of a poisoned arrow, and trekked on."

The train was loaded with newspapermen, among whom T. C. was the most striking. That day in 1950 Vernon Barber and I were on our way to Serowe, the capital of Bechuanaland.

There is honor among journalists, but not much. Vernon, whom everyone calls Jock, though he was born in Yorkshire, had suggested to me that we get off the train at Mafeking and take the next train to Palapye in the evening. This would enable us to waylay both Tshekedi Khama, the Regent of the ruling Bamangwato tribe of Bechuanaland, and Sir Evelyn Baring, the British High Commissioner. T. C. however, was in happy ignorance of this plan, and we proposed that he should remain so.

Thomas Chalmers Robertson is a large man with snow-white hair and a bristling black brigand's mustache. He looks and talks like Ernest Hemingway. A Robertson emigrated from Scotland to South Africa to preach the Word of God among the Boers. His descendants themselves became Boers, but retained their Scottish name. T. C. almost got into Parliament once; but when a Boer heckler made him lose his temper, he bawled: "If it hadn't been for my grandfather you wouldn't have had a God!" This ruined his chance of election. During the Second World War he was one of Jan Smuts's right-hand men and waged war on the Broederbond, the Boer secret society, at the same time that Smuts was fighting Hitler.

The newspapermen were rushing up to Serowe to write a story

with a Biblical parallel. Tshekedi Khama's nephew, Seretse Khama, had married a white girl, Ruth Williams. The newspapermen wanted to find out how Ruth was getting on amid the alien corn. The marriage had raised a violent storm of protest in South Africa. Under South African pressure, the British Government had exiled Seretse. He was in London and had been forbidden to return to Bechuanaland. Ruth was in Serowe, expecting a child. It was a piquant situation.

Bechuanaland is bigger than Texas, but has a population of only 250,000. Tshekedi had been Regent of the ruling Bamangwato tribe for over twenty years because when Seretse's father died, Seretse was only a child. When he came of age, Seretse should have been chief, but his marriage to Ruth had led to exile instead.

Sitting in the train diner watching T. C. drink beer, I thought back to my first meeting with Tshekedi Khama.

: 2 :

MR. PIPPIT, who had been making sucking noises with his pipe, removed it from his mouth and stabbed the air.

"Here come the Kaffirs," he said.

Mr. Pippit was a short man with a short mustache who, between sucks at his short pipe, spoke in short sentences.

The Negro graduates entered two by two. The young men flashed their white teeth in shy smiles, and the girls looked demure. They took their places on the benches provided for them, and gazed about them with pleasurable excitement. They had come here three or four or five years ago, from distant, smoky kraals, some of them the sons and daughters of chiefs. They had sat in lecture halls, diligently taken notes, and read many books. Now they had passed their final examinations and would soon be going forth into the world, as schoolteachers, medical aides, or agricultural officers, or to rule their tribes more wisely than their fathers had done. But to Mr. Pippit they were still Kaffirs.

141

Mr. Pippit, who was the editor of a South African newspaper, and I had come some hundreds of miles for the occasion, which was the centenary of the Lovedale Mission School, in South Africa. Adjoining Lovedale was the Negro university college of Fort Hare, and the Fort Hare students were taking part in the centenary celebrations. That morning we had come up from the small town of Alice, which lay farther along the valley, on the edge of the Ciskei native reserve. Mr. Pippit had been my companion on the journey.

The valley was a green bowl amid blue hills, and the sun glinted on the white lace of a waterfall, high up in the forest. Tiny red and black moving dots on the hillside were grazing cattle, and we could hear the thin, distant cry of a Negro herd-boy.

All through the hot afternoon there were gracious speeches, by the two principals of Lovedale and Fort Hare, and by a Negro professor and a suave and portly English bishop. But one distinguished visitor struck a more vivid note.

The arrival of his followers struck Mr. Pippit momentarily dumb. They had the same effect on me. For they were wild-looking men, wearing animals' skins and carrying spears. They took their places on a bench, with a good deal of jostling and clanking of ankle bangles, then looked around them disdainfully. One of them fixed a stern eye on Mr. Pippit, who blenched.

He whispered rapidly to me, behind his hand: "They're Bamangwato! Tshekedi must have brought them!"

"Tshekedi Khama?" I asked.

Mr. Pippit nodded, and made a fearsome grimace. Still shielding the words with his hand, he muttered: "Damn Kaffir cheek! Just look at those brutes! Now, if I had my way—"

Into the gathering strode a short, broad-shouldered man. He had a round head and a thick, short neck. His black skin shone like satin. He had a rather flattened nose, like a pugilist's, and small flat ears. He wore a plain, dark suit with a white shirt and a dark tie, but his broad shoulders and purposeful step radiated power. He raised a hand, and the men with the spears, who had risen at his entrance, sank back on their bench. Then he sat down quietly and took no further notice of them.

While the portly bishop suavely delivered a carefully prepared speech, with much fluttering of soft white hands, Mr. Pippit imparted a little history.

"That fellow's a troublemaker," he muttered. He was not referring to the bishop. He eyed the broad-shouldered Negro malevolently. "Should have been chucked out long ago. Almost was. But they let him come back. Great mistake, I always said."

"What happened?" I asked.

"The black swine thrashed a couple of white traders." He scowled at the henchmen with the spears, who were shifting their buttocks on the hard bench and yawning openly in the bishop's face. "Thought he was Lord God Almighty. But Evans settled his hash." He chuckled grimly. "Evans of the Broke," he explained.

I had heard of the gallant British admiral. Mr. Pippit glowingly described his African exploit. Admiral Evans, on hearing of the outrage, had marched from Cape Town up to the Kalahari Desert, entered Bechuanaland, and sternly called the Regent of the Bamangwato to account. Tshekedi had apologized. But he had the gallant admiral at a certain disadvantage, for two of the expeditionary force's gun-carriages stuck in the desert sands, and Tshekedi's men, on Tshekedi's orders, helped to pull them out. Also, it transpired that the white traders Tshekedi had punished had flagrantly transgressed tribal law and Tshekedi's hospitality.

"Makes no difference," Mr. Pippit sturdily insisted. "Beggar should have been thrashed himself. Thrashed and then chucked out. Exiled for life. Only way to treat a Kaffir who gets uppity."

The bishop came to a ponderously Christian conclusion amid scattered applause and stepped down with a modest smile. His place was taken by Tshekedi Khama. The broad-shouldered man looked carefully round the gathering. He fixed a particular eye on the gowned graduates. I had expected the voice that came from that powerful chest to be deep, but I had not anticipated the thrilling hint of the trumpet in it. The audience snapped to attention as if a bugle had blown.

He began abruptly. "We Africans," he said, "owe much to the white man. If there had been no white missionaries, there would today be no mission schools, no colleges, and you would not be sitting here today in your graduates' robes. I am not one of you, for I never graduated. When my father died, my nephew Seretse, who is also my chief, was a little boy. They took me from my books and made me Regent of our tribe. So I am still learning."

He smiled and shifted his powerful shoulders.

"One of the things I have learned is that the gratitude we owe to our white friends should always be an African virtue and never be allowed to become an African vice. We Africans are not ungrateful. But we are lazy. We thank the white man for all he has done for us. That is pleasant—and easy. Then we sit back and wait for him to do more for us. That is wrong.

"The bishop, who is the friend of all of us, has told you that Africans suffer certain disadvantages because of their color. That is perfectly true. But I noticed that you all applauded eagerly. Were you applauding because you wanted to do something about it, for yourselves, or because you were hoping that good men like the bishop would do it for you? There are white men who spend their lives fighting for the rights of the Africans. But what are the Africans doing for themselves? You are not children; you are men. Most Africans are ignorant; but how many work hard at educating themselves? Africans are poor; but they are many. They could build colleges for themselves, if each contributed a little. But how many say: 'The white man is rich: let him build colleges for poor Africans'? You will never get anywhere that way. A black man should be proud to be a black man, as a white man is proud of being a white man. But there can be no pride, and there can be no progress, if Africans depend always on white men to do for them what they ought to be doing by their own efforts and their own will. If they do not make this attempt—and they could do it *now*—we Africans

144

will always be poor, ignorant, and backward. It is we who must decide. God helps them who help themselves."

He stopped as abruptly as he had begun, and stepped down amid somewhat bewildered applause. It seemed to be a novel experience for his African audience to be told such things, by an African. The graduates, in their new gowns, looked rather hurt.

I expected Mr. Pippit to approve. He had spent most of the morning telling me that Africans were spineless, unreliable, lazy, and hopelessly dependent on white guidance. I looked at him expectantly.

But Mr. Pippit was gazing open-mouthed at Tshekedi. He looked like a man who had had a rude awakening.

"Well!" he gasped at length. "Of all the Kaffir impudence! Trying to make out that *they* don't need *us!*"

: 3 :

MAFEKING, NORTH of Kimberley and near the Bechuanaland border, is a small, hot town that lives chiefly on memories of its famous siege in the Boer War. When Jock Barber and I stealthily left the train in the early hours of that Sunday morning, the whole place seemed to be still asleep. But outside the railroad station stood a solitary cab with the driver nodding over the wheel.

Not without glee, we watched the train trundle off with its load of newspapermen, carrying them deeper into the desert lands. Then we picked up our bags and hailed the cab. We were just getting into it when a voice bellowed: "Hey!" We turned.

Thomas Chalmers Robertson, looking like a benevolent bull clad in mauve pajamas, had leaped from the departing train, clutching a suitcase. He now surveyed us with a triumphant leer. "Were you planning to leave me behind, boys?"

Jock Barber sighed. "We'll hold the cab while you go into the waiting-room and change," he said resignedly.

Mafeking was slowly and painfully coming awake when we emerged into the streets after a hotel breakfast served by yawning waiters. T. C., now more suitably attired, had told the cab to wait, and we drove off to see Tshekedi Khama. He was living in a small house outside the town.

When we introduced ourselves, Tshekedi smiled politely. But he shook his head emphatically when we started asking him questions.

"I have to see the High Commissioner first," he explained. "That's why I've come to Mafeking."

"Chief," said T. C., "what's your opinion of Seretse's marriage?"

"Ruth is a most charming girl," said Tshekedi cautiously.

"But do you approve of the marriage?"

"I'd rather not say."

I remembered what he had told the gathering at Lovedale: "A black man should be proud to be a black man, as a white man is proud of being a white man."

Barber asked a question: "You stated that you would not remain in the Bamangwato territory if Ruth entered it as Seretse's wife?"

Tshekedi's eyes flickered. He nodded. "I did."

"Well," said Barber, "Ruth is there now."

Tshekedi grinned. "And I am here."

"Do you object to the marriage?"

"I'm not prepared to say."

"Do you think Seretse should become the chief?"

"But he *is* the chief!" Tshekedi protested.

"The British say they'll never let him come back," T. C. pointed out.

"I want Seretse to return," said Tshekedi simply. "I do not agree that because he married a white woman he should be expelled from his own country."

"Then you don't object to the marriage at all?"

Tshekedi smiled. "I never said that. I said that he should not have to leave his own country just because he married a white woman."

146

We could get no more out of him. When we left, Tshekedi courteously shook hands all round.

We returned to the hotel, where T. C. rang up an official and left a message for his old friend Nicholas Monsarrat, who was expected to arrive in Mafeking later that morning by air, in the company of the British High Commissioner, Sir Evelyn Baring.

T. C. proposed to take a shower and lie down. Barber and I went for a stroll in the town. When we returned to the hotel, we walked up to T. C.'s room. As we approached it, a lady left it hurriedly. She appeared distrait.

T. C. was sitting on the edge of his bed, wearing only a top-coat and chewing morosely on a newly lit cigar. Nicholas Monsarrat, also biting on a cigar, looked somewhat shaken.

"That was a district officer's wife," he explained. "I brought her along to meet T. C. I knocked—"

"And I woke up and called: 'Come in,'" growled T. C.

"And I politely let the lady enter first," said Nicholas, "only T. C. was lying on top of the bed with no clothes on. So she left."

"Goddamit!" howled the culprit. "How was I to know you had a lady friend with you?"

Nicholas Monsarrat had not yet published his best-seller, *The Cruel Sea*. This was still a secret between him and his God and the British Navy. He was the British Information Officer in South Africa and was on his way to Serowe to help supervise the *kgotla*, or tribal assembly, of the Bamangwato, at which Sir Evelyn Baring proposed to break the news that Seretse Khama could never become chief.

"More than that I cannot tell you," said Nicholas cheerfully. "Sir Evelyn is going up to Serowe on this evening's train, and I suppose you want to come along. I think it can be arranged. At the moment, he's discussing the position with Tshekedi Khama."

"I hope," said Jock Barber, "he manages to get more out of him than we did."

Nicholas found us seats on the train and followed us into

147

our compartment carrying a flat tin case. T. C. eyed it curiously.

"What's in that?"

"His Excellency's sword."

"Good God!" said T. C., awed.

Presently Baring joined us. He was a tall, pale-faced man, with legs like a stork and a gentle voice. He had a difficult job. The three African territories of Bechuanaland, Basutoland, and Swaziland are "protected" by Britain. South Africa has long wanted to incorporate them, and Seretse's marriage to a white woman increased this desire. The South Africans looked on the mixed marriage as a threat to "white" civilization in Africa. Seretse was thought of as a tom-tom-beating black savage, and what the South Africans said about Ruth was and remains unprintable.

Baring chatted with us affably, but diplomatically confined his remarks to the subject of African bird-life, on which topic he and T. C. turned out to be experts. They were analyzing the habits of the lilac-breasted roller when I fell asleep. When I awoke, Baring had gone and T. C. was bending sinisterly over the sleeping form of Nicholas Monsarrat. He prodded him urgently.

"Nicholas!" he whispered. "Quick! The sword!"

Nicholas sat bolt-upright. He looked agitatedly for his flat tin case.

"What about it?"

"Quick! The sword! Get it out!"

"Why?"

"Because the tribes have risen," said T. C. sepulchrally, "and it's every man for himself."

It took some little time to restore order in the compartment.

: 4 :

WE GOT off the train at Palapye. On all sides stretched flat country covered with thornbush. Palapye consisted of a hotel and a tin shed beside the railroad track.

A car was waiting to take us to Serowe. We bumped over a rough track cut through the bush. Bechuanaland seemed a vastly empty place. The dust churned up by the car hung behind us in a thick spreading cloud. By the time we reached Serowe we were dust from head to foot. T. C., concerned, said he hoped it would not get into Nicholas's flat tin case and tarnish His Excellency's sword.

At the outskirts of Serowe we passed an old Negro in a tattered khaki army greatcoat. He tottered along the side of the road, ringing a hand-bell and calling out something unintelligible in a high, cracked voice. This was the town crier, but we never discovered what he was crying. There was nobody else in sight. Serowe was simply a vast collection of rounded mud huts. Surrounding each hut was a stout thornbush fence, for the capital of Bechuanaland lies in the heart of lion country.

The town was supposed to have a population of 30,000, but the huts seemed deserted. We found the hush somewhat uncanny.

So did the handful of white people who lived in Serowe. They went farther and thought it was positively sinister. At a local trading store we found them discussing the situation. They said it was tense. The Bamangwato, who resented the British action in exiling Seretse, had quit the town and silently melted into the surrounding bush as soon as they heard that Baring was coming to address them. No one quite knew what they proposed to do. Left in the center of the deserted town, the few whites tended to speak in whispers. No one apparently would have been surprised if a spear had come hurtling through a window. T. C. said thoughtfully that at any rate Nicholas had His Excellency's sword.

While T. C. thus did his best to raise the local whites' spirits, at the same time drinking their beer, Jock Barber and I explored Serowe. Narrow paths, beaten by naked feet, wound between the huts. The huts appeared to be laid out on no particular plan, and the paths constituted a fine maze. In a few minutes we were hopelessly lost. The only landmark was a steep red hill, which appeared to have a flat top, reached by a winding path. We climbed up and found the royal graveyard of the House of Khama.

The Great Khama, grandfather of Seretse and father of Tshekedi, was a remarkable man. He became a Christian, and was exiled by his pagan father. When eventually he succeeded his father, his reign was austere. He put a total ban on the consumption of alcohol and spent much of his time seeking out and personally destroying his subjects' concealed beer-pots. He quarreled with his son Segkoma, the father of Seretse and Tshekedi's elder brother. Segkoma was exiled in his turn, Bamangwato history thus neatly repeating itself. The Great Khama lived to be ninety-three, dying in 1923. Segkoma succeeded him, but did not live long. Thus Tshekedi became Regent, ruling in the name of the infant Seretse.

Over the Great Khama's grave on the hilltop at Serowe is a fine monument, of a small deer in flight. Once, when the Great Khama was hiding from his enemies, he took refuge in a thick clump of bush. The stalkers approached, spear in hand, and Khama decided his time had come. He began to pray. As he did so, a little deer, hiding in the same clump of bush, sprang into the open and raced away. The men who were seeking Khama decided that the deer would not have remained concealed there if the bush also sheltered a human being. They abandoned the pursuit and Khama was saved.

We came down off the hill, and a small girl to whom we beckoned led us placidly back through the maze of paths, chattering at us over her shoulder in the Bamangwato tongue, of which unfortunately we did not understand a word. She also giggled at frequent intervals. When we returned to our hosts, they seemed relieved to see us still alive.

They were sitting around talking about Ruth Khama. It was popularly believed among the stampeding newspapermen that Ruth lived in a mud hut whose floor she, as an obedient wife, had to smear daily with cow dung. In fact, Ruth since her arrival had been living in an ordinary European-style bungalow.

Seretse, who had been educated at Oxford, had never lived in a mud hut in his life. Ruth was a girl of spirit.

"I asked her to tea with me," said a lady. "*Naturally* I was curious to see for myself what sort of girl she was. I tried to make her feel at home. After all, here she was, thousands of miles from England, surrounded by blacks." She paused. "Of course, we didn't discuss the *marriage*. But it was all *rather* amusing. Poor dear Ruth committed so many *gaffes*."

She smiled, vinegarily reminiscent.

"I had been writing letters. My notepaper is rather special; it is *hand-woven*. When Ruth saw it, she exclaimed, just like a child: 'I say, what funny notepaper!' You see, Ruth had never *seen* hand-woven notepaper before."

"And did she ask *you* to tea in return?" I asked.

"She did," said the lady vigorously, "and I have never been so humiliated in my life. A dreadful thing happened. One of the black women came into the room. Naturally I imagined she was one of Ruth's servants. You can imagine my horror when Ruth rose, kissed the woman on the cheek, then turned to me and said: 'I'd like you to meet my sister-in-law.'"

She shuddered. "I'm afraid," she said regretfully, "that Ruth is not—a *lady*."

: 5 :

SIR EVELYN BARING'S *kgotla* was like Barbara Fleece's party, in the story by Evelyn Waugh: nobody came.

All the hot afternoon, solemn black soldiers toiled at the traditional *kgotla* ground, an open space surrounded by camel-thorn trees. Sir Evelyn was up at the Residency, putting on his white-plumed hat and doubtless buckling on his ceremonial sword. The black soldiers were drawing white lines to mark the route by which Sir Evelyn and his mounted escort would enter the *kgotla* ground. Their labors were watched by a bored crowd of newspapermen who sat under the camel-thorn trees with their typewriters on their knees, smoking cigarettes and cursing the heat. Also present were a few Negroes. They watched the black soldiers with amusement.

"It is probably an agricultural demonstration," one wag suggested. "They are conserving the soil."

"Or perhaps it is *apartheid*," suggested another.

Nicholas Monsarrat sped anxiously between the Residency and the *kgotla* ground. He counted the number of tribesmen present, then went back to the Residency to report to Baring. Then he came back to the *kgotla* ground to see if the audience might not have increased in his absence.

This went on for some time. The newspapermen became more and more bored; Nicholas grew more and more distraught. The handful of Negroes continued to jeer, and the black soldiers went on sweating in the sun.

Finally a resident commissioner turned up. He wore a topee and a pistol, and he looked very stern. Curt orders were issued. The officials had decided on desperate measures.

Followed by the newspapermen, the resident commissioner went the round of the huts of the tribal headmen. Most of them had discreetly vanished into the bush along with the majority of Serowe's male population, but at last the resident commissioner found one at home. He threw out his chest and marched up to the hut. The newspapermen produced notebooks, and the photographers whipped out their cameras. Everyone waited expectantly.

The headman who had stayed home was a statuesque man who looked like the village blacksmith, which he may well have been. He came out of his hut and folded his massive arms. The resident commissioner cleared his throat.

"Now, I say, look here!" he said. "You've got to come to the *kgotla*, you know."

The headman kept his arms folded and smiled sardonically.

"If you don't, well, dash it all, I may have to arrest you!"

"Ha!" said the headman, very sardonically indeed.

The resident commissioner was now blushing with embarrass-

152

ment. "I'll give you five minutes," he said sternly, "to be on the *kgotla* ground. Only five minutes, mind you!"

The headman spoke. It was rather like seeing an oversize cigar-store Indian come to life. "Nobody will go to the *kgotla*," he said simply. "Unless our chief is present, there *can* be no *kgotla*. Seretse is our chief. Bring him back from England and we will attend a *kgotla*."

He nodded, signifying that the interview was terminated, and turned to walk back into his hut. Then he saw the photographers and smiled broadly. He raised a brawny forearm and pointed. "You take my picture," he commanded.

The photographer thus singled out took his picture.

The headman then retired into his hut, and the resident commissioner retreated, looking shaken.

The correspondent of a British newspaper known for its frequent adulation of the Empire on Which the Sun Never Sets threw his arms despairingly in the air. "This is the end!" he moaned. "I have seen the Empire defied by a lot of niggers!"

"I say, old man," said the resident commissioner, diffidently, "we don't use that word around here. Not done, you know."

We trooped back to the *kgotla* ground. More time passed. It became very hot, even in the shade of the camel-thorn trees. The black soldiers ceased from their labors and stood about, smoking cigarettes. The newspapermen also smoked cigarettes and pecked morosely at the keys of their typewriters. Conversation languished.

Nicholas Monsarrat descended from the Residency and announced that Sir Evelyn Baring had decided, in the circumstances, that there could be no *kgotla*. He added that Sir Evelyn would be pleased if the newspapermen would care to adjourn to the Residency and join him in a drink.

At the Residency, a pleasant white building enjoying such cooling breezes as there were in Serowe, Sir Evelyn appeared, shorn of his glory, in an ordinary suit of clothes, with no plumed hat or sword, and chatted amiably with the press. He seemed inclined to the view that sinister forces were at work and that the people would have flocked to the *kgotla* if they had not been intimidated by certain elements into staying away. The press did not altogether swallow this story, but as they were indubitably swallowing the High Commissioner's excellent whisky, it seemed only decent to let the remark pass in silence.

Afterwards T. C. Robertson and His Excellency went for a stroll in the veld, alone. There was much envious speculation about what they might be discussing and what inside information T. C. might be garnering. When T. C. returned to our midst, we did not beat about the bush: we asked him.

"We were laying bets on which one of us could spot the largest number of different birds," said T. C. simply. "Sir Evelyn won: he spotted ten."

: 6 :

THAT WAS not the end of the Seretse story. Seretse was allowed to return to Bechuanaland, but not to visit his wife. An enterprising newspaperman persuaded the pilot of the plane in which Seretse was traveling to fly low. He then apprised Ruth of the scheme. She was able to wave to her husband, and he waved back. But that was all. The British Government apparently feared a crisis if Seretse Khama were allowed to speak to Ruth Khama. It might have annoyed Dr. Malan.

Finally Ruth had her child, a daughter, and was rather grudgingly permitted to join her husband in exile in England.

The British Government then sent out three "observers" to report on the affairs of the Bamangwato. One of them got lost in the Kalahari Desert. He turned up some days later, burned a bright turkey-red by the sun and suffering from lumbago, but otherwise unscathed. The other two quarreled bitterly in public, while the silent tribesmen watched and wondered about the strange ways of the white man.

Tshekedi was still around. The British Government seemed to feel that, having done Seretse an injustice, the account could somehow be squared by doing Tshekedi an injustice too. So it banned Tshekedi also from entering the Bamangwato reserve, which was his home. But by this time practically everybody had given up trying to make sense of the British Government's policy in Bechuanaland.

In London, in the course of time, Ruth bore Seretse another child, this time a son. Shortly after the birth the British Government announced that no child of Seretse and Ruth Khama would ever be allowed to rule the Bamangwato.

The British tried hard to persuade the tribe to choose a new chief: not Tshekedi, not Seretse, not any son of Seretse. In the middle of 1953, when the affair had dragged on for over three years, the Bamangwato were still without a chief and were still demanding Seretse's return.

Whatever happened to Seretse and Ruth, I was sure of one thing: much more would be heard of Tshekedi Khama, who is one of the most outstanding personalities in the continent of Africa.

XII

SOUTH-WEST AFRICA: DIAMONDS ON THE SHORE

ONE FEBRUARY day in 1952 I flew from Johannesburg to Windhoek, the capital of South-West Africa. The plane passed over a treeless red desert, which presently gave place to a treeless yellow desert. Across the red and yellow deserts wandered the boulder-strewn tracks of dried-up rivers.

A fellow passenger explained: "When there's a drought, life down there is impossible. Sometimes it doesn't rain for five years. But when it does rain, the few roads are impassable and the rivers come down in spate, destroying everything in their path."

I recalled a story Lord Dunsany once wrote about a man who searched for diamonds in those deserts. He found his first diamond only when he was dying of thirst. But as he stooped to pick it up, a river came down in flood and he was drowned.

After the deserts, the plane flew low through hanging curtains of rain, over softly rounded hills covered with bright green bush like the tight fleece on a sheep's back. Lightning flashed and thunder rumbled. We got down on the airfield at Windhoek just before it became waterlogged.

I explored the streets of Windhoek, which means "Windy Corner," and concluded that it must be the neatest town in Africa. It looked like well-kept barracks. But there were some odd contrasts. The broad, clean streets were full of Negroes wearing bright-colored American silk shirts. Tall Herero women wore turban-like headdresses, and Scottish tartan plaids over

156

voluminous petticoats. But most of the stores had German names.

In a German sidewalk café a German band played German tunes. The bandsmen were bare-kneed and wore flower-embroidered tunics. In the intervals of playing they drank foaming tankards of German beer.

After two world wars and two German defeats, the main street in Windhoek is still called Kaiserstrasse. The week before I arrived in Windhoek, the town's German cinemas printed their programs in three languages and in this order: Afrikaans, English, and German. During my stay, German was put first and English last.

The rain had stopped and the sun shone. I drank beer with an Englishman, who kept a disapproving eye on the German waiters. They were large, muscular men who looked as if they had but recently exchanged a Gestapo uniform for a white shirt and a black tie. "I never know," said the Englishman pensively, "whether one of those chaps is going to bring me a drink or lug me off to a concentration camp. War neurosis, I expect."

We listened to the German band.

"German is taught in all the schools here," he explained. "But the Germans are now demanding their own schools. They haven't forgotten that South-West Africa was once a German colony. They'd like to get it back."

He told me what, to him, was a sad story.

"The 15,000 Germans in South-West Africa had a strong Nazi organization before the war. After war broke out in 1939, Jan Smuts interned a lot of them. When the war was over, he deprived 6,000 of them of their citizen rights and threatened to deport them. But he never got round to it, and now Malan has made them citizens again and canceled the deportation order. Since Malan came to power, 5,000 more Germans have entered South-West Africa, and the influx continues."

He sipped his beer.

"Malan gave South-West Africa six seats in the South African Parliament. The total white population of South-West Africa is only 40,000. That means a South-West African vote is worth three South African votes. But it means more. The Germans will soon be running South-West Africa again, you'll see. They've got the brains and the money. And, thanks to Malan, they could easily hold the balance of political power in South Africa as well, if the white South Africans go on quarreling among themselves."

"The Germans," I said, "must be exceedingly grateful to Dr. Malan. He saves them from being deported, restores their citizenship, gives them a vote in South Africa's affairs as well as here—"

He grinned. "Don't you believe it. The Germans know that Malan gave them the vote for his own purposes. He needed their votes to strengthen his position in South Africa against the English there. But now that they've got the vote, they can do what they like with it. In any case, the Germans despise the Boers. The idea of the Boers as a *Herrenvolk* makes the Germans laugh themselves sick. They call Malan the *ersatz Führer*. They know what they want. I think one day they'll get it."

Sam Davis was a large, soft-spoken man who knew all about hotels, real estate, ranching, and newspapers. He had acquired his knowledge the hard way.

"Once, when I was broke," he said, "I tried to get a job as a door-to-door salesman. The wage offered was exactly five dollars and sixty cents a month. I was so broke I would have jumped at it. But they gave the position to someone else. Then I offered to drive the municipal refuse-cart. But they gave that job to a chap who had influence: he was somebody's cousin.

"In those days," said Sam cheerfully, "everyone in South-West Africa was broke. Nobody had any money at all, except of course the illicit diamond-buyers."

"They made money, didn't they?" I said.

"Yes, but it was pretty dangerous. The IDB [illicit diamond-buying] boys spent most of their time dodging the cops. Some of them had narrow escapes. If you were caught, it meant several years in prison. But the boys were smart. I know one man who had a parcel of stones and was tipped off that detectives were watching him. He had to dispose of the stones before the detectives searched him. He didn't have much time. He was staying at a boarding-house, and the detectives took a room next door to his."

"What did he do?"

"He telephoned them, gave a false name, and promised information about himself. He arranged to meet them downtown. When they went out, he parked the parcel of diamonds on top of the wardrobe in their room. The detectives returned, searched him, and searched his room. They didn't find anything, so they had to let him go. Then he retrieved the stones and vanished."

One of the jobs that Sam eventually managed to get was to escort round South-West Africa a delegation of Persian businessmen who were interested in the territory's karakuls, or Persian lambs.

"After I'd accepted the assignment, I discovered to my horror that they could speak no English or German. I knew no Persian. It was terrible."

"How did you get over the difficulty?"

"Thanks to my pious Jewish upbringing," said Sam, "I translated everything into Hebrew, which they understood, and we got on fine."

Sam insisted that in those former days Windhoek had been full of colorful characters. I thought it still was. For instance, there was the manager of Sam's own palatial Continental Hotel. A man of immense, sad dignity, his name was Gustav Aurel Mindszenty. He was a cousin of the famous cardinal, and had been smuggled out of Europe by the Vatican after making an anti-Communist film.

I met an engineer who had flown in, for a day's shopping, from the Orange River mouth, where Sir Ernest Oppenheimer's men dig up about thirty million dollars' worth of diamonds each year. This is the wealth that eluded the Germans when they still owned South-West Africa.

"Is it true," I asked him, "that a toddler armed with a toy bucket could pick up enough diamonds in half an hour to pay a king's ransom?"

He laughed. "Your toddler would require rather more formidable equipment. It's damned hard work. First he'd have to remove about thirty feet of sand. Then he'd have to dig down through a bed of rock and close-packed gravel. If he had been lucky enough to pick the right spot, he'd then recover an average of one carat of diamond for every ton of rock he shifted."

The engineer added, more soberly: "Nevertheless the Orange River mouth is probably the richest tract of country of its size in the world."

Many legends have grown up around this isolated stretch of barren seashore. The diamonds contribute a large share of South-West Africa's revenue. The Orange River mouth is closely guarded. Apart from the physical obstacles, which are considerable, it is about as difficult to get permission to go there as to get into the Kremlin. The area is patrolled by determined men who carry rifles and ride camels. Officially, the 300-mile stretch of coastline is in the keeping of the Administrator of South-West Africa. In fact, Sir Ernest Oppenheimer is the boss.

"What does the place look like?" I asked my engineer.

"You've seen sand-dunes? That's what it looks like."

Thereafter his resemblance to an oyster became so marked that I had to change the subject.

Diamonds are by no means the only source of South-West Africa's present prosperity. I met a karakul farmer who described how he slit the throats of the newborn lambs. "They're only valuable for their fur," he explained. "A lamb must be killed before it's twenty-four hours old. A pelt sells for about two pounds. It's a £6,000,000-a-year industry."

I found the thought of three million newborn lambs having their throats cut depressing, and said so.

"You ought to visit Cape Cross," he said severely. "On the beach there, six thousand young seals are clubbed to death each year. It doesn't mean anything to the lambs, but the seals are different. They *know*. I'd rather kill lambs than chase seals. All the same," he added somberly, "I'm thinking of giving it

160

up. My wife's nerves can't stand it. Once a lamb raised its head and looked at me, and I still dream about it. It made me feel like Macbeth."

South-West Africa has huge, 40,000-acre sheep and cattle ranches. The ranchers sell 150,000 head of cattle a year, for beef. Many of the ranchers are Boers. They poured into the country after the German defeat in 1915. Some of them crossed the border from Portuguese Angola, where they had settled years before. In South-West Africa, they established towns and farms, with Biblical names like Jericho and Jerusalem. But the old Herero names also survive: names like Okahandja, Omaruru and Otjiwarongo.

In addition to diamonds, rich copper and zinc mines in the north, cattle ranches, clubbed seals, and slaughtered lambs, South-West Africa also makes money out of fish.

Sam Davis introduced me to "Boots" Botha, a young South African who had switched from being an air-force pilot to fishing for pilchards, a sort of herring, in Walvis Bay. As a result, he was earning over $80,000 a year, but told me confidently: "Of course the real money will be in tunny when we get round to that." The pilchards were sold to canning and fish-oil companies, and the profits were fabulous. Botha paid one of his deckhands $350 a month.

He told me that three Filipino brothers, Cyril, Tommy, and Gabriel Fernandez, ran several boats, which earned them a joint income of $100,000 a year. "Very decent types," said Botha, and added: "I don't mind having them round to my place for drinks. Although they're colored, they know their place."

: 2 :

ONE OF my reasons for visiting South-West Africa was to learn about the Herero tribe. There were only 33,000 Hereros out of a total black population of 300,000. But the Hereros had conquered and ruled South-West Africa before the Germans, and

161

now they were demanding their land back. So I called on Hosea Kutako.

The old man—he was over eighty—sat under the bare branches of a gnarled tree. In his shabby suit and wide-brimmed hat, his fine face sun-wrinkled, he looked like a dignified Boer farmer—except that he was black, and he hated the Boers.

Near his tree was a concrete communal privy, which oozed sewage toward the concrete tanks from which the 12,000 inhabitants of the Windhoek location drew their drinking-water. All around were dusty, ill-made streets, lined with houses mostly constructed of old kerosene cans. The kerosene-can huts were the homes of the once proud Hereros. The old man was the Hereros' leader.

Hosea Kutako said: "The Hereros have died three deaths. The Germans took our country away from us. We shed our blood in battle, but we were defeated. This was the first death.

"In 1914 the British fought the Germans, and we Hereros joined in the fight. General Smuts sent a letter to Paramount Chief Frederick Maharero asking for young warriors. Smuts and the British promised to restore our land. But when the Germans were defeated, the British abandoned us. We Hereros were dispersed to barren deserts where our cattle could not live—we who had owned more cattle than any other people in the world. This was the second death.

"Now," said Hosea, "the Germans have been defeated again, but this time South Africa wants to annex our country forever. If the United Nations will not help us, this is the third death." He looked at me. "What will the United Nations do? Will they send planes, or land soldiers, to enforce their will?"

"I don't know what the United Nations will do," I said uncomfortably.

We sat in a circle under the tree, Hosea grasping his walking-stick, with his advisers grouped around him. They were all elderly gentlemen of immense dignity, like himself. One of them cleared his throat. "The United Nations," he said gently, "will, I think, do nothing. Malan is too powerful."

I felt that, as far as the United Nations was concerned, he was probably right.

I asked a prosperous businessman in Windhoek: "Why don't you do something about your location?"

He stared at me. "How do you mean?"

"Windhoek is one of the cleanest towns I've ever seen," I told him, "but on your doorstep you've got this ghastly slum."

He shrugged. "If we built new houses, the natives would soon turn them back into pigsties. Besides, give us a chance: Windhoek is only fifty years old! We haven't had time to do much, you know."

In Windhoek itself, new luxury hotels, office blocks, and cinemas were shooting up like mushrooms.

South-West Africa is considerably larger than Texas. The earliest known inhabitants were Bushmen and Hottentots. The Hereros came later. Their own account of their origin is that one day, from an omumborumbonga tree whose stump still stands at the edge of Ovamboland, there emerged a number of virgins who immaculately conceived and bore male and female children. These were the first Hereros.

More probably the Hereros were a westward-wandering branch of Bantu tribes migrating south through Africa in the fifteenth century. The Hereros conquered other tribes, and became a slave-owning aristocracy. They grew so rich in cattle that one of the first white men to enter South-West Africa said: "When a musket is fired, the stampeding cattle of the Hereros shake the veld for miles around with the thunder of their hoofs."

In 1878 the Germans were looking for African colonies. The Herero chief, Samuel Maharero, petitioned Queen Victoria to "establish forts along the coast, take us under your protection, and see that our children grow up more civilized than we have had any chance of being." The British almost acceded to his request, but finally let Germany have the barren territory, over 300,000 square miles of it. Samuel Maharero wrote bitterly: "The British flag flew here. It waved this way and that. We at-

163

tached ourselves to it, and were waved backwards and forwards with it."

Dr. Göring, the father of Hermann Göring, arrived to take over the new colony in the name of the Kaiser. Samuel Maharero told him: "If you do not wish to see your head lying at your feet, you should be out of here and well on your way back to Germany before sunset." Göring asked for British protection and got it. Maharero submitted to German rule. The Hottentot chief, Hendrik Witbooi, warned him: "This giving of yourself into the hands of the white men will become a burden to you as if you were carrying the sun on your back."

Maharero soon found the burden insupportable. The Germans took over most of the Herero land, and traded with the Hereros on the basis of one bag of corn for ten cows. The Hereros rebelled, but Maharero promised to spare all German women and children, and to protect the lives and property of all British and Boer settlers. The rebellion was crushed at a cost of £26,500,000 and many lives. German troops were massacred from ambush by tall Herero women armed with spears and axes.

"What happened next makes an unpleasant page in colonial history," said a German who had lived through it. "I can remember gallows with Hereros hanging from them like bunches of grapes. The rebels were hunted down like wild animals."

A band of a thousand Hereros, led by Samuel's son, Frederick, managed to reach the sanctuary of British Bechuanaland after a long trek across waterless desert. Their sufferings were great, but hardly to be compared with the fate of those who stayed behind. The Germans reduced the Herero population from 80,000 to 15,000. The survivors, men, women, and children, were distributed among German farmers. All Hereros over the age of seven were forced into slavery. In Berlin, Dr. Paul Rehrbach, of the German Colonial Office, wrote: "The Hereros' development into a class of laborers in white service is a law of existence."

My German informant added dryly: "But of course that was not the end of the story of the Hereros. It would be nice if it had a happy ending. But the happy ending, if there is to be one, is still to come."

: 3 :

I TOILED up a steep hill to "the Palace of Ink," to see Dr. Albert van Rhijn, the Boer Administrator of South-West Africa. "The Palace of Ink" was what the Germans called the administrative buildings in Windhoek, which they built and which the South Africans now occupy. Facing the buildings, across a cobbled square, was a red-steepled German Lutheran church. In a large public garden, Negro convicts in red jerseys and white caps were cutting the grass.

Dr. van Rhijn was a large man with a cyst in the middle of his forehead. It glowed like a searchlight as he thumped his desk and denounced the United Nations. He was pretty mad about the United Nations. He was also pretty mad with the world's press.

Foreign newspapermen, he cried, visited South-West Africa, then went away and wrote critical articles. As if that weren't enough, their papers then proceeded to ginger the articles up. "Not content with those poisoned dishes," thundered Dr. van Rhijn, "the American, British, and other foreign editors add their own pepper. We are sick of lies about our treatment of the blacks."

But the chief liar, in his opinion, was not a newspaperman, but a priest: my old friend the Reverend Michael Scott, who spends much of his time being deported from various African countries. Scott had visited South-West Africa to speak to the Hereros. At the very mention of Scott's name, the Administrator turned purple. I left hurriedly, before he should burst.

John Neser, the Permanent Secretary, was more diplomatic. He generously gave me several hours of his valuable time, in which he persuasively pointed out certain facts which, he declared, the critics frequently ignored.

165

"When South Africa took over this territory," said Neser, "the Hereros were only scattered survivors of a once powerful nation. Since then their numbers have doubled and they own 200,000 head of cattle and 5,000,000 acres of land."

Neser further pointed out that South-West Africa's 40,000 whites were trying to do a big job with limited resources. Throughout most of the 1920's and '30's, the territory was deep in debt and depression. "The diamond market had collapsed. Public servants' salaries went unpaid. Farmers were sitting in the middle of thousands of acres of land, but most of them couldn't afford to hire workers, and their own families were living on bread and black coffee."

South-West Africa was still being administered on a financial shoestring. Neser's own remarkable range of jobs seemed to me to be a hangover from the days of austerity. In addition to being Secretary, he was Chief Native Commissioner, Commissioner of Inland Revenue, Director of Prisons, and chairman of the Diamond Board, the Tender Board, the Land Bank, the Fisheries Board, the Native Labour Advisory Board, and the Municipal Advisory Board.

Although I was impressed by Neser's obvious sincerity, I was puzzled to know why the cattle-owning, land-rich Hereros, as he painted them, should have to live in a place like the Windhoek location. On this point Neser's argument was less plausible, if frank. "Without white settlement, there would be no money for the territory's development," he said. "White settlement depends on having black labor."

The South Africans took over South-West Africa as a mandate after the First World War, and their method of getting plentiful supplies of black labor was simple. The area of white settlement, which comprises all of the old Herero and Hottentot land, covers 80,000,000, acres, owned by a few thousand whites. In addition there are 20,000,000 acres reserved for 140,000 Negroes, including the Hereros. But only about twenty per cent of those Negroes actually live in the reserves. South African policy toward the reserves is that "only men who are physically unfit . . . are encouraged to remain there." The able-bodied are expected to "come out to work"—for the whites. Further, it is also the official policy to "discourage" Negroes working for whites in towns and on farms from trying to go into the reserves. The reason given is starkly phrased: "Their services are needed."

When South Africa took over the territory as a mandate, she promised to "promote to the utmost the material and moral welfare and social progress of the inhabitants," meaning the Negroes. The Mandates Commission of the League of Nations was frequently critical of South Africa's methods of keeping this promise. When the League was replaced by the United Nations, General Smuts (who helped write the United Nations Charter) tried to terminate the mandate and simply incorporate South-West Africa in the Union. But he said he would first hold a referendum among the Negroes.

Lord Hailey, the eminent British authority on Africa, asked Smuts's permission to visit South-West Africa to watch the referendum being conducted. Smuts refused. When the results were announced, it was stated that *all* the 160,000 Negroes who live in Ovamboland, the remote northern part of the territory, had voted in favor of Smuts's incorporation plan; not a single person voted against it. In the area of "white settlement," which the whites themselves call "the police zone," 47,560 Negroes were said to have voted for incorporation, and 33,520 against; 56,790 were described as having been "not available for consultation."

Most of the Hereros voted against incorporation. Their aged paramount chief, Frederick Maharero, was still living in Bech-uanaland, under the protection of Tshekedi Khama. One Herero wrote to old Frederick: "The heritage of your father's orphans is about to be taken away from them." Frederick told Tshekedi, who prepared to go to London to plead with the British Government. Under pressure from Smuts, the British refused to give Tshekedi a hearing. (This was before Tshekedi was himself exiled from his own country.)

Tshekedi wrote to Michael Scott, who visited Windhoek, talked with Hosea Kutako and other Herero leaders, and helped

167

them draw up a petition to the United Nations. As a result of this petition, the United Nations rejected Smuts's plan for incorporation.

But Smuts was replaced by Dr. Malan. The new South African Government announced that it would stop sending reports on South-West Africa to the United Nations, and would continue to press for incorporation. Michael Scott returned to Windhoek. This time he was refused permission to visit the Herero leaders. He camped in a dry river-bed near Windhoek, and the Herero and Hottentot leaders visited him in secret. Scott then proceeded to Johannesburg. The Herero leaders had been refused passports to attend the United Nations, and it was decided that Scott himself should go there to present their case again. The Hereros and other tribes collected the money for his fare and sent it to him in Johannesburg. It arrived in the form of silver and copper coins and tattered ten-shilling notes.

When Scott tried to fly to Paris, he was taken off the plane at the last moment by South African officials, who demanded the surrender of his passport. Scott refused to give it up. He got out of South Africa by car, driving across the border into Rhodesia. From there he flew to Paris via the Belgian Congo.

To forestall possible action by the United Nations, Malan rushed a bill through the South African Parliament. This piece of legislation virtually incorporated South-West Africa in the Union, but it did much more. The 40,000 whites in South-West Africa were given their six seats in the Union Parliament, and, as a consequence, a large voice in the conduct of South Africa's affairs.

In Paris, Michael Scott addressed the Fourth Committee of the United Nations. When the South African delegate challenged Scott's right to be heard because he had no authority (from the Union Government) to represent the Hereros, the Mexican delegate answered: "Christ was crucified because He had no credentials to prove He was the Son of God." The General Assembly passed the problem to the International Court, which declared that South-West Africa was still a territory under mandate, and that South Africa could not alter the status of

South-West Africa without the consent of the United Nations. But Malan's legislation presented both the Court and the United Nations with a *fait accompli*. Malan took his revenge on Scott by declaring him a "prohibited immigrant."

: 4 :

THE FOUR-SEATER Ryan-Navion seemed to float in the air as lightly as a soap-bubble. I was the only passenger. Behind us were the purple Auas Mountains, on whose ridges German farmers had built farmhouses like miniature Rhine castles. Ahead of us lay the Otavi Mountains and the town of Tsumeb.

Green valleys slowly opened out beneath us, and we skimmed the tops of hills. At my side, Wulfgang Schenk examined his controls and hummed a gay tune.

"Before the war," he said, "I grew sisal in Tanganyika."

"And then you came here?"

"Not immediately." He smiled gently and pointed. "There are antelope down there."

Far below our soap-bubble, buck were feeding under the trees. They looked like the tiny animals from a model Noah's ark.

"Would you like to have a closer look at them?"

"You mean, go down?"

"Yes, like this."

The soap-bubble tilted. It no longer floated serenely, but screamed earthward, until a wing-tip almost brushed the backs of the startled animals, making them run.

"During the war," said Schenk equably, "I was a test pilot for Messerschmitt. If we see more game, I shall warn you."

It was an exciting trip.

Years before the white man came, the natives worked copper at Tsumeb, which means "green metal." The Germans, who ruled South-West Africa until Germany's defeat in the First World War, operated a copper mine here: between 1907 and 1941, the Otavi Minen und Eisenbahn Gesellschaft (OMEG)

169

produced two million tons of ore. After the Second World War the mine was placed in the hands of the Custodian of Enemy Property, and the South African Government put it up for auction. In 1947 it was purchased by the Newmont Corporation. Newmont produces the copper-lead and zinc concentrates; the American Metal Company sells them. The companies have invested over four million pounds, and pay thirty per cent of South-West's tax revenue. The mine is richer than any single Rand gold mine. Tsumeb, with two thousand whites, has become almost overnight South-West's second largest town.

The resident manager, Jack Ward, and the assistant general manager, John Metz, both Americans, told me that when they arrived, they found the Negroes wearing burlap sacks and living in the usual location of tin huts without sanitation. Poor whites, seeking jobs, kept their families living concealed in the bush, because the mine wanted only single men. Ward and Metz said, with a shrug: "We had to do *something*."

What they did was to pull down the old location and provide the Negroes with $600 houses, sanitary blocks, laundries and washhouses with solar-radiation heating systems, a café, and a social hall. Banana and pawpaw trees were planted around the houses, and the new homes were rented at five shillings a month. If a Negro found this too much, the mine unobtrusively raised his wages. Ward explained diffidently: "We felt like giving them the houses free, but we didn't want them to think we were spoon-feeding them."

The new homes, when I saw them, had lace curtains at the windows, and the native women were busily plying sewing-machines. The company had also built hospitals, and was planning schools (in collaboration with the missions) and churches. Sports fields were being laid out.

The majority of the 2,200 Negroes employed on the mine were Ovambos, recruited on an eighteen-month basis. Fifty per cent of them regularly reported back for a fresh spell of work. The mine could have raised this to seventy-five per cent or more, but was being selective.

Ward and Metz, while politely trying to disguise their true

feelings in deference to South-West prejudices, obviously felt like Mark Twain's Yankee at King Arthur's court. In addition to its mining and rehousing activities, the company had acquired 125,000 acres of farm land, and owned 6,500 head of cattle and a herd of 200 imported Swiss dairy cows; the company pasteurized its own milk. It also grew alfalfa and vegetables for local consumption.

The 650 whites directly employed by the mine had been provided with new homes, a cinema, playing fields, floodlit tennis-courts, and a swimming-pool. The town's nine miles of dirt streets were being paved.

The mine had to bring in thousands of tons of equipment, including generators and boilers, across hundreds of miles of desert; some equipment was brought in tank carriers. The ore is crushed to a fine quality, mixed with acids and reagents, given a bubble-bath, and turned out in powdered concentrate form for shipment.

South-West African wiseacres gave Ward and Metz two years, after which, they were told, they would realize that Negroes prefer to live in pigsties. But Tsumeb may force South-West, willy-nilly, to change its ideas. The farmers were already grumbling that the mine was causing them to lose their black laborers—unless they agreed to pay the laborers more, and improved their rations and housing-conditions.

More American capital may find its way to South-West. Up in the remote Kaokoveld, northwest of Tsumeb, the Bethlehem Steel Corporation has acquired large mining concessions, and a team of American geologists are now probing beneath the desert sands for workable iron ore and other minerals. If deposits are proved, said Bethlehem's representative, Dr. Edwin T. Hodge, a railroad may be built across the mountains, to a new harbor two hundred miles away. The company would first produce pig-iron, and later undertake the large-scale production of steel.

If this happens, another Americanized city will appear in South-West Africa, with new housing schemes for white and black, tarred roads, hospitals, and health, social, and recreation centers.

Wulfgang Schenk was waiting for me at the air-strip. We took off and flew back over all that vast country which had once been the Hereros'. Looking down on it, I thought that though the Hereros would in all probability never get back their land, they and the other Negro tribes of South-West Africa could conceivably get a new deal.

172

XIII

SOUTHERN RHODESIA: IMPERIALISTS IN SHIRTSLEEVES

ONE BRIGHT September morning in 1952 Jane and I took the Great North Road to Rhodesia. I brought the car round to our Johannesburg apartment; we loaded the luggage and set off. In the next few weeks we traveled three thousand miles together, before I went on alone, by air, to the Northern Rhodesian copper belt and afterwards to Nyasaland.

African distances no longer appalled us, though I should still hesitate to emulate the bold example of Arthur Mapleson, of the London *Daily Express*. One day, in Johannesburg, Arthur received a cable from his office. After reading it, he went to the nearest stand and hailed a cab. "Take me to Bechuanaland," he said simply. He and the driver were gone three weeks.

We drove through Transvaal towns, with their sleepy wide streets and outlying farms. The little dorps between the towns were all of a pattern: dusty pepper trees, a row of shops, a filling station, and a Dutch Reformed church. But presently the road shrugged off the towns and the settled countryside, and we entered upon a vast empty plain. Scattered about its perfectly flat surface, like pieces on a chessboard, were mountains shaped like crouching lions.

Jane examined the plain's weird perspectives. "If God hadn't created it, Dali would still have painted it," she said.

We came at last to the broad, sluggish Limpopo River winding through this wilderness. We knew it was crocodile-haunted

173

because Negroes fording it frequently end in the crocodiles' jaws. On the far side of the river was Southern Rhodesia. There were brief formalities at a customhouse. Then we drove over a steel and concrete bridge. Down below we could see hippos grunting and wallowing in the shallows. On the Rhodesian side we stopped at a hotel for tea, which was served in a beautiful garden by black waiters in white starched uniforms.

Five miles farther on, the hotel, its garden, and the stiffly starched waiters appeared in retrospect like figments rioting through the fevered imagination of a wanderer lost in the bush. We began to suspect that the whole thing had been a mirage.

On either side of the road grew tall, thick grass. There were no habitations of any sort in sight. There appeared to be no traffic whatever. The road itself had changed its nature in a sinister manner. It now consisted of two narrow strips of tar, like streetcar rails. The space between was filled with loose gravel, and the strips were slightly raised and had sharp edges. I had to drive carefully to keep the car's wheels on the strips. It was six hundred miles to Salisbury.

When, at last, another car appeared, coming toward us, we hailed it with relief, even though it meant maneuvering off the strips to give the other car room to pass.

"Is this the Great North Road?" I asked.

"Of course." The other driver seemed surprised.

"The countryside seems rather unpopulated."

"Fine lion country," said the other driver enthusiastically. "They shot fifteen between here and Beit Bridge last week."

The tall grass finally gave way to softly rounded hillsides thickly clothed with the beautiful msasa trees, shimmering jade and burning bronze, and then to country still hilly, but harsher, with stony *kopjes* over whose naked rocks fleshy, bulbous baobab trees stretched long, gaunt roots like withered arms. From a bare *kopje* a baboon barked in the noonday heat. Across the road in front of us swiftly slithered a huge striped lizard.

Fort Victoria was like a deserted barracks square. It had a thin military atmosphere, as if soldiers had formerly been quartered here, but had been dead a long time. The sun glared down on a broad empty street, and old men who might once have been colonels drowsed comfortably on verandas. One of them opened a rheumy eye at us.

"Up from South Africa, eh?"

We admitted it.

"Pretty frightful place, they tell me," he said severely, and fell asleep again.

At sundown, a man walked slowly across the empty street and ceremoniously hauled down the Union Jack from its pole outside the post office. Curfew tolled from a bell-tower that formed part of the old fort built in 1891.

When we asked one of the colonels to whom the curfew applied, he said gruffly: "All Negroes must be off the streets by nine. We have to preserve discipline."

We had already visited the public library, where discipline was also being preserved. A notice on the door declared: "As the reading-room is being made a convenience of for luncheon, etc., it will be closed from 1 p.m." Peering through the glass panel, we descried a single row of dusty novels and a woman custodian busy with her knitting. Jane wanted to knock on the glass panel and ask her what the notice meant by "etc.," but I decided we had better not.

At the hotel the only available reading-matter was a local travel brochure, which warned: "Trippers should carry ample petrol, as well as water, food and camping equipment. An axe is also often useful for clearing trees pushed across the road by elephant."

In the morning, fearful that we might run out of gas and be stranded without an axe in the midst of a herd of elephants, I called at a filling station near the hotel. Negroes in blue overalls filled the tank, checked the oil, water, and battery, inflated the tires, and wiped the windshield. When they had finished, they crowded eagerly round me.

"You're from Johannesburg, boss? Take me back there with you. Get me a job in Jo'burg."

I escaped with difficulty and returned to the hotel to find Jane finishing the packing.

"Rather an odd thing happened," she said. "The bedroom 'boy' begged me to take him to Johannesburg and find him a job there."

We drove along the broad main street, which after a few hundred yards ended abruptly and vanished behind us with its few buildings, like another mirage. Five minutes later we were again driving through uninhabited country.

But when we reached the capital town of Salisbury, there was no suggestion of a wilderness. Salisbury was a city of broad streets, shaded sidewalks, and green parks. It was ablaze with flowers. Along the main avenues young trees had been planted. Until they reached maturity, they were protected from the hot sun by thatched awnings. Young women in bright frocks, their eyes likewise protected against the sun's glare by dark glasses, pushed prams along the sidewalk. Traffic lights blinked at intersections, and there were bustling department stores at every corner.

In the crowded, thickly carpeted tea lounge of Meikle's Hotel, a string orchestra dispensed light music. Through the tea lounge barefooted native "boys" threaded their way between the tables, holding aloft blackboards on short poles and ringing bicycle bells attached to the boards. On the blackboards were chalked the names of people wanted on the telephone.

We had a drink with Kenneth Maclennan, whom I first met years ago in Stornoway, in the Outer Hebrides. Since then he had worked in a London bank, and commanded a gun-bristling craft in the Mediterranean. Now, like thousands of other emigrating Britishers, he was seeking his fortune in Rhodesia.

Kenneth had put on weight, but his red hair burned as brightly as ever. He told us that he worked in town, but lived in a house with fifty acres of land attached, and he raised his own vegetables. "At the weekend," he said, "this town is deserted. Everyone goes off to his farm!"

We had to raise our voices to make ourselves heard against the competition of the string orchestra and the shrill bicycle bells. Around us sat tobacco-planters wearing open-neck shirts and khaki shorts, grizzled men who carried themselves stiffly erect and had former Indian Army written all over them, and young men still sporting the handlebar mustaches they had learned to grow in their days in the R.A.F. They all looked very, very British.

"Rhodesians," Kenneth said, "look on South Africa very much as a respectable householder would regard a flourishing brothel doing a roaring trade just across the street. They think that anyone who lives in a place like Johannesburg must be crazy. Is it true that there are riots every night, and that everyone carries a gun?"

"Not every night," I said, "and only every second person carries a gun."

"Is it true that the Boers want to leave the British Empire?"

"Who doesn't?" I quipped recklessly.

A retired Indian Army type at a near-by table rose with a snort and gave me a hostile glare.

In a cool white building in one of the town's broad avenues, I found the Prime Minister of Southern Rhodesia, Sir Godfrey Huggins, smoking a pipe and working at a desk in his shirt-sleeves. He greeted me cordially, and we bawled amiably at each other for half an hour. Sir Godfrey listened to my questions with a hand cupped attentively over his deaf ear, and shouted his replies.

Sir Godfrey was a surgeon as well as a politician. Once a hunter was mauled by a lion in wild country. He was carried unconscious to the nearest outpost, and from there was flown to Salisbury for an emergency operation. When he opened his eyes, he was lying in a white hospital bed. Bending over him was a lean man with a nut-brown face and a brown mustache.

"Who are you?" whispered the hunter.

"I'm the Prime Minister," said the brown-faced man cheerfully. "I've just amputated your left leg."

Southern Rhodesia, Huggins told me with pride, was growing fast. "In five years," he said, "we have increased the white population sixty-three per cent by immigration, doubled the value of farm output, more than doubled the value of industrial output, and raised the national income eighty-five per cent."

The growth was based on a tobacco boom, and on sales of chrome and manganese to the United States.

"The African population is growing too," Huggins said. "That means we must grow more food, quickly. Tobacco isn't enough."

Another man in shirtsleeves, also smoking a pipe, put his head inquiringly in at the door. He was the Minister of Finance.

Huggins rose and shook hands with me. "Go down to the Sabi Valley," he bawled. "Have a look at what they're doing there. Talk to Soffe and Goldberg."

On my way out I passed offices with open doors. Within sat pipe-smoking men in shirtsleeves, working at desks. Most of them had brown mustaches. Above the building the Union Jack floated against the blue African sky.

: 2 :

DOWN IN the Sabi Valley, where malarial mosquitoes rise in clouds, mounted heads of buck made a continuous frieze round the hotel's four wooden verandas. On a shelf in the bar, above the bottled beer, were nineteen lions' skulls. And that was where we first heard of the odd correlation between lion-hunts and the high Rhodesian divorce-rate.

"It's a fact," confided the proprietor's wife, a sprightly and capable woman with hennaed hair and crimson fingernails, and wearing slacks. "If a man goes out after lion, sooner or later he gets clawed. And being clawed by a lion has a curious effect on a man. It turns him against his wife."

A gloomy, gaunt man was leaning against the bar turning a glass of pink gin in his fingers. He had a bald head and a ginger mustache, and wore a bush-shirt. He took a sip of his gin. "There was Tony Smithers," he said. "Tony came into the valley to grow tea. Got married to a very pretty girl, and for six months everything in the garden was lovely. Then Tony went out after lion. But a lion almost got him. That was the end of his marriage. They were divorced before the year was out."

"Lots of cases like that," said the hotel proprietor's wife

178

briskly. "Take my own. My husband was clawed by a lion—it was just digging in for his kidneys when someone else got in a lucky shot. He still has the scars. Like Tony Smithers, he became morose and he wouldn't even speak to me."

She sighed. "I knew it was the shock. You don't get over it in a hurry. I had sheer hell for a whole year. "And that," she added, wryly patting the deep-socketed yellowing skull at the end of the row of skulls on the shelf above the bottled beer, "was his last lion-hunt. *I* saw to that.

"But, you know, some people think elephant are more dangerous. That's simply nonsense. Over in Portuguese East, the elephant come right up to the native huts; and the natives just go out and rattle sticks against tins and yell, and the elephant go away."

"You have elephant here too?" I asked, thinking of the long road we still had to travel, partly after dark.

She nodded. "Plenty of elephant—but rather more lion. Anyway, don't be afraid. If it's night and you find an elephant blocking the road, just switch your lights off and stay in your car until it goes away. They don't like lights."

She was struck by a thought and looked amused. "One thing about going too near an elephant: it's very difficult to take evasive action if you're wearing high-heeled shoes!"

She explained. "We had a lot of elephant round here recently, and some people staying at the hotel wanted to go and have a look at them. My husband would have taken them, but he was over at the colonel's farm"—she gestured at the man with the ginger mustache, who nodded solemnly—"tracking a buffalo. So I said I would. I made them stop the car a good distance away and told them we would have to do the rest on foot. They didn't seem as keen as they had been, but they did as I said, and I led the way.

"It was pitch-dark, and suddenly I almost walked into a bull elephant. I turned to warn the others not to move, but they weren't there any longer—they'd quietly fled back to the car. So I decided I'd better do the same. And then"—she laughed —"I realized I was still wearing my high-heeled shoes! I couldn't

179

run at all. I took off my shoes, carried them in my hand, and *tiptoed* back to the car. I gave these people a proper dressing down, I can tell you. I ruined a perfectly good pair of stockings. But the elephant never paid me the slightest attention. I believe I could have gone up and patted it."

The ginger-mustached man grunted, finished his gin, and left the bar. She looked after him admiringly.

"Wouldn't believe he was eighty, would you? Came up here in 1890 with the Pioneer Column, from Kimberley. When there's a buffalo on his farm, he usually sends for my husband and they hunt it together. But he's a bit headstrong, the old colonel is. One night he went out after a buffalo all by himself, had a shot at it, and didn't know if he'd hit it or not. A wounded buffalo is the most dangerous animal there is; it starts stalking *you*. So the colonel went back home to bed, and in the morning set off with native trackers. The buffalo was lying in the long grass, dead. He'd got it clean between the eyes, first shot.

"I'm a Londoner myself," she added, removing the empty glasses, "but we've been here twenty-eight years. We were in Kenya before that. I love it."

At Chipinga, a little town southeast of Salisbury, all five shops were closed, it being a public holiday. A tattered piece of paper with typing on it, attached to the wooden door of a tin shack, disclosed that the shack was the local bank, but that it was open for business only two days each month. There was a cinema, but it opened only once a week. In the deserted street, a native twiddled his bare toes, and struck melancholy music from a small hand-harp. Big yellow caterpillar-tracked vehicles of the Roads Department roared through the town, scraping the thick dust off the roads. The previous season an energetic new broom in the Roads Department had decided to dig down to the road's foundations and make a good job of it. When the rains came, they turned the loosened soil to solid mud, isolating the entire district. In the heat after the rains, the mud became fine red sand, feet deep. Now they were removing the sand.

Rhodesians talk about roads as people in England talk about

the weather. The two things, in fact, go hand in hand. In a country where people think nothing of motoring two hundred miles to watch a football match and then motoring home again, the state of the roads is important. And Rhodesian roads are bad. To drive on the narrow "strips," often with the glaring African sun in your eyes, is a grueling experience. Round a sharp bend, the road plunges down steeply, without warning, to a narrow bridge over a dried-up river, and ascends as sharply on the other side. The rivers are dry for most of the year; but in the rainy season the dry river-beds suddenly become floods that overwhelm the flimsy bridges and sometimes sweep away motor-cars that are unlucky enough to be in their path.

When we were told that the road from Chipinga to Melsetter had four hundred hairpin bends in forty miles, we preferred to go another way even though it meant adding fifty miles to our journey.

Sunk in its hollow amid the cloud-topped hills, Umtali was praying desperately that the clouds would bring rain. The drought had lasted for months, and a melancholy notice in the hotel toilets said: "It is unnecessary to flush when using the basin as a urinal."

Umtali, far inland from the sea, had a pink-walled custom-house. The border with Portuguese East Africa was near by. The boundary line ran through the property of a former magistrate, whose servant stole all his silver, sat on the boundary fence eating bananas and pelting his enraged employer with the skins, then vaulted the fence to the Portuguese side and vanished into the bush with his loot.

The little town drooped and sagged in the heat. But two men who appeared unaffected by it eagerly explained their plans for increasing the white population of Southern Rhodesia from 150,000 to 1,000,000 in twenty-five years, by further immigration. The basis of the plan was food production, for Southern Rhodesia cannot feed its present 150,000 white and 2,000,000 black people. The key to increased food production, they believed, was the sweltering, malarial, and hitherto despised Sabi Valley.

One night, a quarter of a century ago, a young man seeking a camping site in a piece of virgin bush near the Odzi River hung his mosquito net from the branch of a tree and crawled under it. The patch where he camped became part of the 25,000-acre ranch owned by the five Goldberg brothers. It is divided into six farms and has 4,000 acres under plow and 700 acres under tobacco. It also grows corn, beans, alfalfa, and other crops, and grazes large herds of sleek cattle.

The Goldbergs typify Rhodesia's pioneers of the twentieth-century type. In the depression of the mid-thirties, when tobacco was unsalable, they also had to fight droughts, floods, and pests. Now rich, they do not believe in letting up. The Goldbergs' sober motto is: "In African farming, there is no certain tomorrow."

Deeply concerned with conservation as the prerequisite of successful farming in Africa, the brothers long fought a campaign against their neighbors' unneighborly policy of refusing to co-operate in conservation measures. When Maurice Goldberg was fighting in Italy in the Second World War, he discovered that many of the men with him were also farmers. He formed the Sixth South African Armoured Division Farmers' Association, for swapping views around campfires on crop-yields. Today, thanks largely to the Goldbergs, more and more Southern Rhodesian farmers are becoming conservation- and co-operation-minded.

"For years," said plump Benjamin Goldberg, fingering his spectacles in his Umtali office, "the Sabi Valley was thought fit only for mosquitoes and crazy prospectors. Actually, the valley is no hotter, or more humid, or more unhealthy, than the country around Brisbane, in Australia." The Sabi Valley scheme was launched to create giant cattle ranches and huge sugar estates, as well as to grow food crops. The valley's possibilities are being scientifically assessed by Dr. Charles Converse, who was brought out from Arizona for the purpose. Cautious Dr. Converse has said: "Give me ten years to find out what can and what cannot be done."

"But," Goldberg told me, "already the chief enthusiasts for

182

the scheme are the farmers who actually live in the valley and have a good idea what they can make out of it."

Goldberg pointed out that much depended on how the farmers went about their business. "In the Mazoe Valley, the maize yield fifty years ago was fifteen bags an acre. It fell to three bags, because of bad farming. Now recovery is on the way. Some farmers are back to fifteen bags. Neighbors, on identical soil, are down to two bags."

The other enthusiast for the Sabi Valley is Andrew Cunningham Soffe, an Umtali businessman. Soffe visited the TVA, talked with David Lilienthal, and returned to Rhodesia to get the backing of the Southern Rhodesian Government for his ideas.

Soffe quoted to me a phrase of Lilienthal's: "The things that people, no matter what their race, live by are the same—the soil, the water, the rivers in their valleys, the minerals within the earth."

"In the next twenty-five years," he said, "the big problem of Africa will be, not race, but food." Over most of central and eastern Africa, he declared, the black populations are doubling themselves every quarter-century. "If these mouths are not fed, there will be widespread famine, maybe a relapse into total barbarism."

While I was talking to Goldberg, and to Soffe, Jane went out and found herself a character.

The captain was a thin creature who wore a monocle and looked like Edgar Wallace's lanky Lieutenant Bones. He had lived in Umtali for many years, and the stories about him were legion.

When a large and angry buck charged the captain's car, leaped onto the hood, thrust its antlers through the windshield, and proceeded to drip blood from its slashed throat on the lap of the captain's startled wife, the captain did not lose his head. He got out of the stalled car, went round the side, took several snapshots of the unusual spectacle, then, returning to his shaken lady, amiably inquired: "You all right, m'dear?"

The car itself was an ancient vehicle, for the captain was by

183

no means wealthy. When, after many years, its roof caved in, the captain was equal to the emergency. He simply thatched the hole, and carefully rethatched it every year thereafter, so that the captain's car became one of the sights of Umtali. A similar simple operation put right his refrigerator when it ceased to function. Scorning to place it in the hands of local mechanics, he merely turned it upside down. "Been workin' ever since, good as new," said the captain complacently.

When Jane saw him, the captain was feeling jubilant. After years of precarious ups and downs, he had good reason to think he might end his days in affluence. When a wealthy uncle who lived in the Argentine abruptly announced his intention of visiting him, the captain at first was dismayed. In a long series of letters spread over the years, he had gradually built up a picture of an expanding cattle ranch with rich grazing-land and growing herds. The truth was that the captain had a ranch, but there were no cattle on it. His next-door neighbor, however, had more cattle than he could graze. The captain had an idea. He generously offered to let the other man's cattle graze on his land, without charge, for as long as the uncle from the Argentine was his guest. The offer was promptly accepted.

"He came, he saw, and I conquered," said the captain dreamily. "The old boy congratulated me. Said he hadn't really believed I'd made good, but couldn't doubt the evidence of his own eyes. We used to sit on the stoep and count the cows. Before he went back to the Argentine, he said with tears in his eyes that he was an old man now, and he didn't think he could do better than leave me a good packet, knowin' I'd be able to put it to good use. Rippin' wheeze, what?" asked the captain, in the slang of the London he had not seen since he was in his teens.

The road wound up out of Umtali's oppressive heat, past a clanking gold mine and over the Christmas Pass, toward mountain peaks that hung sunlit in the blue sky. We climbed until the dark Pungwe Gorge lay two thousand feet below us, and there was heather—real heather—on the hillsides. In an hour we had passed from subtropical heat to Scottish mists and windswept uplands.

All these upper slopes were intricately and ingeniously terraced, the terraces being the handiwork of an ancient vanished race. Rhodesia is full of traces of a mysterious, pre-white culture. The country has on its coins a replica of the soapstone bird, possibly of Egyptian origin, that was found guarding the ramparts of the vast, crumbling Zimbabwe ruins by the first white explorers who stumbled on the ruins after hacking their way through the jungle that had long hidden them. (The local natives knew nothing about the ruins or the vanished people who had built them, declaring simply: "It is the place of the dead: only ghosts walk there.")

Many peoples seem to have passed through old Rhodesia. There was long a legend that this was the Land of Ophir, and the Portuguese expended much treasure and lost many men looking for King Solomon's mines. Phœnician coins have been found.

The most startled visitor the country ever had was a learned Chinese who exclaimed over a crude hieroglyphic scrawled with a pointed stick on the mud wall of a native hut in a remote village. It was explained to him that the design was a common one, found on many huts; it had no particular significance. "It is my name," said the Chinese scholar simply. "My family have written it that way for generations."

On these chilly uplands, overtowered by still higher mountains with clouds streaming about their peaks, it was possible to believe anything. The brilliant blossoms of the kaffirbooms burned scarlet against a pearl-gray sky, the tortured sculpture of massive rocks loomed up out of swirling mists, and down below were the forests, damp and menacing.

Beyond the forests was the road to Salisbury, a yellow scar across the plain, hot and dusty, potholed and alive with speeding cars and trucks.

: 3 :

WHEN WE returned to Salisbury we found everyone talking about federation. The plan was to link the two Rhodesias with

185

Nyasaland to form a new British dominion in central Africa. The emphasis was on "British."

"About a third of the whites here have come from South Africa," said a British Rhodesian. "They're welcome, provided they don't bring their politics with them. We don't want a cat-and-dog fight between Boer and Briton like the one they're having now in South Africa. Afrikaners who emigrate here must respect the Union Jack. This part of Africa is going to stay British."

"But of course we understand that," an Afrikaner protested to me. He looked extremely pained. "We Afrikaners are very much misunderstood. We who have come to live in Southern Rhodesia, under the British flag, don't ask much. We only want to be allowed to continue to speak our own language, and we would certainly like to have our own schools and our own churches. We want our children to speak Afrikaans, and to worship in the traditional Afrikaner way. We naturally are interested in what is happening in South Africa, and we could never regard the Union as a foreign country, any more than the British here think of the United Kingdom as foreign. But we are completely loyal to Southern Rhodesia."

"That's just what I mean," said my British Rhodesian friend bitterly, when I quoted this conversation to him. "The British in South Africa are attacked by the Afrikaners for thinking of Britain as 'home.' But Afrikaners who come to Southern Rhodesia think it's all right if they go on applauding Dr. Malan. They want their own schools and their own language. Next they'll want Afrikaans taught in all the schools, and before we know where we are, they'll be claiming Southern Rhodesia as part of the Union."

Another Afrikaner living in Southern Rhodesia preferred to view the whole matter from a different angle. "All the whites must stand together," he said. "Quarrels between British and Boer are stupid. They face a common danger in the black man. The British here need the Afrikaners, for Britain is far away, and is in any case preparing to sell out the white man everywhere in Africa; whereas South Africa under Dr. Malan offers protection to all men who are ready to help in defending white civilization." He smiled. "There is going to be trouble from the Africans, and also from India. Then you will see how quickly the British in Rhodesia will turn to Dr. Malan for aid."

Salisbury, like every town in South Africa, had a Negro location. Called Harari, it was about five miles from the town, on the wrong side of the railroad tracks. Old brick slums were being replaced by a new type of "elephant house." Made of concrete, with slightly humped roofs, these houses looked from a distance like a troop of elephants. They also looked bare and depressing: we had the feeling, perhaps unjustified, that in a few years they too would be slums, that to become slums was their destiny, and that their dispirited builder had also felt this in his bones when he erected them.

In the older part of the location, some of the people lived in huts made out of old rusted oil-drums, with thatched roofs. On the outskirts were barrack-like sheds, with boarded-up windows, which housed a few wretched Indian families.

There was in fact little difference between the Rhodesian and the South African way of life. Negroes were segregated. Cinemas were called "bioscopes," as in the Union. Social life consisted largely of "sundowners" and "morning teas."

A five-man delegation from the International Confederation of Free Trade Unions had arrived in Salisbury in the course of a study-tour of Africa. Leaders of the Southern Rhodesian Trades Union Congress went gladly to the airport to meet the distinguished visitors. At the airport it was discovered that one member of the delegation was a Negro who had been born in the Congo.

It was a delicate situation. The leader of the delegation was a Lancashire trade-unionist, named Bagnall. He was tactfully taken aside.

"We've booked accommodation for you and your colleagues at a hotel."

The man from Lancashire expressed gratification.

"Of course, in the circumstances, you won't mind splitting up?"

"What's that, lad?" asked Mr. Bagnall.

"We thought your—ah—friend from the Congo would prefer to go to the colored quarter. We can find a man who will put him up. Very respectable colored schoolteacher."

Salisbury, during our visit, was trying very hard to pretend that the ICFTU delegation were nonexistent. I sought them out and found them after some difficulty. They had refused to split up and, as a gesture of defiance, were all living in the colored quarter. The man from the Congo was looking amused. The man from Lancashire was striding up and down in a rage.

"Bah goom, lad!" he said. "This beats all! Not much democracy around here, is there?"

Jane and I went to hear a lecture on race relations by a clergyman who was reputed to be Salisbury's leading and most daring "liberal." "Most people think he's a bit of a Bolshie," we were warned. "But what he insists on is that after all the native is a human being, just like ourselves."

The meeting was held in a church hall. The audience sat on hard wooden chairs and listened attentively.

"There are times," the clergyman boomed, "when we white people have our patience sorely tried. We see the garden 'boy' lazing on the job, or some sulky 'girl' smashing our best china. In the factories, agitators encourage the aborigines to form trade unions. Despite all we have done for them, there is today a grave spirit of unrest among our Africans. Faced with this situation, some of us are sometimes almost tempted to the cold, clean solution of the machine-gun." He smiled sadly and raised a plump hand. "But no! We must always remember we are Christians. We must forbear."

We visited a farm near Salisbury, where we were hospitably received by a monocled retired brigadier who looked like John Buchan's Dick Hannay at the age of seventy.

"I don't like the Boers," he told us, "but at the same time you've got to admit they do know how to handle natives." He polished his monocle. "But of course the British way is best. I grow tobacco, breed pullets, and treat my natives justly but firmly."

: 4 :

WE FOUND the road between Salisbury and Bulawayo speckled with dusty little gold-mining towns. The mines had names like Bright Outlook, Mugs' Luck, Hidden Secret. They frequently changed hands.

One day a man in Gatooma strolled into the saloon and disgustedly tossed down a drink. "Let's play poker dice for the next round," suggested his neighbor; in Rhodesia, the bartender keeps a cup and dice under the counter for this purpose.

"No," said the disgruntled miner, "I'll play you poker dice for my mine; if I win, I'll buy you a drink."

The other man won the mine. Unfortunately for the loser, that mine later yielded one million pounds' worth of gold. But this is exceptional.

In hot, dry Gatooma an enterprising local poet had persuaded a shopkeeper to put samples of his verse in the window; handwritten on cheap ruled notepaper, they were flanked by tins of snakebite serum.

A Britisher who had emigrated to Rhodesia and lived in Gatooma had been there only a few days when he had an alarming experience. "They told me to be careful about snakes," he said. "My house has an outside lavatory. There's no waterborne sewerage. The bucket is removed each night through a hole in the back of the tin shack.

"I was in there one morning when I heard a hissing noise. I jumped up"—he looked apologetically at Jane—"from where I was sitting, and rushed into the house."

"In East London it was tarantulas," said Jane composedly. "Go on."

"I told my wife what had happened, and she handed me my shotgun. 'Don't let the kids come near,' I warned her.

"I went back and opened the lavatory door. I was half hoping the thing had gone away, but the hissing was louder than ever. I felt I couldn't miss in such a small space, so I shoved the muzzle of the gun in through the door and banged away."

189

When he finally ventured within to see what damage he had managed to inflict, he found a dead goose behind the bucket.

At Gwelo, we met Mrs. Jeannie Boggie, who in two fascinating volumes had written the story of Rhodesia's pioneers. A small spry woman with a broad Scottish accent, she owned valuable tracts of land around the town, and had conferred on Gwelo a unique memorial: a tall tower commemorating, not the human pioneers of 1890, but the oxen, mules, and donkeys that made their journey possible.

The late Major Alexander Boggie was a formidable man. He had served in the French Foreign Legion, and all his life had a taste for challenging people to duels. Brave as a lion, he suffered from a lisp. When he thought anyone was making fun of him for it, he advanced on the offender and demanded: "Do you prefer pithtols or thwordth?"

When the major died, he was buried in the churchyard. Mrs. Boggie subsequently had a difference with the minister and decided to remove her husband. She had a vault built for him on her farm, directly outside the front door. "They brought his bones in here, and I laid them out myself on that couch where you are now sitting," said Mrs. Boggie, making us jump. "He was all there except his left kneecap. I never found what happened to it."

Cecil Rhodes and Starr Leander Jameson are buried in the Matopo Hills, near Bulawayo. Eagles have their eyries near by. The graves of the two great men are marked merely by flat stone slabs over which scamper purple-bodied lizards with mustard-colored tails. The lizards looked well fed.

Rhodes was the fourth son of a twice-married English rector who had nine sons altogether. Cecil's brothers were soldiers and farmers; he himself was destined for the church. But the adventurous Cecil joined his brother Herbert in Natal, and later followed him to the diamond diggings at Kimberley. Herbert died in 1879, in Nyasaland. A spark from his pipe exploded a demijohn of gin from which he was pouring himself a drink. Cecil, who was not exactly a teetotaler himself, was always angered by any suggestion that Herbert was a drunkard. But he described another brother, Bernard, as a "charming loafer." And when a third brother, Arthur, submitted to him a claim for compensation for maize destroyed on his farm during the Matabele Rebellion, Rhodes scribbled across it: "This is the most impudent that has yet been submitted."

Rhodes, his partner in the diamond mines Alfred Beit, and his chief lieutenant in Rhodesia, Dr. Starr Leander Jameson, were all born in 1853. Rhodes was already a diamond millionaire in Kimberley when he returned to Britain to study at Oxford, where he dazzled fellow undergraduates by casually pulling handfuls of diamonds from his trousers pocket. He matriculated at Oriel College in 1873, but did not take his Oxford degree until 1881.

The conquest of Rhodesia began in 1888, when a bearded Scottish adventurer named Rudd persuaded the Matabele chief Lobengula to sign a treaty with Rhodes's British South Africa Company. The Pioneer Column entered the country in 1890. Lobengula made war and was defeated in 1893. His land was shared out among the whites by Jameson. In 1895 the conquered country, three times the size of England, was officially named Rhodesia.

Rhodes made treaties with native chiefs before proceeding to take over their territory. Rudd was only one of his emissaries. Another he sent east, to the kraal of Chief Gungunyana, a savage potentate who wore wine-colored satin waistcoats and frequently chopped off his wives' heads.

This emissary was still in his early twenties. After he had agreed to undertake the mission, Rhodes as an afterthought asked: "By the way, you are not married?"

When the answer was "No," Rhodes exploded with relief. "Thank God! If there's one thing I hate, it's having a widow weeping and wailing on my doorstep."

There are men still living who knew Rhodes well. Jimmy Davies worked on the railroad that Rhodes had built from the Portuguese port of Beira to Umtali. "There were thirty to forty deaths a day from malaria and blackwater fever," he told me. "A glass of water cost half a crown. The port was full of Japa-

191

nese geisha girls—the Scottish stationmaster bought one for five pounds and they lived happily ever after.

"One day Rhodes came down to see how the work was getting on. They were unloading a boiler from a ship, and it slipped over the side, taking Harry Graham with it. When they hauled him out, poor Harry had an arm off. There was a lot of cursing and swearing, for we all liked Harry. Rhodes stood watching, twiddling his wide-brimmed hat between his fingers, behind his back. He went very white, and then he turned and walked quickly away without a word. Next day there was a notice up in the workshops: 'Mr. Rhodes takes strong exception to bad language and the next man heard swearing on the job will be immediately dismissed.' "

Rudd, who secured the concession from Lobengula, was helped by two missionaries, Helm and Carnegie. Helm's daughter, who was still alive in Bulawayo, told us how as a little girl she had lived with her father at Lobengula's kraal.

"The king's city was entirely surrounded by a tall wooden fence made of saplings, with four entrances, all heavily guarded. Round the perimeter, within the fence, were the huts of the people. Lobengula's royal kraal consisted of a house, a wagon-shed, and enclosures for the king's cattle and goats. There was a kraal for the sacred black oxen, and an enclosure where the whitened bones of cattle slaughtered in sacrifice were scattered. Near Lobengula's house, close to the goat kraal, was the *indaba* tree (palaver tree) where he conferred with his advisers.

"Lobengula was hospitable to white traders and missionaries, but refused to be converted to Christianity, or to give up any of his tribal customs. 'I am too old to change,' he said."

Periodically the witch doctors would smell out a plot against the king's life. This would be followed by a night of bloodshed in which men and women were clubbed to death. In one purge Lobengula had his own sister strangled. The whites who stayed at or near the royal kraal were powerless to prevent these massacres.

"He was quite a nice man, really," Helm's seventy-eight-year-old daughter told us, while her grandchildren gathered round to hear her tell the story again. "No worse, after all, than any of the English Tudors. My father was very fond of him."

Rhodes's Pioneers were recruited from "the shires, the clubs and the professions." They came in quest of gold, land, and adventure.

The Pioneer Column crossed the Limpopo and hacked their way through forest. Their ox-wagons creaked up Providential Pass, with Lobengula's *impis* (warriors) hanging watchful and hostile at their flanks. When they gained the high plateau, their troubles had only begun. In that first year of 1890, as they began to clear the bush, mark out farms, and create little townships of tents and grass huts, they were struck by drought and then by terrible floods.

The food-wagons could not get through. No crops had yet been sown. Men dying of malaria and starvation crawled on hands and knees to the huts of neighbors, begging for help. Meanwhile more men, and women and children too, were crossing the Limpopo to enter the promised land. The wagons covered only ten miles a day. On the long trek, children were born, and many of them were buried beside the trail. The parties were attacked by lions and sometimes also by savages. Everywhere malaria and blackwater fever took a deadly toll. One man, who strayed from the wagons and was lost in the bush for forty-nine days without food, tried to drown himself in a pool that proved too shallow. Then he tried to hang himself from a tree, but the branch broke. He was rescued by another party of trekkers, who found him living inside an anthill. He was walking on all fours and was completely out of his head.

The settlers had barely begun to farm when rinderpest swept all their cattle away. The Matabele rose in rebellion. In the little towns like Fort Victoria and Fort Salisbury the women and children took refuge in the jails, several families to a cell, while the men went out to fight.

Bulawayo, which means "Place of Slaughter," stands on the site of Lobengula's kraal. It is an impressive-looking town, for Rhodes commanded that the streets should be broad enough for a wagon drawn by sixteen oxen to be able to make a U-turn.

In 1952 a census had just disclosed that there were 32,000 white people living in Bulawayo, which had therefore outstripped the capital, Salisbury, with its 22,000. This statistical victory had generated a certain smugness.

"We really have a terrible traffic problem," a town official lamented. "You ought to see Bulawayo at the rush hour." The rush hour was at five in the afternoon, when all the shops and offices promptly closed and everyone raced off to play tennis. Then the midsection indeed became a maelstrom of traffic: in one street we saw as many as ten cars waiting to cross an intersection.

Half an hour later the streets were utterly deserted. Bulawayo does not cater to those who love night life.

But Jimmy Gilchrist, a spruce man with a monocle, begged us not to be deceived by the town's prim atmosphere. He recalled the days when angry wives stormed the club with sjamboks and shotguns to retrieve their erring husbands from the gaming-tables.

Jimmy drove us to his imposing home, Fortune's Gate, and royally dined and wined us. Later he took us to a charity ball. The grounds were lit with fairy lanterns. Champagne flowed freely. Sleek limousines deposited sun-tanned, Empire-building men in evening kit, and ladies in velvet gowns.

Our host, a white-haired man with the benevolent manner of a Wodehouse peer, beamed upon the gathering but kept looking at his watch. A large bulldog followed closely at his heels. At midnight he snapped his watch shut. "Well, well," he said genially, to the bulldog, "time all these good people went home, eh, Towser? Early to bed and early to rise, what?"

We took the hint and departed.

: 5 :

THE ROAD from Bulawayo to the Victoria Falls runs for the most part through thick, primeval forest. But about midway there is a large coal mine.

We came out of the trees and there below us was a man-made wilderness of crisscrossing railroad tracks, puffing locomotives, mountains of coal, and sooty brick houses. Everything, including the one hotel, was inches deep in coal dust.

Beyond Wankie, trucks rumbled along the road in the blazing heat, between the green walls of the forest. But not far from the mine there was a game preserve, whose animal inhabitants included numerous giraffe and five hundred elephant.

The preserve is not fenced and the elephants and other fauna frequently wander across the road. When we came to a large sign beside a narrow wooden bridge which said: "Beware of Elephant," we were inclined to take it lightly, until we met a truck-driver who had had a shattering experience—or rather had just managed to avoid having one.

He was carrying a load of several tons of glassware from Bulawayo to Lusaka, in Northern Rhodesia, when he found the road blocked by a herd of elephant. "They made no move to get off the road," he said. "I couldn't risk a collision. So I stayed where I was. I camped beside the truck, and they held me up for three days."

Two white-coifed nuns passed us in a jeep. One was driving, and the other tranquilly read a book. The forest was full of missions, of diverse denominations. Their trim buildings and schools stood in clearings just off the road, crowding one another like competing banks on opposite street corners.

The Africans call the Victoria Falls "the Smoke that Thunders." Out of deep gorges cut by the Zambezi River, white spray rises and hangs in the air, a curtain of vaporized water visible from miles away. David Livingstone wrote that "such loveliness must have been witnessed by angels in their flight." Rhodes, who had a lesser mind, arranged that the railroad bridge across the Zambezi should be so built that the spray of the falls descended on the trains. There were hippos in the river, and crocodiles on its sandbanks. In the midst of all this was a gigantic luxury hotel.

To reach the lip of the falls from the hotel, we went in a heavy iron trolley, covered with a strip of awning and pushed along a set of rails by sweating Africans. The distance was about a mile. We passed the perpetually drenched statue of Livingstone, gazing from under his peaked cap at the falls he found, and perhaps pondering the fate of the black people he vowed to succor in the name of God. Before the trolley reached its terminal, the natives pushing it were wiping the streaming sweat from their faces with their elbows. They were clad in rags and were barefooted. They pushed with bursting lungs, their faces gone gray with strain. The white tourists sitting on the trolley chattered brightly among themselves, and remarked on the heat, all except one man, who suddenly and violently remarked: "By God, look at these poor devils! I'd rather walk," and got off.

Thankfully we followed his example, and reached the falls dripping with sweat ourselves. But the Africans only scowled, thinking we were trying to get out of tipping them.

Over the Victoria Falls pour seventy-five million gallons of water a minute, generating six million horsepower, but nobody has deemed it worth while to replace the heavy hand-pushed iron trolleys with a light electric railway; Africans are cheaper.

Perhaps that was why, wherever Jane and I went in Rhodesia, Negroes always clustered round our car with its Johannesburg number-plate. White Rhodesians expressed only loathing for "Jewburg," the City of Mammon; the one ambition of most Rhodesian Negroes seemed to be to get there.

Across the Zambezi was the town of Livingstone, which has an airport for British jet airliners traversing Africa, and the land of Northern Rhodesia.

XIV

NORTHERN RHODESIA: COPPER BELT

THE PASSENGERS in the Viking included an infant in a basket and a British businessman with a brief-case. We were flying over the waterless bush of Northern Rhodesia. South of us was the Zambezi; to the north lay the thick forests of the Congo.

"We were damned fools to invest money in places like Persia," said the businessman suddenly. "We should have invested more here. Africa is the continent of the future."

"Mainly desert," I said.

"What about the great lakes?" he countered. "Think of the mineral wealth." He was one of those who dreamed of a great new British dominion in central Africa stretching from Rhodesia all the way to Kenya. In British Africa the spirit of Rhodes, who went about splashing the map with red paint, lives on.

Meanwhile there was the copper belt, with its four huge mines amid the red, thirty-foot-high anthills.

Ndola was a hot and dusty town. It had one long, straight street, down the center of which grew mahogany trees, whose trunks were surprisingly painted white. The white paint was to protect the trees from voracious ants, which in Rhodesia eat everything, including the houses. The white paint also protected the trees from drunken night drivers.

The dust settled at evening, a clean cool wind blew, and the sky blazed with brilliant stars. But indoors every light attracted insects. My white mosquito net blackened under a swarm of beetles, bugs, moths, and spiders. The light-switch was by the

197

door, across the room from the bed. I braced myself, put off the light, stumbled forward in the darkness, lifted the net with its clinging insect burden, and crawled between the sheets.

With Eric Bridges and his wife, I drove the thirty-eight miles from Ndola to Kitwe, near the Nkana copper mine.

On the way we passed the tall, thick columns of teak trees, which have luminous bark and look like pillars lit from within.

The population of the copper belt was growing rapidly—too rapidly for amenities to catch up. In Ndola a public lavatory had been turned into temporary offices for an overflow of health-department clerks. Wooden boards were nailed over the toilets to provide seats. In Kitwe a bank was constructed of sheets of corrugated iron, nailed together.

But at Nkana the white miners and their families were living in large airy bungalows with beautiful gardens. More than half of them were recent immigrants from South Africa. A lady from whom we asked directions stopped watering her flowers, came to her garden gate, and answered us in Afrikaans.

A white miner, Bridges said, earned, with his copper bonus, about $420 a month. The mining companies also provided heavily subsidized houses, cinemas, and clubs. White miners at Kitwe possessed not only motor-cars, but also small yachts, which they sailed on an artificial lake. To make the lake, water had been pumped out of the mine and dammed. The miners of Kitwe also had their own speedway track.

"Are they happy?" I asked a company official.

"They're human," he said dryly, "which means that, whatever they've got, they want more."

The mine's Negro workers were housed with their families in a separate township. Two-roomed houses were laid out in neat rows. The African township had a large red-brick hospital and a social center. Interspersed among the little houses were open-sided structures with thatched roofs for shade, where the Negroes sat drinking beer and wine.

By the side of the road was parked a truck from which the Negro driver was selling fish. "The fish comes from two hundred and fifty miles away," said Bridges. "It used to be carried here in hundred-and-fifty-pound head-loads." The Negro fish-salesman gave us a cheerful wave of his hand as we passed.

The mine town of Nkana looked brand-new, as if its stores and cinemas and one hotel had been imported in one piece, as they almost literally had been. In the hotel, though it was still early in the day, white miners off duty were drinking whisky and playing poker. The losers bought the drinks.

At the hotel we waited for Jock Brotchie. When he arrived he proved to be a dour-seeming Scot with an air of not suffering fools gladly. Later, as he conducted us round the Nkana copper mine, he thawed out and revealed himself to be a genial mine of information.

Giant cranes, capable of lifting eighty-ton loads, seized and hoisted buckets of slag. Green flames shot from giant smelters. Copper was decanted in molten rivers. The smelters were fed by cut-down forests. Southern Rhodesia's Wankie coal mine could not provide enough fuel, because of the long rail haul and a truck shortage, so gangs of Negroes armed with machetes were cutting down the forest for miles around the mine, to feed the furnaces.

Amid blistering heat and clanking din, the minehead hoists were like Euclidean exercises in aluminum-painted steel, etched against the clear blue African sky. A mine-cage, which carried one hundred and twenty men and traveled at a rate of two thousand feet a minute, was raised and lowered half a mile by an all-automatic, driverless hoist.

In the mine's copper refinery, a Negro sitting far above our heads in the moving cabin of a ten-ton crane operated levers that dipped copper sheets in great vats of acid. The Negro earned thirty-five cents a day. Near by, a white man, also by sitting and moving a lever, poured molten copper into moving pans. His basic wage was about eleven dollars a day .

A tall stack sent copper-colored smoke up into the blue sky. Round its base were hundreds of red anthills. In the neighboring jungle, monkeys chattered from the trees, and big birds whistled shrilly. In clearings amid the trees were the thatched, round mud huts of Negroes who did not work on the mine. But they had taken to bicycles, and the roads swarmed with them.

The roads about the mine cut straight through the jungle, and also clean through the anthills, which they sliced neatly in half. There were too many anthills for the road to try to go round them; and most of the anthills were twenty feet wide at the base, as well as being thirty feet high. One road, a narrow tunnel boring through a forest of close-packed, straight-boled trees, continued to Elisabethville, in the Belgian Congo. Stanley and Livingstone passed this way, before there were any roads. One of the first roads to be built in the area overlaid an old Arab slave trail.

With copper selling at over $700 a ton, the four big mines of the Northern Rhodesian copper belt were earning $154,000,000 a year. In the heart of Livingstone's "Darkest Africa," the Pan American Constellations flying between New York and Johannesburg passed by night over green-flamed furnaces and the gleaming scattered lights of jungle-girt towns. A new Rand was in the making.

: 2 :

LAWRENCE CHOLA KATILUNGA, a forty-five-year-old Negro with bulky shoulders and a small black mustache, chewed happily on a stick of sun-dried venison, which the South African Boers call *biltong*. To Katilunga, the biltong was a symbol of victory.

Katilunga is the president of the copper belt's forty-thousand-strong African Mineworkers' Union. He had just called his men back from a strike that had lasted three weeks and had cost the mines $560,000 a day in lost production. The strike ended in big pay increases for the black miners.

In addition to their pay, the Negro copper-miners get free rations. But when they went on strike, they had to buy their food. It was expected that the union's funds would soon dwindle. But the miners had been stockpiling biltong, which

Katilunga described as "our iron rations." This enabled them to hold out.

The Negroes' trade union was organized after the Second World War, with the active support of the British Government, by a ginger-mustached and blue-eyed Scotsman called Bill Comrie. Few whites in Northern Rhodesia, including the 5,000 white copper-miners, who are themselves strongly organized but frown on Negroes' following their example, believed it could lead to anything but trouble. Instead, the union had proved a great success. A Northern Rhodesian Government official, a senior labor officer, told me: "In negotiations with the employers, the union leaders have shown themselves astute and knowledgeable." After organizing the union, Comrie stepped completely out of the picture, handing the union over to the Negroes themselves.

On one occasion the Negro miners challenged the white miners to a contest: each would work one shift, to see who could produce the most copper. The white miners refused. An engineer employed at Nkana told me bluntly: "We could replace all the whites with blacks tomorrow, and increase our output."

Katilunga explained that his union collected a shilling (fourteen cents) a month from each member, through a stop-order system. He said: "My father was a tribal blacksmith. He forged spears for the warriors. I entered the mine as an unskilled worker, and became a skilled rock-breaker. But I still earned only a twentieth of the wage of a white miner doing the same work."

He complained: "The companies bring in white men as 'learner miners.' They know nothing about the job. A Negro 'boss-boy' has to show them what to do. But they are still the bosses, and the Negroes who teach them are still 'boys.' The white learner starts at about ten dollars a day. The 'boss-boy,' who has been in the mine maybe for fifteen years, gets only one dollar and twelve cents a day."

The strike began when the African Mineworkers' Union demanded an all-round increase of thirty-five cents a day for its members. For seventy-five per cent of the Negro copper-miners this would have meant a one-hundred-per-cent pay raise; for the highest-paid Negro miners it would have meant a twenty-five-per-cent raise.

Surprisingly, the companies at no stage denied that they could afford to give the Negroes such an increase. They admitted that in five years dividends paid to stockholders had risen from seventy-five to two hundred per cent. The argument used by the companies was that such increases would upset the "traditional" Negro wage-level throughout Northern Rhodesia.

Years before, in 1947, the British Government had set up a commission to examine the color-bar in Northern Rhodesia. The outcome was the Dalgleish Report, which recommended that the color-bar should be gradually broken down and that Negroes should be allowed to do jobs hitherto reserved for whites.

"The Dalgleish Report is still on the shelf," Katilunga told me, "and we want it taken down and implemented. Until that happens, we are going to press for more and more pay increases. In the end the companies will be compelled to let Negroes operate more machines and do more skilled work. Otherwise they will simply have to pay us high wages for low-skilled work. It's up to them."

After talking to Lawrence Katilunga in Kitwe, I drove out to see Tommy Fox-Pitt. On the way, we ran into a storm of flying ants. They descended on the car in swarms, their bodies hitting the windshield like bullets. After a few minutes the windshield was smeared half an inch thick with dead ants, and the wipers ceased to function.

It grew dark. The unlighted, potholed track ran through thick forest. Finally the car could go no farther. I got out and walked. Stumbling through the trees in pitch-blackness, I wondered what would happen to me if I missed Fox-Pitt's bungalow. The next place inhabited by white men on this route was Elisabethville, in the Belgian Congo. Through the trees a lantern waved, and a cheery British voice hailed me. Thankfully, I directed my footsteps toward it.

In a book-lined room, crimson moths fluttered round the

paraffin lamp set in the center of the dinner table. Other insects, unidentifiable, crawled across the tablecloth. At one point a scorpion fell from the ceiling into my host's soup. Calmly he removed it and called for another plate.

In the Second World War, Fox-Pitt commanded a destroyer. When the war ended he was appointed provincial commissioner in the Fort Jameson area of Northern Rhodesia. It was a farming district. The farmers sold their produce through a Government-controlled marketing board. When Fox-Pitt discovered that Negro farmers were paid less for their produce than white farmers, apparently solely because they were Negroes, he violently attacked both the system and the Government. He was asked to resign.

This passion for justice was, it seemed, hereditary. "My grandfather," he recalled with a twinkle, "was a British major-general. Kitchener was fighting in Egypt. My grandfather brought a regiment to Port Sudan. By an oversight on the part of the War Office, his men were not provided with boots. He refused to let his men land until the boots arrived. This set back Kitchener's campaign by some weeks. My family has always insisted on fair play."

Fox-Pitt was outspoken about the color-bar. Despite his distinguished war record and his silvery hair, he was regarded as an "agitator." He said dryly: "The Government watches me closely. My mail is censored. The results have occasionally been amusing. Once a letter addressed to me was seized by the police. But it fell off a police car in the center of Kitwe. A passer-by picked it up, saw it was addressed to me, and kindly delivered it by hand."

I had been warned that Fox-Pitt was a "Communist." Anything less like an agent of Moscow than this gentle but determined former naval commander it would be difficult to imagine. Surrounded by his dog-eared books, he lived alone in his bungalow in the heart of the forest, with only crimson moths for company.

"Do you have much contact with the Negro copper-miners?" I asked.

He shook his head. "They no longer need white help. They are on their own."

But in the Kitwe hotel a white man blustered: "The niggers are getting out of hand, and it's all the fault of white agitators like Fox-Pitt. Letting down their own race . . ."

: 3 :

LUSAKA, THE capital of Northern Rhodesia, is just another hot, dusty, one-street town. But it has politicians instead of miners. In the center of a big green lawn, fringed with crimson and yellow cannas, a Union Jack hung limply on its pole. Facing the flag was a three-story yellow building. This was the Secretariat, where the Northern Rhodesian Legislative Council meets.

The "Legco" assembled in a small room with yellow walls and a gold-and-white ceiling. There were twenty-three members, of whom two were Negroes. The Speaker and the Clerk of the House wore wigs and black robes. Round the walls were fading pictures of Cecil Rhodes and other celebrities. A slowly revolving fan reposed untidily on a chair. Members of the public sat at the back, under a wall clock and a golden eagle. The division bell, rung to summon absent members to the debating chamber when a vote is about to be taken, was also used to announce intermission for the tea, when the members of the Legco flocked into an adjoining room for a ten-minute break each morning and afternoon.

Some of the shops in Lusaka had hatches opening on the sidewalk. White customers walked into the shop to be served at the counter in the normal manner. Negroes were not permitted to enter the shop, but were served through the hatch, while they waited on the sidewalk.

A Northern Rhodesian Government official invited me to lunch. While his white-clad Negro servants helped him to beef and vegetables, he discussed the "native problem."

"All this talk of advancing the Negro is so much sentimental twaddle," he said. At his elbow a servant waited patiently with a dish of potatoes. "These people are unteachable. You might as well try to teach baboons." He took some potatoes and impatiently waved the dish aside. "They are fit only to live in the bush, as they have always done."

Outside, a truck driven by a Negro roared past.

Other Rhodesians had different ideas. The Government was making films for distribution among the bush villages, and the Negroes were buying large quantities of cheap "saucepan" battery radios. A propaganda campaign urged: "Have *your* chief buy *your* village a 'saucepan.' "

Louis Nel, who was handling the distribution of films, drove me twenty miles out of town to his farm, Rockwood. Surrounded by dogs and Siamese cats, we dined off excellent mutton.

At the age of thirty, Louis, who was born in the copper belt, was filled with nostalgia for the "old days." "Kitwe had only three hundred white inhabitants. There was a lot of malaria and blackwater fever. A birth was an event, but there was a funeral a day."

During the depression, in the early thirties, when the price of copper went down to seventy dollars a ton, the unemployed white miners lived in houses constructed out of packing-cases and kerosene cans. "But those were great days," Louis insisted.

To collect material and ideas for his documentary films, he often went off alone into the bush and stayed away for weeks. On one occasion he walked two hundred miles in ten days, living mainly on sweetened tea. "When the body is tired," he explained, "the mind is clear." He had an enormous affection for the black folk with whom his work brought him into close contact.

The two Negro members of Legco, Dauti Yamba and Paskale Sekota (they were not elected, but were appointed by the Governor), were living at a Government rest-house in Lusaka. This was a tactful way of getting round segregation: neither of them would have been admitted to a hotel. When I called, rather early in the morning, Yamba was strolling around in his pajamas. He hastily changed. They were both small men, not much over five feet. Both had been schoolteachers. They were in their late thirties. Yamba had rugged features and a large nose. Sekota had a round, boyish face.

They were indignant about Lusaka's shop "hatches." Yamba said: "Rhodesians virtuously denounce Malan's *apartheid* in South Africa, but there is no real difference."

Sekota remarked cynically: "They keep saying that they want 'partnership' between white and black—with one 'partner' inside the shop and the other being served through a hatch."

I said: "In South Africa—and in Southern Rhodesia, for that matter—there are no Negroes in Parliament, not even appointed ones."

Yamba added: "Down there a black man's money is as good as anyone else's, but he gets no political rights. Here, there has been some political advance, but even so, a Negro is still treated as a 'nigger.'"

Sekota said: "There *has* been progress here compared with South Africa. And Rhodesia is becoming rich. I believe the day will come when Negroes from the south will begin to trek up to Rhodesia to find jobs, instead of the other way round." He added thoughtfully: "What Northern Rhodesia needs is more black immigration."

I had just come from a meeting with whites, all of whom had assured me that the solution of the "native problem" was to bring in more white people. I reflected that it all depended on the point of view—and the color of your own skin.

: 4 :

ROY WELENSKY is the biggest thing in Northern Rhodesia, in more ways than one. A huge man, standing over six feet, he weighs 272 pounds. He has large, bushy eyebrows, like those of John L. Lewis, whose career his own has in some respects resembled. Welensky has a peculiarly sweet smile and a soft, gurgling voice, both unusual in so large a man. He is also the political boss of a country larger than Germany.

"The mass of the Africans are incapable of understanding politics," Welensky said. He told me a story to prove it. When it was proposed to federate the two Rhodesias and Nyasaland, Negro copper-miners marched in a body to their white foreman. "We are against ventilation," they said. "Our leaders say we must oppose it." Welensky explained: "They confused 'federation' with 'ventilation.' They thought it had something to do with the working of the mine."

We sat in the living-room of his unpretentious home. Welensky wore a crumpled white suit, and had his bulk wedged in an oversize chair. The atmosphere was cordial, but conversation was difficult. Welensky kept open house, and people kept dropping in. Most of them were men in their shirtsleeves. Welensky introduced them and hospitably invited them to help themselves to whisky or beer. He himself drank only water, and did not smoke. But as the gathering grew, the room was filled with tobacco fumes. Welensky's guests sat round the room, drinking his beer and whisky and talking loudly among themselves. Several conversations were going on at the same time. Welensky sat in the center, obviously enjoying himself. He was like a monarch presiding over a rowdy court. His visitors were mostly miners and railroad men. They treated him as one of themselves, without any outward show of respect. One or two of them jeered good-humoredly at something he had said in Legco. Welensky grinned lazily back. "Bet you think you could have done it better, Jack," he said. Yet somehow there was no doubt at all about who was boss.

When the other visitors had all gone, drifting off in twos and threes, Welensky said gently: "Would you care to hear some music?"

He lumbered toward a big radio-phonograph, and began to play records. His favorite composers, I discovered, were Stravinsky and Bach.

Officially, Welensky is only "chairman of the elected members" in Northern Rhodesia's tiny Legislative Council. As a British colony, Northern Rhodesia is technically run from Whitehall. It has a Governor, Sir Gilbert McCall Rennie,

K.C.M.G., M.C. In fact, however, Northern Rhodesia is run by Welensky. Though he is a Companion of the Order of St. Michael and St. George, he dislikes even the trappings of colonial subservience to the United Kingdom. Recently, when fellow members of Legco arrived in Lusaka for the Council's opening session wearing white colonial service uniforms and ornamental swords, Welensky threatened: "If this goes on, I'll wear an engine-driver's overalls and carry an oil-can as my badge of office."

Welensky, who is forty-six, was born in Salisbury, the capital of Southern Rhodesia. His father, Michael Welensky, was a Polish Jew, who, however, moved to Sweden. Subsequently he emigrated to South Africa, where he married a Boer girl, Aletta Ferreira. She became Roy Welensky's mother.

In 1890 Michael Welensky and his young Boer wife joined the northward trek of Cecil Rhodes's Pioneers across the Limpopo into Rhodesia, which was then called Mashonaland. The virtually unmapped territory lay under the shadow of the powerful Matabele king, Lobengula, and his dreaded impis. Every white man carried a rifle.

Roy Welensky went to school in Salisbury until he was fourteen. Then he started to earn his living. For a while he was a barman, in a hotel chiefly patronized by tough, hard-drinking gold prospectors. He also served behind the counter of a "Kaffir store" in the bush, selling cheap goods to Negroes who lived in mud huts. When he was seventeen, he began working on the railroad. At this time also he became a boxer and wound up as heavyweight champion of Southern Rhodesia.

In 1933 the railroad sent him to Northern Rhodesia. He was allotted a clinker-and-cement house at 24 Central Avenue, Broken Hill, where he still lives.

Welensky drove the mail train in and out of Broken Hill. When regular passengers were late in arriving at the station, the train waited for them. The train also stopped between stations to pick up passengers who hailed it. At that time, the white population of Northern Rhodesia was only seven thousand.

The railroad men had a strong trade union. Welensky was an active union man. He became chairman of the Broken Hill branch of the union, and was elected to the union's national council. In 1938 the railroad workers and copper-miners of Broken Hill joined forces to nominate Welensky for a seat on the Legislative Council. He has represented Broken Hill in Legco ever since. But he still has his engine-driver's ticket, and officially he is still on unpaid leave from the railroads.

Welensky's predecessor in Legco had been the distinguished pioneer Sir Stewart Gore-Browne, who wore a monocle. The nominated, later elected, members were in a minority. They were called the "unofficials," and usually they listened respectfully to the "officials," who were all civil servants. The Governor always had the last word. The "officials" were in the main urbane and cultured men, who wrote poetry and studied the classics in their ample spare time.

"Welensky," says an old friend, "burst into the stuffy atmosphere like a preview of the atom bomb." When one of the "officials" got up and declared with pride that in the past year Northern Rhodesia had added three miles to the length of its railroad, Welensky said scathingly: "Put it in inches, sir; it will sound more impressive."

Welensky, representing the copper-miners and railroad workers, formed a Labour Party. This was an unheard-of thing to do. The colony was not supposed to have political parties at all. But Welensky's new party contested five of the eight "unofficial" seats in Legco and won all of them.

When the Second World War began, the Governor appointed two of the "unofficials" to his Executive Council. Welensky was one of the two who were chosen. On the Executive Council, he was given the job of Director of Manpower.

Welensky threw himself into his task with characteristic vigor; but by doing so, he stood hard on many a fellow trade-unionist's bunion. He had already dissolved his Labour Party. When the copper-miners threatened to go on strike for more pay, Welensky banned strikes. He agreed to the summary deportation of the copper-miners' leader, Frank Maybank, on the ground that Maybank's activities were holding up vital production. On one occasion, waiting on a railroad platform for a train, he heard a railroad worker express admiration for Hitler's treatment of Jews. Welensky, the former heavyweight boxing champion, promptly knocked the anti-Semite flat.

When the war ended, Welensky's job as Director of Manpower ended with it. For his wartime services, he accepted the C.M.G. But he soon made it clear that he was highly unsatisfied with the unrepresentative character of the Legislative Council. The composition of Legco was altered to meet his wishes. The new body had ten elected members and only nine "officials." It also had two Negro members, chosen by their fellows but requiring the Governor's approval, and two white members appointed to "represent African interests." Welensky was leader of the elected members.

The Governor's Executive Council—performing the functions of a cabinet, with the Governor presiding—still had seven "officials" as against five "unofficials." In theory, "Exco" could override the wishes of Legco. In practice, the "officials" on Exco have always bowed to the wishes of the "unofficials," who take their instructions from the elected members of Legco. As the elected members, all white, take their lead from Welensky, who has never been seriously opposed by any white political group in Northern Rhodesia, this makes Welensky the boss.

"The population of Northern Rhodesia," Welensky told me, "works out at six to the square mile. There are only 40,000 whites living among 1,500,000 Africans. The Africans are rapidly increasing their numbers; the African population is expected to double itself in twenty-five years. But only once in the past five years has Northern Rhodesia been able to feed itself. We need more whites, to raise our economic standards. We must also grow more food.

"One day the Africans will have fully equal political rights, but they still have a long way to go. We whites want the Africans as partners; but we don't think they ought to be running the country just because they are in the majority. In a situation like this, the two *races* must agree to work toward equality. White must not dominate black, and black must not dominate white." Welensky did not deny that at present, and for a long time to come, the whites must be the senior partner.

On the subject of his favorite project, federation, Welensky said: "If three men are walking down a dark road, they'd better walk together, not separately."

One of the things that made the road dark, in his opinion, was Boer nationalism and consequent anti-British feeling in South Africa. By origin a Jew, whose father was born in Warsaw but emigrated to Africa, Welensky would be rightly offended if anyone suggested he was anything but British. Like many Rhodesians, North and South, he feared Afrikaner infiltration. Half of Northern Rhodesia's recent white immigrants, one third of Southern Rhodesia's, had come from the Union. A federation in control of its own internal affairs, but still stoutly loyal to the Union Jack, would be a bulwark against Boer nationalism.

When not finding a Boer under his bed, Welensky is apt to discover a Communist or an Indian. He thought there was a lot of Communist propaganda among the Negroes. For allegedly preaching Communism, Northern Rhodesia had just deported to England a young white immigrant, Simon Ber Zukas, who ironically was also a Polish Jew.

The Indians, too, were infiltrators. They greatly outnumbered the whites in Kenya, Tanganyika, Uganda, and Nyasaland. In Northern Rhodesia itself, their numbers were rapidly increasing. I gathered that, in Welensky's view, Nehru, Malan, and Malenkov all had greedy eyes fixed on British Africa, and he hardly knew which was worst.

"What about black nationalism?" I asked. "What about the color-bar, in Lusaka shops and on the copper mines?"

He moved his enormous shoulders, not impatiently, but like one who has mountains to move and can move only one of them at a time. He looked at me from under his bushy eyebrows and smiled his singularly sweet smile.

"It took me a long time to begin to understand Stravinsky,"

he said. "Such strange discords! But in the end it becomes music."

He seemed to think it a good, ambiguous note on which to end the interview. Perhaps he was right.

XV

NYASALAND: THE LOST ONES

NYASALAND, WHICH is slightly larger than Indiana, is a difficult place to get at. You can go from Beira by rail, or from Salisbury by road. But I flew.

We crossed tight-packed ranges of cloudy mountains, and the bumpy trip of one and a half hours from Salisbury was enlivened for me by a companion who had made two previous flights on this route.

"The first time," he said, "the port engine got on fire, and we had to turn back. The second time was by charter plane. I was the only passenger. We flew on for a long time, and finally the pilot said: 'How good are you at reading maps?' " 'Why?' I asked, and he said cheerfully: 'Because I'm lost.' "

As a matter of fact, very few people get killed flying in Africa.

We landed at Blantyre. Julian Theunissen was waiting for me with a dusty Chevrolet. On the way into town from the airport the car stuck in a swamp. Helpful black men put stones under the wheels, making a causeway over which, with much pushing and heaving, we lurched back onto dry land.

Blantyre was being blistered by a particularly vicious sun. The paint was cracking on the houses, and the town's main street danced in a heat haze. There were few white people about. It was the siesta hour and they were all asleep. But the Indian-owned stores were open for business, and all along the street black men wearing garments like long white nightgowns sat on shady verandas treadling busily at sewing-machines, which they operated with their bare feet. In Nyasaland it is the men who make the clothes: the women work in the fields.

Before proceeding by road to Zomba, we had lunch in Blantyre, in a small, dark hotel dining-room, heavily protected by mosquito screens. In Blantyre, as I discovered later, the mosquitoes really mean business. We lunched with Harry Ellis, who sold books to Africans. Ellis said: "The British Council tries to interest them in T. S. Eliot—God knows why—but at the moment they are more fascinated by the working of the internal-combustion engine. I sell dozens of books about motor-cars. Meanwhile they operate sewing-machines and ride bicycles."

On the way to Zomba, we passed an African woman trudging along the road with a child wrapped in a blanket on her back, a huge bundle on her head, and a big umbrella held aloft to protect her and the child from the fierce sun. Outside Limbe, there was an imposing home with turrets.

"Macaroni Castle," said Theunissen. "It was built before the war by an Italian tea-planter. During the war the few Italians living in Nyasaland were interned there."

In the bar of the Limbe hotel an African stood in the corner, motionless as a cigar-store Indian. Round his neck was a cord supporting a tray, as if he were selling popcorn. What he was actually selling were books. The tray contained an assortment of paper-backed literature. The titles included S. J. Perelman's *Crazy like a Fox* and D. H. Lawrence's *Sons and Lovers*. I concluded that the people of Nyasaland were a well-read lot, a conclusion that Theunissen's conversation certainly supported. A handsome young man with curly hair and a dark mustache, he was a South African by birth. His talk was lively and informative, and the home that he and his wife had made for themselves at Zomba overflowed with books.

The bar of the Limbe hotel, besides having a literary section, sold ice cream in addition to whisky and draught beer. Nyasaland, I reflected, was an African country with unusual attributes.

Beyond Limbe the countryside was hilly, green, wooded, and extremely beautiful. We might have been in an English shire, except that through the trees we glimpsed Nyasa huts, looking like shaggy dogs. Built of mud, they had thick, topheavy thatching, which came down low over the tiny openings that served as windows.

Nyasaland is a long, narrow strip of land attached to its lake, which is large enough to be called an inland sea. There are few roads, and half of them are impassable in wet weather.

"It's the old-style district commissioner's paradise," said Theunissen, and explained: "Elsewhere in Africa, communications are now too good. A district officer is on a short lead, attached to the Secretariat. Here, when you're out in the field, you're strictly on your own. A Nyasaland D.C. still spends at least twelve days in every month traveling round the countryside—and he does it on foot! The result is that he knows the people not as a mass, but as individuals. When he arrives at a place he is welcomed as a friend of the family."

Theunissen, who had been working in the Secretariat at Zomba, was shortly going back into the field as a D.C., and seemed very happy about it.

Zomba had a large hospital for Africans. It also had, opposite the hospital, a prison, which turned out to be a dignified piece of architecture with nothing forbidding about it. The Secretariat was an extraordinary affair: a red-brick pile, with many outside wooden staircases creakily clinging to it, and a maze of stone corridors, all in the shadow of a five-thousand-foot mountain. The handful of whites at Zomba, all civil servants, had a club, which combined cinema, bar, and library. There was also a playing field. As soon as we arrived, Julian changed into jersey, shorts, and football boots. He was scheduled to play in a match immediately. Whites were playing blacks. I sat on the club's long veranda with Mrs. Theunissen, consuming cooling drinks, while Julian and his teammates pursued a ball in equatorial heat.

The football match was the most energetic thing I saw in Nyasaland. Though pretty, it is not a country conducive to great exertion.

As we watched the football game, a lean man dropped into a deck-chair beside me. He was an agricultural officer. Two years before, he said, there had been a serious famine, so bad that many African children were abandoned by their parents. Now the administration was trying to improve the Africans' farming methods. It was not an easy task.

"We tell them: 'Grow more; think of your grandchildren.' They don't seem very interested in the fate of their grandchildren. A popular saying here is: 'Tomorrow is ten days away.'"

The Africans, he said, owned and cultivated widely scattered strips of land. Attempts to get them to practice a mild form of collectivization had not met with much success. Nyasaland had few real villages. The people lived in small family units, in the bush. The authorities were trying to create villages, by regrouping.

"When a man wants to plow or to gather in his crops, he calls his neighbors from miles around to help. To attract them, he has to throw a big beer party. The result is that there is more drinking done than plowing or harvesting. The administration," my informant added calmly, "has now forbidden beer-drinking before lunch."

About forty thousand Africans, he went on, worked on the white-owned tea estates. The minimum wage for an African worker was two dollars and forty-five cents a month, excluding rations and a hut, which the employers provided free.

"It doesn't seem much," he said, "but most of the workers do only a few hours a day. Often they don't work in the afternoon at all."

The contract was for thirty days. "But an African may decide to go off after a couple of weeks, accept a 'ticket' elsewhere, and come back when it pleases him, to finish his first 'ticket.' If he doesn't come back at all, the employer can't do much about it. Some planters offer a bonus to workers who agree to finish their thirty-day stint inside forty-five days.

"The truth is," the lean man finished, "most of the Nyasa just aren't interested in earning cash. They've got plenty of land of their own. Labor is scarce and employers are at a disadvantage."

216

An African on the field adroitly dribbled the ball, then shot it into the white goal. The spectators clapped, and the lean man raised his voice: "Oh, good shot!"

: 2 :

EARLY NEXT morning, before six, Julian Theunissen drove me to the top of Zomba Mountain. The road was steep and winding. Rapidly we rose above the hot green plain, and the air grew cool. Everything sparkled in the sunshine. Directly below, the Secretariat dwindled to a shining doll's house.

The road was so narrow that it was impossible for two cars to pass. On one side the mountain towered, a sheer wall; on the other side was a sheer drop. An ingenious arrangement had therefore been devised. At the side of the road a large board announced that ascending vehicles could proceed only during the first quarter of each hour. A similar notice at the top warned descending vehicles that they could launch out on their downward journey only between half past and quarter to. In this way, ascending and descending vehicles could never meet— unless someone had a breakdown, or lingered to look at the view.

"Suppose someone did," I asked Julian.

"Well," he said cheerily, "it hasn't happened yet. Why worry until it does?"

From the top of the mountain the range of visibility was two hundred miles. In the distance were the mountains that marked the border of Portuguese East Africa. Lake Chilwa was a blinding disk under the sun, like a brimming lake of molten silver. From the green plains below, hills rose solidly, rounded, complete, but still far beneath us, as if we were examining a huge map in bas-relief.

Excursions to the top of the mountain were understandably frequent. They provided an immediate relief from the heat of the valley; and amid cool trees where English flowers grew, there were mountain streams full of fat trout. Being exiled to Zomba, I thought, need be no hardship for nature-loving Englishmen.

"But we are too small a community," Julian said. "You can't imagine the amount of gossip we manage to generate about one another. It's worse than a small-town university."

The words gave me an important clue, I felt, to the spirit of Zomba. The people were all busy and hard-working, and they were keen on their work. They could talk for hours about such matters as soil conservation, village hygiene, and the Shire Valley Plan, whereby it was hoped to control the flow of water south from Lake Nyasa and thus irrigate many thousands of acres of land for tea and rice. But they were only a handful of white men and their wives, living in the heart of a rather remote African country. Everything was, relatively, on a small scale. This made things more manageable than in more sprawling territories, with their miles of empty semi-desert lands. But at times the weight of sheer boredom, of feeling isolated and out of it, must be crushing.

"Here," said Julian thoughtfully, "we're awfully respectable. White-sahib stuff. But in Blantyre they drink rather a lot."

As we drove back down the mountainside, Julian told me that the local language, Chinyanga, had no abstraction terms. "We have to translate everything into Chinyanga English, then into Chinyanga proper. Chinyanga English is rather like Basic English: everything has to be made concrete." He chuckled. "It's going to be awfully difficult to explain 'federation' in Chinyanga."

"How," I asked, "will you explain 'partnership' to an African who takes you at your word and expects the immediate abolition of the color-bar, which is something he can see and feel?"

But Julian shook his head. "There's no color-bar in Nyasaland."

Back at the Secretariat, after an enormous breakfast to satisfy an appetite that the mountain air had sharpened, I put the same question to Mr. Gwonde.

Gwonde played a curiously dual role. He worked at the Sec-

218

retariat, which meant he was in the pay of the administration. At the same time he was a leading member of Nyasaland's African Congress, a political organization that aimed to remove the British administration as soon as possible and so clear the way for an independent Nyasaland.

The white official in whose department Mr. Gwonde performed his clerkly duties said tactfully: "Of course, you will want to see him alone. He must feel perfectly free to say anything he likes about white rule. So I suggest the pair of you take a walk."

Mr. Gwonde was excused from his duties, and he and I walked up and down one of the Secretariat's winding stone corridors while I asked questions and Mr. Gwonde answered them.

"There is an economic color-bar," said Mr. Gwonde cautiously. He spoke very good English, and wore "European" clothes: a neat dark suit, with collar and tie. Most of the white officials at Zomba wore open-neck shirts and khaki shorts. "An African clerk in Government service may earn over one thousand dollars a year. This, of course, is very much more than most Nyasas earn, even those who have their own land. He also gets a free house. But an African clerk who occupies a post formerly filled by a white man gets only half the white man's pay."

Gwonde readily agreed that, though the standard of African education in Nyasaland is high compared with that in some other territories, thanks to the work of the numerous missions, the bulk of the Nyasa people were still a long way from being capable of running their country by themselves. At the same time he complained that too much money was spent on salaries and pensions for white Government officials. "It leaves too little for African education, and for improving African farming."

The Nyasaland African Congress, he admitted, had only 900 members—out of a total African population of 2,000,000.

There are 2,000 white people in Nyasaland; but there are 3,000 Indians. The Indians, though more numerous than the whites, seemed to have no political ambitions. The whites wanted to federate with the Rhodesias. The Africans opposed federation, which they felt would end forever any possibility of Nyasaland becoming "independent." The truth seemed to be that Nyasaland was too poor to be able to stand on its own feet. To the whites, this was so self-evident that they could not understand the Africans' opposition to federation.

The pleasant Mr. Gwonde returned to his clerkly duties and, presumably, to dream about a "free" Nyasaland. In another office in the Secretariat's maze of stone corridors a white official described for me the extent of Nyasaland's poverty.

"Compared with Northern Rhodesia," he said, "Nyasaland is relatively densely populated—over fifty-five people to the square mile. And over eighty-seven per cent of the country is owned and occupied by the Africans themselves. But each year 150,000 Nyasa men go looking for paid employment in other territories —the Rhodesias and South Africa. Some come back and some don't. The ones who don't are known as the Machona—'the Lost Ones.' This is Nyasaland's tragedy."

"Why do they leave?" I asked.

He smiled grimly. "Recently we made a detailed survey of an area called Domasi, near Zomba. The area covers roughly a hundred square miles and is fairly typical. Most of the people were suffering from tuberculosis or syphilis. Farming methods were extremely primitive; consequently crop yields were low. The average *family* income, translated into terms of cash—except that of course they don't handle cash—was a few pence a day. Most families had hangers-on—aged parents, blind uncles, crippled cousins, idiot brothers and sisters. If you lived in a place like Domasi, wouldn't you want to get out?"

"Yes," I said.

"That's the explanation of the Lost Ones," he said.

The British Colonial Development Corporation has spent about three million pounds on Nyasaland since the end of the Second World War. I discussed the corporation's schemes with a very angry young man who had recently resigned from it.

"What happened to some of the money spent in Nyasaland," he said, "may explain why the corporation has been running over-all losses of two million and three million pounds a year.

In Blantyre, the C.D.C. built homes and offices for its Nyasaland staff, at a cost of eighty-five thousand pounds. The idea was to encourage the production of palm-nut oil, rice, and tobacco. The houses and offices were not built in the town itself. The corporation, instead, bought fifty acres of land in a valley near the airport. The houses had beautiful parquet floors, and the offices were extremely up-to-date. That was three years ago. Today the C.D.C. staff in Blantyre consists of one accountant and one stenographer. The houses with the beautiful parquet floors are standing empty. The corporation would like to sell them, but nobody will buy. The valley is full of mosquitoes, and the road to it is impassable in wet weather.

"The corporation," he continued remorselessly, "also launched a fish-catching and canning scheme on Lake Nyasa. The fishing industry was controlled by a Greek. The corporation spent thousands of pounds, but the Greek still controls the industry. The corporation has now abandoned that project too. The Greek bought some of the expensive fishing-boats that the corporation had imported. He got them at knock-down prices."

"Who was responsible for the muddle?" I asked.

"Fabian Socialists," he said darkly. "Fabian Socialists."

: 3 :

BACK IN Blantyre, I heard a good deal about Fabian Socialists. Duthie Hess, the editor of the *Nyasaland Times*, was scathing about the visit that had been paid to the territory by the Creech-Joneses. Creech-Jones was Colonial Secretary during the term of office of the British Labour Government.

"Mrs. Creech-Jones," said Hess, "took a trip into the bush. She caused quite a sensation. Women left off pounding their mealies and gathered round her. Pagan chiefs sent their wives along in batches. When they were all assembled, Mrs. Creech-Jones addressed them on the need to organize themselves politically, and to form discussion circles."

I gathered that much heartburning had been caused among

the white ladies of Blantyre, whose organization, it was alleged, Mrs. Creech-Jones had declined to meet. A reason for this might have been that, among the males of Blantyre, the white ladies' organization was vulgarly referred to as "the Naggers."

Duthie Hess believed that he had a mission in life to teach Americans to drink tea, which, after tobacco, is Nyasaland's chief export.

"When I was in America," he said in a shocked voice, "I often asked for a cup of tea. I was invariably presented with a pot of hot water and also with a small bag on a string. When I asked what this was for, I was told that it was to dip into the pot. The bag contained tea leaves." He shuddered. "In Nyasaland we grow very good tea. But we are handicapped by the rail freight charges, which are monstrous.

"The same applies to our tobacco. The distance from Blantyre to the port of Beira is no greater than from Salisbury to Beira. But Nyasa tobacco has to pay a freight charge of £7. 10s. a ton, whereas Southern Rhodesian tobacco pays only £1. 10s. a ton. The reason is that Southern Rhodesia subsidizes its tobacco exports, through low freight charges, out of the profits on its mineral exports. Nyasaland has no minerals to export."

Hess believed that federation might help to iron out those anomalies.

Hess denounced British Socialists for putting unwanted ideas into hitherto unsophisticated Africans' woolly heads. Like many Englishmen in Africa, he was especially outraged by Britain's experiment of giving virtual self-government to Negroes on the Gold Coast.

"Now the Nyasa have been encouraged to believe that they can take over this country and run it for themselves," he said. "The white man has been in Nyasaland only fifty years or so. When we arrived, the tribes were fighting one another, and all of them were at the mercy of Arab slave-traders. We put an end to tribal wars, and ended the slave trade. But now they want us to get out."

I spent my last evening in Nyasaland at a club in Blantyre.

Everyone agreed that it was too hot to eat, so we drank instead. It was an exclusively male and exclusively white affair. Gin loosened a good many tongues.

"The blasted Indians are only waiting for the niggers to get rid of us," said a stocky man in an open-neck shirt, showing a triangle of hairy chest. "Then they'll move in."

"It's already happening in East Africa," said a tall gloomy man with a bald head. "And it's all the fault of the Colonial Office. The way they kowtow to those wogs makes me sick."

"That's why we've got to have federation," said the hairy-chested man. "The Rhodesians won't stand any nonsense from coolies."

"Get rid of the Colonial Office influence and everything will be all right," said the bald man. "Whitehall is the nigger in the woodpile. But if we were running our own show . . ."

"I was up in Kenya before I came here," said a man with sweat patches under his armpits. "That's Indian country now, brother. The white man hasn't got a look-in."

"But what shocks me, coming from South Africa," said a man in khaki shorts, "is the way you let your nigs put it over you. I'd like to see a Kaffir in the Union just walk off a white farm when he felt like it! Our coons know what a sjambok is, all right."

"It's those fellows up at Zomba," explained the hairy-chested man. "All those la-di-da regulations. No penal provisions to protect the white farmer against his own niggers. Nothing to make them work. They fine you if you look at a nigger sideways. And look at the amount of land the natives have got! All of Nyasaland, you might say. Land that *we* could put to proper use."

"All comes back to the Colonial Office," insisted the bald man.

"Run our own show . . ."

"Put these niggers in their place . . ."

"Federation, that's the answer . . ."

"The Rhodesians aren't softies, they know how to . . ."

223

"Damned Socialists in London . . ."

"Breaking up the good old Empire, that's what they're doing . . ."

I walked back to the hotel through the empty, hot little town. It was a suffocating, tropical night. Huge globes of stars burned brightly in the sky. An outside wooden staircase led up to my bedroom, which opened on a creaking veranda. In the morning I would be driven out to the air-strip. Meanwhile there were the mosquitoes to contend with. They came at you with a sharp *ping!* and in Blantyre they seemed especially hungry. I crawled under the mosquito net and lay in bed listening to the mosquitoes. I thought of the hard-working, isolated white men in the Secretariat at Zomba, worrying over problems like syphilis, tuberculosis, witchcraft, the chances of famine. Meanwhile, each year, 150,000 Nyasas left their own country, to find work and food elsewhere and to be swallowed up in the shantytowns and mine compounds of distant Johannesburg, many of them never to return.

And I thought of the lonely, aggressive, gin-drinking men I had left at the club, perplexed by their problems, angrily looking for scapegoats for their troubles.

It seemed to me that the Lost Ones were not only blacks.

XVI

BRITISH CENTRAL AFRICA: "FEDERATE AND FLOURISH"

AFTER CONSIDERABLE heart-searching, the British Government decided to go ahead with the federation of the two Rhodesias and Nyasaland. The heart-searching was caused by the fact, well known in London, that the five million Africans in the three territories were opposed to the plan.[1]

A scheme was devised to "safeguard African interests." The natives, whose greatest fear was the loss of their land, were assured that they would lose none; and an African Affairs Board was proposed to scrutinize federal legislation and to detect any racial discrimination. The theory was that the Colonial Office could then step in and prevent any discriminatory laws from being passed.

I was not surprised to find that Africans who gave any thought to such matters remained highly skeptical. There was a shocking cynicism about their attitude, which must have pained many white supporters of federation. One of the Africans told me: "The only drawback to those beautiful safeguards is that, once the federation is a going concern, the Colonial Office will never dare to interfere with the whites who will be in control on the spot, no matter what they do. When Britain handed over South Africa to local whites, we Africans were told it was inconceivable that Great Britain would permit any whittling down of the

[1] In 1953 the following figures were published on the white populations (round numbers): Southern Rhodesia, 160,000; Northern Rhodesia, 43,-000; Nyasaland, 4,400—a total white population in the new Federation of British Central Africa in excess of 207,000.

225

black man's rights. Look at what's going on in the Union now!"

The whites in the three territories, numbering fewer than 200,000, did not share the Africans' opinion. Although many of them were vehemently opposed to federation in the form proposed by the British Government, it was because they thought it ridiculous that African rights should be safeguarded at all. In order to relieve their fears, Sir Godfrey Huggins cheerfully announced that there was really nothing to worry about. Since the white minority would have a huge majority in the federal parliament, there was little danger of the blacks getting uppity. And the white majority in a federal parliament would never be such fools as to allow themselves to be swamped by black M.P.'s. Nor need the white voters fear being swamped by black voters, despite the fact that blacks outnumbered whites in the three territories by twenty-five to one. For, though Africans in Southern Rhodesia were theoretically entitled to an equal vote, they had to pass property and educational tests which few blacks could meet. If the number of black voters threatened to become too large, all the whites need do was to use their majority in Parliament to raise the property and educational qualifications for voters. To show how easily this could be done, Sir Godfrey made the hurdles for voters in Southern Rhodesia twice as high as they had been before.

Sir Godfrey's clincher concerned the African Affairs Board. If, he said, the board in actual practice made a nuisance of itself by repeatedly rejecting laws proposed by the federal parliament on the ground that they were discriminatory, the obvious course would be for the federal parliament to abolish the board. Sir Godfrey, who knew his Colonial Office, apparently had no fear that the Colonial Office, if faced with such a situation, would really venture to do anything about it.

To bolster Huggins's appeals to the whites to support federation, Roy Welensky early in 1953 flew to Southern Rhodesia and addressed a number of meetings. At Wankie the white coalminers nervously asked if, under federation, Negroes would be allowed to do jobs that had hitherto been reserved for white men. Welensky replied with spirit: "If you're afraid that black men are capable of doing your job, you can't be much good. If you think the white man is superior to the Negro, what are you afraid of?"

A further meeting addressed by Welensky, this time in Salisbury, was held in a tobacco-auction hall. Only whites were admitted to the hall. It was discovered, however, that there were not enough chairs. When more chairs were sent for, they were brought in by Africans. Then the Africans were cleared out again, and the door was locked. The Africans seemed to resent this. One of them, probably a Communist, was overheard to say: "It's our future as well as their own they're discussing." In the course of his speech, Welensky stressed the need for race partnership in order to make federation a success.

Sir Godfrey also addressed meetings. They were quiet and gentlemanly affairs. Speaking in cinema halls discreetly placarded with exhortations to "Federate and Flourish," Sir Godfrey reiterated the points he had already made. He was genteelly applauded.

At this juncture the Reverend Michael Scott unexpectedly turned up in Rhodesia and addressed gatherings of Africans. He advised them to oppose federation, but to do it peacefully. He then went on to Nyasaland and made similar speeches there. One of his points was that the Africans might take the matter up with the United Nations.

Rhodesians were outraged to be thus classified with Dr. Malan, whose attempt to incorporate South-West Africa the United Nations, thanks largely to Scott, had frustrated. Their answer to Scott, however, was the same as Malan's. "We shall never be masters in our own house," a Rhodesian fumed to me, "until we can stop fellahs like Scott coming in and stirring up the blacks." If you don't like what a "fellah" is saying, he implied, the proper way to shut him up is to knock him down. A good many Rhodesians shared this simple view. So apparently did the British Government, which deported Scott from Nyasaland as an "undesirable."

The Huggins government held a referendum in Southern Rhodesia on the issue of federation. Among those who took part were 400 Africans who were eligible to vote. The ballot was secret, but as there were 40,000 white voters, the outcome was scarcely in doubt. Federation was approved by a handsome majority. Many whites who were still dubious about the safe-guards for African interests and the possibility of the Colonial Office continuing to intervene in Rhodesian affairs were swung over by their aversion to "fellahs" like Michael Scott. If Scott told the Africans that federation was bad for them, then, they argued, it must be good for whites.

The Federationists were understandably jubilant. They were so much so that, though a section of them continued to talk solemnly about race partnership, another group yielded to the temptation to let the cat out of the bag.

"Our future course is clear," said one of these. "As soon as we have secured the civil and military power, we shall act." He twiddled his cocktail glass triumphantly. "We certainly don't intend to have the same sort of trouble as they're having in South Africa and Kenya, by Jove. We shall nip it in the bud, by gad."

He became confidential. "After all, there are only a few score of Africans who are a real menace. Damned intellectuals and trade-union chaps, and agitators of that sort. If they try to put up any sort of a show, we'll clap the lot in jail, by gad. The rest will shut up, all right. The *real* African is a very docile chap. All he needs is a bit of firm handling." He drained his glass. "We must be firm, but just, and we'll soon have him respecting the white man as he used to do."

XVII

TANGANYIKA: OF MEN AND MONKEYNUTS

WE FLEW the length of Lake Nyasa, going north. Below us, drifting over the shining surface of the lake, wispy black clouds formed and dissolved, like steam rising from a boiling pot. Six dots were dugout canoes, in which the Nyasa fishermen brave the violent storms that sweep almost daily across this inland sea. And then, for several hours, we saw nothing but bush.

Tanganyika is bordered on the west by three great lakes, and on the east by the Indian Ocean. It is more than twice the size of California. But two thirds of it are infested by tsetse fly, and therefore almost uninhabitable by man. It is seemingly empty and endless bush country.

But down there, I knew, when the moon rose like a yellow eye and even the most stunted trees threw long shadows, other shadows moved. The tribes still have the cult of the lion-men, who stalk their victims at night, with sharp knives fastened to their hands for claws.

There are other oddities. A British district officer once came out of the bush to find the elders of a village squatting in a circle, gazing sadly at something lying on the ground. They told him that a hostile witch doctor had caused the sacred tree of this village to fall.

The young D.O. blinked, for the sacred tree still stood. On the ground where the old men gazed, there was nothing at all. But no word of his could persuade them of this.

He finally had the witch doctor brought before him and told

229

him to take the spell off the people. When the man refused, the D.O. said: "Very well, I shall prove to them that the tree still stands, for I shall hang you from one of its branches."

Only as the noose tightened round his neck did the witch doctor submit. Gravely he pronounced the proper incantation, and the D.O. saw the elders' eyes follow the phantom tree as it rose from the ground and was restored to its place.

A Britisher on our plane, himself a former district officer, nodded when I recalled this story. He said calmly: "I once arrested a bunch of rain-making wizards who had caused a drought and were demanding a terrific fee for ending it. I kept the blighters in jail *until they lowered their price.*"

"And then did it rain?"

"Of course."

We landed at Tabora, on a long red-gravel runway, beside a large tin hut. All around stretched the sea of bush. But growing close to the tin hut were bright flowering bougainvillæas. The hut was furnished with comfortable chintz-covered chairs, and there were tables spread with English magazines. Waiting for the plane were youngish men and middle-aged men with leathery skins and topees; pretty, brisk young women, very English; and numbers of small children. The children hugged toys, and the young women carried parcels wrapped in brown paper. They chatted casually, as if, having just done their shopping, they were waiting for a bus to carry them home, instead of for a plane that would take them hundreds of miles over the bushlands. There are only 17,000 white people in the whole of Tanganyika, but they seem to have "settled in" better than any other white community in Africa.

While the plane refueled, the former district officer told me: "The whites occupy only 0.8 per cent of the land. They're not allowed to have any more. White immigration isn't encouraged, though there is plenty of land—not tsetse-ridden, either. There are 7,500,000 Africans, and they own 6,500,000 cattle. Last year one African paid £500 income tax; the usual native tax is 5s. a year."

One of the leather-skinned men, his topee stuck on the back

of his head, chipped in. "The Chagga, who grow coffee on Mount Kilimanjaro, do even better than that. Their Co-operative Union is at Moshi. The Co-op offices at Moshi cost £200,000 to build. They've got a community center, and every guest-room has a bathroom attached. They've also got shops, a library, a reading-room, and a printing press; a restaurant to seat 250 people, and an assembly hall to seat 750. The Chagga did all this themselves, with their own money. The Co-op's roof-garden is better than anything the whites have."

He laughed. "Last time I was there, the Co-op printing press was busy with an order it had just received. The African manager showed it to me. It was the rules of the European Club in Moshi. And one of the rules was that the club admitted only whites."

He added that Tanganyika's chief crops were cotton, coffee, and sisal. In recent years the prices of those products on the world market had risen respectively by 400 per cent, 500 per cent, and 650 per cent.

From Tabora we flew southeast over more bush, toward the Indian Ocean. When we reached the coast, the plane flew out to sea, then circled back over a green and purple bay edged with white sand fringed by palm trees. Small islands of green vegetation floated in the water, which was so clear that, as the plane dipped, we could see large white shells gleaming on the sea bottom and a moving something that looked like an octopus. Then we were rushing low over the tops of the palm trees and over rows of thatched native huts.

When the plane door was opened, heat hit us: the steam heat of a Turkish bath. Walking the short distance from the plane to the airport buildings, I dripped with sweat. So did everyone else. While my passport was being examined, I could feel the shirt on my back begin to melt. And there was a strange smell. An all-pervading odor filled the long, bamboo and thatch building. Everyone, very faintly but unmistakably, stank. This, I discovered, was unavoidable in Dar es Salaam in the hot season.

"You can bath as often as you like," the man who shared my cab told me sadly. "It won't make any difference." He paused. "Dar es Salaam means Haven of Peace." He paused again. "But most people just call it the Arse-hole of Africa."

I drove to a hotel and secured a room heavily hung with mosquito netting. A large-bladed fan, like a plane propeller, whirred in the ceiling. It was still hot. I felt I needed a drink.

In the hotel's central courtyard, open to the blue sky, a tall palm tree grew beside the reception-desk. On the other side of the desk was a London-type telephone booth. You pressed button A to make yourself heard, and pressed button B to get your money back if the number was engaged.

A short man with a shining red face and a wet neck, which he was continually wiping with his handkerchief, hospitably insisted on buying me a drink. As soon as he had done so, he started talking about Tanganyika's famous groundnut scheme. Groundnuts are peanuts. He called them monkeynuts.

"The monkeynut scheme," he said emphatically, "is one big mess."

"I believe it lost a lot of money."

"Thirty-six and a half million pounds sterling down the drain," he asserted.

"What went wrong?"

"Everything."

He mopped the back of his neck and drank his beer. He wore khaki shorts, and his white shirt was unbuttoned all the way down the front.

"The idea was to clear 2,400,000 acres of virgin bush with tractors and bulldozers; then grow monkeynuts. Britain needed margarine; the world needed fats."

"That sounds reasonable."

"On paper," he insisted. "Only on paper. Only to chaps sitting in a blank office in the blank City of London, dreaming about a blank Africa they'd never even seen.

"Here's what happened in practice. They couldn't get enough bulldozers, so they imported some from the Philippines. When they arrived, the chaps who had to drive them found they'd been lying in sea-water for five years.

"They built an oil pipeline up from the coast. That was to fuel the bulldozers, the tractors, and the jeeps. When they got the pipe laid and gave the signal to commence operations, out spouted mussels and part of the Indian Ocean instead of oil.

"They started a railroad, but when it was half finished, they found nobody had decided yet where it was to go.

"The bulldozers got mucked up. So did the tractors. The bush was a lot tougher than they'd imagined. There wasn't enough water, and it seems nobody had thought of that. They built a sawmill to cut up the trees into logs, but there was no way of transporting them. And, brother, they didn't grow many monkeynuts!"

He laughed.

"All this was happening in an area where Africans live in mud huts without windows and with skins on the floor. The Africans came and gaped at the bulldozers and the tractors. They'd never seen anything like them. But finally they got the idea: the white folk wanted monkeynuts. Only they didn't seem to be growing any.

"So the blacks returned to their own *shambas*,[1] where they were growing monkeynuts without any trouble, and then came back to the big camp. They went round the campfires at night, where the men were sitting, cursing the plan and wishing to God they'd never got mixed up in it. And they said: 'You like nuts? Want to buy some?'

"And these chaps, who hadn't even *seen* a monkeynut yet in Tanganyika, bought monkeynuts from the Africans to eat with their beer!"

"How do you know all this?" I demanded.

He chuckled. "I was one of the suckers who came out from England to work on the scheme. I quit. Now I'm on my way home."

"What has happened to the scheme?" I asked.

[1] Gardens, cultivated plots of ground.

233

"Oh, they've cut it down from 2,400,000 acres to 240,000, and they still hope to grow monkeynuts. I'm sure they will, too. Only, on the basis of what the scheme has cost already, each individual monkeynut is going to cost about half a dollar!"

Subsequently I made further inquiries about Tanganyika's groundnut scheme. It was a painful subject, and most people preferred to draw a veil over it. But my first informant's facts, I discovered, were substantially correct.

In the evening, when the air grew slightly cooler, I went for an unrewarding walk in the town. Dar es Salaam consisted of a collection of low, flat-topped white buildings, all smelling slightly of sewage.

I was looking in the window of a shop whose stock seemed to be composed mainly of very old fashion magazines—I should still like to know what a 1938 Vogue was doing there—when two affable strangers walked into my life.

One was a tall South African and the other was an American ship's radio operator. The South African, who lived in Dar es Salaam, had befriended the radio operator, who was lonely. They were driving along in the South African's car when they saw me and, it seemed, had decided that I looked lonely too.

"We propose," said the South African, whose name was Wallace, "to drive along the beach in search of cooling breezes. Would you care to join us?"

I said I would.

The place they took me to was, in fact, called the Ocean Breeze. There was a dance band, and a dance floor the size of the surface of a rather large office desk. Fans kept the air in motion. Outside, palm trees nodded their heads and a large moon was beginning to silver the beach and the sea.

"In another hour," said Wallace, "Dar es Salaam will begin to look almost beautiful. The magic of the tropic night will grip you." He added: "Of course, everyone will still stink a little."

Fuller, the ship's radio operator, was a large, serene man who said little but, when he laughed, chuckled right down to his

234

belly. The secret of his serenity was that he was writing a "great novel."

"Usually there isn't much for me to do on board the ship," he said. "I have lots of spare time. That's why I took the job in the first place. I love to write. I meet people, and I write about them. I've been to lots of places, too. One day my work will be hailed for what it is: a great literary masterpiece. Then I'll quit the sea and settle down in Boston. That *is* where John P. Marquand comes from, isn't it?" he asked anxiously.

"How long have you been writing your novel?" I asked.

"Not long. About ten years. I like to polish."

Wallace pointed out a small man with a short, pointed beard. "That's Elroyd Hitchcock."

"Who is Elroyd Hitchcock?"

"The sisal king. He's a millionaire."

Sisal, Wallace explained, is a green and spiky plant that is grown on large plantations in Tanganyika. It requires a large labor force, and it is difficult to handle, for its sharp needles puncture the skin and produce grievous sores. Mr. Hitchcock, I gathered, owned not mere acres but square miles of sisal.

Tanganyika, Wallace told me, had several millionaires. There was an enormously rich Indian who owned most of Dar es Salaam. He rode about in a huge black limousine and was completely "Westernized"; but his wife wore a heavy gold veil and a brilliant red sari.

There was also John Thorburn Williamson, Tanganyika's diamond king. Williamson, who had been a lecturer in geology at McGill University, in Montreal, arrived in Africa with one fixed idea: to find diamonds. He studied De Beers operations in South Africa. Then he decided that Tanganyika was the place.

For five years Williamson lived in the bush, where he grew a large black beard. Almost everyone thought he was crazy. One of the exceptions was an Indian lawyer in Dar es Salaam, named Chopra, who financed him.

One day Williamson came out of the bush with a small bottle that had contained hard candy. It was now full of diamonds.

235

Naturally, Williamson declined to say where he had found them. But Williamson's Diamonds was launched on a startled world. A large area was secured by Williamson and fenced off. Mining operations were begun. "In ten years," said Wallace, "Williamson has netted about £12,000,000—nearly $34,000,000. He says he's sitting on a bottomless diamond mine, and he is probably not exaggerating. He presented Queen Elizabeth of England with a coronation gift: a pink diamond worth £250,000."

Williamson's fabulous mine, Wallace added, was a very difficult place to get at. First, it was deep in the bush, up near Lake Victoria. Second, the whole area was strictly guarded. Only Williamson's own planes, flown by his own pilots, were permitted to land on the air-strip he had had built on the mine property.

"Once a year, on his birthday, which is in February, he throws a big party," said Wallace. "All the guests are flown in by Williamson's own planes. He also flies in a couple of dance bands, from Nairobi. The party usually lasts for three days."

From the Ocean Breeze we moved on to a night-club called Chez Margot, which appropriately was owned by a French-woman. It had lovely pictures on the walls. It was an odd place to find some of the best work of the French impressionists.

"I am from Paris," said Chez Margot's owner simply. "I knew them all."

In the midst of this a handsome Greek walked in.

"That is George Arnautoglu," whispered Wallace. "You should see his yacht. He—"

"Don't tell me," I said. "I can guess. He's a Tanganyika millionaire."

: 2 :

THE SUNSHINE in Dar es Salaam was so strong that being exposed to it was like being beaten over the head with a club. Along the seafront, separated from the ocean by a blinding white road, was a collection of thatched huts. This was the Sec-

236

retariat. The Legislative Council of Tanganyika was housed in the Aga Khan Boys' School. In the entrance hall of the school were glass cases containing mounted butterflies and stuffed birds.

The actual debating chamber was a room about 120 feet long and 80 feet wide. Its five doors and six windows all stood open. Outside, in the eye-searing sunshine, the sea glared like blue glass, and the leaves of the palm trees rustled with a tinny sound. Even at nine o'clock in the morning the air that entered the debating chamber was like the breath of a baker's oven. In the ceiling, seven huge three-bladed fans whirred noisily in an attempt to reduce the temperature.

At the far end of the chamber was a dais flanked by red and yellow silk curtains. Behind the dais was a Union Jack; but sewn on the flag was an oval containing the head of a rather silly-looking giraffe. On the dais, in a high-backed white chair, sat His Excellency Sir Edward Twining, the Governor of Tanganyika.

The members of Legco raised their eyes to him respectfully; Sir Edward glared back at them through horn-rimmed spectacles, preserving an immense dignity despite the butterflies, the stuffed birds, and the giraffe.

The Governor was a large man with thin, graying hair and a gray mustache. While members rose to speak one after another, he fidgeted and frowned. Finally he took off his spectacles and impatiently bit one of the bows. He had the air of a man who has an urgent appointment elsewhere and is being delayed by trifles.

Below him the members faced one another in two rows: fourteen "officials" and fourteen "unofficials." They included a burly South African who had been a celebrated Rugby footballer, a British ex-brigadier with a rosy bald head and a jutting jaw, a Cypriote, and a sprinkling of Indians and Africans.

The members were debating a new constitution for Tanganyika, which Sir Edward Twining had played a large part in devising. The plan envisaged a legislative council of twenty-one "officials" and twenty-one "unofficials." The "officials" would all be "British subjects of white descent." But the "unofficials" would consist of seven whites, seven Indians, and seven Africans. The seven whites would represent 17,000 people of their own race. The seven Indians would represent Tanganyika's 72,000 Indians, and the seven Africans would represent 7,500,-000 Africans.

Nevertheless, a lot of whites in Tanganyika, and a lot more across the northern border in Kenya, had attacked the proposals as radicalism, verging on Bolshevism.

In the legislative council the whites would still have 28 votes against 14, not counting the Governor's, and even assuming that the Indians and Africans voted as a block, which seemed doubtful. The London *Times* had attempted to quiet the whites' fears by pointing this out, and calling the proposed constitution "an assertion of principle which would in fact have no direct effect on the balance of legislative power." It seemed a fine, cautious, British way of putting it.

All the members who spoke in the debate, both "officials" and "unofficials," praised the new constitution. Nobody had a word to say against it. Most speakers managed to drag in a coy reference to the outstanding wisdom of His Excellency. When such tributes were paid to his political genius, Sir Edward got into a fine fret of impatience and bit his spectacles more savagely than ever.

When the hands of the clock pointed to eleven, he restrained a member who was obviously about to launch into a speech agreeing with everything that everyone else had said, and gruffly announced the tea break.

I thought the explanation of his growing impatience was now unveiled: first, Sir Edward was a modest man and these reiterated references to his sagacity embarrassed him; secondly, he wanted his tea. It turned out I was quite wrong. There was nothing at all self-effacing about Sir Edward, and though he probably did want his tea, he had a much more pressing reason for wishing to stem the loquacity of the speakers.

The members trooped out into the entrance hall, where they

proceeded to drink very hot, in fact scalding tea, and to munch sausage-rolls, amid the glass cases of butterflies and birds. Sir Edward arrived among them rather like a charging buffalo and seized a leading "unofficial" by the arm.

"Bill," he pleaded, "for God's sake get your team to cut the cackle. I'm supposed to leave on a huntin' safari before lunch, but if your chaps go on exercisin' their jaws the way they're doin', I'll never get away today!"

Sir Edward Twining, at close quarters, looked like Teddy Roosevelt. He seemed to have many of that great man's attributes. He traveled extensively throughout his huge territory, and loved to arrive in some distant village, complete with mounted escort and wearing a white-plumed hat, gold epaulets, and a ceremonial sword. Having thus impressed the aborigines, he would change into a bush-shirt and shorts and call for the African equivalent of bringing on the dancing girls, by which he meant sitting under a tree with the local chief, drinking native-brewed beer, and swapping hunting yarns.

On one occasion, accompanied by Lady Twining, he attended a meeting of Indian Girl Guides.

"And what did you do to win your badge?" he asked a small Guide.

"I won it for archery," she answered shyly.

"Ha!" said Sir Edward bluffly. "Bow-and-arrow stuff, eh? You ever hear of William Tell? He shot an apple off a fellah's head. Think you could shoot an apple off anybody's head?"

"Yes," said the small Guide boldly.

"We'll soon see about that," said His Excellency, and, procuring an apple, he placed it on his wife's head and commanded the Guide to shoot.

She did so, happily transfixing the apple instead of Lady Twining, who underwent the ordeal with commendable calm.

Sir Edward greeted me affably, but seemed uncertain of my status.

"You're not one of those United Nations fellahs, are you?" he asked sharply.

When I said no, I wasn't, he seemed relieved, and presently, matters having been so arranged, bustled off for his safari.

I was introduced to two African members of Legco: Chief Adam Sapi, a slightly dandified but dignified man with a small black mustache, who wore a gay butterfly bow tie and a gleaming white suit; and Chief Kideha Makwaia, a pencil-slim man with a boyish face, though he was in fact in his mid-thirties.

Makwaia was Chief of the Sukumu. He had been educated first at Makerere College, in Uganda, then at Oxford. In Sukumuland, which is south of Lake Victoria, an area the size of Wales is being cleared of tsetse fly, he explained. When the job is done, a million Africans will be able to live there. They will sell their surplus cattle for slaughter and, they hope, become rich.

"The 7,500,000 Africans of Tanganyika," Makwaia told me, "are divided into about 120 tribes. The tribes are about equal in numbers: no one tribe predominates."

"What do they think about the proposed new constitution?" I asked.

He smiled ruefully. "Even in Dar es Salaam, where there are 60,000 Africans, I doubt if even 200 are sufficiently advanced to understand the proposals. It's our job to persuade them that this is at least a step in the right direction."

Tanganyika, he added, was spending almost one million pounds a year on education. The number of teachers had gone up from only 400 in 1938 to about 2,000. But there was still a long way to go.

I went along to the Secretariat. White men in shirtsleeves, all British colonial civil servants, were working in the thatched huts.

"We are spending twice as much on education as on police," one of them told me. He added that Kenya, even before the Mau Mau troubles, was spending £1,500,000 on its police force. "Dar es Salaam has very little crime. In the whole of Tanganyika, there have been only 760 serious offenses in four years."

On the other hand, penalties were severe. The sentence for an assault was seven years' imprisonment and a flogging; for bur-

Courtesy AFRICAN DRUM

A member of the Basuto gang that calls itself the "Russians" and terrorizes other Negroes in wealthy Johannesburg's crowded slums.

A "street" in Orlando, a Negro shantytown in Johannesburg. BELOW, Pat Duncan (on crutches) and Manilal Gandhi (wearing glasses), joint defiers of Malan. Both were jailed.

Both courtesy AFRICAN DRUM

High veld and low. Typical Karroo heavily grazed sheep land in the high, dry plateau of the Cape Province. BELOW, a rich Transvaal low-veld farm where subtropical conditions permit the blooming frangipani tree in the foreground and the citrus orchard beyond.

Both courtesy South African Information Office

The tragic land. A typical horseshoe-shaped Zulu kraal, with the cattle kraal in the center. BELOW, a typical beehive Zulu hut. Both photos show severe erosion of barren land.

Both courtesy South African Information Office

Basuto kraals. A rundown one on the edge of a European farm in the Orange Free State. Note erosion, center. BELOW, a better kraal in the Transvaal.

The Ndebele people of the Transvaal live in beautifully decorated huts; girls are carrying water. BELOW, a Tlokwa kraal in the Transvaal. Note typical rock outcropping, sandy soil, and vegetation.

Both courtesy South African Information Office

Natal, the English stronghold, is mountainous and beautiful.

One of the vast citrus estates wrung from the reluctant land of Southern Rhodesia.

Northern Rhodesia. The colonies of immensely destructive termites appropriately look like deserted graveyards. BELOW, interior of an Ila hut, where poverty and beauty meet.

A tea-growing area in Nyasaland, with 10,000-foot Mount Mlanje in the background.

Married women of the Kikuyu, the Kenya tribe terrorized by Mau Mau. Huts and granary on stilts in background.

Both courtesy British Information Services

Contrasts in Kenya. The Turkana, akin to the Masai, inhabit a vast semi-arid district. BELOW, cultivating a plantation in constant struggle against rank growth.

Both courtesy British Information Services

Mount Kenya, 17,040 feet high, in all Africa second only to Kilimanjaro in Tanganyika. BELOW, looking away from the mountain toward the Aberdare Range, a rugged hide-out of the Mau Mau.

Both courtesy British Information Services

Belgian Congo. The vast 26,000-acre Elisabetha palm-oil plantation owned by Unilever. BELOW, at the northernmost bend of the Congo River, dugouts rush to greet the bimonthly river boat. By LIFE photographer Dmitri Kessel.

Both © TIME *Inc.*

The Gold Coast. Its first Negro Prime Minister, Kwame Nkrumah, and supporters in Accra. BELOW, a typical market scene in a smaller town, Tarkwa, which rents stalls to traders.

Both U.K. Govt. photos

Heavy erosion at the edge of the Nigerian jungle.

Bilili country. To the north, the Nigerian jungle trails off to grasslands and then to deserts inhabited by Moslem tribes.

Jebba, at a main river crossing in Northern Nigeria, is little influenced by European civilization. BELOW, Kadzebi, a hybrid town in Togoland.

glary, ten years' imprisonment and a flogging. Another official cautiously admitted that such sentences seemed "slightly vindictive." He said, however, that the Government hoped to abolish flogging altogether.

A cheerful pipe-smoking man with very short shorts and knobbly knees told me of the visit to Tanganyika of a United Nations mission.

The mission consisted of a Siamese prince, an American, a New Zealander, and a representative of the Dominican Republic. On arrival, it announced to the Africans: "Our mission has come to see the conditions under which you live and work, and the progress that has been achieved. We will report to the Trusteeship Council what we have seen and heard."

This official said dryly: "Some people here thought it was awful cheek for the mission to make an appeal of that sort direct to the Africans, over the heads of the Tanganyika Government. Actually, everything went off quite well. We didn't feel we had anything to hide, and of course the British are running this territory on behalf of the United Nations."

He chuckled. "So far we've had two missions. The first one included a Russian. He went about asking people: 'What is the *exact* income of an African peasant?' It was pretty well an impossible question to answer. Some African peasants only grow enough to feed themselves and don't handle cash at all. Others earn quite a lot—ranchers, and the Chagga coffee-growers, for example. But when anyone fumbled the question, the Russian snapped triumphantly: 'So! The Government then takes no interest in the welfare of the people!'" He sighed. "Very trying chap altogether."

: 3 :

A BRITISH colonial official in Dar es Salaam asked me home to lunch. We rattled briskly through the hot streets in his small English car. "The door on your side doesn't shut properly, I'm afraid," he said. "Do you mind holding it? Don't fall out. I know you won't mind the window being broken, we need all the air we can get." About £36,500,000 has been expended on the groundnut scheme, but the handful of white men who carry on the day-to-day administration of Tanganyika are not paid high salaries.

We drove to a suburb of large, solid, gloomy houses. He pointed to one of them as we passed.

"A German missionary lived there. During the war all the Germans were interned, of course. The military wallahs took over the missionary's house. The commanding officer had a huge portrait of the *Führer* on his wall. It stood just behind his desk. Chaps paraded before the C.O. sometimes didn't know whether they were saluting him or Hitler."

My host's own house in this former German suburb was large, rambling, and somewhat tumble-down.

"You'd like to wash your hands before I let the missus know we're here?"

"Yes, please."

"It's in there."

The lavatory was separated from the scullery only by a thick green curtain. Pots and pans were being banged in the kitchen. The living-room was enormous, with very high ceilings, and it was almost cool. Bookshelves were stuffed with great quantities of rather tattered paper-backs. On the walls hung Picasso prints.

My host was a large brisk man and his wife was a large cheerful woman. We sat down almost immediately to lunch, for he had to get back to his office. Lunch consisted of tinned sausages, fish, and fried potatoes, all served up together. I eyed the steaming mound on my plate with apprehension. The clean shirt I had put on for the occasion was already sweat-soaked. But they both ate heartily and with apparent enjoyment. The main course was followed by a sort of trifle, over which had been poured the better part of a bottle of sherry.

"The white farmers are mostly opposed to the new constitution," my host explained. "Of course, their affinities are really with the white settlers up in Kenya. They'd very much like to join hands with them in a sort of united white front. But only about a thousand of the whites in Tanganyika are farmers. The rest of us are civil servants, missionaries, employees of banks and big commercial houses, and so on. Therefore the set-up here is quite different from Kenya. Probably just as well," he added dryly.

"But even our white farmers don't all think alike," his wife pointed out. "For instance, Hitchcock, the sisal king, who has his estates at Tanga, knows he has to get along with the big Indian sisal-growers. He's all in favor of race harmony."

She quoted a recent statement of Mr. Hitchcock: "It is my view that an imposed white leadership is today an anachronism and will surely defeat its own objects. Leadership, whether by Europeans, Asians, or Africans, will emerge on its own merits!"

"He's absolutely right," her husband said approvingly. "The truth is that here in Tanganyika the races have been thrown together quite a lot, thank goodness. Williamson, the diamond king, regards Chopra, the Indian, as his friend as well as his business partner. Here in Dar es Salaam the whites and the Indians get along fine. And, of course, the whites themselves aren't only few in numbers, but are a pretty mixed lot into the bargain. There are more Greeks than people from Britain."

"You ought to hear Frank Anderson on that subject," she said to me.

"Who is Frank Anderson?"

"He grows seed-beans. He's probably the world's most successful grower of seed-beans. He has twenty-nine varieties on his farm up in the Northern Province, and he sells them all over the world."

"And apart from growing beans?"

"Frank is looked on as the political leader of the white farmers in Tanganyika," said my host with a rather wry smile. "When I say 'white,' I mean, of course, 'British.' Frank thinks it's shocking that Greeks and other lesser breeds should have got a foot in here. He also is deeply perturbed by what I believe he refers to as 'the Indians' stranglehold.' He further thinks that 'the salvation of the African lies through hard work,' by which I suspect he means working hard for white employers."

"I suppose he's terribly British and pukka sahib."

"He's an Australian who came here via Tokyo. He first tried growing coffee and lost all his money. For a while he traveled around in a truck, selling photographs. Now he does very well."

My hostess said: "He denounced the groundnut scheme as a plot to introduce large-scale Jewish immigration. He doesn't much care for Jews either, you see." She shrugged. "The Overseas Food Corporation, which ran the groundnut scheme, has sold its oil pipeline, which cost £400,000, to the Government of Israel for £250,000. I don't know whether Frank would regard that as sinister confirmation of his theory."

"Of course, the white farmers resent the fact that the Africans in Tanganyika have been left in possession of all their land," said my host. "It means that the Africans show no overwhelming desire to 'come out to work' for low wages. Therefore the whites say the Africans are lazy and good-for-nothing."

The conversation drifted into other channels. With considerable knowledge they discussed the historical theories of Arnold Toynbee, the place of Picasso in contemporary art, and a new book by a leading novelist. All the time I was conscious of the heat, of the fact that all three of us smelled faintly of perspiration, and that the room was pervaded with the heavy odor of fried sausages.

My host glanced at his watch and rose. "I must get back to town. I have to draft an official letter to Sir Seyyid Khalifa Bin Harub, the Sultan of Zanzibar!"

: 4 :

OPPOSITE THE hotel with the palm tree in the courtyard was a large church. Outside the church, between it and the hotel, the most zestful Negroes I ever saw were digging up the road. Despite the appalling heat, they threw themselves wholeheartedly into the business of destruction. Naked to the waist, their black bodies oiled with their own sweat, they swung picks and shovels

244

like Trojans, singing as they worked. The whole road was marked off with ropes and red lanterns. In front of the hotel, at little tables under gaily striped umbrellas, people sat imperturbably drinking beer amid swirling clouds of dust and grit.

Behind the hotel, half a block away, was the office of the *Tanganyika Standard*. In a room just large enough to hold his desk, Alan Joseph Neville pecked thoughtfully at a typewriter. He was a lean man with a large black mustache and large spectacles, and he wore khaki shorts and rolled-down socks. The room and the desk were littered with galley-proofs and copy, so that he looked as if he were taking a sort of paper bubble-bath.

When I asked him to come round to the hotel for a drink after work, he shook his head. "You come with me to my place up in the hills," he suggested instead. "It will be lot cooler there. Stay the night."

I accepted gratefully.

The moon shone brightly as we drove off in Alan's little Austin. The road had a dirt surface and was very narrow: a silvery tunnel through the dense forest to which the tall, thin palms that grew near the town had quickly given place. Alan drove carefully.

"The two things to look out for on this road," he said, "are lions, and trucks abandoned by African drivers. The trucks are the more dangerous. Africans are very casual about trucks. They go off and leave them in the middle of the road, without lights." We bounced along, keeping a keen lookout for abandoned trucks. After a while Alan added thoughtfully: "Of course, there are leopards too."

Alan's home was seventeen miles from Dar es Salaam. He had built it himself. It had a thatched roof, and boards were placed loosely along the rafters to provide ceilings for the separate rooms. Kerosene lamps provided the illumination. The windows of the house were covered with strong wire netting. Alan did his cooking on a stove on the veranda. His wife, he explained, was away visiting relatives.

"At night," he warned, "it's not a good idea to go out on the

245

lawn. Too many inquisitive leopards prowling round in the bush."

"You have a gun, of course," I said.

He looked sheepish. "As a matter of fact, not."

All around stretched the bush in the bright moonlight, vibrant wth humming insects. The main thing was that it was cool. I could understand Alan and his wife risking the leopards in order to escape the heat of Dar es Salaam.

He insisted that I have his wife's room. Her photograph stood on the dressing-table: she was extremely pretty. One gold dance slipper was kicked half under the bed. After Alan had left me, I looked for a while at his wife's picture, and thought about the leopards. I decided she must be brave as well as beautiful. I sat down and read a book. Outside, the bush was still silvered by moonlight, beautifully mysterious, and now utterly silent, the insects having abruptly ceased their humming. Next door Alan began to snore. I went on thinking about the leopards. Finally I blew out the lamp and crawled under the mosquito net. In a few minutes, the leopards forgotten, I was sleeping like a log.

When I woke, wind was briskly rattling the windows and it was raining. Moreover, it was still cool.

Alan, the perfect host, brought me hot shaving water. He was laughing merrily. "The water was full of mosquito larvæ," he said. "Wriggling little chaps. Breakfast on the back veranda in five minutes."

We ate fried eggs, chipped potatoes, and fruit salad and drank coffee. While we did so, he proudly explained his domestic arrangements. There was no water supply, but a large tin drum collected rainwater. He had installed a bath, complete with faucets, which was attached to the drum. He had also supplied himself with a radio-phonograph. This imposing machine stood in one corner, but it had a handle at one side, and a large, old-fashioned horn speaker.

"Of course, the radio part doesn't work," Alan said cheerfully. "I bought the case and put in a phonograph. It's wound by hand, but I wouldn't part with it, or my horn speaker. The tone is terrific." In the evenings he listened to Bach and read the historical works of Arthur Bryant, a writer to whom he was partial.

After breakfast Alan said: "You'll find the whatsit at the bottom of the garden. It's quite safe here in daylight, absolutely no leopards. Privacy guaranteed, too. You'll see."

At the bottom of the garden was a small reed hut, reached by a well-worn path. Just outside the hut was a wooden turnstile. When you passed through, a hand-painted sign announced to all further comers that the hut was now occupied. When you departed through the turnstile, the sign swung round to show its reverse side, making it clear that the hut was once more vacant.

"It comforts shy people," Alan said.

Presently we got into the car and bounced in the direction of a near-by kaolin mine, believed to contain the world's largest deposit of china clay. All around was dense forest. The soil, however, was milky white.

Alan said: "Hugh Elliott—he's now administering Tristan da Cunha—was wandering in those parts when he stumbled on an old German railroad tunnel, about two hundred yards long. The tunnel, built before the First World War, was of course overgrown with trees and bush, but was perfectly dry inside. The Germans, unknowingly, had driven it right through a hill of almost solid china clay." Now the stuff was to be run, in solution, through pipes straight into ships in the harbor of Dar es Salaam.

Alan also told me about a Canadian company operating a mine at Mpanda. The company did not know whether to call it a lead mine, a copper mine, a silver mine, or a gold mine: all four metals were present in payable quantities.

"The chief problem in developing Tanganyika is going to be labor," he said. "About half a million Africans are now in paid employment, at Dar es Salaam, on the sisal estates, and so forth. But most of those who work for hire are attracted more by adventure than by cash. The Mpanda mine offered wages above the average, but the only effect thus far has been that when the Africans have earned what they need, they just quit work and go home. You can't run a mine on that basis."

"What do they need?"

"Enough money to pay their poll tax—five shillings a year—and to buy a few blankets."

But on the way back to Dar es Salaam, we passed on the road a number of Africans, going home from the kaolin mine. They had changed from their working-clothes into gaudy shirts, chalk-striped trousers, and green pork-pie hats. All wore dark glasses with wide white rims, which gave them a carnival appearance. One man was festooned with bright copper kettles and an alarm clock. Balanced on his head was a small tin trunk, on top of which his green pork-pie hat rested. They all rode brightly shining new bicycles. Acquisitiveness, if not culture, had come to this part of Africa.

Alan drove me to the air depot, and presently I was bumping over the road to the airport. The bamboo and thatch waiting-room was an oven. Outside, the sun glared on the apron. Sweat trickled down my neck. A plane had just come in, and the debarking passengers flocked into the waiting-room after passing through customs. They edged away from everyone else with worried looks, then gradually began to edge away from one another. I knew what their trouble was: they were conscious of beginning to stink.

When the call came, I thankfully took my seat in the plane. We taxied out, turned, and raced along the runway to become airborne. Soon the thatched huts, the palm trees, and the low white buildings of Dar es Salaam were dwindling as they receded. Beneath us was the blue-and-green bay, with its sweep of golden beach. And inside the aircraft it was mercifully cool.

248

XVIII

KENYA: "DON'T LOSE YOUR HEAD"

From our altitude the country looked flat, brown, and empty. It was like an enormous pancake under the sun. But ahead of us the sunlight glittered on a fairy mountain rising abruptly from the plain, sparkling like a giant cake covered with sugar icing. It was still the most impressive sight in Africa.

The pilot changed course, and presently we were sliding smoothly past Mount Kilimanjaro, so close that a wing-tip seemed to brush the snow. Passengers hastily produced cine-cameras and crowded the windows. As we circled, the engines droning lazily in the thin air, we could see naked cliffs of brown granite, with snowdrifts piled at their foot. There was a glacier, and hanging bunches of long-pointed icicles, like frosty fruit; then a great stretch of virgin snow, dazzling white and un-marked. The passengers peered and the cameras whirred. Then the plane stopped circling, we flew back onto course, and the vast ice-clad mountain receded like a dream.

Below us the country was once more flat, brown, pancake-like. In a few minutes we would begin losing altitude as we approached Nairobi.

The plane's wheels touched the runway and we rolled at speed, the engines shouting. With the tail down, the field flashing past seemed oddly tilted. Then slower, for a dignified right-about. The field righted itself, and the propellers stopped turning. We unfastened seat-belts, jammed on hats, and crowded awkwardly out of the plane and past the many-armed Nairobi airport signboard, which supplied such information as that Jo-

249

hannesburg is two thousand miles to the south and Khartoum is two thousand miles to the north.

Sean Browne was waiting for me beyond the barrier, and we drove off in his car. Down near the airport the narrow streets were crowded with Indians, as I remembered them. The Indian stores still displayed bales of bright-colored cloth, and the houses were still close-packed and slummy, with rusting tin roofs and flaking white paint.

"What's new?" I asked.

Sean flipped the wheel to pass a truck filled with African policemen in slouch hats and dark-blue uniforms. They all carried rifles.

"The Mau Mau shot a police inspector last night," he said. "And they got Tom Mbotela. His body was found in the Burma Market, after the big fire. They slashed him to death with *pangas*." (A *panga* is a short, heavy, sharp-edged knife, rather like a butcher's knife, which all Kikuyu men carry. It is used for cutting down banana trees.)

"How's the war going upcountry?" I asked.

"Bloody awful," said Sean, who is an Irishman and does not mince his words. "When you were here last, the Mau Mau gangs had only knives. Now they've got Sten guns."

"Who's supplying them?"

"The British."

"Oh, come on."

"It's a bloody fact," said Sean seriously. "The Mau Mau have been holding up police stations and pinching rifles, Sten guns, and plenty of ammunition. They're well armed now. They've got uniforms, too."

"Same old muddle, in other words, only worse?"

"Same old muddle," said Sean.

He pulled open the glove-compartment fitted under the dashboard. Inside was a revolver. "I never travel nowadays without that. The Mau Mau ambush cars."

We drove to the New Stanley Hotel, in Delamere Avenue. The hotel looked the same, with its striped awning over the entrance. Shiny motor-cars still went in dignified procession round the big traffic circle, where Lord Delamere's statue looked thirstily into the saloon of Torr's. The avenue was the same, with the trees growing along the center and the smart-looking shops. But the people had changed. When I had been here before, on the pavements jostled spruce white men with an outdoors look, who wore hats with leopard-skin bands; Kikuyu men in rags, and their shaven-headed women; and Indians in smart suits. The white men still wore bush-shirts and wide-brimmed hats, but many of them were gaunt and bearded, and they all carried guns. There were few Kikuyus to be seen, and the Indians walked with an apprehensive air.

I had always thought the marble foyer of the New Stanley Hotel looked like the setting for the first act of a satirical play by Noel Coward about this happy breed that built the Empire. It was invariably crowded with bronzed men who drawled a hunting anecdote while waiting for cocktails. This time they were grimmer, and their anecdotes were all about hunting down "Kukes." In Kenya, a "Kuke" is a Kikuyu tribesman. They stood around as they had always done, but they no longer looked ineffably bored. Some had forgotten to shave that morning. Others had untrimmed black beards of several months' growth. All had bandoliers strapped round them and wore holstered revolvers on their hips. Some carried Sten guns on their backs.

I peeped into the big lounge. The tall white-robed waiters in their red fezzes still served tea and pushed trolleys of sandwiches and cakes from table to table. But the people who sat at the tables no longer looked like gay, idle chatterers. They had a grim and at the same time a bewildered look. They were like people whose comfortably upholstered universe has suddenly developed cracks.

One man who preserved at least an outward imperturbability was my friend Humphrey Downes. There was nothing surprising in this. I knew from experience that if a bomb were to start ticking under his chair, Humphrey would first finish his drink then call languidly for a waiter to remove the infernal machine before it made a bally mess. He was seated at a table with his wife, Arabella, consuming pink gins. When Sean and I joined them, Humphrey called for more pink gins. Then he looked at me from under lazily lowered eyelids and crossed his long legs.

"Back for more fun?" he asked sweetly.

"More work," I said.

"Going upcountry?"

"Yes," I said.

"This time," said Humphrey gently, "you'd better carry a gun. Preferably two."

"It's really bad up there now, is it?"

"Tolerably bad," said Arabella lightly, fitting herself to her husband's mood. But I thought she looked strained, in so far as anyone as pretty as Arabella could display a haggard look. "All rather tiresome, really."

It was the affected boredom that Nairobi had always worn like a garment, which it was now pulling tighter around itself to keep out certain drafts, and I should have known better. But, as had happened before, it annoyed me.

"Well, you seem to have plenty of well-armed characters on hand to protect you," I said; "so I suppose Nairobi is in no immediate danger." I raised my gin. "Here's to long life."

Humphrey laughed. "You think we've all gone a bit round the bend, what? You detect an unseemly state of flap?"

"I can't see the Mau Mau invading the New Stanley Hotel and rudely disturbing the cocktail hour," I said bluntly.

"We try to preserve complete calm," said Humphrey. "We try not to lose our heads."

Arabella giggled. "People say to one another: 'Don't lose your head, dear.' Decapitation is not nice."

The Mau Mau were collecting heads. The corpses of some of their victims had been found with the heads off. But that was "upcountry." Here in Nairobi, I thought, all that was far away, so people like Humphrey and Arabella, who made a joke of everything, made a joke of that too. I felt angry.

"I don't imagine Nairobi's night life has been much affected, though," I said. "Do you still go night-clubbing?"

Sean kicked me under the table.

"Haven't been to a night-club for quite a while," said Humphrey, lighting a cigarette. "Life has been rather hectic lately," he added vaguely.

"We are reformed characters," said Arabella gravely. "We hardly drink at all."

I looked at the pink gins. "So I see," I said.

Sean kicked me again under the table.

I said: "You'll be telling me next that Humphrey stays home to protect you, rifle in hand."

Humphrey said: "Since the incident, yes."

"What incident?" I asked.

Arabella twiddled the stem of her glass. She looked guilty, as if it were all her fault.

"My father and mother were attacked, you know," she said. "A gang got into the house. They were rather—badly slashed. They're old. It was a bit of a shock for all of us. My father and mother had never done anyone any harm. It was pretty frightful."

Sean was looking at me reproachfully. Arabella didn't look at me at all. I suddenly realized that there were lines in Humphrey's face that I hadn't seen there before.

"This happened in Nairobi?" I asked.

"In Nairobi," said Humphrey. "About ten minutes' drive from where we're sitting." He leaned forward to stub out his cigarette. "That's why people say: 'Don't lose your head.'"

: 2 :

NEVERTHELESS THE Nairobi night-clubs early in 1953 still flourished and were even more hectic than I remembered them. In East Africa a favorite quip is: "Are you married or do you live in Kenya?" Noel Coward might satirize it, but Michael Arlen, the fashionable English novelist of the gay 1920's, is still its prophet.

Sean and I dutifully did the rounds, for after talking to Humphrey and Arabella I wanted to see how the night-clubs were faring in this new head-hunting atmosphere, with mutilated corpses practically on their doorsteps.

At the top of a steep flight of red-carpeted stairs, the first thing we were asked was, not whether we were members, but if we would kindly check in our guns.

Sheepishly Sean handed over his revolver. Still more sheepishly, I confessed I didn't have one.

A small plump man in evening dress took Sean's gun, ticketed it, and nonchalantly tossed it in a drawer of his desk, which he locked. The drawer was full of nickel-plated hardware. In a cupboard behind him were stacked Sten guns.

"We have to be careful," he apologized. "People are a little edgy these days. They've got a bit of a chip on their shoulders."

"I thought they shot the Mau Mau, not one another," I said.

He shrugged. "Sometimes they don't care whom they shoot. Last week one fellah found another fellah dancin' with his wife. He reached for his gun and the other fellah reached for *his* gun. Fortunately they were both damn bad shots, but the band had to buy a new drum. Now we make them leave their guns at the desk."

A dance orchestra was pounding away and people, all in evening dress, were standing four deep at the bar. Sean recognized a friend and we pushed our way through. Two men were conducting a loud argument. Between them, a girl in a white dress, perched on a high stool, was powdering her nose and thoroughly enjoying herself.

"She came with me," said one of the men. "You bastard, I tell you she came with me."

"I don't care who she came with," said the other man. "She's damn well dancing with me now."

"Cynthia," the first man appealed, "you came with me."

"Don't be a bore, Frank," said Cynthia. "I came with you, but I'm dancing with him. Is that clear?"

"But you're going home with me," said Frank.

"Buy him a drink, somebody, for God's sake," said Cynthia.

"You're going home with me," Frank repeated.

"Trouble with you, old man," said Cynthia's new boy-friend,

a tall, broad-shouldered, lean-hipped type who looked and spoke like George Sanders, "is that you're drunk." He did not use the word "drunk," but employed a more vulgar expression.

"He certainly is drunk," said Cynthia, not using the word "drunk."

"I'll show you who's drunk, you bastard," said Frank, doubling up his fists and lurching forward.

Two other men took him firmly by the shoulders, swung him round, and propelled him out of the bar, shouting threats over his shoulder as he went.

Making his voice falsetto, George Sanders sang: "Daddy wouldn't buy him a Mau Mau."

Everybody laughed.

Sean's friend said: "Pretty quiet tonight, actually. This place doesn't liven up until around three. Then everyone's really stinking."

After a while Sean retrieved his revolver, and we went down the steep flight of red-carpeted stairs.

In the next night-club we visited, a fat man with a red face was holding the floor.

". . . so I was getting bloody tired of it. That evening after dinner and a few drinks I called my boys together. When they were all squatting in front of the veranda I went out. 'All right, you bastards!' I told them. 'I know you're all in this Mau Mau business. You want my head for a Christmas present, so you can bloody well come and get it. Come on: here's my head still on my shoulders, you bastards, come and get it!'"

The fat man grinned round the circle of faces. "What d'you think happened?"

"I think you were bloody blotto, old man," said a bored voice.

"I *was* bloody blotto," said the fat man. "But they were bloody well terrified. Not one of them dared to move. 'All right, you bastards,' I said. 'Now I'm going to come and get *you*.' I went down there among them and kicked their behinds and gave them all a good sjamboking. 'Now get the hell off my farm, the lot of you, and don't come back,' I said. And, by God, they didn't lift a hand to defend themselves."

255

"You're a marked man now, chum," someone said. "They'll lay for you, you mark my words."

"Like hell they'll lay for me," said the fat man. "I shoot first and ask questions afterwards, by God. Just let one of those Kukes put a foot on my land, that's all."

"What do you do about labor if you've cleared off all your Kukes?"

"I've got Kipsigis," said the fat man, referring to another African tribe. "Kipsigis hate the Kukes' guts. You can depend on Kipsigis. They're too damned stupid to start anything. They know the white man is boss."

In the third night-club, a British newspaper correspondent I had met on my last trip to Kenya was involved in a heated argument with two men in evening dress and a woman in a white fur coat. He rose thankfully when he saw us and introduced us. The two men grunted perfunctorily and the lady gave us an icy smile. Then they went on with the argument.

"I say you newspapermen are a lot of bloody Bolshies," said one of the men. He was drinking brandy and had a parboiled look.

"Ought to be run out of the colony," said the other man, who had a pursed-up mouth and a high, aggrieved voice.

"If you're not on the side of the damned Kukes," said the parboiled man, in a loud bullying voice, "why are you always running down the white settlers?"

"Look," said the correspondent wearily, "we're not running down anybody. We're here to report the facts—"

"Facts!" jeered the man with the pursed-up mouth. "The facts are clear enough. All the damned Kukes ought to be shot."

"Strung up in batches," said the parboiled man. "Confiscate their land. Take hostages from every village and shoot ten Kukes every time there's a Mau Mau outrage." He took a gulp of his brandy.

"The overseas press," said the lady in the fur coat, "do *not* report the facts. They suppress them. They still talk as if Kikuyus were human. It is disgraceful."

"Look," said the correspondent again. He sounded desperate.

"If you can give me a single fact that the newspapers haven't reported—"

"Certainly," said the lady promptly. "Last week, in Nairobi, a white girl was raped."

"The Mau Mau don't bother to rape people," said the correspondent wearily. "They behead and disembowel them. Madam, I am reporting a war, not your local crime. In most cities rape is, unfortunately, a fairly regular occurrence."

"Not by black monsters," said the lady. "Elsewhere, the victims at least have the consolation of knowing that they were not raped by blacks; only by people of their own race."

The correspondent choked. "Excuse me," he said. "You were saying?"

"I was saying that the outrages being committed here should horrify the whole world, but apparently they don't."

"It's a tough world," said the correspondent. "The world—I admit it—is in a mess. But it's not just here, you know. They're fighting a war in Korea too, and in Indochina."

"That," said the lady firmly, "is different." She leaned forward. "The point is that such things have never happened before to *us British.*"

When they had gone, the correspondent mopped his brow. "You have heard the Voice of the White Settler," he told me. "How to win friends and influence people."

"I gather they dislike the press."

"You don't know the half of it. One reporter was chucked out of his hotel because he was seen speaking to a Kikuyu politician who's a member of Legco. They wanted to tar and feather Jimmy Cameron because his paper criticized the color-bar."

He looked at his watch. "Let's get out of here and go round to the Press Hut. There might be a late bulletin."

The streets of Nairobi were dusky and deserted. We could hear the faint throbbing of a dance band from one of the night-clubs, and mechanical voices issued tinnily from a cinema with an overloud-speaker system.

I knew the Press Hut of old, and wondered if Watkins-Pitch-

257

ford were still there. It was a grass-grown wooden bungalow in an open unlighted space near the Law Courts. We stumbled across the uneven ground.

"If the Mau Mau wanted to bag a journalist," said the British correspondent gloomily, "they couldn't have a better place for an ambush."

"Anyone who takes a pot shot at the press in Nairobi," said Sean cheerfully, "is more likely to be a white settler than a Mau Mau."

Watkins-Pitchford was sitting in his office, large and affable as ever. "The bulletin is being typed," he said in a suitably hushed voice. "Copies will be available in a few minutes."

"Anything big?"

"Rather an unfortunate day," said W.-P. "They bagged another loyal chief—we'd just given the poor fellah his M.B.E.[1]—and a couple of other loyal Kikuyus were burned alive in their huts. Oh, yes: and they've dug up the bodies of several women in the Kiambu reserve. Strangled, as usual. Always been a hotbed of Mau Mau, the Kiambu reserve," he added sadly.

I recalled the early days of Mau Mau, when the Press Hut was a rather more rollicking place. Mau Mau then was little more than a joke in somewhat poor taste, and Nairobi's white officialdom treated it accordingly. I remembered one press conference at which two uniformed, bemedaled, and bewhiskered brass-hats looked coldly at the assembled newspapermen, whose presence in Nairobi they resented as an intrusion. One of the brass-hats rose, coughed, and glanced at a sheet of paper that had been handed to him.

"Well, not much to give you chaps, rahlly, I'm afraid," he said. "Men *believed* to be members of a Mau Mau gang broke into a dairy farm and stole a cow. Don't think even you fellahs can manufacture much of a sensation out of that, what?"

The other bemedaled gentleman coughed and tugged his companion's sleeve. They whispered together, in short hisses.

The first bemedaled gentleman then got up again. "Sorry," he

[1] Medal of the British Empire.

258

said. "Bit of a slip in the typing there. Seems 'cow' should read 'can.' Can of milk, y'know. Cows unscathed. That is all."

There was general laughter.

In those days white officialdom was hardly prepared to admit that such a thing as Mau Mau could exist at all in a well-run British African territory. But that was before Eric Bowyer was found slashed to death in his bath, and before the Mau Mau organized snipers and whole regiments in the Aberdare Mountains, to make ferocious war on the white settlers.

: 3 :

WE STUMBLED back across the grass to the main road, and I went up to my room in the New Stanley. Lying in bed under the mosquito net, I could hear, only too clearly, the tinny music and wailing mechanical voices from the cinema across the street. It was the Indians' night, and the cinema was showing an Indian film. From past experience, I knew the noise would go on for a long time. After that, there would be loud voices in the street, and the slamming of car doors. But the white night-clubs would continue until dawn, and the thin pounding of jazz would go on echoing like the sound of distant tom-toms.

The last time I had been here, the New Stanley had as its guests Clark Gable and Ava Gardner. They were making a film in Kenya, about Kenya. Miss Gardner made few public appearances, but every day Mr. Gable lunched under the scrutiny of worshipful eyes.

A Metro-Goldwyn-Mayer unit took over almost an entire floor of the hotel, and there was much coming and going of heavy-jowled men who wore dark glasses, chewed on large cigars, and looked very executive.

One of them seized upon me. "You're here on an assignment for *Time* magazine?"

"Yes."

259

"Then, boy, I've got something for you. Something big."

I followed him, mystified.

He led me into a room that had been turned into a dressing-room. It was quite bare, but in one corner, resting on a sort of pedestal, stood a pair of high-laced boots.

"There you are," he said proudly. "These boots."

"What about them?"

"They are Mr. Gable's boots."

"They look fine," I ventured.

"You don't understand," he said irritably. "These are the boots that Mr. Gable wore in actual combat in World War Two! The actual boots! In real combat! You want a picture?"

"I'm here to report on the Mau Mau," I explained.

"Oh, that!" He waved a hand, which held a large cigar. "I can tell you something about that."

"Go on."

"I can tell you here and now, the whole thing has been grossly exaggerated. It will not interfere for one second with the making of this picture."

On subsequent evenings, as I sat in the hotel lounge, I heard the yowling of cats echoing through the building. They began usually about eleven and continued for an hour.

"I wish," I said fretfully, "someone would do something about those cats."

My companion looked at me. "Cats?"

"Can't you hear them?"

"Those aren't cats," he said. "It's a recording of a jackal calling to its mate. The MGM men play it over and over. They're trying to get the right pitch for a scene in the picture."

I remembered this and other episodes as I lay unwillingly listening to the tinny music and wailing voices from the cinema that was running the Indian film. Nairobi had changed a good deal—or had it?

On my last visit to Kenya I had spoken to Eliud Mathu, the Kikuyu leader. Then he had still been hopeful about the Kenya situation. Everyone had seemed hopeful. It all seemed a long time ago. I must find out where Mathu stood now.

260

But I would not see Tom Mbotela, the other "moderate" Kikuyu leader, who had been a Nairobi city councilor. Apparently he had been too moderate for the fanatics. One day he went walking in the Burma Market. The police found his mutilated corpse in a gutter. And I would not see Roger Ruck, who, standing outside the farmhouse of murdered Eric Bowyer, had boasted: "They'll never get me." But they had got him all the same.

What had happened to once peaceful Kenya? What circumstances had created the Mau Mau?

261

XIX

KENYA: SHINING MOUNTAIN

THE FIRST time I went to Kenya, in early 1952, I flew with a man who at my request explained the country's race policy.

"There are 35,000 whites, 100,000 Indians, and 5,500,000 Africans inhabiting a country about the size of France," he said. "Actually, most of the people live in one third of the country: the 'Highlands,' which are the fertile part. That's where the Kikuyus have their reserves, and the whites have their farms. The rest of the country is mostly desert, or suitable only for cattle-ranching. The Masai have a lot of territory, but it's pretty barren. The coastal strip round Mombasa is mangrove swamp. The Highlands are the real Kenya.

"The chief thing to remember," he went on, "is that we don't have any color-bar. We have a culture-bar, which is quite a different thing. If a man is civilized, he can go anywhere and do any job, no matter what his color is."

It seemed to me that Kenya must be a sort of Shangri-La, happily shielded from the rest of troubled Africa by its two shining mountains, Mount Kilimanjaro and Mount Kenya.

Nairobi was hot and dusty. I called at the Secretariat, which quaintly had its offices on the top floor of the Law Courts, and spoke to Victor Matthews, the Financial Secretary. He was a big, gray-haired man, with, I thought, big ideas.

"You can't develop a country without developing the people in it," he insisted. "That is what Kenya's Ten-Year Plan is for." He took off his dark-tinted spectacles and polished them vigorously. "Of course, we get a certain amount of kicking from some of the farmers and planters." He grinned mischievously. "Development costs money and they object to paying taxes. But as the sisal-growers have declared seven interim dividends in the past year, I don't think they're in danger of bankruptcy." He grew serious again. "We definitely need industries, and of course these should be in private hands. I'm no Socialist. But industry can't get itself established, can't expand, without roads, a certain minimum of public works—above all, trained workers. We must have schools. At present, the majority of the Africans, including the Kikuyus, are still primitive. The danger is that they will be used as human tools. We've got to turn them as fast as possible into tool-users, for our own sakes as well as theirs.

"In Nairobi," he went on, "there are about 70,000 Africans, mostly Kikuyus. Their living-conditions are frankly bad. They've flocked into town, out of their overcrowded reserves. Here they live in townships, which are now so overcrowded that several families occupy one house, and at night they hang the babies round the walls suspended in sacks, because there isn't room for them on the floor. We've got to clean that up. Another Nairobi problem is that there are seven African men to every African woman. The reason is that the African urban worker still has an umbilical cord attaching him to his land in the reserve. He comes here to work, but he leaves his family behind. It's an unhealthy, unnatural situation. He's got to be either a full-time peasant or a full-time factory worker. In either case, he must have his family with him. That means facing up to the inevitable growth of a permanent urban African population. If the African is going to have his family in town with him, his wages must rise so that he can maintain his wife and children. For his wages to go up, his skill must be increased. That's why we must have more schools, more technical training of all kinds."

Victor Matthews, it seemed to me, talked more common sense than anyone I had met before in Africa.

The United States Information Service had an office in Nairobi. When I went there with George Kinnear, the editor of the *East African Standard*, I found the staff dispensing Cokes and sausage-rolls to a number of shy young Africans.

"Let me introduce you," said Kinnear, "to my fellow editors. Each of these chaps runs a newspaper for Africans, in the various languages of the colony. We have a little session here once a week, when we discuss our common problems."

The discussion was eminently friendly. "Elsewhere in Africa," said Kinnear afterwards, "the intelligent African, the 'intellectual,' is in danger of becoming frustrated and embittered because of the color-bar. Here in Kenya we're trying to overcome that, by encouraging those chaps and helping them along."

It all seemed very sane.

I drove out of town to visit Eliud Mathu, a forty-year-old Kikuyu who had been educated first at Fort Hare University College in South Africa, then at Oxford. He lived with his handsome wife and five children in a well-built house in the Kikuyu reserve, fourteen miles from Nairobi. He was a large man, with a small black mustache, a warm handshake, and a brilliant smile. He had an orator's trick of suddenly opening his eyes very wide, to show all their white, and flashing his gleaming teeth. Mathu was one of six Africans who were members of the Kenya Legislative Council, and Victor Matthews had spoken highly of him to me.

"Go and see Mathu," he had said. "That's the sort of man the Kikuyus will become."

Mathu was optimistic, and bursting with ideas. "Matthews is right," he said. "We need more schools, more technical training. But we also must have more land. The Kikuyu reserves are overcrowded. Of course, many of the white farmers are reluctant to hand over any of their land to Kikuyus. They look at the state of the reserves and say: 'If we hand over land to those people, they will ruin it as they have ruined their own.'" He shook his head good-humoredly. "The point is, you can't teach people to make good use of land unless you give them sufficient land to make good use of! People can't be taught to farm properly up in the air!

264

"But it will come," he said confidently. "We and the white people are learning to understand each other. In the last ten years I've seen big changes in race attitudes here. There's been a great change for the better."

It all sounded just fine.

: 2 :

THE CROWD applauded, keeping a discreet eye on the Princess. On the field, the Duke galloped his pony after the rest of the team, swinging his polo stick. In the distance the snowy top of Mount Kenya glinted white under a blue sky.

I had come up to Nyeri, a distance of a hundred miles from Nairobi, on a road that was often rough and rutted and was always dusty. The red dust whirled up by the cars hung for long minutes in the air after the cars had passed, and then settled like a pall on the fields, turning them rusty. The bushes at the side of the road were red, not because their leaves were normally that color, but because of the thick red dust that lay on them.

All the way through the reserve, on both sides of the road, were round, thatched huts of mud. They crowded the hillsides and were clumped together in forest clearings. There were so many of them that they covered the countryside like clusters of anthills. On the roofs of some of the huts, etched against the sky, men were busy mending or replacing the thatch. Women toiled in the fields, distant figures bent patiently over their work. But frequently we passed a Kikuyu woman walking barefooted in the red dust at the side of the road, bent double under a heavy head-load of thatching or a huge bundle of faggots. Usually a man, her husband, walked ahead of her, carrying no load, carelessly swinging his walking-stick. Seen thus at close quarters, a Kikuyu woman looked less than human. She was a shriveled creature, flat-chested, with a tight-skinned skull that had been shaved to total baldness, a scrawny neck, and leathery ears, which had once been pierced with holes for large wooden disks and which now hung, ornamentless, almost touching her

265

humped shoulders. Her skinny body was tightly wrapped in an earth-colored blanket. When she removed her head-load, the tight leather strap that had held it in place had worn a deep, permanent groove across her wrinkled forehead.

I had come to Nyeri to see Princess Elizabeth and her husband, the Duke of Edinburgh. The people of Kenya had presented them with a forest lodge as a wedding gift, and they were staying there during their visit to the colony. There had been garden parties and street processions in Nairobi, and on the lawns of Government House the Princess and the Duke had shaken hands with plump white bishops, slim Indian ladies in silk saris, British colonels, turbaned Hindus, and various African chiefs, one of whom turned up clad in skins and ostrich feathers and with a ball of ivory attached to a sliver of wood skewered through his lower lip.

Today the Duke was playing polo with the white farmers of Nyeri, and people had come from miles around to watch. Lined up outside the wood and bamboo clubhouse, with its waving Union Jack, were dusty Daimlers and ancient Rolls-Royces. An African soldier, wearing a red fez, blew a bugle to mark the end of each chukker.

Crowds had gathered all along the route from Nairobi to Nyeri. African school-children, boys and girls, stood on high banks and waved small Union Jacks. Almost naked African tribesmen leaned on their tall spears and watched the road, as patient as storks. A wrinkled tribal elder, wearing a money-box in the shape of a pink elephant round his neck, and with silver coins in his ears, herded his wives into line and then paid no further attention to them, looking straight ahead when one of them spoke to him. Other Africans had painted their faces and bodies vermilion, green, and scarlet, in broad streaks and loops and whorls, and pranced excitedly up and down the road. Everybody seemed happy.

The happiness of the whites was more genteelly expressed. They were all dying to see the Princess, but it would have been infra dig to crowd the veranda and have a good look. They contented themselves with standing about at a discreet distance and occasionally turning their heads toward the royal presence for a quick peep.

They could be less inhibited toward the Duke, since he was galloping about the field in full view.

"I like his seat on that horse," said a grizzled ex-colonel who wore a spotted silk scarf round his turkey-red neck, and a billy-cock hat at a rakish angle.

"Seems quite a decent sort of chap, all round," said another cautiously.

Young or old, they were all lean, whipcordy men, mostly in white silk shirts and riding-breeches. When they were not discussing the Duke, they talked about horses. Nearly all of them had double-barrel names, like Carew-Smith, Tatham-Waters, and Stoke-Potter.

"Of course, nowadays we're an impoverished lot," said the club's vice-president cheerfully. "Don't you believe all those stories about black sheep, remittance men, and checkbook farmers. The Happy Valley crowd are nearly all gone. The war and taxes finished them." He laughed. "There are still one or two chaps living on their wives' overdrafts, as we say, but in the main the farmers around here have to work jolly hard, and the young ones especially are fearfully keen."

He broke off to applaud gently, with his eyes on the field.

"Good shot, that."

"How much does a man need in actual cash to start farming in Kenya?"

"Oh, well, things have gone up a lot, you know. He'd need at least five thousand pounds to start with, I should say. Can't expect to see any return on his money for the first few years, of course."

"I don't see how you can expect to get many more white people on the land, if that's what it costs. Yet everyone tells me the urgent need is to increase the number of white farmers."

"Yes, it's quite a problem."

"Couldn't you have smaller farms? Subdivide some of the very big twenty-thousand-acre ones?"

"Yes, I believe there's been talk of that, but I hardly think it can come to anything. Most fellahs like to have a lot of land, you know. Wide-open spaces and all that sort of thing."

Some of us were invited to spend a night at Treetops, which the Princess and the Duke planned to visit later in the week. Treetops was a bungalow that had been built in the branches of a giant fig tree, overlooking a forest pool. The pool was frequented by game—rhino, buffalo, elephant—and these could be watched in comfort and safety from the tree-house.

A white hunter arrived in a shooting-break, a sort of open-sided station-wagon, to escort us to Treetops. He was a tall, lean, almost excessively handsome man, with gentle blue eyes and a large brown mustache. He wore a white silk shirt, a spotted silk scarf, and a hat with a leopard-skin band. He also carried a rifle.

We drove into the forest. Large butterflies fluttered between the trees. The forest, hot and silent in the afternoon, had an after-lunch somnolence which, our guide warned us, was possibly deceptive. "Bound to be lots of game about, only you can't see it."

The shooting-break stopped in a clearing, and we got out. A narrow path wound through the trees. The white hunter, who was a former Indian Army major, gripped his rifle.

"I'll go first and you follow, in single file. No smoking, please, and as little noise as possible. I'll warn you if I sight anything. If a rhino pops up, run like hell for one of the tree-ladders." He explained: "We've built sort of ladders up lots of trees. They're for you to use if there's trouble. Don't bother about me, I'll look after myself." He patted his rifle.

At brief intervals along the path, slats of wood had been nailed to tree trunks, to make rough ladders. Each time we passed one, there was a distinct hastening of pace among our party to reach the next. It was rather like a game of musical chairs. When the major paused, we all paused until he beckoned us to proceed. He paused several times, peering round bends in the path. Sometimes he also raised his head and sniffed the air. "I can always smell a rhino coming," he assured us confidently.

When we came within sight of the tree-house, after a scary

walk of half a mile or so, the major cautiously proceeded ahead on tiptoe. He returned, still on tiptoe, and breathed: "No rhino; but there's an elephant on the other side of the pool. I don't think there's anything to worry about, but absolute quiet, please."

Also on tiptoe, and holding our breath, we followed him at a snail's pace to the foot of the big tree. "One at a time," he whispered. "When you're on the ladder, you'll be able to see the elephant. But don't stand too long, we've all got to get up, you know."

A long ladder led to the branches on which rested the treetop bungalow, which was a large wood and canvas affair, securely lashed into place, with two jutting verandas.

We crept up the ladder. Beyond a brushwood fence lay the forest pool. On the other side of the pool, a medium-sized elephant, its large behind turned to us, was swishing its tail and slowly flapping its ears. With the major urging us on from the rear, we ascended the ladder, eyes fixed on the elephant, until we stood in the tree-house itself.

"All clear," said the major briskly, his brown mustache popping up through the trapdoor after us. He hauled himself lithely up, rifle and all, and stood beside us. He glanced at his watch. "Well, soon be dark, sun goes down pretty fast around here, so we'll haul up the ladder and make ourselves cozy and safe."

A hand-winch hauled up the ladder, which, once it was raised, rendered the tree unclimbable even by leopards, the major explained. Breathing rather more heavily, he concluded his labors. "There! You can smoke now, we're too high up for the scent to carry, but still not too much noise, please."

"I don't suppose even you would venture through the forest without your rifle," someone said.

"Well," the major admitted, "I have done, once or twice. I can smell rhino, you know; and there are always the tree-ladders along the path. But I certainly wouldn't advise anyone else to try it."

At this point a voice from below called loudly: "Hey! You up there! Let down the ladder!"

269

At the foot of the tree, a small, bald, pugnacious figure, wearing a bush-shirt and carrying two cameras, stood my friend Dmitri Kessel of *Life*.

The major turned pale, but immediately lowered the ladder, and Dmitri scrambled up.

"My dear fellow!" said the major, distressed. "How on earth did you get here?"

"I got a cab from the hotel, then I walked," said Dmitri.

The major made a noise that sounded like "Ch'k! Ch'k!" "You took a great risk," he said severely. "Why, you don't even carry a gun!"

Dmitri waved a hand. "Aw, I don't put any stock in all that wild-animal stuff." He peered interestedly over the edge of the veranda on which we stood. "Say! There's an elephant!"

We all felt that Dmitri had introduced a note of unwelcome anticlimax into what had been for the majority of us the most exciting moments of our lives.

: 3 :

MY DRIVER on the trip to Nyeri was a Kikuyu, a broad-faced man with a merry brown eye. He told me a great deal about his people's attitude to the other tribes and other races who lived in Kenya.

There are over one million Kikuyus, which makes them the largest single tribe. But there are also the Masai, the Meru, the Embu, the Luo, the Wakamba, the Kipsigis, the Sambura, the Turkana, the Somalis and others. But the Kikuyus predominate in the "settled" (meaning the white) areas.

My driver had been born in Nairobi, and he had a supreme contempt for the other tribes. "Savages," he said, expertly flicking the ash of his cigarette out of the window. "The Masai live on cow's blood and milk. Their children don't go to school. The Kipsigis are stupid. The Sambura and Turkana are dangerous children who go about armed with spears and bows and arrows."

He had equally uncomplimentary remarks to make about the other tribes.

"That's why the whites say they like the other tribes more than they like the Kikuyus," he said. "Because the other tribes are just stupid savages who still think the white man is a god. But the whites have to employ the Kikuyus, because the Kikuyus know how to work. They can handle plows and tractors. Some white farmers have tried employing Kipsigis, but the Kipsigis, though they work for a very low wage, break all their machinery. The Kikuyus," he insisted, "are the only *civilized* Africans in Kenya."

I looked out of the car window at a shriveled Kikuyu woman plodding along in the dust, bent double under a head-load of wood while her lord and master strode ahead, carrying his walking-stick with a jaunty air. But I said nothing.

My driver had decided views, also, about the whites, and the Indians.

"They're not bad people, most of them. But they don't begin to understand the Africans, and they don't want to. They just want the Africans to be obedient servants. They dislike Kikuyus because, unlike the other tribes, the Kikuyus want to be treated as men, not as children. That makes the whites really angry. When a Kikuyu wants to talk to them, as one human being to another human being, they just think he's being impertinent. They say: 'Look at all we've done for them! How ungrateful they are!' Just like a man who can't understand that children grow up, that they too are human beings like himself, that they have a right to be heard. Then they say: 'The Kikuyus are not only ungrateful; they're lazy, they lie, and cheat, and steal.'

"They invent stories about our bad habits, to make themselves feel superior, and therefore entitled to own all the best land, and to run the country without consulting the black man. For the whites came here and stole the land they now have. It wasn't all Kikuyu land, as some Kikuyus claim, but it was African land. The whites say that when they came here, the land was empty, so they thought they could take as much as

271

they wanted. But nobody could really be as simple as that. The truth is, there had been a famine, and smallpox, and rinderpest, and many people had died, and those who didn't die had temporarily moved to another part. But the land was still theirs; they hadn't given it up.

"The whites, in fact, knew this very well; for when they did come across villages, and chiefs, they made agreements with the people, who allowed the whites to use the land, and to pay rent for it. But the chiefs who made those agreements weren't *selling* the land; it was never theirs to sell. A chief could rent part of the tribe's land to strangers, but he could never sell it—any more than the mayor of New York could sell the city of New York, or the caretaker of a building could sell that building. In Kikuyu tribal law, land could never be sold.

"I think the whites knew this very well; but they afterwards pretended that they had bought the land outright, though they paid almost nothing for it. And that's how they came to possess the White Highlands, and why the Kikuyus now work for them as laborers on land that is really the Kikuyus' own land."

He lit another cigarette.

"I suppose what's done can't be undone, but the whites ought in fairness to give us some of that land back. It's not as if they needed it all, or even used it all. Great areas of the whites' land aren't being used by anybody. But still they won't let any Kikuyus share it, or even allow them to buy some of it. They say it must 'stay white.' And in the meantime the Kikuyus can't even feed themselves off the little land they have. Of course that compels most of them to go out and work for the whites, for a few shillings a month and a handful of porridge.

"All the same," he went on, "I'd rather work for a white man than for an Indian."

"Why?"

"Because the Indians pay even less than the whites do, and make you work harder," he said promptly. "They also cheat the African even out of what they've promised him, if they can. They own all the stores, trade with the Africans, and overcharge them. They get all the best jobs—jobs that Africans could get

272

if the Indians weren't here. The white man is at the top of the ladder; the African is at the foot; and the Indian is in the middle, blocking the African's way up."

"The Kikuyus go to school?"

"Oh, yes. We're not fools like the Masai, who despise education. Of course, there aren't nearly enough schools for Africans; but the Kikuyus are thirsty for education."

"What school did you go to—a mission school?"

He shook his head. "No, I went to one of our own Kikuyu schools."

"What are they?"

"The Kikuyu Independent Schools were started by Jomo Kenyatta," he said with a ring of pride in his voice. "Jomo said the mission schools were all right so far as they went, but the missionaries were just like all the other whites; they didn't really understand the Africans. We Kikuyus have our own customs, created over a long period. The missionaries tried to break them down."

"What sort of customs?"

He looked a little uncomfortable. "Well, we believe in female circumcision."

"Do you?" I asked skeptically.

"It's a Kikuyu custom," he said stubbornly.

As an educated man from Nairobi, I think he was rather ashamed of female circumcision; but for some reason he felt he had to defend it.

"Then," he went on hastily, and argumentatively, "why should a man *really* be prevented from having more than one wife? Lots of peoples practice polygamy. There are good reasons for it. If a woman's husband dies, tribal law says the dead man's brother must marry her, to protect her and her children. If he is already married, must he divorce his first wife? Or let his brother's widow starve? But the missionaries declared that polygamy was sinful. When we asked why, they said it was in the Bible. When we read the Bible, we discovered that most of the people in it had more than one wife, just like us!"

"Tell me more about Jomo Kenyatta," I suggested.

273

At once he relaxed, grinning. "Jomo is a great man," he said. "In what way?"

"He's an educated man. He has more education than any of the white people you'll meet in Kenya," he boasted. "He's been away, in London and Paris. He went to London University, and studied anthropology. He wrote a book about the Kikuyu tribe and its customs. That's why the whites here hate him. He's a black man who's got more brains than they have, and has proved it."

"What does he do now?"

"He runs the Kikuyu Independent Schools, and he's president of the Kenya African Union. The whites have tried to trap him and put him in jail, but he's too clever for them. They put other Kikuyus in jail, but they can never catch Jomo. He just laughs at them."

"But how does he live? How does he earn money?"

My driver grinned more broadly and his brown eyes twinkled. "Jomo knows how to look after himself. He's got a big house, and a car, and he can afford to do himself well. He's smarter than any white man. He beats them every time."

"That's why you admire him," I said. "Not so much because he teaches that female circumcision is all right, but because he is a black man who outsmarts the whites."

He considered my statement quite seriously. Then, to my surprise, he nodded. "Yes," he said simply. "I suppose that's why I admire him. If you were a Kikuyu, wouldn't you?"

In the Nyeri area, I spoke to a district commissioner, a lean, brown-faced man who looked with loathing at the papers on his desk and with longing at the sunshine outside.

"Kenya seems a pretty peaceful spot," I said, "compared with some other parts of Africa."

He wrinkled his nose. "Does it?"

"Well," I said, "you don't have any real trouble, do you? I've heard a few grumbles, but on the whole everybody seems fairly contented. I get the feeling that they're at least prepared to sit down together and discuss their problems sensibly."

He smiled. "A little concession here, and another concession there: peaceful argument and a spirit of compromise?"

"More or less," I said.

He shook his head, but hesitated a moment. Then he leaned forward across his desk. "Take my word for it, there's going to be big trouble here before long."

"I didn't hear any suggestion of that in Nairobi."

"No," he said bitterly, "you wouldn't hear any suggestion of that—in Nairobi. Because the fatheads in Nairobi prefer to shut their eyes to what's brewing. I could tell you about reports I've sent in that have just been chucked into the wastepaper basket of—never mind who. But, believe me, we chaps out in the country, we *know* what's going on. And it isn't funny."

"What is it that's brewing?"

His eye had wandered to the window, and suddenly he smiled and pointed. "That chap out there could tell you a lot more about it than I—if he cared!"

I turned. Passing the window, in the road outside, was a remarkable-looking man. He was broad-shouldered rather than tall, and he was inclined to be paunchy, but he carried himself as arrogantly as an emperor. He had one of the finest heads I had ever seen: very large, with a broad, calm forehead—a sculptor's dream. His skin was black, and he wore a very black beard. In one hand he carried a huge walking-stick, with a carved head —an elephant's head. The sun flashed fire from a large ring he wore on one finger.

"Who is it?" I asked.

"His name is Jomo Kenyatta." The commissioner smiled thinly and without amusement. "In a few moments he'll be coming in to see me. We'll greet each other affably, and I'll offer him a cigarette, which he'll politely accept. He'll wait for me to give him a light, which I shall do. Then we'll talk. He'll look at me reproachfully, call me 'Mr. Commissioner,' and sigh that he's a much misunderstood man. He'll complain that I have policemen watching him—which is true. As I have absolutely nothing against him that I can prove, I shall have to be very careful and noncommittal. He has influential friends in

London, if not in Nairobi, and he'd have me chucked out of the service if he could. We shall fence with each other for some time, and then we shall politely shake hands and he will go away.

"But he knows I would give my pension to be able to nab him and put him away for good; and I know that he would snuff me out like a candle tomorrow if he thought he could get away with it. He's the most dangerous man in Kenya, but if I said a word against him in public, he'd sue me for slander, and probably win!"

"What is it you're afraid of?"

"Ever hear of Mau Mau?"

"Never."

"You will."

On my way out, I found myself brushing past the bearded man with the huge walking-stick: he was waiting to enter the commissioner's office. I muttered an apology, and he gave me a grave, gentle smile. His brown eyes were sad, and at the same time they seemed to be mocking me. He stepped politely aside to let me pass, but I could feel his eyes following me down the path. They seemed to be gently sizing me up. Then, as I turned my head, he turned on his heel and went into the commissioner's office.

: 4 :

NEWSPAPERMEN OF various countries, but mostly British, were assembled at the Outspan Hotel in Nyeri. The Princess and the Duke were installed a few miles away at Sagana, the cedarwood lodge presented to them by the King's loyal subjects in Kenya. The press had been permitted to take pictures of its chintzy interior, and even to take a picture of the Princess opening the front door with a golden key on arrival. But thereafter they were politely requested by her secretary to go away and play, which they were not loath to do.

The countryside was beautiful. Mount Kenya, snowy and

276

often cloud-capped as well, towered above the thick forest during the day, and hung brilliantly moonlit in the velvet sky by night. There were streams full of fat rainbow trout, and there were horses to ride.

It was generally agreed by all the newspapermen present that Kenya was a lovely land inhabited by gentle people, and that few softer assignments had come their way for many a long day.

There was a splendid golf course next to the hotel, on which purple-faced ex-colonels in canary-yellow sweaters played daily. Their ladies sat on the hotel's stone terrace, partaking of tea. Nyeri might easily have been a hill station in India under the raj.

The newspaper men and women had eagerly or shudderingly climbed the ladder into the treetop house where the Princess and the Duke were to spend a night watching game, and Eric Sherbrooke Walker, the owner of Treetops, had explained how the royal couple would be entertained while waiting for the rhinos and elephants to appear. He admitted there had been a slight contretemps, baboons having broken into Treetops almost on the eve of the royal visit and caused havoc. "They tore up all the lampshades we'd installed and ate all the toilet paper," he confessed. The correspondent of the *East African Standard* was much ribbed because his paper, in reporting this incident, mentioned the lampshades and added: "The baboons also removed other royal equipment."

The press were not permitted to approach Treetops after the Princess and the Duke had arrived there, but they were allowed to wait beside the main road to watch them return to the royal lodge. When the official cars emerged slowly from the forest, the Princess smiled and waved, the Duke bowed, and the reporters removed their hats. They then returned to the hotel and to their typewriters to inform a waiting world that the Princess and the Duke had seen an abundance of game, and that the Princess had left Treetops looking particularly radiant and no whit fatigued by the experience.

We were in the midst of writing this story, and thinking rather more seriously about lunch, when a white-faced official called us hurriedly together and announced that in the early hours of that morning, and of course unknown by anyone in Kenya until a few minutes ago, King George VI had died in his sleep.

It was a British journalist who first recovered his professional composure, and began his story by saying that Elizabeth was the first English monarch ever to become Queen while spending the night up a tree.

The royal visit to Kenya had abruptly broken down in tragedy, and the newspapermen were dispersed before the storm like blown leaves. There would be urgent cables of instructions, perhaps long-distance telephone calls, awaiting them in Nairobi, from their various offices in different parts of the world. The obvious and only thing to do was to get back to Nairobi as fast as cars could be requisitioned.

But the professional eye can never stop taking notes, and even in the midst of sudden stress the newspapermen could not help observing the manner in which the retired colonels and their ladies took the news. On the golf course, the men paused for a moment, straightened themselves—and then went on with their game. On the terrace, tea continued quietly to be served.

The hotel put a large notice in the lobby, saying simply: "Owing to the death of His Majesty King George the Sixth, there will be no film performance in the lounge this evening."

A black limousine carried the new Queen of England and her escort to Nanyuki airport, where they were to board an airplane to take them to Entebbe, in Uganda, and then straight to London. A handful of newspapermen stayed to watch the car leave, and stood at the side of the road with their heads uncovered as it swept past in a cloud of red dust.

Though few then knew it, a cloud was hanging over all Kenya, and a terrible storm was about to break. The hurried royal departure, in an atmosphere of sudden tragedy, marked the end of a chapter, and the opening of a new and dreadful one.

XX

KENYA: "I WINGED A KUKE"

I RETURNED TO Kenya a few months later in time to see the beginning of the Mau Mau reign of terror.

Jomo Kenyatta and five other African leaders had been arrested. They were alleged to be "managers of Mau Mau." All were members of Jomo's Kenya African Union. A state of emergency had been declared. Troop-carriers rumbled through the streets of Nairobi. In Nairobi, and in the reserves, thousands of Kikuyus were being rounded up for taking part in Mau Mau ceremonies. Helping to round them up were Somalis and Turkana tribesmen. I wondered what my friend the Kikuyu driver thought of it all.

I visited the headquarters in Nairobi of the Kenya African Union. Although the Kenya Government declared: "KAU is the mother of Mau Mau," the organization was still allowed to function. Kenyatta's post of president had been taken over by a Negro named Fanuel Walter Odede.

Young British soldiers, the Lancashire Fusiliers, walked about the streets. They wore black berets with yellow ribbons, and had a rather lost and bewildered look. The Nairobi headquarters of KAU were in a dingy building in a poor Indian quarter. I climbed a dark staircase and knocked at a peeling door.

Odede was a fat-faced man going slightly bald. He looked like a black Mussolini. He had studied veterinary science at Makerere College, in Uganda, but had returned to Kenya to become first a journalist and then a politician.

Helping him to run the reorganized KAU were Wycliffe Wyasya Work Awori and Joseph Anthony Zuzarte Murumbi.

279

Awori had a thick cap of fuzzy hair and big strong teeth. He wore a white shirt and a black bow tie. He was a Negro business-man, who did a big trade in the buying and selling of crocodile-skins: his friends jokingly called him "the crocodile king." He also owned a flour mill and a chain of Negro stores, and farmed a thousand acres of land in Nyanza Province, up near Lake Victoria.

Murumbi was the most interesting of the trio. A tall, serious, spectacled man, he had been educated in India, and was a skillful lawyer. He had won three British medals in the Second World War. His father was a Goan, and his mother a Masai. He himself was married to a Somali girl.

Neither Odede nor Awori were Kikuyus. They were both members of the Luo tribe.

Sitting behind a desk and twiddling a pencil, Odede told me earnestly: "We deny emphatically that the Kenya African Union ever had any connection with the Mau Mau. But, if there *is* a Mau Mau element in KAU, be sure we shall purge it completely." He said that all KAU asked for was more education and economic opportunity for Africans, and a gradual extension of the franchise. Awori and Murumbi agreed.

I noticed that Jomo Kenyatta's picture was still prominently displayed on the wall.

I drove out to Eliud Mathu's house, in the reserve. Everything seemed normal. I got no feeling of tension. Kikuyus whom I passed on the road showed no hostility toward a white face. On the contrary, they grinned cheerfully. Perhaps, I thought, the whole thing had been exaggerated.

Mathu greeted me warmly. He still flashed his white teeth and rolled his eyes, showing the whites. But he expressed only disgust about the Mau Mau.

"The Kikuyus are damn fools to fall for this voodoo stuff," he said vigorously. "Damn fools."

"Is it just voodoo?"

"Of course. Mumbo-jumbo. They walk under arches of banana-tree branches, and eat sheep's eyes." He wrinkled his nose. "Like children."

"What will happen next?"

"The Government will suppress it. It's a setback, of course. But we'll get back on the proper road. I'm not pessimistic about the future. Kenya is all right."

I went to see Sir Evelyn Baring at Government House. I had last met him in Bechuanaland, when he was High Commissioner. Now he was Governor of Kenya.

Government House is a large white mansion with many green-shuttered windows, set amid flowery lawns on a hill overlooking Nairobi. It drowsed peacefully in the sunshine. A large cat slept in the shade of the portico. A clean-limbed young Englishman chatted brightly to me while I waited for the Governor to be free: Baring, he explained, was giving an audience to a number of troubled bishops who wanted to talk about the Mau Mau. "It's a bit of a knock for them," he said cheerfully. "The missions were the first to get it in the neck. The Kikuyus refuse to go to church any more, and they've taken their children away from the mission schools."

"The Mau Mau is anti-Christian?" I asked.

He laughed. "I don't think Christianity ever went very deep here."

Presently he led me briskly along a broad corridor, and across a large room with brocaded chairs and tinkling glass chandeliers. Despite this formality, the atmosphere was not stuffy: on a marble mantelpiece someone had left a dismantled fishing-rod. He knocked at a door and ushered me into the Governor's presence.

Baring was as I remembered him: a tall, rather pale man with a lean, handsome face and very long, thin legs. His speech was a cheerful gobble, like a turkey with an Oxford accent. He asked me to sit down and crossed his long legs.

"Jomo spent five years in Moscow," he said, adding dryly: "With results that you might expect. The Mau Mau organization has definitely been plotting to undermine the Kenya Government. It began with a lot of speech-making in the villages. Then the oath-taking started. Crime followed. They started by murdering Christian Kikuyus, headmen, Government-appointed chiefs. The idea, of course, is to create chaos and put an end to law and order. But the Mau Mau is essentially anti-white."

"Do you think the Kikuyu Independent Schools had anything to do with it?"

"Well, look here!" Baring exclaimed. "Jomo organized the schools. And the schools started teaching the children hymns in which the name 'Jomo' was substituted for 'Christ.' "

He quoted a sample of the "literature" being distributed by the Mau Mau: "We shall be the knives and the whites shall be the meat."

"What are you going to do about it?"

He crossed and uncrossed his legs and spoke rapidly. "Well, we'll crush it, of course. But that isn't enough. We must have a two-prong policy." He held up two fingers. "First, crush and destroy the Mau Mau. Second, institute various reforms. The land question is a big *indaba*: we'll probably need a commission of inquiry on that. But we can improve housing of Africans here in Nairobi, and try to raise Africans' wages. Oh, yes, there are some legitimate grievances."

"Do they explain the Mau Mau?"

"Not quite," said Baring dryly. "Disemboweling people is not the usual way of remedying economic ills, however strongly you may feel about them. No; the Mau Mau is a terrorist, anti-Christian, anti-white organization, run by men who are out to achieve power for themselves. But we'll deal with it."

Later I watched Baring open the Legislative Council. For the occasion, he wore a black hat with white feathers draped over it like custard on a pudding, gold epaulets, a bemedaled dark-blue tunic with embroidered cuffs, dark-blue trousers with broad gold braid, black shoes with spurs, and a sword with an ivory handle in an ornamental scabbard. He also, rather disconcertingly, wore spectacles with horn rims.

The members of Legco yawned and fidgeted while Baring read a flat speech about building roads and dams. The speech contained hardly any reference to the Mau Mau or its causes. One irreverent member looked at Baring and whispered derisively to another behind his hand: "As our Empire shrinks, our uniforms become more and more Ruritanian."

Afterwards I spoke to Colonel Ewart Grogan, the oldest member of Kenya's legislative body. The gallant colonel in his youth had known Cecil Rhodes, and on one occasion had walked all the way from the Cape to Cairo, on a dare. When I asked Colonel Grogan what should be done about the Mau Mau, he answered cheerfully: "It will be a bit of a rat-hunt, I suppose. But we'll come out on top all right." He had the air of a man who thought life was not complete without a bit of trouble from the natives now and then.

: 2 :

THE POLICE station was a bare, sun-baked building with a tin roof, set squarely in the center of a bare yard. Two sweating policemen lugged a large wooden box across the hot yard and put it down near the high fence.

Other policemen carried large banana-tree branches, heavy with green foliage, which they set up in the form of a rough arch. They were reconstructing a Mau Mau oath-taking ceremony.

One of the policemen proceeded to open the box. "Better stand back a bit," he advised. "This is going to be rather niffy."

Out of the box tumbled the disemboweled and dismembered body of a gray cat. Tied round its neck was a long piece of string. It had also been strangled.

Holding the dead cat by the string, and with the two fingers of his other hand firmly clamped over his nose, the policeman hung it from the banana branch.

A young policeman turned pale and reeled back a pace. "Jesus!" he exclaimed. "What a stink!"

The smell of the rotting carcass powerfully filled the yard.

"They first kill an animal and hang it on the arch," the policeman in charge of the demonstration explained. "Then the initiates pass through the arch seven times: once for each oath.

283

In addition, they have to drink the creature's blood, and eat its eyes."

He enumerated the oaths in their correct order:

"The first oath binds a man to help expel the whites from Kenya, by whatever means the Mau Mau decides.

"The second oath binds him never to betray another member of Mau Mau. The penalty for breaking this oath is death by strangulation or decapitation.

"The third oath compels those who take it to be at the disposal of Mau Mau at all times, and to obey the Mau Mau orders unquestioningly.

"A man who takes the fourth oath pledges himself to help Mau Mau killers dispose of the bodies of victims.

"Those who take the fifth oath are pledged to leave their village when the call comes, and join a Mau Mau guerrilla band.

"The sixth oath binds a man not to come back from a killing expedition without the head of a white man.

"The seventh oath is a vow to follow Jomo Kenyatta wherever he may be, and to set him free."

The policemen began taking down the arch and putting the body of the cat back into the box.

"We found these things in a hut near Nairobi," said the policeman in charge. "Unfortunately we were just too late to catch the oath-takers; or the secret oath-administrator, who was rather more important for our purpose." He added: "But we did dig up a few bodies buried near the hut. Suspected informers, presumably. They had all been strangled and buried in sacks with the ropes still round their necks. Just like the cat, you see."

"You can't do anything with people like that," said one of the policemen violently. He looked as if he were going to vomit. "The best way is to shoot the bastards: shoot all of them."

: 3 :

COLIN LEGUM of the *Observer* had flown in from London. He sat on the veranda of the Norfolk Hotel in Nairobi, smoking a

284

cheroot and blinking through his spectacles like a benevolent owl.

"I have hired a car," he said, "from Sir Eboo Pirbhai. We shall take a tour through the White Highlands, talking to the people and coming to grips with the situation." He announced this like a politician who proposes to confer favors on deserving constituents.

Sir Eboo Pirbhai was the Aga Khan's vizier in Nairobi. Thirty thousand of Kenya's hundred thousand Indians are devout followers of the Aga Khan. Sir Eboo also owned a garage and filling station.

"The Leuenbergers would like to come too," I said.

Colin waved an expansive hand. "Why not?"

Hans Leuenberger was a Swiss photographer. He wore a brown velvet jacket and looked like Prince Albert carrying a Leica. He had soft, brown eyes and an air of gentle wonder. He and his wife, Charlotte, a tall girl with a short haircut, had driven down to Kenya from Abyssinia in a *Volkswagen*. On the way, they slept in the bushes as far from their car as possible, to avoid the attention of bandits. They did not carry a gun. Before that they had been in Afghanistan.

"Hans," said Sean Browne, "looks like gentle Jesus meek and mild, until you discover he has spent the last twenty-three years wandering in fifty-two different countries, and raising hell in most of them."

When he reproached Hans for exposing his wife, who looked like a startled fawn, to such perils, Hans replied gently: "She is not fearful."

We set off on the road that runs through the Kiambu reserve and dips down sharply into the Rift Valley. From the top of the rise the valley lay at our feet like a gigantic frying-pan. A tiny chocolate-colored train puffed across its flat expanse, and on the other side were distant blue mountains. The sun-warmed air quivered like molten gold.

"Beautiful," said Colin.

"The Arabs," said Hans reflectively, "of all the people in the world write the most colorful poems. This is because in their desert lands there are no colors and forms, no melodies to disturb their imagination. Kenya is too beautiful to have poets or painters. It has the Mau Mau instead.

"In northern Syria I once met a sect who believe that God gave the earth to the Devil to govern; otherwise, they asked, how could it have got into such a mess? They give most of their money to their priests, who live well and have visiting-cards with peacocks printed on them, the peacock being a reincarnation of the Devil. It is as Nietzsche says: the earth is beautiful, but has a disease called man."

He was always full of such cheerful little items.

"Be quiet, Hans," Charlotte ordered.

We descended into the Rift Valley.

Near Lake Naivasha there was a pleasant hotel with the hospitable atmosphere of an English country pub. In the evening the local white farmers crowded into the bar. When we entered, drinks were set up by those kindly souls. They wore checked shirts and corduroy trousers and looked a sunburned, hard-working lot. They were also very English.

"The first thing to understand about the Kukes," said a large man who was drinking gin, "is that they've only been fifty years out of the trees. Kukes are savages."

Colin politely ventured to dispute the point. The large man banged his empty glass on the counter. "Never mind about chaps like Mathu! Oh, I grant you they can learn a few tricks. So can baboons. But give them half a chance and they're back in their old mumbo-jumbo ways. Here, have a drink."

Colin had a drink.

"The missionaries thought they had them converted," said the large man gloomily. "Converted, ha ha! The minute the missionary's back was turned they were holdin' blood-drinkin' ceremonies in their filthy huts. Hence the Mau Mau."

"All Kukes are filthy by nature," said a man with a drooping mustache. "Look at the way they treat their women. They turn them into beasts of burden."

"Full of filthy sex, too," said a third man. "I found my 'boys' were pinnin' up pictures of half-naked film stars in their huts,

286

torn from magazines. I made them take 'em down. Giving themselves ideas about white women."

"It's because their own women are so damned ugly," explained a fourth man. "Shriveled old hags with no teeth, most of them."

"Give me the Masai every time," said the large man who was drinking gin. "There's a fine-looking people for you! Pure savages, of course, but they respect the white man."

"The trouble with the Kukes is that they're overeducated," said the man with the drooping mustache. "Some of them have been to school, so they think they can chuck us out of Kenya and take over." He laughed.

"The Masai hate their guts," said the large man. "If the Government had any sense, it would turn the Masai on the Kukes. Give them their spears and tell them to go ahead."

"If the Kukes ever did get our land, the Masai would soon take it away from them," said a man who had not spoken before. The prospect seemed to please him.

"That's why it's better for us to have the land," said the large man. "Better for the Kukes themselves. Better for everybody." He disposed of his fourth gin and said hospitably to Colin: "Have another drink."

"Personally, I'd rather have Kipsigis working for me every time," said the man with the drooping mustache. "But they can't handle farm machinery. Too stupid."

"The Kukes can handle farm machinery, all right," said the large man gloomily. "You've got to hand it to the blighters. They learn fast. Of course, it's just like teaching animals to do tricks. It doesn't really mean anything."

"Only fifty years out of the trees," somebody repeated.

"And they're a lazy lot."

"God, but they certainly are lazy! Won't do a hand's turn unless you're constantly at their behinds."

"Treacherous, too."

"Well, look at this Mau Mau business. I never thought Kukes had enough guts to start a thing like that."

"They don't have guts," explained the large man. "They only

attack in bands. They'll run all right if they know you're armed."

At this point the door opened and a girl entered the bar. It was a thoroughly dramatic entrance. She advanced swiftly across the floor and then came to a sudden halt. In one hand she held an automatic.

She had long golden hair, and wore a tight knitted sweater. Her delicate cheeks were flushed, and her blue eyes were bright with pleasurable excitement. She looked extremely beautiful.

She waved her automatic and in a high, clear, English voice, full of girlish enthusiasm, cried: "I say, chaps! You'll never guess what!"

"What, Nell?" asked the large man.

She waved the automatic again. "I've just winged a Kuke!"

"Good God!" said the large man, adding: "Have a drink."

"I will," said the golden-haired girl. She tucked her automatic into her purse. "It was all too fearfully thrilling. I was driving over from the farm, when I thought I saw someone in the bushes at the side of the road. You know, lurking! I stopped the car and hullooed, and he started to run. It was a Kuke all right. So I fired. And," she added triumphantly, "I'm almost sure I winged him!"

Colin lowered his voice. "I think we ought to go," he said.

The farmers had gathered around Nell and bade us only perfunctory good-bys.

When we got outside, into the cool night air, Colin said: "I think I've had too many gins. Did I imagine that girl, or—?"

"You had too many gins," I said. "But she was real."

Hans said happily: "In Eritrea they have a drink made of fermented honey which leaves no hangover."

: 4 :

FATHER LAZZARO was surprisingly young to be in charge of a mission. He was an Italian priest from Venice. The mission buildings stood in the midst of a maze of neatly tilled terraces and banana groves. Dogs barked furiously at us as we approached the gate, then changed their minds and wagged their tails. From the open windows of a schoolroom came the sound of girls' voices singing a hymn.

We drank coffee with the father. He thoughtfully nibbled a biscuit, and said: "The Mau Mau came here. I was walking in the fields when two men suddenly sprang on me. They threw me to the ground without a word, and began to beat me with the flat blades of their *pangas*. One of the nuns came on the scene. When she saw what was happening to me, she screamed and began to run away, to fetch help. One of the men who was beating me drew out a revolver and fired a shot at her. She was wounded, but not too badly; the bullet grazed her head. Then the men, alarmed by her screams, I suppose, left me lying on the ground and fled into the bush."

"Why?" I asked. "Why should they attack you?"

"They hate all the whites, because they believe that the whites stole their land," he replied simply. He did not seem resentful.

An African priest to whom we spoke was less charitable. He had been threatened by the Mau Mau, and was a badly scared man. "They should shoot a few people, publicly, in each location," he said violently. "That would soon put an end to it." He was all in favor of hostages and reprisals.

All along the narrow winding roads in the Fort Hall district we met troop-carriers. In a forest clearing, tents had been pitched. There was a radio van, with a tall, slender mast. Near the tents, surrounded by barbed wire, about fifty Kikuyu men squatted sullenly on the ground. All were dressed in filthy rags. They were Mau Mau suspects.

"You just need to look at them," said a white soldier disgustedly, "to see they're only fifty years out of the trees."

We came to the Beck farm in the late afternoon. Colonel Beck was a jovial man who wore a monocle on a black ribbon. He also wore a battered hat with a broad brim, a checked shirt, and riding-breeches. The farmhouse was merely a whitewashed cottage with a long veranda, perched on the lower slopes of the Aberdare Mountains. When we drew up, Colonel Beck was seated on the veranda, reading a novel by Thomas Mann. He greeted Colin cordially, for they were old friends.

Beck was a German aristocrat who had fled from the Nazis. Now he and his son were farming in Kenya. "None of us around here makes any money," he said cheerfully, "but it is a good life."

"Despite the Mau Mau?" I asked.

Colonel Beck made a noise that sounded like "Pfui!"

"My 'boys' are not interested in Mau Mau nonsense," he said. "I treat them well."

He ushered us in, made us sit down, and insisted that we drink German beer. He also produced what he described as a small snack. The snack consisted of cuts of cold ham, hard-boiled eggs, sardines, and loaves of freshly baked bread. While we ate, he built up a huge fire. "It gets cold here in the mountains," he explained. We had barely finished the snack when he seated us at table and produced soup, fish, boiled mutton, more eggs, more beer, and bottles of wine.

"You have no appetite," he complained. "I thought, after your long journey, you would be starving."

Presently the Becks' nearest neighbors dropped by: a lean Englishman with graying hair, and his blonde wife. Somewhat disconcertingly, the lady wore a black velvet cloak over an evening gown. She looked as if she were on her way to a ball. On her wrist was a black velvet purse. Rings gleamed on her fingers. Her nails were crimson. Her blond hair looked freshly permed. She wore very high heels.

Charlotte, who had been traveling over dusty roads all day, gave her a swift, dirty look.

The lady dropped her velvet purse on a side table with a heavy clunk. "I get so tired of carrying that damned revolver around all the time," she complained.

Her husband said: "We came over in the truck. Hope you don't mind riding back in it. The roads are pretty bloody."

Colin was to spend the night with the Becks. The rest of us were going to the neighbors' farm.

"Colin and I will probably sit up all night, arguing by the

fire," said Beck. "I know Colin. He loves to argue. But you three will have a good night's rest."

"Bit rough and ready, of course," said the Englishman. "Built the place myself, you know."

After a while the Leuenbergers and I followed our hosts out to their truck. The mountains loomed black above us. It was bitterly cold.

"Hope I can get the damn thing started," said the Englishman.

Beck, carrying a lantern, saw us installed. The truck roared into life, and off we lurched. I noticed that our host had a rifle on the seat beside him.

He had not exaggerated the state of the roads. The truck bumped, groaned, shuddered, strained at stony hills, and floundered in thick mud. We were thrown up in the air to land with a thud, and tossed from side to side.

The Englishman explained: "We patrol this stretch every night. Bit of a fag, when we have our normal work to do as well during the day. Got to be done, of course. They're bound to try to burn down the farmhouses."

"How far is it?" I asked, trying not to bite my tongue off.

"Oh, not far—about ten miles. This is the easy part: gets a bit rougher farther on." He complained: "Some blighters have shut up their farmhouses and pushed off to Mombasa. Government shouldn't allow it. It means the rest of us have to look after their property as well as our own."

"Have you had much Mau Mau trouble in this area?"

He carefully aimed the truck at a high narrow bridge and charged it. We surmounted the hazard safely.

"Well, not much actual Mau Mau, as yet. Always the odd bit of witchcraft going on, of course." He laughed. "Found it quite useful at one time. We kept our own tame witch doctor on the farm. If anything was stolen, we set him to smell out the thief. The 'boys' were terrified of him. He always came back in triumph with the stolen article. Never asked him any questions. He knew how to go about it, all right."

The farmhouse was a long log cabin of uncertain shape. It had obviously been added to from time to time. Inside, there were different floor levels, unexpected short flights of steps, and numerous doors.

"For its size, the place is a regular maze," said our hostess proudly. "Sometimes we get lost ourselves. But he'd never done even carpentering before." She glanced fondly at her husband.

"Damn roof leaks," he said gloomily. "Can't seem to find the holes, somehow."

A dachshund wandered in, followed by two more. There were also a number of Siamese cats. The Englishman stopped and scratched a dachshund's ear. "Hope you don't mind animals," he said. "We've got lots."

He showed us to our rooms. "I'm afraid we're all a bit scattered," he apologized. "And, by the way, none of the doors have locks. Never seemed to need 'em, before all this business started. Any of you got a gun?"

We said no, none of us had a gun.

"Pity; there's only one rifle. I keep it beside my bed. My wife could lend you her revolver if you're nervous, but I shouldn't think you'd need it, actually. You'll be all right. If you hear a bit of a scuffle outside, don't worry: we let the dogs roam around all night." He grinned. "If anybody tries to get at you, just yell; I'll come at the double. Good night, all; sleep well." He retreated, taking his flashlight with him.

"He talks as if we should be afraid," said Charlotte scornfully.

I thought: "That's all right for you, you've got a husband to protect you." I didn't even have a dachshund. But I didn't like to say anything. This tall, proud, beautiful girl might conclude I was nervous.

"In Russia, during the war," said Hans chattily, "I once slept in a room with four German soldiers. In the morning two had had their throats cut by Soviet peasants who crept in, without disturbing the rest of us."

"Good night," I said coldly.

The windows of my room looked toward the forest, which came to within a hundred yards of the house. Bright moonlight lit up every twig of the trees in the garden. But the forest was a black and menacing mass. The Mau Mau gangs were forest-dwellers.

I drew the curtains, got into bed, and switched off the bed-side battery torch.

In the morning I found our hostess busily plying a needle while her husband smoked his pipe and read a book about humus and crop rotation. She was wearing much-patched slacks, with her revolver stuck in a hip pocket.

"I'm making thick curtains," she explained, "for the windows. The ones we have are almost transparent. If the Mau Mau attacked they could easily see to shoot through."

It did not seem to me much of a precaution in a house that lacked locks on the doors, but I let it pass. Kenya, I thought, had hitherto been such a peaceful place that these people were not yet accustomed even to the idea of violence.

The white settlers still baffled me, and still do. They drank imported Moselle, and kept tame witch doctors; they lived in rather rickety old farmhouses with leaking roofs, but this was evidence of their genuine love of the land. Now the Mau Mau was casting a long shadow over the lonely bungalows. Perhaps the essence of the tragedy was that the whites, who loved the land, forgot that the black man loved it with an equal passion. I had heard so many white settlers exclaim in exasperation about the Kikuyus: "If they're well treated, what more do they want?" Both sides were fighting for an existence rooted in the soil.

We breakfasted off elegant silver and china, in a long room whose cedar-log walls were decorated with stags' heads. Kikuyu servants, wearing long blue smocks, padded silently about. Our hostess poured coffee, and put her revolver down among the silver.

"I keep sitting on the damned thing," she complained.

We drove back in the truck to the Beck farm. When I had a moment alone with Colin, he asked: "Did you sleep well?"

"Yes."

He looked at me suspiciously. "You did?"

"Of course."

"I didn't sleep a damned wink," he said. "I kept waking up and looking out at that forest."

I did think he looked a trifle hollow-eyed.

Beck offered to drive us up into the Aberdare Mountains. It was not an offer we cared to refuse. Since the Mau Mau troubles had begun, very few whites except soldiers had been on the mountains. I wondered, however, how he proposed to get us there. There were no roads. The range, thirteen thousand feet high, separated the areas of white settlement lying east and west of it. His answer was to produce his own truck.

Though this was a daylight ride, it was even more nightmarish than our drive the previous night. The truck charged at steep grassy slopes, and twisted and turned to avoid the trees. There were times when it canted at an angle of forty-five degrees. We clutched at the sides and at one another. The thought of breaking a leg and having to be jolted in a helpless state back down the track was not pleasant.

But the trip was worth the trouble. We came out on a flat meadow, and white-tailed buck fled from us down the farther slope, to be lost in a valley where grew cedar trees and wild olives. The early morning air was fresh and stinging in our faces, and every leaf and blade of grass looked as if it had just been created. It was like being present in the dawn of the world, and I understood why all its people, white and black, loved Kenya. It seemed a pity they had to kill one another to prove it.

"If the Aberdares are really the lair of the Mau Mau, then they are down in that valley somewhere," said Beck soberly, pointing to the trees into which the buck had fled.

He turned the truck and we went back down our side of the mountain. Behind us the trees seemed to be watching.

: 5 :

NEAR NYERI, where I had seen the new Queen of England drive away in a black limousine, we spoke to a man who had been a brigadier. Now he was in Military Intelligence, fighting the Mau Mau. He had a sealed-lips air, and strove hard to give the impression that he could tell us many hair-raising things if only he cared to. I nevertheless had the feeling that he knew very little more than the people in Nairobi, who so far as I could see were almost completely in the dark and were being extremely nonchalant about it. But he said one illuminating thing.

"I met Jomo Kenyatta once," he told us. "I've never forgotten it. He's a thoroughly intelligent man. He talked so persuasively, I found myself beginning to agree with him!"

"What did you do about it?" asked Colin.

"I got a grip on myself and said: 'Steady, old chap! Remember, he's black, you're white!'"

In Nairobi we had been told that on no account would any of us be permitted to take a trip in one of the light spotter aircraft that were flying daily over the Aberdares to try to locate Mau Mau gangs. Hans had very much wanted to take aerial pictures of the terrain where the war would be fought, if there was really going to be a war.

When we mentioned the matter to an official in Nyeri, he looked surprised. "Certainly you can go in one of the planes, and take as many pictures as you like," he said. "I'll arrange it."

It could not, however, be arranged until the next morning, and Colin and I had people to see at Thomson's Falls and Nakuru. Hans said he would rather wait in Nyeri and take a plane ride. Charlotte said she would go up too. When the official looked a little dubious, she said tranquilly: "I do not get sick, ever."

So we left them, and Colin and I drove on to Thomson's Falls, which consists of large, half-timbered dwellings whereby Englishmen in exile have managed to import the atmosphere of a Tudor village into the land of their adoption. At the hotel we asked in vain for a bed: the place was full up. We decided, however, to have a drink before driving on through the night to Nakuru.

"It's so important," said Colin, "to talk to the people and get their point of view."

He was not long left in doubt as to what their point of view was.

In the bar of Barry's Hotel sunburned men in checked shirts were drinking gin and discussing Kukes. They turned and stared as we entered. "Strangers!" said a tall ginger-haired man in a checked shirt with a large revolver stuck in a holster on his hip. "Have a drink, strangers." He swayed like a tree about to fall, so that I had an impulse to cry "Timber!" With difficulty he focused his eyes on Colin's face. "What's your name, stranger, and what's your business?"

The London *Observer* is a solid, conservative paper, and Colin is understandably proud to be attached to it.

"My name is Legum," he said. "I am a correspondent of the *Observer* and . . ."

The tall man seized Colin, who was a good head shorter than he, pulled out his revolver, stuck it in Colin's ribs, and bellowed: "Another bloody Bolshie!"

In the ensuing silence, the bartender turned pale. Two other men crept upon Ginger from behind.

"Keep talking to him," a third man whispered agitatedly in Colin's ear.

"The *Observer*," said Colin coldly, "is read by the best people in London." He wriggled where the gun touched him. He said afterwards that it tickled.

"Have a drink, ole man," someone pleaded with Ginger.

Very slowly Ginger's eyes went out of focus again. With equal slowness he let the gun point to the floor. He then keeled over very gently, but was prevented from falling by the two men who had crept up behind him.

The bartender tapped me on the shoulder. "Better get your friend out of here," he advised.

We went on our way, toward Nakuru.

"What was the matter with him?" demanded Colin. "Apart from being drunk, I mean. Even drunks don't normally pull guns on total strangers."

"He was Harpic," I said, quoting Humphrey Downes.

Harpic is a much-advertised fluid for cleaning lavatory bowls.

296

Its makers claim that it "goes right round the bend." Being "Harpic" had become a well-known malady in Kenya since the start of the Mau Mau. People were going right round the bend in many parts of the country, including Nairobi. Becoming Harpic included, in most white settlers, developing a violent antipathy to all persons who were obviously not white settlers; and especially to newspapermen, who were suspected of criticizing Kenya's way of life.

: 6 :

AT NAKURU we were given beds at the Stag's Head Hotel. In the morning I put a call through to the White Rhino Hotel at Nyeri, for I was worried about our Swiss. I had visions of their tiny plane hitting the mountain and strewing their remains among the wild olive trees.

"It is Charlotte," said the voice.

"How did everything go?"

"I was not sick," she said complacently. "The pilot and Hans were sick. It was very bumpy. But Hans took good pictures." She added: "He was sick twice."

I told her we would see them both in Nairobi.

Colin had gone to call on the district commissioner. He returned in haste. "There's been a Mau Mau murder on the Kinangop. A white farmer called Eric Bowyer was cut to pieces in his bath. His two African servants were slaughtered in the farmhouse kitchen. We'd better go there."

The Kinangop plateau was south of Nyeri, on the west side of the Aberdare range. We drove past the soda lake near Nakuru, a white expanse ringed with pink flamingos, and presently turned off the main road into the hills. It had been raining, and in places the track that led to the plateau was solid mud. Off this track lay isolated farmhouses. We spoke to a British major with a wooden leg. He and his wife were not afraid, but they were very angry.

"A beastly thing," said the major. Bowyer, he told us, was a middle-aged man, who lived alone on his farm, and kept a *duka*, a small store for selling goods to Africans. "He was an extremely generous chap and was very fond of the Kukes. He was the last man I'd have thought they'd go for."

The high, wind-swept plateau was beautiful country. Green wheat rippled for miles around. It had been Masai country, but the Masai were given other land in exchange for it, as far back as 1911. Not until 1948, however, did white settlers begin to farm it. In the short time since then they had done a marvelous job of clearing and planting. The plateau was a clean and sunny but still immensely lonely place.

By the time we reached Bowyer's farm, the bodies had been removed. The police were in possession, and bloodhounds were tracking the suspected killers deep into the surrounding hills. On the muddy road near the farmhouse we spoke to a small, stocky, dark man who introduced himself as Roger Ruck. He was a farmer and a neighbor of Bowyer.

We talked in the roadway. A chill wind blew and we stamped our feet as we talked, to keep them warm. Trucks had churned up the mud, leaving deep tracks, and heavy clouds lowered over the hills where the police with their bloodhounds were seeking the killers.

"Bowyer was slashed to bits," said Roger Ruck, who had a black stubble of beard, and whose lips were pale. "All the fingers of one hand were gone. After they killed him, they disemboweled him. When we tried to lift the body out of the bath, bits of his bowels began to slide down the drain." His face worked. "Bloody Kukes!"

Ruck told us there were about twenty farmers with their wives and children living on the plateau. "We have to look after ourselves," he said. "There aren't any troops at all in this area. Our wives are living together, with the children, in a sawmill for protection. The men patrol the farms, but there are only a handful of us." The farms, he said, ranged in size from five thousand up to sixty thousand acres of land.

Mrs. Ruck drove up. She was a pretty, fair-haired girl, with a lovely complexion. Ruck introduced us to his wife. "She's been nursing Kukes," he said bitterly. "She's a qualified doctor. She looks after their children, and hands out medicines to the sick."

"Not any more," said Mrs. Ruck. "After Bowyer, I'd rather tend animals."

Ruck said: "I fought the Italians in Abyssinia during the war. But the Italians had the right idea. I wish we had old Graziani here now. He'd drop Kuke bastards from airplanes."

Mrs. Ruck said, but half-heartedly: "You don't really mean that, Roger." She glanced nervously at us.

"I'll tell you one thing," Ruck said, "and you can print it. These bastards won't get me the way they got Bowyer. From now on, so far as I'm concerned a dead Kuke is a safe Kuke." He repeated: "They'll never get me."

That was the beginning of the real Mau Mau terror. Other white farmers would go the way of Bowyer—including Roger Ruck.

Weeks later, when I was back in Johannesburg, I read that the Mau Mau had killed not only Ruck, but his wife and child as well. One night a servant of the Rucks knocked on the farm-house door. He told Roger that a Mau Mau oath-taker was hiding in one of the huts on the farm. Roger got his gun and went out. It was a trap, and he was slashed to pieces on his lawn, before he could fire a shot. Mrs. Ruck ran to her husband's aid and was also murdered. The killers then entered the farmhouse, where the Rucks' child lay asleep. They broke down the door of the room and cut the child's throat.

When I read this account, I remembered Roger Ruck and his wife standing talking to us on the muddy road, near Bowyer's farm, and Roger Ruck saying angrily: "They'll never get *me*."

: 7 :

IN NAIROBI, the Indians gave a party for Fenner Brockway and Leslie Hale, two British Socialist M.P.'s who had come to Kenya to investigate the Mau Mau problem. Neither Mr. Brockway nor Mr. Hale was *persona grata* with the white people of Nairobi.

299

or for that matter with the white settlers of Kenya as a whole. They clearly fell into the category of "bloody Bolshies." There was consternation that they should have been admitted to the colony at all, and loud questions were asked in the Legislative Council.

When Brockway and Hale landed at Nairobi airport, they were met by a cheering crowd of Africans and Indians. (The police seized the opportunity to arrest a number of Africans in the crowd as Mau Mau suspects.) Disapproving whites noted that Hale emerged from the airplane wearing sandals and no socks, and the next morning an enterprising aviator flew over the Indian home where the two Socialists were staying, and dropped a pair of socks on its roof. The general opinion among the whites was that it was Hale who should have been dropped from the airplane instead.

A party was held for the Socialists in a large house in Parklands, a superior Nairobi suburb. When Colin and I drove up, we found rows of motor-cars already parked, and two bearded white troopers watching the proceedings. The authorities were keeping a close eye on the two Britons.

We were received by an Indian lady wearing a sari, and ushered into a room packed with people who were standing in groups or squatting on divans, all engaged in earnest discussion. The party had overflowed onto a back veranda, where more people were standing and eating curry.

Awori, the "crocodile king," was there, and so was Joseph Murumbi. In the main room someone started a phonograph, and a number of small Indian girls demonstrated an Indian dance. Brockway and Hale, glasses in hand, wandered in from the back veranda. The little Indian girls gravely danced toward them and retreated, their shiny black pigtails swinging, and Hale looked somewhat startled. He had the air of a man who, setting out in all good faith to deliver a resounding political address from well-worn notes, to an audience of familiar faces, found himself plunged unexpectedly into a fancy-dress ball. I noticed that he was now wearing socks.

Brockway kept an affable smile fixed on his face and nodded amiably whenever anyone spoke to him. Everyone was now talking at once. A man sitting cross-legged on a divan was arguing vehemently about the need to teach Africans to drive locomotives. Awori was talking loudly about crocodiles. Murumbi struggled through the crowd with a glass in each hand, looking anxiously for anyone who did not yet have a drink. The smell of curry and other rich Indian food drifted in from the back veranda. The phonograph played wailing Indian music, and the troop of small Indian girls threw themselves into ever more violent contortions, writhing like pigtailed boneless wonders. The lady in the sari looked pleased: her party was a great success.

Outside, in the dark road, the two bearded troopers walked up and down, listening to the music and the hubbub of conversation, and straining their ears to catch some snatch of subversive talk. In the clubs of Nairobi, white citizens were downing gins and declaring vehemently that bloody Bolshies who hobnobbed with Indians and Africans should be tarred and feathered. In mud huts in the near-by Kikuyu reserve, Mau Mau initiates were taking the oath, vowing to kill all traitors and white men, and drinking the blood of slaughtered animals from a bowl that the oath-administrator passed round.

In the Aberdares, in the scattered lonely farmhouses, the white farmers were hugging their rifles and listening intently for the first warning sound of a Mau Mau attack. Since Bowyer's murder you knew what to expect: if you relaxed your vigilance for an instant, the disemboweled bodies of yourself and your wife and children would be found by the police in the morning.

A slim young African, wearing a gray suit and a white silk tie with brown spots, buttonholed me and eagerly explained: "The Mau Mau, of course, is purely an invention of imperialist exploiters. It is a plot, an excuse to imprison and persecute Jomo Kenyatta, an innocent man and a great savior of the African people. There is no such thing as Mau Mau: it does not exist."

Hans and Charlotte had come to the party. The young African seized on Hans. We escaped into the garden, and presently Hans joined us.

"In Switzerland," he said, "we have a wine called Twann which makes all who drink it very angry and confused. I think that in Kenya they have all been drinking Twann."

"Not just in Kenya," I said.

XXI

KENYA: GALLOWS ON THE GOLF COURSE

So HERE I was back in Nairobi, I thought, as I lay under the mosquito net in my hotel bedroom, listening to the wailing Indian music from the cinema across the road, and thinking of those previous visits to the Land of the Shining Mountain.

Once again I had flown into Kenya past the snows of Kilimanjaro, and spoken to Sean Browne and to Humphrey and Arabella Downes, and visited the dreary night-clubs where the young men drank gin and carried guns. Nairobi was a thin and brittle place where tempers were too easily frayed, and too many illusions were nurtured on gin. It was an unsubstantial Mayfair miraculously transported to the tropics; a ridiculously out-of-date Mayfair close to the equator, incongruously swarming with Indians and on the edge of still raw Africa. It was not so much a town as a collection of stage props, with comic pukka sahibs playing loud and angry roles.

I winced as I recalled some of the illusions I myself had nurtured on my first visit. Victor Matthews and Eliud Mathu had seemed to me to be reasonable men, with fine, sound ideas for the future. But Matthews had vanished from the scene, and Mathu, they told me, was "discredited": hated by the fanatics among his own people for being "moderate," and criticized by the whites because he refused to abandon his hopes for a better deal for the black men in Africa. The Mau Mau had smashed through those bright but flimsy hopes, splintering them into hatred and muddle.

Now there was murder in the streets. Mau Mau gangsters rode in death-cars disguised as taxicabs and shot down their victims on the sidewalks. Everyone in Nairobi went armed, and the gun-dealers no longer had guns to sell. When I had last been in Kenya, the Mau Mau bands had been armed only with *pangas* and a few stolen revolvers. Now they had rifles, Sten guns, and uniforms. They attacked police stations, burned whole villages, and ravaged the countryside like an invading army. Kenya was at war.

I did not like Nairobi, but it was a place you kept returning to if your job was to report on Africa; for what was happening there might be the dismal future pattern for a whole continent in turmoil. Nevertheless, when at last the cinema across the way closed and the wailing Indian music and loud mechanical voices ceased, I resolved to stay as short a time as possible in Nairobi, and to get upcountry as quickly as I could, to where this war was really being fought.

"You'll have to keep a good lookout on the road," said the man who sat across from me at breakfast. He was a spruce, soldierly-looking man, who spoke crisply. "They've started ambushing cars and destroying bridges. The army have also put up roadblocks." He grinned at me. "It all makes life very difficult for travelers. If you turn a corner and find a barrier across the road, it may be the Mau Mau, or it may be an army roadblock. If you stop and it's the Mau Mau, you've had it. If you don't stop and it's the army, they'll shoot." He smeared marmalade on his toast. "And it's very difficult to tell whether it's the Mau Mau or the army until it's too late to do anything about it," he concluded cheerfully.

I drove along a familiar road, through the Kiambu reserve, where the skinny Kikuyu women still stumbled along under head-loads that would shatter the spines of pack-mules, past the thickly clustered thatched mud huts like shaggy beehives. According to Kikuyu legend, the women were in a state of bondage for past misdeeds. Once upon a time, the legend ran, the Kikuyus had queens, and the queens were ruthless tyrants. All Kikuyu women were exalted, and their men were their slaves.

So the men put their heads together and decided that on a certain day they would make all the women pregnant. This not inconsiderable feat having been achieved, the women were simultaneously rendered helpless in childbirth, and from that time on, the men had been the masters and the women had been their slaves.

Beyond the reserve the country was beautiful. Giraffes nodded their tall necks on the plains, and the nandi flame-trees were ablaze with bursting crimson buds against the pale blue of the sky. Suspended in the sky was the bright snowy crest of Mount Kenya. Even the Aberdares seemed peaceful, with cloud shadows chasing over their dappled sides. Looking at them, you had to remind yourself that it was in the Aberdares that the Mau Mau bands had their lairs, and that this mountain range lay like a vast scorpion in the heart of the White Highlands, its sting pointing south to Nairobi and its head toward Thomson's Falls.

From the thick tangled forests on the upper slopes, the Mau Mau struck repeatedly at the scattered white farms. About those forest thicknesses a bearded white commando leader told me: "We were on maneuvers with the Lancashire Fusiliers. The soldiers passed us only the breadth of a tree trunk away. We could hear them stumbling past, but we couldn't see them. They neither saw nor heard us. If we had been Mau Mau—" He grinned in his black beard and made a crude gesture across his throat with a calloused hand.

This was the deadly game of hide-and-seek that went on day after day and week after week up in the mountain forests.

Pausing at Nyeri, I saw an astonishing sight. The colonels' ladies still drank tea and gossiped on the stone terrace of the hotel, but the colonels in their canary-yellow pull-overs were no longer playing golf. Instead, the golf course was fenced with barbed wire and, visible from the hotel, there towered a grisly erection behind corrugated-iron walls. It was a portable gallows, for hanging condemned Mau Mau prisoners, and it had been brought down to Nyeri from Thomson's Falls for a batch of local executions. The colonels' ladies watched it while they drank their tea, with a grim satisfaction.

In the saloon of Barry's Hotel at Thomson's Falls, men in checked shirts sat on high stools with gun-butts sticking out of black leather holsters on their hips. Other, bearded men, commando riders, shouldered their way in with Sten guns slung on their backs. Thomson's Falls had gone Wild West. They drank a good deal, and there was a raw bitterness in their talk, like the harsh bite of a buzz-saw.

A tall, red-faced man hitched up his gun-belt and gulped down a brandy. He was having an argument with an older and quieter man, with gray hair.

"Jesus Christ!" said the red-faced man. "You talk as if you thought Kukes were human."

"They're not all Mau Mau," said the other man. "Personally, I still trust my 'boys.' After all, they've been with me twenty years, most of them."

"They're the bastards you should trust least," said the red-faced man angrily. "The Meiklejohns kept saying *their* 'boys' were all right. Meiklejohn is dead, and his wife almost bled to death. Bingley and Ferguson trusted their Kukes: they're dead too. Gibson said his 'boys' would warn him if he was in danger: who let Gibson's murderers into the farmhouse?

"Nobody told Roger Ruck the Mau Mau were hiding on his farm. When he spoke to one of his 'boys,' the Kuke grinned and said: 'Yes, *bwana* (boss).' He didn't say: '*Bwana*, it's all decided, we're going to kill you tonight.' When Ruck's wife was doling out medicine to sick Kukes, they didn't tell her: 'Look out, they're sharpening the *pangas* in the huts.' Oh, no; they just grinned and thanked her for the medicine. When the Rucks' six-year-old kid went toddling round the farm, the Rucks' Kukes didn't say: 'Little *bwana*, we're going to kill your father and mother, then break down the door of your room, while you scream and scream, and cut your throat.' They just grinned and said: 'Good morning, little *bwana*; you look well, little *bwana*.' "

The red-faced man spat. "Trust your Kukes after that, do you?" he demanded.

The older man looked abashed.

306

They were very bitter at Thomson's Falls, at Naro Moru, at Ol Kalou, on the Kinangop, and in all that country infested with Mau Mau. In a pathetic attempt to protect their almost defenseless farmhouses, the farmers had put wire screens, no thicker than chicken-coop wire, on their verandas, and kept large dogs. No farmer's wife, when her husband was out patrolling with his rifle, was ever without her revolver strapped to her waist. Pretty Margaret Campbell Clause, who lived at Thomson's Falls, changed her infant's diapers with a revolver ready to hand on the nursery table, lying next to the baby's rattle, while she talked to me.

The farmers were especially bitter about the politicians in Nairobi. One farmer said vehemently: "They sit on their fat behinds in their nice offices and make up soothing speeches, when what we need are more soldiers and more guns. The way they're fighting the Mau Mau, it could go on for years. But how long can *we* go on? Night after night you lock the doors, and see to the guns, and kiss your wife and kids good-night, and wonder if you'll see them alive in the morning. When a 'boy' comes in to lay the table for breakfast, you don't know whether he'll be alone or have a Mau Mau gang at his heels.

"Up here we have *no* protection, except ourselves. Some of us can't farm any more. We're out on commando patrol all the time. So for a week or two weeks you go out into the mountains and leave your farm to be run by your wife, with the help of your parents or hers.

"My father and mother are helping run my farm. They're not young any longer, and the strain is killing them. I bought them a radio." He laughed derisively. "They don't dare switch it on! It might drown the other noises they're always listening for. But what can I do? All my life savings are in the farm. Nobody would buy it, anyway, if I tried to sell it. Nobody in Kenya is such a bloody fool as to want to buy a farm today!"

A commando leader explained how the Mau Mau gangs were sought by patrols, bloodhounds, and native trackers who were almost as keen on the scent as bloodhounds. He said: "Sometimes we run smack into a gang and have a running battle. We try to take prisoners, to get information, but they're either unwilling to talk or they're scared. They know what will happen to them if they talk and the Mau Mau get hold of them afterwards. 'Traitors' are beheaded, disemboweled, buried head-down in the ground, burned alive. So when we take prisoners, we have to make them more afraid of us than they are of the Mau Mau."

He did not say how this was done, but his voice was savage.

: 2 :

TWO SOLDIERS who had preceded me on the road to Thomson's Falls were ambushed. Their car was pockmarked with bullets, and the windshield was smashed. One bullet went through the driver's leg, a second shattered the other soldier's kneecap. The wounded driver carried on and brought them both to safety.

"You were lucky," a farmer told me briefly.

The farmers, no longer able to trust Kukes, of whom it was rumored that at least seventy-five per cent were secret sympathizers with the Mau Mau, were clearing thousands of men, women, and children off their farms. Near Ol Kalou, I found a towheaded young policeman in an open-neck khaki shirt supervising one such operation.

"Where will they all go?" I asked.

"Back into the reserves."

"But the reserves can't feed the people in them already!" I protested. A district officer near Nyeri had told me gloomily he expected a famine in his area before long.

The young policeman shrugged. "That's the Government's *indaba.*"

"Well, how do you get them back to the reserves?"

"Oh, they go in trucks, and the Government is laying on trains as well."

I visited a farmhouse where commando men had collected. It was the headquarters of the patrol whose duty it was to see that the evicted Kikuyus actually left and did not hide in the hills and return later to their huts.

308

"What exactly is the drill?" asked a young man nervously, looking dubiously at the rifle that had been thrust into his hands. Until he volunteered for duty against the Mau Mau, he had been a clerk in Nairobi.

"After midnight, you can shoot any Kuke who doesn't halt when challenged."

"What do we do with the ones who halt?"

"You shoot just the same, stick *pangas* in their hands, and say they tried to escape."

There was grim laughter.

On the way back from the farmhouse, two angry farmers barred the way, standing in the middle of the road and waving their arms. The towheaded young policeman halted his jeep.

"What's the trouble?"

"Look here," exclaimed one of the farmers. "You blighters said the Kukes would be transported today. We've got about a thousand of them rounded up and dumped down at the Ol Kalou railroad siding. Now we're told there won't be a train for days!"

"I'll look into it," said the young policeman.

We drove to the siding. Shiny, hot in the sun, the rails stretched into the distance endlessly. Beside the track squatted human beings, goats, cattle, sheep. Kikuyu men wore tattered army greatcoats, caps, mufflers: the rags of the white civilization that was now sending them back into their reserves. Their legs were bare and skinny under their coats. Most wore no shoes. The women ranged in age from young girls to withered hags with shaven skulls. Some suckled infants. Two black children with running noses and hair the color of dirty gray wool sat on the ground guarding a pile of cooking-pots. The cattle, skinny, reddish-brown beasts, chewed the tough, sparse grass resignedly. Sheep and goats wandered across the empty tracks. The goats gave off a powerful smell.

A half-witted Kikuyu youth wearing a single garment like a nightshirt, full of holes, tried to climb into the jeep. His face was smeared thick with white clay, his head shaved and covered with sores. The young policeman cuffed him, and the half-wit ran away, holding his head and uttering unintelligible sounds. The young policeman got out of the jeep. Presently he came back, looking disgusted.

"Some bastard has mucked it up properly," he said. "Nobody seems to know anything about a train."

"What will happen to the people?"

"They'll just have to wait until something can be done about them. Of course, they could always go to the transit camp at Thomson's Falls, but that's full up already."

The transit camp at Thomson's Falls occupied a large open space and contained about fifteen hundred Kikuyus, kept behind barbed wire. All of them had been evicted from white farms. Once their papers were cleared, they were sent off in batches to the reserves. Those suspected of serious complicity in Mau Mau were detained. The people behind the barbed wire went quietly about their business of cooking food, mending their clothes, and washing themselves. One man was washing his feet in a tin bucket. Another was making himself a pair of shoes from an old tire tube. A third was staking out a sheepskin on the hard ground, to dry it in the sun. Two children sat peering through the fence at a dead sheep lying outside. Many of the people, men and women, squatted on the ground, wrapped in their blankets, just staring. Their eyes were without expression.

A white man was seated at a table in the open, going through a collection of passes and calling out names. He wore a flat-topped hat with a wide brim, a khaki shirt, and corduroy trousers. Behind him stood a tall Negro soldier, wearing a greatcoat and a red fez.

"We're screening them and getting them out as fast as we can," the man in the flat-topped hat explained. "But over a hundred a day keep coming in, for every hundred we shift out."

Outside the camp stood a line of ten or twelve open trucks. In these, people leaving the camp were storing their belongings, then quickly climbing aboard themselves, the women handing up their children. There they crouched down and stared about them. A man passed holding a struggling sheep against his chest.

There was very little conversation. Watching the Kikuyus get into the trucks were a number of tall, slim men, with arrogant, smooth-skinned faces, almost as pretty as girls. They wore triangular red cotton hats, and carried spears and bows and arrows. These were Sambura tribesmen who were acting as guards.

The trucks were rapidly filled. Then they began to move off, in clouds of red dust, jolting over the rough track that led away from the camp. The Sambura guards climbed aboard the moving trucks and stood upright among the crouching Kukes. The trucks painfully climbed a steep rise and vanished one by one over the top of the hill. The last glimpse of them, amid the swirling red dust, showed the tall, upright figures of the red-capped Sambura, clutching their spears and bows and arrows and still looking disdainful or amused.

I drove back to Thomson's Falls. At the police station, a small gray-stone building with a green-painted tin roof, white men in uniform were excitedly going through the contents of a wooden box that a commando patrol had just brought in. The commando leader, a tall, dark-haired man with a long nose, wearing a blue jersey with leather shoulder-pads, and with a Sten gun slung on his back, explained: "We found a Mau Mau hide-out in the forest. They'd dug a tunnel leading to an underground room. The whole thing was damn well camouflaged. But they'd been cooking, and one of our chaps spotted the smoke coming up through the ground. They must have heard us approaching and beat it, but we found this stuff." He nodded toward the box.

A police official was going through some papers from the box. The papers consisted mostly of tattered school exercise-books, their yellow pages scrawled with painful writing. "It's a complete record of Mau Mau in this district," he exulted. "Names of members, everything. What a find!" He peered. "By Jove, they've even written down the name of the chief oath-administrator, and I believe I know the chap! Cunning brute—I'd never have suspected him."

He rang a bell, and another police officer entered and saluted. "Yes, sir?"

311

"Look here," said his senior, "there's a chap in this district called Karimi, isn't there?"

"Yes, sir."

"Then have him brought in at once. Good God, man, he's the chief oath-administrator in this area, and he's been operating right under our noses!"

The other officer's face changed. "Are you sure, sir?"

"Of course I'm sure. Look for yourself!" He thrust the tattered exercise-book toward the doubter.

The junior police officer scratched his nose. " 'Fraid we've made a bit of a blue, in that case, sir."

"What the hell d'you mean?"

"Well, sir," said the junior officer apologetically, "we've had Karimi in the camp, for screening, for the past two months. He seemed all right, and we let him go yesterday." He blushed. "I signed his pass myself."

: 3 :

ON THE way to Kitale, beyond Eldoret, families of giraffe grazed peacefully by the roadside, like cattle. Kitale was a typical up-country cow town, with a broad main street, a single hotel, and a club where everyone got drunk. Twenty-five miles from Kitale, in the shadow of Mount Eldoret and near the Kenya-Uganda border, was Kapenguria, with its *boma*, or office of the district commissioner. Near Kapenguria was a small red-brick school-house, standing next to a plowed field. The schoolhouse was no longer functioning as one, but had been turned into a court-house. Here Jomo Kenyatta and five other Africans were on trial for "managing the Mau Mau."

The rough winding road from Kitale to Kapenguria was heav-ily guarded. Halfway along it, a yellow-painted armored car with a turret and a two-pounder gun watched for trouble. The sol-diers who manned it had a radio transmitting set and were armed with rifles and Sten guns. Two more armored cars stood outside the improvised courthouse. All motor-cars on the road were

312

stopped, and their occupants politely asked to show their papers.

Each day Kenyatta and the other five prisoners were brought to the courthouse in an open truck from the Kapenguria *boma* jail. They wore handcuffs and were guarded by African soldiers armed with rifles.

I watched the six men descend from the truck and go into the building, where the handcuffs were removed. Each morning they were permitted half an hour with their counsel before being marched into the courtroom. They were being defended by a British Queen's Counsel, Denis Nowell Pritt, as well as by an Irish barrister, a Nigerian lawyer, and an Indian.

Pritt was a sharp-nosed little man with very sharp eyes behind his spectacles, and thinning gray hair. He was sixty-five years old. Loudly he complained of the bad road over which he had to travel each day to attend the trial. He declared that the trial should have been held in the comparatively civilized surroundings of Nairobi, and contemptuously brushed aside the Kenya authorities' argument that in Nairobi the Crown witnesses would certainly have been intimidated and quite possibly murdered.

Pritt was so much disliked by the white settlers, all of whom believed that Kenyatta and the other five accused should have been shot or hanged out of hand, that the Kenya Government had provided him with a bodyguard. The bodyguard was a tall, well-muscled young policeman who followed Pritt about with a heavy tread, never taking his anxious eyes off him, like a nursemaid in charge of an unpredictable child. His anxiety was justified, for Pritt, who had objected volubly to having a bodyguard at all, shook off the nursemaid whenever he got an opportunity.

Pritt invited me to meet the accused. I wondered if Jomo Kenyatta would recall our previous meeting; if he did, he gave no sign of it. He shook hands, grinning and showing a big front tooth that protruded over his bearded lower lip.

He wore an open-neck orange-colored shirt, corduroy trousers, and a broad leather belt embroidered with colored beads. I had been told that it was because of his fondness for this sort of belt, which is called a *kenyatta*, that he had received his name. His real name was Johnstone Kamai. As a child he had been taken care of by a Church of Scotland mission; he was suffering from a spinal complaint. Brought up and educated by missionaries, he was now charged with "managing" the Mau Mau, whose avowed aim was to destroy all missions and drive all white men into the sea. The name "Jomo," which he had adopted early in his career, meant "Burning Spear."

Jomo and the other five prisoners grouped themselves around a table and discussed their case with Pritt. Fred Kubai, who was supposed to be Jomo's chief lieutenant, was a big man with a beard and mustache. Achieng Oneko was tall and thin, with a narrow skull and a long, lean face. Two other bearded prisoners were Kunga Kurumba, and Bildad Kaggia, who looked like a diminutive Haile Selassie. The youngest was Paul Ngei, clean-shaven, with a small round head and angry eyes.

These men had been teachers, journalists, politicians, even preachers. All were members of the Kenya African Union. They were either dyed-in-the-wool conspirators, as all the white settlers thought; or else they were innocent men, imprisoned and persecuted because they had dared to criticize white rule in Africa, as most Africans, not only in Kenya, firmly believed. Grouped round gray-haired Pritt in the bare little prisoners' waiting-room at Kapenguria, they looked harmless enough.

Jomo dominated his fellow prisoners. When they were brought from the waiting-room into the courtroom, he led the way, briskly swinging his arms and thrusting out his broad chest, like a soldier on parade. He appeared fitter and less paunchy than when I had last seen him, at Nyeri, before the Mau Mau terror began.

The courtroom looked just what it really was: a classroom in a small country school. The spectators sat on wooden chairs, facing the teacher's desk, which had become the magistrate's bench. Behind the bench was a long blackboard and, on the wall above it, a color portrait of the Queen of England, wearing a crown.

Against the wall, on the magistrate's right and the spectators' left, was a narrow bench. The prisoners sat on this, their backs to the windows. In front of them, penning them rather closely against the wall, was a stout wooden bar, resting on two uprights. On either side of them stood an African policeman, wearing a red fez, a blue jersey, and khaki shorts.

Facing the magistrate's bench, but a little in advance of the public who occupied the whole of the back portion of the classroom, were Pritt and the other defense lawyers, and, directly under the magistrate's bench, the prosecutor, a large man with a boyish face, who wore a black alpaca jacket and chalk-striped gray trousers.

The people who had come to watch the trial were mostly local white farmers and their wives. The men sat in their shirtsleeves. The women were bareheaded and wore cotton dresses. They whispered among themselves and consumed fruit drops, which they carried in tins. One woman passed the time industriously working at a piece of tapestry on a wooden frame.

The magistrate, Ramsley Thacker, had a plump, square face, a strong nose, and thin black hair brushed straight back off a square forehead. He took copious notes as the trial proceeded.

Most of the prisoners had copied Jomo's style of dress. Kubai wore a leather jacket and khaki trousers, Ngei a red shirt. Kurumba had khaki trousers, but Kaggia had on a neat dark-blue suit, and Oneko wore a green tie and well-creased brown trousers. They leaned on the wooden bar in front of them, listening intently, but showing little sign of emotion.

The course of the trial had been marked by storms. Pritt declared that to hold it in so remote a place amounted to a denial of justice. The magistrate took this as a personal reflection and charged Pritt before the Supreme Court in Nairobi with contempt. This charge failed, but there followed angry scenes between Pritt and the prosecutor, Anthony Somerhough. Like all lengthy trials, the Kapenguria trial also had its dull patches. But there was nothing dull about the conclusion of it.

In a courthouse more heavily guarded than ever, with armored cars outside and sandbags and barbed wire round the doors, the magistrate began a long summing up. Military planes flew overhead, for the authorities still took seriously the Mau Mau threat to set Kenyatta free. A piquant touch was added by the Duke of

Manchester, serving in Kenya as a police reservist, who checked passes as people entered the courtroom.

Storm clouds rolled up, and lightning flashed ominously from cloud-wreathed Mount Elgon. The courtroom became so dark that the magistrate had to halt the proceedings while kerosene lamps were brought in. Then, while the lightning spasmodically split the gloom, he found Kenyatta and the other five guilty and sentenced them to seven years' imprisonment.

The Mau Mau had threatened the magistrate's life, and this threat was also treated with extreme seriousness. As soon as the trial concluded, Thacker was whisked off in a motor-car, with armed escort. All other traffic was held up while he got away over a heavily patrolled road lit with flares. A special plane awaited him, to fly him out of Kenya altogether, to Entebbe in Uganda. From there he was flown direct to London.

Jomo and the other five immediately lodged an appeal against the judgment.

: 4 :

ITS GRAY stone softened by green climbing plants, the solid-looking house fitted snugly into the hillside. Beyond the terrace there was a sharp drop to the valley, and the windows of the house looked straight across at the blue-misted mountains on the other side. There was a smooth green park planted with sturdy trees, and riding-horses were being saddled before breakfast. Michael Blundell came out of his front door, lightly swishing a riding-crop, and a groom touched his cap to him. The scene might have been laid in an English shire, except that the groom was black and in his other hand Blundell carried an automatic pistol.

At the Stag's Head Hotel in Nakuru, a notice at the reception desk invited guests to park their revolvers, rifles, and Sten guns before going in to dinner. Round the corner, in the Rift Valley Club, the club members, wearing regimental ties and looking collectively like David Low's Colonel Blimp, drank their gins and cursed the Mau Mau. Otherwise Nakuru looked the same as when I had last seen it.

From the Stag's Head I telephoned Michael Blundell, and he cordially invited me to drive over to his farm, twenty-five miles away. At intervals along the road were white signposts pointing the way to other farms. On the hillsides were perched country houses with broad lawns, dominating neatly plowed fields. This was the heart of the White Highlands, where Kenya's gentlemen farmers owned many thousands of fertile acres. Michael Blundell was the first gentleman.

"It's a long way from Yorkshire," I said.

He smiled agreeably, like a man who knows he has come a long way. "When I arrived in Kenya, eighteen years ago," he said, "I was taken on as a farm pupil. I had to learn the business the hard way. When I bought this land"—he waved a hand at the park with its handsome trees, the creepered house with its stone terrace—"it was virgin bush." Before the Mau Mau troubles began, he was offered £75,000—$210,000—for his farm at Subukia, and turned the offer down.

Now barely forty, Blundell is also the political leader of the Kenya white settlers. I had seen him in Nairobi, striding briskly through the dim corridors of the Memorial Hall, where the Electors' Union has its offices, and at meetings of the Legislative Council. If Kenya ever gets "self-government," which is what the white settlers really want, Blundell will be Prime Minister. Should Kenya, Tanganyika, and Uganda ever be welded into a new British East African dominion, which the whites would also like to see, Blundell will be the boss. Meanwhile, with his fair, close-cropped hair, boyish smile, and blunt features, he looks like a farmer and a Yorkshireman. Meanwhile, also, there is the Mau Mau.

After Blundell had returned from taking his six-year-old daughter, Susan, for her morning ride, we sat down to a hearty English breakfast: grapefruit, porridge with cream, eggs and bacon, coffee. Sharing the meal were Blundell's wife, Geraldine, a silvery-haired creature of elfin charm, and a young man with a ginger mustache, Douglas Everard.

Formerly a policeman in Palestine, Everard was Blundell's bodyguard. Blundell had received a series of crudely written letters from the Mau Mau leaders. "You and your family will all die," said one of those sinister communications, "and be sure your deaths will not be easy."

While we were at breakfast, the telephone rang. Everard went to answer it. "Just the usual check-up," he said, sitting down again.

Blundell explained apologetically: "The police ring my number every few hours, to make sure the wires haven't been cut. Bit of a nuisance," he added.

Outside, seen through the diamond-pane windows, the lawn glistened smoothly in the morning sunshine. But as I looked, an African policeman strolled slowly past, with a rifle on his shoulder. He was on sentry duty. And both Blundell and Mrs. Blundell, I noticed, took their automatics with them wherever they went.

Blundell conducted me round the farm. With pride he showed me his prize Guernsey bull, his mill for grinding corn, and his neat asparagus fields. "I grow them and a chap next door cans them," he explained. Wherever we went, Everard trotted obediently along. Up at the house, Mrs. Blundell was looking after Susan—with the African policeman patrolling the garden path with his rifle.

Blundell read my thoughts. "Yes, it all seems a bit fantastic, doesn't it?" He smiled. "But I've got to think of Geraldine and Susan. It would be stupid to take risks."

Thinking of Roger Ruck and his family, I fervently agreed.

"One night we were wakened by someone knocking at a window," Blundell said. He smiled at Everard. "That was before we had Douglas to protect us. It was a kid, a child of one of the Kikuyu farm workers. We let her in, of course, and she sobbed out her story. Poor kid was terrified out of her wits.

"A Mau Mau gang was on the farm. They'd arrived in secret a couple of nights before, and they proceeded to torture several of my workers into taking the oath. They got them into a hut and beat them up. One man was almost strangled to death before he gave in. I was going about the farm on my normal business, you understand. I spoke to those people several times in the course of the day. Not one of them dared warn me that there was a Mau Mau gang on my land, threatening and torturing them. Until this little kid crept out by night and gave us the alarm I knew absolutely nothing about it." Blundell paused.

"We managed to round up most of the Mau Mau people," he went on. "And the oath-administrator turned out to be a young Kikuyu I knew well. He was a well-educated, politely spoken chap—a carpenter by trade, who'd done odd jobs about the farm. He was the last man I'd have suspected. Now do you wonder why a lot of us farmers find it difficult to trust any Kikuyu?"

At dinner that evening there were candles on the table, and behind our chairs stood "boys" in white gowns, wearing red sashes and red fezzes. They changed our plates and filled our glasses with silent deftness. Blundell watched me watching them and smiled. "They're not Kikuyus," he said.

He told me a story. "I made a broadcast, advising the farmers to discharge their Kikuyus, or, if that wasn't possible, never to allow a Kikuyu into the house after nightfall. The broadcast was much criticized. I was told such advice was drastic, unnecessary, and brutal. But the sad truth is that many if not most Kikuyus have been compelled to take one or more of the seven Mau Mau oaths. The oath has a terrible binding power. Once a Kikuyu has taken it, even under duress, he feels bound to keep it.

"My broadcast talk was partly in the interests of the Kikuyus themselves. I know a Kikuyu who worked for a farmer for over twenty years. One day he went to his *bwana*. 'I'm leaving,' he said. 'They made me take the oath. Now if I get a chance to kill you, I won't be able to trust myself. So it's better that I should go away at once.' "

Blundell grinned. "All the same, my broadcast had some odd results. Soon afterwards a peppery old ex-colonel puffed up to me in Nairobi. 'By gad, Michael,' he said, 'you were absolutely right: I didn't want to sack my "boy," but I wasn't going to let him catch me bending, either. So when he brought in my meals, I sat at table covering him with a shotgun at every course. After two days the beggar left me. Guilty conscience, what? Fellow was obviously a Mau Mau all the time. Just shows you can't trust a Kuke!' "

After dinner Everard took me down a long passage to the back door of the house. He satisfied himself that the door was locked and bolted. Seated in the stone passage, drowsing over a brazier, were three African police guards. They were wrapped in their greatcoats against the cold night air of the mountains; they all clasped rifles.

As we returned to the living-room, the telephone rang. "Damn that thing," said Everard. "Police checking up on us, I suppose." It was.

In the living-room, Blundell sat in a chintz-covered armchair near the big log fire. Mrs. Blundell was curled up in an armchair opposite him. Beside Blundell's chair was a rack of English magazines, Punch and the Tatler among them. He wore spectacles, which gave him an older look, and he was reading the air-mail edition of the London Times. His automatic lay on the arm of his chair. Mrs. Blundell had her automatic on a small table beside her. She was sewing.

"A typical peaceful Kenya scene," said Blundell dryly, looking up as we entered.

The curtains were drawn across the windows. The big room, with its chintzy furniture and tall pink-shaded lamp standards, had a cozy English look. Outside, in the garden, the African policeman no doubt patrolled with his rifle. At the back of the house were the three guards. The log fire crackled pleasantly.

Once Blundell got up from his chair to cross the room to mix himself a drink. Everard, who had been gazing into the fire, looked at him and then meaningly at Blundell's chair.

"Uh-uh!" he said.

Blundell almost blushed. "Sorry," he said.

He went back to his chair, picked up his automatic, and carried it with him across the room.

"Douglas insists that we do it," Mrs. Blundell explained. "He says he wants us to acquire a habit of vigilance."

Everard said quietly: "Gibson, one of the chaps the Mau Mau killed, was found dead on his own living-room carpet. His gun was on a side table a few feet away. He'd left it to cross the room to switch on the radio when they burst in on him."

There was no need to ask who "they" were.

Presently Blundell put down his *Times* and began to talk.

"I used to think most of our problems in Kenya could be solved by reforms, especially economic ones," he said. "But I've come, reluctantly, to the conclusion that you can't fight a thing like Mau Mau with more schools and more lavatories."

He went on: "In one way, but perhaps not the way some of our critics think, we whites are to blame for Mau Mau. The Kikuyus have acquired our civilization faster than any of the other tribes. It's we who've forced the pace—partly, of course, for our own selfish ends. But we've compelled the Kikuyus to try to assimilate two thousand years of civilization in fifty years. The result has been mental bewilderment and spiritual frustration.

"Mau Mau is a deliberate turning back to the primitive: it's atavistic. Of course, it's thoroughly anti-white, and anti-Christian. That is because the white men, including the missionaries, put this strain on the Kikuyu mind, under which the Kikuyu mind has temporarily broken down. They're rebelling against us primarily because we have taken away from them what they had—their tribal customs, their laws, their whole social structure—and we have put nothing really satisfying in its place."

Privately, I thought the color-bar as practiced in Kenya might also have something to do with it, but I did not like to say so. In any case, Blundell had gone on.

The chief mistake the British had made in Africa, he thought, was shrinking from deciding what would be good for Africans, and then going ahead and doing it, letting the chips fall where they might. "We have forgotten that we are an Imperial People," he said sternly, sounding the capital letters.

"Do you think that other people—not Africans—are supplying the Mau Mau with arms and ideas?" I asked delicately. It was a ticklish question, for I had heard many white settlers make such an allegation more specifically.

Blundell hesitated. "No, I don't," he said. "Not quite in the way you mean. But, you know, the Indians would like to see the British chucked out of Africa. They believe they could do a deal with the Africans, because of their brown skins. India has a colonizing eye on this part of the world. Indians resent our presence, for a number of reasons. They'd like to take our place in Africa."

So we had come back to the color-bar, after all.

322

XXII

UGANDA:
THE BISHOP AND THE CROCODILE

THEY WERE having an air display at Entebbe, the capital of Uganda. Vampire jets screamed across the blue sky like silver arrows shot into the equatorial sun. They trailed their vapor over the shining surface of the lake, then returned to power-dive above the nervously ducking heads of the crowd. A Vickers Viscount showed its paces, and an Ethiopian plane with the Lion of Judah painted on its side was whooshed into the air by its special rocket burst.

For days Africans had been converging on Entebbe from all parts of Uganda. They trudged along Uganda's red roads, past the banana trees and the cotton-fields, or came on bicycles, with the girls riding pillion and clutching their cycling swains' waists. But the Kabaka of Buganda, King Edward Mutesa II, came from his hilltop palace in Kampala in a big black limousine, with his pretty young Queen, the Nabagereka, at his side, wearing a pink silk dress and a hat with ostrich feathers.

A party of British newspapermen had been flown in from London specially for the event, but I arrived alone and unheralded and did not even know there was to be an air show. I just wanted to visit Uganda. When I pushed my way through the crowds and went behind the scenes in search of my old friend Tom Parry, whom I vaguely knew to be working for the Uganda Government in some capacity, I found the event being conducted with somewhat less than the traditional British phlegm and stolidity.

323

A tall, thin man with a gray mustache stood wringing his hands and emitting a curious wailing noise. He looked like one of P. G. Wodehouse's peers who had lost his prize-winning pig. He clutched at my arm as I passed and fixed me with a hopeful if watery blue eye.

"I say!" he ejaculated. "Have you by any chaunce seen Miss Smythe-Hopgood?"

I shook my head. "I'm a stranger here myself."

Though disconcerted, he managed a toothy smile. "Fact is," he confided, with a small giggle, "Miss Smythe-Hopgood has got His Excellency's speech. Bit awkward, what? You haven't by any chaunce seen Miss— But no, of course not; you don't *know* them, do you? Only, you see, *she* might know where Miss Smythe-Hopgood would be, and *then* I could give H.E. his speech."

He shook his head ruefully, and vanished in a swirl of people, all looking as harassed as he.

I finally found Tom Parry, talking to a fat man with a blue chin and a very young man wearing horn-rimmed spectacles and a serious look. He greeted me joyously and introduced his companions. They were lecturers who had been sent to Uganda by the British Council. Then he looked at his watch.

"It's about time for the Governor's speech."

"If they've found it," I said.

Tom turned on me a look of bleak horror. "Don't tell me they've lost it *again!*"

"How often does it happen?" I asked.

"I must find Miss Smythe-Hopgood!" said Tom agitatedly, and dashed off, perspiring freely.

I turned my attention to my two new friends, who were silently regarding me with that look of nervous disapproval with which I had by now become familiar in those British African colonies every time I opened my big mouth too wide. To break the ice, I asked: "Tell me, to whom do you lecture, and about what?"

The very young man with the horn-rimmed spectacles looked

appealingly at the fat man with the blue chin, who cleared his throat in a portentous manner.

"We lecture," he said, as if he were about to commence a lecture now, "to the native school-children, y'know."

"Good," I said, thinking of all those millions of Africa's children who, God knew, badly needed all the instruction they could get; "fine. And you lecture on—?"

The blue-chinned man cleared his throat again. "Well," he said, "at the moment, y'know, we're dealing with T. S. Eliot."

"His poetry," explained the very young man.

"The inner meaning," said the blue-chinned man proudly.

The tall, thin man with the gray mustache came by. "You haven't," he asked, "by any chaunce seen some of the newspaper fellahs?"

I denied all knowledge of the newspaper fellahs.

He shook his head and giggled nervously. "Dear, dear! Then I seem to have lost them. They went off to Kilembe this morning. I fear they will not find it easy to get back. No transport. Someone seems to have overlooked their transport back."

He drifted away, then returned. "But I found Miss Smythe-Hopgood," he said triumphantly. "So it's all right about the speech."

His Excellency the Governor of Uganda duly delivered his speech, probably being in ignorance to this very day how near he came to not making it. Afterwards we were shepherded into a large hall for the exhibition of photographs illustrating the Progress Made by Uganda.

Tom Parry took me round and seemed anxious to have my opinion. I inspected the photographs. They showed the Governor having tea with a native chief; the Governor opening a new hospital; the Governor having tea with a bishop; the Governor giving a garden party. The Governor was featured in other roles, as they say, too numerous to mention. In nearly all of them, however, he wore a white uniform and a hat with white plumes. He looked indefatigably gracious. It was a terrific exhibition, if you wanted to study the Progress Made by the Governor. There wasn't much about Uganda.

: 2 :

THROUGHOUT THE Empire, wherever British colonial servants forgather, Entebbe is famed for its gardens, tennis-courts, and golf course, which are among the Empire's finest. Entebbe is almost exclusively populated by British colonial servants, who tactfully assist King Edward Mutesa II and his three neighboring "protected" monarchs to run the four Negro kingdoms that mainly constitute the green and fertile little country called Uganda.

I was staying at a hotel in Entebbe. The hotel's wide green lawns faced Lake Victoria. From the terrace one could watch the Empire-builders plodding off across the smooth lawns every morning and afternoon to their tennis and golf. Each golfing Empire-builder had in attendance on him a covey of black caddies.

I sat on the terrace with Jim Larkins, who was a mining engineer. He also had a rough, red neck and strong views.

"They're all so bloody genteel!" boomed Mr. Larkins. "When you talk to them about copper and cobalt, iron and phosphates —and this country's full of minerals—they look at you as if you'd told a dirty story in a lady's presence." He drank beer moodily. "The other day I was talking to one of them about the mine at Kilembe. When I'd finished, he sighed and said: 'Ah, well, I suppose change must come to Uganda—though it seems a pity. But at any rate I hope you *thrusting* chaps will leave us our tennis'!"

He pointed to the wide smooth lawns, which were dotted by melancholy, slow-moving black figures, who were making leisurely sweeping motions with their arms, each looking like a half-awake Father Time.

"When Winston Churchill came here, 'way back in 1908, he had a look at the lake, and he had a look at the river—this is

326

the true source of the Nile, you know—and then he went up and had a look at the Ripon Falls. And he said: 'What fun it would be to make the Nile begin its long journey by going through a turbine!'

"Well, they're still talking about vast electricity schemes. But their lawns are still scythed by hand!"

"You are a disgruntled, embittered, *thrusting* man," I said. "But even you must admit Uganda is a very *peaceful* place. If you compare it with Kenya, just across the border—"

"Uganda," said Larkins, "is the place where all the clocks have stopped. It's still living in Victoria's cozy reign. Tennis and afternoon tea. Have you been to afternoon tea in Entebbe?"

"Not yet," I said.

"You wait," said Larkins ominously.

"What do they do?"

"I was once asked to afternoon tea by the Under-Secretary for Agriculture or somebody. I asked if I could bring a pal along, and he said: 'Sure.' My pal was in the Government service too. He didn't seem at all keen, but I dragged him along. It almost caused a diplomatic crisis.

"You see," Larkins explained, "my pal was the Under-Secretary of Posts and Telegraphs or something. And in Entebbe the Under-Secretary of Posts and Telegraphs ranks below the Under-Secretary for Agriculture. So they do not mingle socially. Nor do their wives. They incline the head slightly when they pass each other on the street, but that is all."

"How many whites are there in Entebbe, all together?" I asked.

"About two hundred and fifty," said Larkins.

"How do the social inferiors amuse themselves, if they're never asked to tea by their betters?"

"They sneak off to the Indian cinema in Kampala."

I forsook Larkins, who had work to do, and sneaked off to Kampala myself.

Seen from any one of its seven hills, the town had a pretty and pleasing air. The houses, all pink and cream, tumbled down the sides of the hills into picturesque, crowded, narrow streets.

327

The souls of the people were well catered for. Dominating the town were a Roman Catholic cathedral, an Anglican cathedral, a glittering white mosque, and a Hindu temple. On one of the remaining hills was the palace of the Kabaka, and on another the red-roofed buildings of Makerere College.

But when I descended from my hill, the town at closer quarters proved to be less pleasant. These crowded picturesque streets had a flyblown look. The shops, mostly owned by Indians, were dusty, with sad interiors. Kampala was a smaller and barer Nairobi, without any of Nairobi's superficial main-street smartness.

I called on A. C. Duffield, the brown-eyed editor of the *Uganda Herald*. On his office wall hung a souvenir of the Allied campaign in Abyssinia: a road-sign that he had personally removed from outside an Abyssinian village.

"We were in a pretty tight spot," explained Duffield. "I didn't think we were going to get out alive. I decided that if we ever did, I should have something to remind me of the place. There wasn't anything to take except that road-sign, so I took it."

Uganda, said Duffield, was really progressing, despite Larkins's grumbles. He admitted it was progressing mainly because of men like Larkins. Work was being done on the country's mineral deposits. Textile mills were going up at Jinja. Above all, a vast hydroelectric project was planned, based on Winston Churchill's old idea of making the Nile start its journey by diving through a turbine. The scheme, said Duffield, would produce thirty-four times Uganda's present electric power. Duffield wasn't at all sure what the country would do with all that electricity, if and when it really got it. He was also skeptical about the Government's plan to buy up, compulsorily if need be, cotton-ginneries now owned by Indians, for handing over to African co-operatives. The reason for the Government's move, he explained, was that the Negroes, who grew the cotton, were highly distrustful of the Indians, who bought it for ginning. The Government was planning to avert possible race tension. So were the Indians, who were highly conscious of the Negroes' feelings toward them and in a possibly belated spirit of appeasement had just built a commercial school for the Negroes' exclusive use.

In Uganda, as in East Africa, the Indians (40,000) vastly outnumbered the whites (5,000), but were themselves outnumbered by the Africans (5,000,000).

I left Duffield writing an editorial about cotton-ginneries, and toiled up the hill on which the Kabaka's palace stood. The palace was a low, red-roofed building, surrounded by a stockade of tough elephant grass, eight feet high. The palace had a silver cupola, and above the entrance was a black shield with crossed spears. Outside the gate of the stockade, a Negro sentry wearing a red hat marched briskly up and down, shouldering a rifle. Near the palace, and also encircled by a stockade of elephant grass, was the home of the Prime Minister, or Katikiro.

Though Uganda is a peaceful place, its recent politics have been turbulent. The job of Katikiro is no sinecure. Attempts to assassinate previous Katikiros have taken such forms as setting fire to them while they lay asleep in bed, and taking pot shots at them on the steps of one of Kampala's cathedrals.

There is nothing very surprising in this. Uganda politics have always been riddled with intrigue, move and countermove sparked when occasion demanded by murder. Edward Mutesa II was educated at Cambridge, is an honorary colonel of the Grenadier Guards, is no stranger at Buckingham Palace, and likes to be seen wearing gray flannels and a regimental tie. But his grandfather, Mwanga, worshipped crocodiles.

When the first white missionaries invaded Mwanga's kingdom, in the nineteenth century, they came in two rival batches, English Protestants and French Roman Catholics. Mwanga frowned on both groups, and finally murdered an English bishop and had some scores of Christian Negroes burned alive.

The other Christian Negroes banded together against Mwanga, who was forced to flee. But then the Christian Negroes split into two groups, Protestants and Catholics, and began a civil war. The British then stepped in, in the person of

Captain Lugard, later made a lord, and took everyone, including Mwanga, under their protection.

If Uganda's innumerable crocodiles are no longer openly worshipped, there is still a good deal of respect for them. This is because they are believed to contain the souls of the departed great, including Mwanga himself.

About the time I was there, a small crocodile was discovered in the Kabaka's ornamental lake, which is about the size of a Hollywood star's swimming-pool. There was considerable mystery as to how the crocodile had got there. But people remembered that the little lake had once been the sacred lake where Mwanga kept a sacred crocodile. The inference was clear: Mwanga had come back, disguised as a croc.

The hardheaded men of the Uganda Game Department were not particularly interested, however, in this aspect of the crocodile. Their job is to kill crocodiles and other pests. So they descended upon the Kabaka's lake to dispatch the crocodile. But the crocodile proved elusive, so the lake was drained. When it was emptied, there was still no sign of the crocodile. It had apparently got away.

Shortly afterwards great rains swept down on Uganda. There were damaging floods. Rivers burst their banks.

But that was not all. Concurrently with the floods, every river, lake, and swamp suddenly swarmed with crocodiles. There were crocodiles everywhere. They came out on the flooded roads, and signs had to be hastily erected, warning travelers that if they saw a crocodile waddling toward them along the road, it was real, not an illusion. Several travelers had narrow escapes.

The Kabaka's subjects had their own perfectly simple explanation of the phenomenon. The crocodile that got away really had been old King Mwanga. Justifiably annoyed by the attentions of the Game Department, he had loosed a crocodile plague on the land.

In his stockaded palace the Kabaka thoughtfully fingered his regimental tie, but said nothing. It was generally believed, however, that, as between the martyred crocodile who might or might not have been his grandfather, and the murdered bishop who had been Uganda's first martyr for a different faith, his sympathies lay with the bishop.

: 3 :

I WATCHED King Edward Mutesa II open a session of the Lukiko, or Parliament. He wore a black gown with a frilly white shirt-front, and occupied a tall-backed, heavily carved chair that stood on a dais covered with leopard-skins. A white-haired bishop, a white-tunicked British officer, and the Negro M.P.'s, some of whom wore shapeless white robes like long nightgowns, listened intently. The speech was extremely dull.

King Edward arrived to open his Parliament at the head of a medieval retinue. The procession included the royal hangmen. This was a reminder of the times when the King of Buganda ruled like a Tudor, crushing his powerful feudal nobles or enlisting their aid in war, as the occasion demanded. The Kabaka today has little or no real power, but he still insists on due respect being paid to him. Recently a noble kinsman entered the Kabaka's presence and carelessly omitted to raise both hands in the air, the traditional form by which his subjects greet the King. The Kabaka's kinsman seemed to think that he might waive this old-fashioned salutation, possibly because he, too, was educated at Cambridge and no longer believed in such stuff. He received a rude awakening. King Edward had him locked up for a whole day, and afterwards, commenting on the incident, said severely: "In my father's time that fellow would have had both hands chopped off at the wrists."

Nevertheless the Kabaka is even more circumscribed in the exercise of power than most constitutional monarchs. The British, though they do it tactfully, really rule the country, through British colonial servants. Such political assassinations or attempted assassinations as have occurred have been mainly the work of disgruntled nobles, jockeying for royal favor. The ordinary people go on growing their cotton placidly. They own their own land; and many of them are rich enough to hire other, foreign Negroes to work it for them. Negroes flock in from Ruanda-Urundi, the Belgian-mandated territory next door, to be hired by Uganda Negroes: Uganda appears to have no sharp-edged political or racial problems.

There are, however, two political parties, the Bataka Party, and the Farmers' Union Party. Both claim to represent the peasant masses, and their demands include higher prices for cotton and other products, and the replacement of Indian cotton-ginners by Africans. The Bataka Party is led, from abroad, by Kumu Mulumba, who used to be a Roman Catholic teaching brother. In 1947, Mulumba's followers raised money to send him to London to present a petition to the British Government. Mulumba duly presented the petition, but decided not to come back. Cynics declared he was leading the life of Reilly.

In Mulumba's absence, another mission-taught African aspired to political leadership: a young man called Ignatius Musazi, who formed the Farmers' Union.

Outside Kampala there was a red road lined with vegetable stalls and mud huts. Between two vegetable stalls, a wooden shack had a hand-painted sign tacked above the door. This was the headquarters of the Farmers' Union. It was occupied by a Negro wearing a green tweed jacket over his white nightgown. He was looking thoughtfully at a typewriter and sighing heavily at intervals. The sheet of paper in the typewriter remained blank.

He greeted me with the minimum of cordiality and, when I explained that I wanted to see Mr. Musazi, said briefly that Musazi was away. Away where? Somewhere "in the country." When would he be back? Nobody knew.

The Union secretary, if he were the secretary, was playing the cards close against his chest. This was probably because, after a riot in which the Farmers' Union was allegedly involved, the Uganda Government politely but firmly placed Musazi under house arrest. Relations between the Farmers' Union and all white men had since been somewhat cool. Finally giving it up, I left my card and went on my way. I never heard from Musazi.

Others told me he was having a tough time. Mulumba's long absence had not after all left a vacuum that Musazi was able to fill. On the contrary, Mulumba had strengthened his position. For when things went wrong, Musazi got the blame, because he was on the spot; whereas when the Negroes scored a political gain, Mulumba, from London, confidently assured his followers that he was responsible. "I spoke to the Colonial Secretary, and he fixed it." So Mulumba was getting all the credit and Musazi was receiving most of the kicks. It seemed to me that however assiduous the people of Uganda might be as cotton-pickers, politically they must be pretty simple. I'd have liked to talk to Musazi, to know what he thought about it. He was the proverbial prophet without honor in his own country. I felt sorry for him.

: 4 :

FROM THE Farmers' Union shack I walked stickily into Kampala —it was an extremely hot day—and gratefully flagged a taxi to take me to Makerere College. The cab was a small Ford Anglia, and its Negro driver had festooned the hood with pretty red flowers. We puffed up the hill to the college like a small mobile garden.

In the college entrance hall a number of Negro students were reading the notices pinned to a large board on the wall. Males predominated. When a couple of girl students appeared and one of the men addressed them, they giggled nervously and hastily departed.

While I waited for an audience with the college principal, Dr. de Bunsen, I read the notices. The College Dramatic Society was presenting Noel Coward's *Present Laughter*, with an all-Negro cast. The "Bookshop Essay Prize" had just been won by G. W. B. Gowa. A note attached to this announcement stated: "For this year's essay, 'Violence' was the most popular subject among students. It proved an unfortunate choice for most. The

333

subject lent itself to vague generalities and to waffle. It was decided to award the prize to Gowa because his essay contained concrete references to Buddha, Christ and Gandhi."

I was still trying to follow the line of reasoning, which struck me as somewhat peculiar, when two of the men students began a discussion at my elbow. One was a burly fellow, wearing a turtle-neck sweater and what English undergraduates call flannel bags—no white nightgown. The other, who was thin and earnest, wore spectacles, a red tie, and a gray suit.

The one in the sweater said accusingly: "I have now had an opportunity of perusing your article, in which you criticize my approach to the Lake District poets. I thought your argument was weak."

The thin and earnest one took off his spectacles and polished them defiantly. "It seemed to me," he retorted, "that you had sought to cover up serious deficiencies in understanding by resort to the camouflage of ironical hyperbole."

I decided that the emissaries of the British Council had not visited Uganda in vain, and followed a beckoning secretary upstairs to the office of Dr. de Bunsen.

The principal received me warmly. He was a tall, youngish man, with a pipe gripped between his teeth. He looked very English: the sort of man you would expect to find strolling through a spinney with a hunting dog at his heels. What he did have, curled up under his desk, was a large white dog of indeterminate breed, with a fresh gaping wound in its neck.

"He's always getting into trouble," said Dr. de Bunsen, patting the dog affectionately on the head. "Came in like that this morning, and I didn't have the heart to chuck him out. Mind you don't get any of his blood on your trousers." He wagged a finger at the dog. "Disgusting animal! That'll teach you not to fight with other dogs."

Dr. de Bunsen had formerly been Director of Education in Palestine, "until," he said with a hearty chuckle, "they threw us British out." The college, he explained, had 400 students, which number would soon be raised to 600. Only 13 of the students were women.

"We badly need more girls. They're shy, poor things. The country has a long tradition of female inferiority. But our girls are in great demand—for taking part in plays, and so on. Trouble is, they get so much of that sort of thing to do, they don't pass their exams."

Students at the college took the degrees of London University. Most of them came from Kenya, which had more schools than Uganda. But there was a Persian from Zanzibar, and two Ethiopians from Addis Ababa. There was also one Indian.

"We do try to link the courses that students choose with definite training for a specific profession," said the principal. "And we have a hospital here, where most of the surgery is now done by Africans who have been trained at Makerere. Of course we want African doctors to set themselves up in private practice. At the moment, though, in return for their bursaries, or scholarships, they work for the Government."

He got up from behind his desk. "Now let me show you round." The white dog uncurled itself from under the desk and followed us to the door. "No, sir!" said the doctor sharply. "You will jolly well stay here—nasty, bleeding animal." He closed the door on the dog, and we went on our way.

We passed a number of students, carrying books under their arms, who greeted the principal respectfully. Dr. de Bunsen beamed on them. In the library, students were poring over books and magazines. Sunlight filtered down the long corridors. Somewhere a bell tolled. The college had a peaceful, academic hush. Outside, students strolled on bright green grass, and insects droned in the flower-beds. A white lecturer perched on a sun-splashed wall was smoking a pipe and talking to a group of young Negroes who stood about him with their hands in the pockets of their flannel bags. Not many miles away, in Kenya, white troopers were hunting down Mau Mau gangs, and armed Kikuyu were attacking white farmhouses.

Uganda was a peaceful contrast. But I wondered, as I drove off in my flower-bedecked cab after saying good-by to Dr. de Bunsen, how Noel Coward, the Lake poets, and the camouflage of ironical hyperbole would fit in with the sort of made-over

335

Uganda that men like Jim Larkins were dreaming about: a bustling Uganda busily manufacturing textiles, mining copper, and raising the level of Lake Victoria to produce more electric power. The dusky young men in the flannel bags had come a long way from Mwanga-style crocodile worship. But were they going in the right direction? I did not think you could fight disease with quotations from the classics, or grow more cotton with quips by Noel Coward. Makerere, it seemed to me, had too genteel an air for a country still pretty full of tropical squalor. Uganda needed more rugged pioneers and could dispense for a while yet with ivory-tower specialists, and with *Present Laughter*. The young men of Makerere might make either good dons or bad agitators; but what Uganda required was good engineers.

And where, also, did the tennis-playing whites of Entebbe fit in? Entebbe was like a green bush full of twittering birds, the twittering being mainly over trivialities. In grim Kenya there was death in the afternoon, but in Uganda there was only the tinkle of teacups. Henry James, I thought, would have loved it, but would Henry James have made a good colonial administrator?

Drinking beer on the terrace of the hotel at Entebbe, facing the green lawns and the shining lake, Jim Larkins savagely underscored those doubts. "The men who run Uganda," he said, "are strangling themselves with their old school ties. Most of them are pretty snooty. You wouldn't mind them being so snooty if they were competent; but when most of them are so incompetent, you wonder what the hell they've got to be so snooty about!"

He scowled at the lake. "You saw those jets the other day. They were mostly being flown by lads with broad Yorkshire accents who'd never been to Eton. They're a different breed from those Colonial Office wallahs. Engineers and mining men are moving into Uganda. They're a different breed, too. They'll build airports, dam rivers, create new towns. I don't think Entebbe is going to like it, because it may interfere with the tennis; but Entebbe will just have to lump it. Africa is changing, and Uganda can't escape change, any more than can Kenya, or

South Africa. Malan wants to keep his 'niggers' down. The British colonial servants would like to preserve Uganda as a museum of interesting 'native' customs. But the new emerging Africa is different from either."

He raised a hand and pointed to the west. "Over there you'll find the twentieth-century revolution in full blast. They don't cut their lawns with scythes. They use motor-powered mowers. They're mining uranium, making railroads, building shipyards, and putting up factories. They haven't got any crazy color complexes, and they're not rigid with etiquette and red tape. But why don't you go to the Belgian Congo and see for yourself?"

So I did.

XXIII

BELGIAN CONGO: CONGO FURNACE

I PLANNED TO fly from Entebbe, the capital of Uganda, to Usumbura, which is the capital of the Belgians' mandated territory of Ruanda-Urundi. But things didn't quite work out that way. We flew over Lake Victoria, dotted with tree-choked islands and sandbars where crocodiles rested like wet black logs, into thick cloud. The plane bumped like a bus with a flat tire on a rough road, and there was no visibility at all. This went on for over two hours, and the radio operator must have been having a busy time. The truth was that, though we were not exactly lost, most airfields were telling us we could land where we liked so long as it wasn't on their field. Tropical downpours, no doubt sent specially by the vengeful ghost of Mwanga, had flooded hundreds of square miles of this part of Africa. We were bumping about in a shroud of cloud somewhere between Entebbe and the Mountains of the Moon, and nobody wanted us.

Finally we began to nose our way cautiously downstairs. The racing black clouds parted for a fleeting second to show a lake beneath us. Nobody, except possibly the pilot, seemed to be sure which lake it was. We circled a wooded shore and then made for a patch of bare and stony ground on top of a hill and looking about half the size of a cricket pitch. The plane's wheels hit what presumably passed for a runway, and we roared exuberantly toward a small stone building, jerking away from it only when it seemed certain that we must pass right through it.

The plane stopped, panting. The motors died. After this, nothing happened for a long time. We could see people moving about inside the solitary building, but none of them seemed greatly interested in us.

Eventually a gangway was hauled out from its hiding-place and pushed reluctantly toward the plane. The door was opened, and we descended.

We were led into the small building and formed in a queue in front of a desk. Behind the desk sat a small plump man with pale eyelashes, in a blue uniform. He stamped our passports between puffs at a cigarette.

The passengers included a sallow, black-haired man with deep circles under his eyes, and his companion, a tall woman with flat-heeled shoes who looked like a man dressed up in female clothing. The lady spoke sharply in French to the official behind the desk.

"This is not Usumbura!"

"No, madame. Everything will be explained at the air office in town."

"But where in God's name are we?"

"It is Costermansville, on Lake Kivu."

"That is ridiculous. We were to fly from Entebbe to Usumbura. Usumbura is on Lake Tanganyika, not on Lake Kivu! Have we, then, descended on the wrong lake?"

"Everything," said the official stolidly, "will be explained at the air office in town."

A small bus that had seen better days arrived on the airfield with much wheezing and groaning. Into this we were piled with our luggage. The sallow man and his grim companion had several large suitcases between them. The lady kept up a scathing running commentary on the inefficiency of all airlines, and made the Negro porters rearrange her luggage twice.

The bus jolted down the hill and toiled through a gloomy forest, over a very bad road. At frequent intervals we passed marching gangs of Negro convicts. Chained together, they were clad in rags and looked thoroughly miserable. They did not raise their heads as the bus groaned past them.

After an interminable journey we came suddenly to a pretty town on the shore of the lake. A long cobbled street ran downhill to the lake. The houses looked neat and attractive. It was like coming out of the African forest into a bit of transplanted Europe. The bus halted outside the air office. Porters began to unload the luggage. Inside the office a beautiful blonde in a tight blue tunic explained how we had come to Costermansville instead of arriving at Usumbura. The tall woman who looked like a man immediately joined issue with her.

"The plane," she said angrily, "had no right to be diverted. We have paid—"

"Madame," said the blonde, smiling seductively at the sallow man, who merely looked glum, "can proceed to Usumbura by car."

"Who will supply the car?"

"The airline, madame. It is of course without charge."

"Then we shall take it."

"What," asked another passenger, "is the road like to Usumbura?"

The blonde smiled upon him dreamily. "Monsieur, I will be frank with you. There has been much rain. I think the road is very bad."

"Then I shall stay here," said the passenger hastily. "It is already getting dark."

The sallow man coughed. "Perhaps we, too—"

"We go to Usumbura," said the tall woman.

In for a penny, in for a pound.

"I'll go too," I said.

The car, when produced, turned out to be a small stationwagon. But most of the space was already taken up with crates of vegetables and cases of beer. My luggage consisted of one grip. Nevertheless there was very little room for three passengers and my companions' several large suitcases.

"Remove this other stuff," commanded the tall woman.

"No, madame," said the driver. "It must at all costs be delivered to Usumbura."

"The beer cannot be essential."

"It too must go."

The tall woman turned to me. "Monsieur, I think it would be better if you remained in Costermansville tonight."

"Or you could leave some of your luggage to be forwarded," I suggested.

She tightened her lips. "We shall all be extremely uncomfortable. And you heard the girl say the road is very bad."

"Unfortunately I have urgent business in Usumbura."

She turned away, thwarted.

Finally everything was stowed away in the station-wagon, which bulged. A Negro appeared from nowhere and sat beside the Belgian driver: he would take turns at the wheel. My two companions occupied the remaining seats. I perched on a case of beer and hoped that the rest of the luggage would not descend on my neck. The lady sat bolt upright and shot poisonous glances all round. It was like riding with Lady Macbeth.

Outside Costermansville the road became a series of hairpin bends winding up steep hills and hanging over ravines. It was already dark, and now it began to rain. The surface of the road was slippery, and the station-wagon skidded several times. I began to wish I had stayed behind in Costermansville.

When we had gone some twenty miles, a Negro soldier appeared out of the darkness, waving his arms in the middle of the road. The station-wagon stopped. The soldier approached the driver and handed him a rain-sodden scrap of paper. The driver read it, nodded, and proceeded to turn the station-wagon.

"The road to Usumbura is blocked," he explained. "A tractor overturned and they cannot move it until morning."

We returned to Costermansville.

: 2 :

I WOKE up in an outsize bed, situated in what appeared to be a small ballroom. Facing me was a built-in cupboard, with three enormous doors. Scattered about the ample space were square tables and round tables, armchairs, chairs with straight backs,

341

and chairs with sloping backs. I threw back the bedclothes, crawled the few feet to the edge of the bed, and got out, feeling like Gulliver among the Brobdingnagians. A brisk morning walk across several acres of parquet floor brought me to a door leading to a white-tiled bathroom, probably no larger than a small town's ball park. Immersed in hot water in the bath, I remembered where I was.

At the air office the beautiful blonde had been still up and around, though it was well after midnight, and seemed not a bit surprised at our reappearance. She had arranged hotel accommodation, and I had been swiftly separated from my companions—which occasioned me no pain at all—and driven out of town to what appeared to be a wooded peninsula on the lake shore. Amid the woods nestled a hotel like a large Swiss chalet, and I had been conducted to the bedroom where I had just awakened.

I breakfasted at a table overlooking the calm lake, with an excellent view of the pretty houses on the other side. My table companion was an engineer from Tanganyika named Leslie Ramsden, who during the war had frequently dropped into Yugoslavia as a member of an airborne tank-corps unit, and who climbed mountains for recreation.

"Everything in the Congo is big," said Leslie. "The Congo itself is eighty times the size of Belgium. The result is that the Belgians in the Congo like doing things on a large scale. They have the longest river in Africa—the Congo with its tributaries is *navigable* for six thousand miles—some of the highest mountains, the biggest forests, and the tallest people. They mine most of the world's uranium. And they have a Ten-Year Development Plan while other countries, including Russia, are content with Five-Year Plans." His face lengthened. "They also have a very high cost of living."

Leslie had come to the Belgian Congo for a holiday and was finding it exceedingly difficult to get out. He had been marooned in Costermansville for some days by the heavy rains.

"When I saw my bill I almost fainted. It ran into thousands of francs. I telegraphed to Tanga for more money, but there was some delay, and by the time the money arrived, I still owed more than I had."

Despite telegraphing, he was currently some two thousand francs in arrears, and did not see how he was ever going to catch up, because by the time more money arrived, he had run up another, bigger bill.

"Meanwhile," I said, "you are eating an excellent breakfast and enjoying a wonderful view, so why worry?"

The lake was like a mirror, reflecting slowly moving clouds that bound the silent hills with white cords. After the rains the air was fresh and everything sparkled. We might have been in Switzerland.

The manager of the hotel had recently arrived from Antwerp. He was a brisk Belgian with bright ideas. He had installed a large cocktail lounge, and he also had a fixed notion that what his customers required for their full enjoyment was plenty of music. He employed a Negro to feed records all day to a large phonograph. The records he had chosen fell into three categories: grand opera, hot jazz, and the crooning of Frank Sinatra. Arias, boogie-woogie, and Sinatra followed one another in strict rotation across the turntable, and pursued the hotel guests into their bedrooms and bathrooms and halfway across the lake.

Lake Kivu, at 4,789 feet, is the highest lake in central Africa. It is also a place of great natural beauty. Consequently many of the 70,000 Belgians in the Congo, who sweat it out in Léopoldville, mine copper in the Katanga, or supervise cotton and palm-oil plantations in the sprawling humid north, go there for holidays. But the rains had kept many people away and the lake hotel was almost empty. The new manager from Antwerp was seizing the opportunity to extend his premises. New annexes were going up, and Sinatra and the bawling Italian tenors had to compete with brisk hammering and the noise of a cement mixer.

A Negro carpenter who was wiping the honest sweat from his brow looked to me like a Nyasalander. When I asked him, he said he was.

"How did you get to the Congo?"

343

"I walked," he said simply.

Ramsden inspected a new cement doorstep with professional interest. Then he looked up at the cloud-filled sky.

"The next time it rains," he told the man from Antwerp agreeably, "you'll have puddles."

Staying at the hotel was a Swiss medical missionary. He was a tall, gaunt man with a worried look. He said grace lengthily before each meal, ate quickly, then rushed off to a near-by hospital, his face lined and his shoulders bowed with care. In time he shyly confided to us the reason for his woe.

"For years," he said, "they have been training Congo women as nurses. They have a big hospital here; everything is very modern, very spick and span. Under supervision, the nurses are excellent. The patients could not get better care. But when the nurses are left to themselves, they seem to go to pieces. Bandages are carelessly tied and filthy. Patients are neglected. This, you understand, is after years of training." He shook his head despairingly. "One sometimes almost gives up hope."

Ramsden and I borrowed the hotel manager's station-wagon and Negro driver and had ourselves conveyed into town, where we strolled about the steep cobbled streets, stopping off frequently to drink beer. The first thing the Belgians in the Congo do, when they have built a town, is to add a brewery. We found the beer of Costermansville excellent. It was pleasantly cool in the town. The neat, high-peaked houses, the placid lake, did not seem to belong to Africa at all. Some of the homes, we were told, belonged to évolués: the educated, "advanced" Negroes whom the Belgians accept, at least in theory, as social equals. (Most of their grandfathers were cannibals.) But we did not see any évolués marching into cafés and bars. We were assured that if they did, they would receive precisely the same service as whites. Perhaps they just weren't thirsty.

A newspaperman in a strange town invariably and instinctively makes for the nearest newspaper office. I persuaded Ramsden to go along, and after some difficulty we found it, in a back yard in a back street. Despite its unimposing situation, it had an imposing title: the *Centre Afrique, Journal Indépendant du Congo Oriental et du Ruanda-Urundi*. It was edited by a tall, thin, intelligent Belgian, ably assisted by his intelligent and charming wife.

This attractive couple explained a point that had been bothering me: how was the Congo being developed on an annual budget of under 80,000,000 francs? That, they said, was just the little budget, for the payment of officials' salaries and other small change. But then there was the extraordinary budget, totaling annually over 600,000,000 francs; and on top of that was the Ten-Year Plan, estimated to cost 660,000,000 *dollars*.

After this exposition, the pair of them, chattering excitedly like squirrels, abandoned their own immediate labors to produce bluebooks, documents, editorials, and discourses by the Governor-General, out of which they built up for me a graphic picture of the Congo and how it was run.

The Belgian Congo rests on a tripod of the Belgian State, Big Business, and the Roman Catholic Church. It is a paternal despotism. Nobody in the Congo, either among the 70,000 whites or the 11,000,000 blacks, has an effective political voice. The Governor-General himself, despite the pomp surrounding his big palace in Léopoldville, takes his orders from Brussels and passes them on down through layers of obedient officials.

The Ten-Year Plan has earmarked $40,000,000 for the educating and $125,000,000 for the housing and health needs of the politically voiceless blacks. Tribes may own land, but not individual Negroes. On the other hand, Negroes are encouraged to become skilled workers, and are so employed in the Congo's multiplying factories. If they elect to go to night schools for further technical training, they get paid for learning. Negroes may also borrow money from the Government, for building white-style homes for themselves, or for setting up their own small-scale enterprises. The paternalist state fixes minimum wages, minimum food rations, and minimum standards of housing for Negro workers. Private firms do not kick about this, partly because to kick against state decrees in the Congo is to risk being kicked out altogether, partly because the state is itself a large shareholder in the biggest concerns, which set the pace and dictate the business morals of the smaller fry. Negro trade unions are permitted to exist, but have about as much real influence as, say, a street trader in Moscow. Negroes work in banks and business houses as well as in factories, and may rise to high positions: those who do are the *évolués*. In the upper social strata, mixed marriages, between white and black, do infrequently occur, and when they do, nobody makes a fuss about them. About one million Congo Negroes work in white-run factories and mines, accounting, with their wives and children, for about forty per cent of the Congo's total black population. Of the remainder, a good proportion grow food, cotton, and palm oil either on their own land (but under direction and, where necessary, by compulsion) or on white-managed plantations, many of which make a South African farmer's six thousand acres look like a small cabbage patch. The rest of the Negroes, who have so far managed to evade the eye of the work-compelling Belgian big brother, live carefree in the thick tropical forests and just go fishing.

"Fifty years ago," said our instructors proudly, "the Congo did not have a single road."

"And now you have roads, with Negro convicts working on them," I said.

They did not blink an eye. "Africans who commit crimes, or who do not produce the cotton quota, may certainly be compelled to work for the state."

I let it pass. "Tell me more about your development."

The Congo is spending a lot of money on the education of the Negroes. There are about two million Negro children attending schools. It spends even more on the physical welfare of the black population. Workers, their wives, and their children get free or near-free medical attention. Women are encouraged to have their children in hospitals. The bigger private companies build hospitals and clinics but not merely for their own workers: all the Negroes in their district are encouraged to use them. The result has been a material and in some cases startling reduction in mortality rates from disease, and especially in infant mortality.

"But who pays for it all?" I asked, not being skeptical, just inquiring.

The riches of the Congo are being developed by giant Belgian corporations, working hand-in-glove with the state. The resulting structure has almost a Soviet look, though this resemblance, I was hastily assured, is only superficial. At the very top is the Société Générale de Belgique, where Belgian cabinet ministers and Belgian bankers hobnob and hand out orders. Next biggest is the Comité Spécial du Katanga (CSK), which was established as far back as 1900, with the job of developing 111,000,000 acres of mineral-rich land, and which laid the strong foundations of the Congo's present copper, cobalt, tin, and uranium fortunes. The state owns 66 per cent of CSK, which in turn owns a quarter share of the Union Minière du Haut-Katanga (UMHK), which does the actual producing of the copper, cobalt, uranium, and so on. The UMHK is a $250,000,000 outfit, with mineral rights over an area bigger than Belgium. Each year it pays out some $50,000,000 to the Government, and half of that to its private shareholders. The Société Générale, the CSK, and the UMHK are the three biggest noises in the Congo.

But they by no means exhaust the list. There are, for example, the CFL (Chemin de Fer du Congo-Supérieur aux Grands Lacs Africains), which controls railroads; Huilever, which has a palm-oil concession over 4,000,000 acres; and such organizations as Sogelec (electricity), Sogechim (chemicals), and Inéac (Institut National pour l'Étude Agronomique du Congo Belge), which was established in 1933 to direct all agriculture in the Congo and which today has far-flung laboratories, meteorological stations, and experimental farms over the whole one million square miles of the Belgian domain in Africa.

Later I checked on all this information to the best of my ability, and all of it, as far as I could judge, was perfectly accurate; but when it was first given me, I looked somewhat dubiously from the glowing faces of my two informants round the crowded little office where they produced their small newspaper. I also thought of the bad road to Usumbura, and the ragged convicts I had seen on the road into town from the airport.

They understood my look and laughed.

"You have come into the Congo by the back door," said the editor of the *Centre Afrique, Journal Indépendant du Congo Oriental et du Ruanda-Urundi*, cheerfully. "Go to Léopoldville. Go to Elisabethville. See for yourself."

It began to rain again as Leslie Ramsden and I started back to the lake hotel. Leslie looked at the black clouds overhead and groaned. He was worrying about his finances again. That evening, with maps spread on the floor, he tried to work out a way of escaping from the Congo back to Tanganyika, even if there should be no available plane. We finally decided he would have to walk across to Lake Victoria, catch a lake steamer to Entebbe, and fly from there to Nairobi, where he might be able to get another plane to Tanga: the whole operation would probably take a month or two.

That evening the hotel manager announced that all main-line air services had now been resumed. The situation was saved.

Next morning, early, we set off in the hotel station-wagon. The other passenger was the Swiss medical missionary, still brooding about the shortcomings of Congo nurses. The hotel manager from Antwerp came to say good-by. The big phonograph was still churning out grand opera, jazz, and Frank Sinatra. It was raining, and the new cement doorstep had puddles, just as Ramsden had said it would.

I had changed my plans, deciding to go straight to Elisabethville and then on to Léopoldville. At the air depot in town, arguing vehemently with the beautiful blonde in the tight blue tunic, were two familiar figures, the sallow black-haired man with the deep circles under his eyes, and the tall woman in flat-heeled shoes who looked like a man dressed in female clothing. They were surrounded by their several large suitcases. When I got into the air bus and drove away, I left them there, arguing. They were still trying to get to Usumbura.

: 3 :

THE PLANE was late in departing. There were few passengers, but no waste of space: the seats up front were heaped with automobile tires, and there were crates of live chickens down the aisle. Instead of the usual air hostess there was a smart young Negro, male, in a stiffly starched white uniform. He stood at the back of the plane all the way.

The DC-3 got out of cloud at about six thousand feet, and we stayed at that altitude. Below us dense forest was broken by great stretches of perfectly flat country which was a vivid emerald in color. We passed over two rivers, both running strongly and colored a bright red. Gauguin would probably have loved the Congo. But presently all this faded like a dream, giving place to the more familiar African bush as we flew south. This arid bushland, down near the border with Northern Rhodesia, is the treasure-house of the Congo, the Katanga. It contains the great copper and cobalt mines and, not far from them, Shinkolobwe, the world's largest and most closely guarded uranium mine. There is a chunk of uranium from Shinkolobwe in the museum at Elisabethville, and visitors are warned not to go near it with loaded cameras: it is so radioactive that it immediately fogs their film. This museum specimen is as close as any visitor ever gets to the Congo's uranium. Shinkolobwe is strictly out of bounds to everyone, including Belgians.

I landed at Elisabethville and was driven to the Sabena guest-house, which is something to see. The room I was given was not so large as the one I had had at Costermansville—it was only the size of a full suite—but the bathroom attached was more opulent. Water, scalding or cold according to taste, came out of chromium faucets the size of fists, and hanging on a heated roller were several tent-size fleecy towels. I scrubbed, feeling like Nero amid this splendor, then dined in the guest-house's large restaurant off lobster and red wine to the soft music of sighing violins. After which I went to bed.

Elisabethville's newspapers next morning had startling, inch-high headlines. A Government decree, freshly signed, authorized the shooting on sight of any persons found within the boundaries of the Shinkolobwe uranium mine who had no right to be there. As the decree itself ran to only about three lines of print, the newspapers had had to fill up their headline space somehow. They had done so in various ways. Theories to account for the official action included the discovery of "American journalists" lurking behind the bushes near the entrance to the mine, and the uncovering of a Communist plot whereby Red agents were smuggling away samples of uranium handed over to them by Negro workers.

I rang up a friend of mine and arranged to meet him in town at the Leopold II Hotel.

Elisabethville has pretty streets, some of them cobbled, and is surrounded by pleasant green meadows. The houses are picturesque, with high-pointed slate roofs and red-painted doors and windows. As in other parts of the Congo, you don't get any feeling of being within a thousand miles of Africa. Elisabethville also contains the imposing offices of the CSK, the UMHK, and other giant corporations. The creation of Elisabethville was *decreed*, in 1910. There was nothing there at all. Then a provincial governor said there ought to be, and there was. This is a good example of how the Belgians have set about their task in the Congo. When they arrived in the Katanga, its population consisted of cowed Negroes and warlike Arab slave-traders, surrounded by cannibalistic tribes with sharp-filed teeth.

I stopped frequently to admire the gardens, filled with tropical blooms, and the handsome statues in the town's large squares. Women, wearing shorts, were bicycling briskly about with shopping baskets attached to their handlebars. Men, in white tropical suits, were sitting at tables on the sidewalks, drinking beer. I looked to see if there were any black *évolués* among them, but the *évolués* of Elisabethville were apparently not making free of the cafés any more than the *évolués* of Costermansville had done. The beer-drinkers were exclusively white.

My friend, who shall be nameless because he is still there and the Belgians may still be resentful of snooping American journalists, was waiting for me at the Hotel Leopold II. We ordered coffee and were served in addition with stickily sweet buns.

"What's all this about Shinkolobwe?" I demanded.

He chuckled. "I thought you would ask. You can forget it."

"Do they usually shoot people on sight around here?"

"Not as a rule. But they're a little nervous at the moment—so many people are interested in uranium."

"There must have been some specific happening to produce the new decree."

He chuckled again. "There was. A couple of 'intruders' were found near the mine. But the true story is that they turned out to be two Belgian schoolboys who were birdnesting in the woods."

"How about 'lurking American journalists'?"

"Well, we had a couple of American newspapermen here. They were writing articles about the Congo. They got on fine until they started asking questions about Shinkolobwe. They were put over the border, protesting."

"But look!" I said, protesting myself, "the Belgians are selling their uranium to the United States, aren't they? If these were *bona fide* newspapermen, they were entitled to ask questions, so long as that's all they did. Nobody was obliged to answer the questions."

"The Belgians are scared of Americans who ask questions," said my friend. "In fact, they're scared of Americans period. They say: 'Belgium is so small, America is so large. Perhaps Americans want to take over the uranium and mine it themselves.' "

"That's ridiculous."

"Of course. But the Belgians aren't rational on the subject. They've got this stuff, which wasn't even worth much a few years ago, and now it's the biggest thing on earth. They're terrified of it. They're like a man who has been handed a billion dollars, in bills, and has nowhere to bank it. They suspect everybody, but chiefly they suspect the two nations who're most interested in uranium: America and Russia. They see 'poor little

Belgium' as the small man who's got clutched to his bosom what the big fellows want. They peek under the bed each night, looking for two things: Reds and Yanks. And when they see anything, they scream like a frightened spinster, even when it turns out to be only two schoolboys gone birdnesting."

"Going back to the two American newspapermen," I said, "did they manage to find out anything about the uranium?"

He shook his head. "No. If they had, I doubt if they'd have been put over the border."

"What would have happened to them?"

"God knows. The Belgians don't want any trouble. But they're scared men, and scared men act funny."

He said it with a smile and I think he was partly pulling my leg. Partly.

"What about this alleged Communist plot?" I asked.

His smile faded. "I just wouldn't know."

"But you're here, on the spot. You must hear things."

"I wouldn't know," he repeated. "Nobody knows *anything*— about Shinkolobwe. I don't even know what the mine looks like, what area it covers, how it's guarded, how many people work there; it may have electrified fences a mile high, and tall watch-towers and guards with machine-guns; or on the other hand it may be just an ordinary-looking mine like the copper and cobalt outfits, which are big but strictly normal. I wouldn't know; and I've got no intention of trying to find out."

I thought over what he had said. "I don't think I'll bother to try to get to Shinkolobwe," I ventured.

"No; if I were you, I shouldn't bother. Not unless you want to leave the Congo, quite quickly."

Presently we were joined by a fair-haired young American who was in business in Elisabethville.

"It's a funny atmosphere," he admitted. "I don't know whether to describe it as the iron hand in the velvet glove or the velvet glove in the iron hand!"

He gave me an instance.

"I had a chap working for me, a Negro foreman. We got on pretty well. He was intelligent and curious. He asked me a lot of questions about the U.S. One of the things he was interested in was trade-unionism. As you probably know, the Negroes aren't forbidden to form trade unions here, so I thought there was no harm in giving him the information he wanted."

He paused. "I'd like you to get a clear picture of this chap. He was no radical. He liked to do a fair day's work for a day's pay, and he saw to it that the men under him did the same. I'd say that in the States he'd have been all for the A.F.L. and a bit dubious about the C.I.O.—not," he added hastily, "that I personally have anything against the C.I.O. Anyhow, he was pretty interested in everything I told him, and I knew he was passing it on to some of the others.

"Well, one day he didn't turn up to work. I waited a couple of days, thinking he might be sick; then I got worried, and started making inquiries. Nobody could tell me anything. I went to officials. They regretted they couldn't help me. They would have to go into the matter. Finally they reported that my man had suddenly left the district altogether—with, I may say, some days' pay due to him. No, they couldn't tell me why he had gone, or where, or how I could contact him. They advised me, quite kindly, to forget about it."

The young American fixed me with his very clear blue eyes. "All this," he said slowly, "in a country where a man, especially a Negro, has to carry papers all the time, and to report when he enters a district and when he leaves it; where you can't move, be you white or black, without having to inform some official who you are, what's your business, and your mother's maiden name."

"What further steps did you take?" I asked.

He shrugged. "I'd done all I could. I didn't take any further steps. I wanted to stay in business here."

I thought of the Northern Rhodesian copper belt, less than two hundred miles away, and of Lawrence Katilunga's strong black union there. I wondered just how long, despite their politer version of an Iron Curtain, the Belgians could keep "their" Negroes insulated from trade-union developments that little bit farther south.

The American said it cost a Belgian firm in the Congo an

average of $7,000 a year for each white employee—wages plus social services, which often included free or subsidized housing. "There's a lot of inflation as a result. At the same time there's an acute shortage of skilled workers. But the powers that be are opposed to large-scale white immigration from Belgium. Instead, they're breaking their necks to train Negroes to do the jobs."

"Who are the big bosses around here?" I asked.

He laughed. "There aren't any. Even the top men in Elisabethville must refer all questions of high policy to Brussels for decision. They're in the same position as His Excellency the Governor-General in Léopoldville. I doubt if he could answer you a single important question without getting Brussels' okay on it."

"How much Communist propaganda is there?"

The American shook his head. "I don't know," he confessed. But my friend looked self-conscious.

"I've got a theory about that," he said. "I think there may be quite a lot. I believe it comes in through what I call 'the Arab tunnel.' It comes right down from the Middle East. Don't forget that there are millions of Negro Moslems. The Arabs want to get back into Africa, where they used to be quite a power. The whole of this area, the Katanga, was once under Arab domination."

It was certainly a novel theory. In Kenya I'd heard the white settlers mutter that the real menace to them, in Africa, was India. They also said the Indians used Communist techniques and Communist propaganda to turn the Negroes against the whites, with the aim of grabbing Africa for themselves. Down in South Africa, Malan was muttering the same thing. Now, in the Congo, I heard it was really the Arabs who were the plotters.

My friend correctly interpreted my skeptical look. "Perhaps 'official secrecy' is making us all inclined to see bogies," he confessed.

The American laughed. "Seeing bogies is a favorite occupation around here. The Belgians are very touchy about American designs on their uranium. They also fear that Britain's self-government experiments in the Gold Coast and Nigeria may upset their Congo apple-cart. On the other hand, they're just as afraid that Malan's repression of the Negroes in South Africa will touch off a black revolt throughout the continent. And of course, they're dead scared of Russia, and of Communism."

"Meanwhile," I said, "you get along fine if you don't open your mouth too wide, and keep at least one eye shut."

He nodded, a little grimly. "That's it," he said.

Near and around pretty Elisabethville sprawled the great mines of the Katanga, including the forbidden Shinkolobwe. Here Negroes with grotesque tribal tattoo markings on their bodies, who had not long been out of the bush, learned to handle, with confidence and efficiency, the white man's twentieth-century tools. It was perhaps not quite the miracle that some zealous publicists of the Congo made it out to be, since, after all, Negroes not much less primitive had been doing similar work in the gold mines of the Witwatersrand for some time. Nevertheless, there were significant differences. Here on the Katanga the Negroes lived a normal family life and were not kept in compounds. Further, they were encouraged to increase their skill and so to earn for themselves a higher economic status: there were no rungs on the economic ladder legislatively marked "For Whites Only," as in South Africa.

All the same, I wondered if the Belgians weren't handling other stuff just as dangerous and as liable to explode in their faces as uranium. Everyone in Elisabethville, the Pittsburgh of the Congo, seemed highly and uncomfortably conscious of that iron hand of "security" inside the velvet glove of paternalism, uplift, and social welfare. The whites were just as conscious of it as the blacks. From Brussels, it might look like an inevitable adjunct of the highest idealism in carrying out a wonderful but complicated job; but here on the spot the atmosphere was apt to seem a little oppressive. In Elisabethville, I found myself instinctively tightening up inside every time I passed a policeman, or entered any of the numerous lairs of officialdom and produced my papers for inspection by a junior clerk. It wasn't a very good feeling. I kept remembering the Negro foreman who had vanished overnight after taking an undue interest in the mechanics and methods of orthodox American trade-unionism, and the two American journalists who had been politely but firmly put over the border because they asked too many questions.

After witnessing the smooth, scientific running of the Katanga, the Congo's treasure-house and powerhouse, nobody but a fool could fail to admit that the Belgians were doing a big job supremely well. But men are not machines. Man, even when he is tattooed all over, has recently lived in the bush, and has had a cannibal for a grandfather, is first and foremost a political animal. The Congo can't be isolated from change; and political change is surely sweeping over Africa. Among the Negroes, it takes the immediate form of deep resentment against the handful of whites who rule the continent—for ruling it, for being topdog, for just being white. I didn't see how the Belgians could escape that either. In the Congo there surely was resentment against white rule, against even white paternalism, certainly against the refusal to grant the black majority any political voice, and against the imposition of fairly arbitrary decrees. That resentment might or might not be fed by Communist propaganda; but it would probably exist anyway. It was of course true that the Negroes had long been accustomed to having to obey the whims of their own chiefs. But the white man himself had changed that. And the chiefs, however tyrannical, had been black; the new bosses, however paternalistic, were white, alien.

Such questions, I thought, must certainly be bothering the Belgians themselves. I wondered if I might find some of the missing answers in Léopoldville.

356

XXIV

BELGIAN CONGO: OYSTERS ON ICE

On the flight from Elisabethville to Léopoldville the plane descended for refueling at a place called Luluabourg. The airstrip was some distance from the town and there was nothing to see but a line of trees. We walked across a flat meadow to the airport buildings. There were a small restaurant and a lavatory. The door of the "messieurs" stood wide open, exposing the urinals. It had stuck fast some time back, and it was impossible to close it. There was a window, also immovably open, which looked directly into the "dames." No one seemed to worry about this, except me. Everyone hurried to the lavatory, and there was much flushing of water.

I consumed the omelet, cold meat, and tea set before me, and watched the air crew consume theirs. The pilot was a short, square man with a large black beard. He had powerful shoulders, and black hair grew on his wrists. With a cutlass between his teeth and a knotted handkerchief instead of a visored cap, he would have made a fine film pirate.

Presently he and his companions were joined at table by the crew of another plane that had just landed. They greeted one another jovially. A bottle of wine was produced, and when it was quickly emptied, it was followed by another. There was much hilarity.

But then my pilot pulled out his watch, and immediately everyone became grave. They looked solemnly at one another. When my pilot rose, with a heavy sigh, the other pilot rose also. The two men gripped hands in a silent farewell. Followed by his

357

crew, my pilot walked slowly out to the waiting plane, and the other airmen watched them go. They shook their heads and began to drink what was left of the wine, but listlessly, without enjoyment. I wondered if perhaps they thought poorly of our chances of getting safely to Léopoldville, and braced myself for a perilous journey.

The distance from Elisabethville to Léopoldville is 2,337 miles. The Belgians' huge domain is practically a continent within a continent. Most air travel is over thick tropical forest. Severe electrical storms are frequent. Thunder rumbles like artillery over the silent forest, lightning splits the sky, and the rain tumbles down like a thousand Niagaras. But on this occasion nothing of the sort happened. We took off without incident, and flew without a tremor all the way to Léopoldville. Presently I fell asleep.

When I woke, we were over the Congo, turning, coming down to land. On the farther shore was the French town of Brazzaville. Below us sprawled Léopoldville. Suddenly a mechanical insect appeared, quivering and hovering directly beneath us, before shooting off nervously on its own course over the town. From its tail there streamed a long trail of white smoke. It was the helicopter that flies over the town daily, spraying the houses with DDT in an endless war against mosquitoes and malaria. We swept in low over the scattered buildings fronting the river and landed at the airport.

I got a cab and drove to the Regina Hotel, stopping at the local Cophaco on the way. Cophaco is another of those monster Congo enterprises, with branches everywhere. It sells drugs. In Johannesburg, Louis Kraft, the Belgian-born secretary of the South African Institute of International Affairs, had advised me that the minute I got to Léopoldville I should equip myself with a remedy against stomach upsets. He obligingly gave me the name of one. According to Louis, anyone who spent more than a few days in hot, humid Léopoldville was bound to come down with the grippe, and the only sensible course was to face up to this certainty and be ready to deal with it.

I do not like taking drugs and usually forget when traveling in the tropics to swallow my anti-malaria tablets, but I will not deny that this time Kraft had scared the pants off me. He is an intense man who bulges with brains and whose spirit burns like a thin bright flame. When he lays down the law on any subject, he is utterly convincing. There is nobody of my acquaintance who knows more about Africa than he does. He spends his time amassing facts and statistics, varying this with occasional forays into the jungle in search of gorillas. His idea of a correct opening conversational gambit is likely to be startling. Once he arrived at a luncheon party and found himself seated next to a shy young girl, whose shyness was not abated by the fact that she was the only female present. Louis took compassion on her, sitting silent and awkward, and he determined to break the ice and make her feel at ease. He waited for a lull in the talk and then, turning to her, said loudly: "There is an African tribe whose female members on approaching the age of puberty enjoy eating earthworms. This is believed to have some sexual significance. What do *you* think?"

When I told Louis I was going to the Congo, which he knows well, he looked at me thoughtfully for a moment and then said: "It is of course certain that you will have bouts of diarrhea, and in all probability the sun will give you splitting headaches. The only thing to do is to be prepared for this and, when you feel an attack coming on, take the appropriate remedy, retire to bed, and hope for the best. With proper precautions, an attack should not incapacitate you for more than a day."

So I stopped at Cophaco and asked for Louis's recommended medicine, and Cophaco supplied it. When I got back in the cab, I read the label on the bottle. It declared enthusiastically, in French, that the bottle contained pills that were "a sovereign cure for putrid dysentery." I drove on to the hotel, clutching my pills and wondering how soon I could expect putrid dysentery to strike me down.

Outside the hotel, under striped awnings, people were sitting at little tables, drinking locally brewed beer. Across the way, other people were similarly seated at tables on the sidewalk, outside a café. This was the capital of the Congo, and this broad boulevard could be taken to be the very center of the Congo's new civilization, which was fast turning ebony-skinned ex-cannibals into modern men who juggled with ledgers and were at home with rock-drills: it boasted of having already produced 10,000 *évolués* and to be producing more at the rate of 2,000 a year. I looked eagerly around, hoping to see a black *évolué* seated at his ease at one of the little tables, drinking his beer and acknowledging the fraternal salutes of his white friends and social equals. But no: as at Costermansville and Elisabethville, the only black men in sight were barefooted waiters, obviously not *évolués*. I was disappointed and began to feel that these *évolués* were a haughty lot, who had become swollen-headed and were consequently too proud to be seen in the company of whites. I did not, as some carpingly critical visitors to the Congo have done, begin to conclude that the *évolués* did not exist at all. I knew they existed, because I had seen photographs of them in official Congo publications. In these photographs they invariably looked well fed, well dressed in European clothes, and all obviously happy and wearing delighted smiles. Just like official photographs of laughing Soviet citizens.

: 2 :

I PUSHED aside the mosquito net and blinked at the barefooted boy who stood grinning at me from the foot of the bed, holding a cup of tea in his hand. He was literally a boy, being about fifteen. When I spoke to him, he answered me in French, put down the tea, grabbed up my shoes, and vanished.

It was seven a.m. I put on a dressing-gown and went out on the balcony of the bedroom to have an early morning peep at Léopoldville. The sky was filled with thick cotton-wool clouds and the air was stickily damp with a threat of great heat. In the broad street below, Belgian women, wearing shorts, were bicycling briskly on shopping expeditions, with their shopping baskets fastened to their handlebars, as in Elisabethville. Chairs were neatly stacked on the sidewalk outside the café across the way, which was not yet open. Next to the café was a tall apartment house, with balconies. On one of the balconies, facing me, a woman in a dressing-gown was looking sleepily around her. On another balcony stood a white man, smoking a cigarette: as far as I could see, he was completely naked. At one end of the street was a large square, with a large statue in the center. At the other end were trees dotted with brilliant flowers, and a mango tree heavy with fruit.

I came in from the balcony to find my shoes returned, highly polished. I bathed and dressed and went along a huge stone corridor and down a gigantic staircase to an enormous dining-room. It was getting hotter by the minute. Two men walked past me on their way to their table, and the backs of their thin drill shirts, between the shoulder-blades, were already patched with sweat. Nobody wore a jacket or tie. I ate two rolls with butter and jam, the jam being a sort of apple-rhubarb mixture, and delicious, and drank two cups of very weak, very sweet and scalding tea. When I peeped into the pot, I saw that the tea was suspended in the hot water in a little bag, and wondered if I should write and tell Duthie Hess in Nyasaland about it.

Outside the hotel, taxicabs were lined up. When I walked toward one, I was instantly surrounded by barefooted Negroes, yelling at me in French and pointing to the other cabs. I decided to ignore them and pushed my way on to the one I had chosen. Its driver saw me coming and obligingly leaned back from his seat and opened the rear door for me. I leaped in and he slammed the door shut on me and immediately revved his engine and shot off at perilous speed. When we had got round the first corner he slowed down and asked me in French where I wanted to go. I told him, then turned and looked back through the rear window. The other Negroes had come panting round the corner, but when they saw that we were still in motion, they halted and contented themselves with shaking their fists and yelling insults after my driver. I decided they were not *évolués* and withdrew my attention from them.

I visited a few places in town, including the post office, the airline office, and the *"Population Blanche,"* to recover my passport. The *"Population Blanche"* is that part of Belgian official-dom which deals with travelers in the Congo. It has an insatiable appetite for passports, which it likes to hold on to and study before returning them to their owners. Before doing so, it makes the travelers fill out forms, which are detailed questionnaires dealing with where you were born, and when, and what you are doing in the Congo, and containing such trick questions as what your mother's full maiden name was and when *she* was born. Hotels ask their guests similar questions, and presumably the *"Population Blanche"* officials check the answers with the information in the passports and pounce triumphantly on anyone who gets any of the answers wrong. No European—that is, any person who has lived in Europe—can object to this procedure, which is merely copied from the dismal practice of most countries on that continent.

As I drove about the town, my wonder grew. I decided that what Léopoldville needed most was a shave and a haircut. There was lush vegetation everywhere, with shops and other premises scattered about in this jungle. Wherever there was a break between buildings, the vacant space was filled with bushes and flowering trees. This made for picturesqueness, but it also made it difficult for the stranger to know if he was still in the center of the city or heading for the suburbs. As a matter of fact, I never did find the main street of Léopoldville, assuming it has one; though I gathered that the city was more or less grouped round the statue of Leopold II, near the Regina Hotel. There is much somewhat strained veneration of Leopold in the Congo.

This monarch not only founded the Congo Belge, with the assistance of Stanley, the newspaperman who discovered Dr. Livingstone; for some years he claimed it as his personal domain. About the turn of the century, horror stories concerning Leopold's Congo kingdom were rife. It was further alleged by critics that Leopold was as lecherous as he was cruel and rapacious. Modern apologists prefer to say that the King led an "unconventional private life." The horror stories, of enslaved Negroes and "red rubber," tend to be dismissed with an elegant shrug. The Belgians are naturally annoyed that their King should be picked out for special opprobrium, and point out acidly that other colonial powers do not exactly have clean hands. It is also true that the Congo has since made great strides in progress. But the apologists for Leopold have certainly gone too far. If the skirt-chasing and gold-loving King envisaged a noble and uplifted future for his dusky Congo subjects, he certainly managed to conceal the fact from his contemporaries; and so did Stanley, whose apparently genuine admiration for Dr. Livingstone went hand in hand with treatment of Negroes which would scarcely have won the approval of the great Scottish missionary and explorer. Today, however, Leopold officially is getting post-humous credit for reforms and advances instituted by better men, who rightly recoiled from atrocities committed during Leopold's regime, if not with his personal approval, certainly without causing him any sleepless nights.

The expanding town of Léopoldville was shooting up out of the lush vegetation like a well-nourished mushroom. Building was going on everywhere. There was at least one office building twelve stories high, and others were rapidly climbing skyward. The stores presented a deceptively dull appearance, because window-display artists were apparently in short supply. A store might have nothing in its window but a couple of half-unpacked crates; but inside you could buy anything from costly jewelry to rare perfume. I got an impression that the stores did not have to entice customers to buy; the customers queued up for the privilege: hence the lack of display. Like most towns in Africa, Léopoldville was growing like a bamboo shoot and booming like a cannon.

But it was hot. The sunshine was a blinding glare, the brilliant flowers dazzled the weary eye, and even the effort involved in climbing out of the cab and crossing the sidewalk made me sweat like an overworked horse. Léopoldville also seemed to have temporarily outpaced its sewerage facilities in its headlong ex-pansion; sometimes, at the corner of a street, rich decaying smells cloyed the air as if a compost heap or a large neglected cheese were concealed below street level. This, I thought, might account for the ready sale of remedies for putrid dysentery. On the other hand, the beer-drinking Belgians and their briskly bicycling womenfolk all looked not only healthy, but hearty.

I drove past the Governor-General's palace, which drowsed with its closely shuttered windows in ample grounds. There was about as much sign of activity as there is around most of the palatial official residences scattered throughout Africa, which always look as if they were the centers of a permanent siesta. I got out of the cab at a less pretentious group of buildings which housed Léopoldville's working officials, produced my letters of introduction, and made inquiring noises. An impressively tall and exquisitely polite Negro supplied me with an armchair and tiptoed from the anteroom. He returned presently to inform me that the man I'd wanted to see was out, but that I could expect him at the hotel.

I was finishing coffee after consuming a well-cooked sole when M. Boucher descended upon me like a small whirlwind. (Boucher is not his real name, but in the Belgian Congo, perhaps more than in some other places, Government officials who permit themselves to express sentiments that are not merely carbon copies of their superiors' platitude-laden gobbledegook risk censure. M. Boucher was a highly intelligent man who could on occasion be pleasantly cynical about Belgium's great civilizing mission in the Congo, and I do not want to expose him to the risk of any misunderstanding.) He was a small man with well-brushed gray hair and an infectious smile. He bustled up to me and swiftly introduced himself. We shook hands.

"You have finished lunch? Good. I have a car outside."

A moment later we were on our way. The Negro cab-drivers lurking in ambush at the entrance to the hotel made a concerted rush for me as I appeared, but M. Boucher merely raised a hand and they slunk back to their cabs. His own car was a 1948-model Ford, which, he told me proudly, had already done over 100,000 miles on the Congo's roads and seemed good for another 100,000. It had a brisk and eager air, like its owner, and sailed smoothly along.

"Léopoldville," explained M. Boucher, who spoke excellent

English, "consists in reality of two cities, one for the whites, one for the blacks. The Negro population has doubled itself in five years, and is now a quarter of a million. The white population is 12,000. Negroes must carry identity cards, to which are attached their tax receipts. There is a strict curfew after seven p.m., but it applies to both whites and blacks. That is to say, after that hour no Negro may enter the white city, save by special permit, and no white may enter the Negro city. I shall now take you to the Negro city."

Black Léopoldville was larger but at the same time seemed more compact than white Léopoldville. We drove along a broad street lined with homes, which varied from shacks to stoutly built European-style dwellings. Each home, however, had a garden. The streets swarmed with people, women and children predominating. The women wore bright cotton dresses, some of which had the alphabet printed all over them. Others had pictures of airplanes. The most popular pattern, however, was a symmetrical arrangement of six spark-plugs.

"In the early days," explained M. Boucher, "we had only four-cylinder cars. Then came the six-cylinder job. The Negroes call an attractive woman a six-plug girl."

We got out of the car and he led the way into the market-place. Women in bright dresses squatted on the ground beside mounds of produce. They were offering for sale manioc, dried fish, green-and-brown-striped caterpillars, and blackened lumps of elephant meat. They also sold beads, bangles, carvings, charms, matches, screw-nails, hand-mirrors, combs, and Negro medicines, probably cures for putrid dysentery. Most of the women had babies, either strapped on their backs or crawling, naked, among the mounds of food.

After spending a while in the market-place we walked back to the car. There was a loud droning overhead, and we caught a glimpse of the helicopter spraying its DDT. "The war against disease," said M. Boucher, "is constant, and successful. The houses are regularly inspected and the Negroes are compelled to keep them clean. We have periodic checkups for tuberculosis and venereal disease. The hospital is free, except that patients are expected to pay for their food." None of the Negroes bothered to look up at the helicopter.

We drove past the hospital and a couple of schools. "Education," M. Boucher explained, "is free, but not compulsory. There are also classes for women, who are taught cooking and sewing." He pointed out a two-story house. "The Negro who owns that is employed by a bank. His salary is one hundred and fifty dollars a month. He belongs, in fact, to the new Negro middle class. We are very anxious to foster the growth of a middle class among the Negroes, as promoting stability. Negroes may either rent homes or build and own their own. In the latter case, they may borrow the money from the Government, the loan being repayable over a period of thirty years."

All Negro workers, he said, were protected by the laws that laid down minimum wages, minimum food rations, and a minimum standard of housing; and of course all the Negroes enjoyed free health services.

He stopped the car again, and I followed him obediently into a small timber yard. A number of men were making furniture. One of them approached, smiling and wiping his hands on his apron. All three of us shook hands vigorously.

"This fellow is a black capitalist," said M. Boucher. "As you see, he turns out chairs, tables, and so on. He began his little factory on a state loan, which he has completely paid off. Now he puts all his profits back into the business, which is growing. But he is also building himself a fine new house."

He translated his remarks into French. The black capitalist grinned and nodded his head.

"How many workers do you have in your employ now?" M. Boucher asked him.

"Only nineteen," said the man frankly. "At one time I had twenty-seven, but eight of them were no good, so I sacked them."

"You see," said M. Boucher, delighted, "he really is a capitalist."

We inspected some of the tables and chairs, which were very

366

well made. Then we shook hands again with the boss and bade him farewell.

From the furniture factory we drove some distance, arriving finally at an imposing building that M. Boucher explained was an art school for promising young Negroes. We entered and were greeted by a bearded young Belgian, smoking a cigarette in an elegant holder, whom M. Boucher introduced as Brother Marc Stanislas. Brother Stanislas called to a young Negro who was bent over a wood carving and clapped him on the shoulder. "This one is well thought of in Brussels," he said. "His work has already won prizes there." The young Negro grinned shyly. He was one of the handsomest men I have ever seen, with broad shoulders and fine sensitive hands. We inspected the work of the school, which ranged from small clay models to elaborately carved bookcases and superb heads in wood. "Unfortunately," said Brother Stanislas, "we also must train them in commercial art, so that they may make a living. But we hope of course that they will continue with their more serious work."

From the art school M. Boucher drove me to an open piece of ground dominated by a huge stadium. Near by was a large open-air swimming-pool where Negro youths were playing water polo. We entered the stadium, which had tiers of stone seats ranging dizzily upward and reminded me forcibly of the Colosseum. "But the Colosseum seated only 50,000 spectators, and this stadium seats 72,000," said M. Boucher. "It is used for ball games, and also for bicycle races. Games are played at night as well as during the day. The stadium is equipped with 142 arc-lights. Guess how many men were employed to build it."

I said I had no idea, but supposed it was a considerable number.

"Only three white men, supervising two hundred and fifty Negroes," he said.

He grinned. "Yes; like the Romans, we believe in bread and circuses. We think it is better that the Negroes should shoot goals in a stadium like this than that they should shoot us in the streets!"

I pondered this remark as we drove back toward "white"

367

Léopoldville, but was given very little opportunity for meditation. We visited in turn a shipbuilding yard, a chemical works, a shoe factory, a soft-drink plant, and a jute mill. The factories were light, airy, and modern and the Negroes who tended to the machines seemed to have little to do but pull levers. The jute mill was turning out about half a million bags a month, and the entire output was absorbed locally, but it was planned to step up production to eight million bags a year, which would leave some over for export. The works manager, surprisingly, was not a Belgian but an Englishman. I asked him if the Negroes were good workmen. He said cautiously: "They're first-class so long as you keep a fatherly eye on them, but a man can have been doing the same job for ten years and if you leave him to himself he'll bungle it as badly as if he'd never seen a machine in his life." And I thought of the Swiss medical missionary and the African nurses at Costermansville.

: 3 :

IN LÉOPOLDVILLE I never suffered from dysentery or any other internal ailment, and my only headaches were strictly legitimate hangovers from such attractive but potent beverages as iced rum punch, as concocted by a Luxembourger who had lived in Jamaica, and a fascinating green liqueur called, I believe, Izarra. After a while I stopped using a mosquito net: the DDT-spraying helicopter effectively kept the city free of mosquitoes.

I was waiting for M. Boucher and two friends. Meanwhile I read an article in a local magazine. The article expressed severe displeasure over the conduct of certain citizens. It said:

"It has come to our notice that recent immigrants from Belgium are tactless and crude in their behavior towards the Africans, among whom they have come to live. They are harsh to their servants, who have rightly complained. But the matter goes deeper and is more serious. 'Evolved' persons have been insulted by those people, who have on occasion been actually overheard using the term 'nigger.' The matter, we understand, is engaging the attention of the authorities, who take a grave view. Such rude behavior on the part of immigrants, which harms relations between the different races, poisons an atmosphere hitherto harmonious, and does disservice to the Congo's civilizing mission among the less advanced aborigines, will not be tolerated. We should like to warn those people that there is not only a standard of conduct to be maintained, but laws that are to be obeyed. The man who behaves in this fashion will not make a good colonist. Any repetition of the offense would deserve, and ought to receive, the penalty of the offender being removed back to whence he came. We mean, in short, deportation."

I tried to imagine such an article appearing in a South African magazine, but the imagination boggled and I gave it up. Anyway, it was time to go down to dinner.

M. Boucher's two friends were a cotton planter from upcountry, a fat man with prematurely white hair who looked like Sydney Greenstreet, and a handsome young man with a small mustache and a pink-and-white complexion, who appeared to be some sort of army captain. We were dining at a fashionable restaurant and the manager appeared in person to ensure that everything would be to our satisfaction. I looked around to see if any *évolués* might have honored the place with their presence, but I was out of luck again: all the diners were white.

I immediately raised the matter of the magazine article I had been reading, and everyone approved its sentiments. M. Boucher said the authorities were cognizant of the position and would indeed take drastic action if anything of the sort occurred again. It was in fact one of the reasons—indeed, the chief reason —why the Government had set its face against large-scale, indiscriminate white immigration, despite the colony's rapid economic growth and the serious labor shortage. "We do not," he said apologetically, "wish to have here a similar situation to what you have in South Africa. One of our great fears is that events in the Union may one day send a wave of discontent

369

throughout the continent, which would include us among its victims."

"On the other hand," said the planter, "we do not look with favor on the mania for Negro self-government which has gripped the British in West Africa. The vast majority of our aborigines are, you understand, still primitive. To talk of their trying to govern themselves is absurd. We must be firm; but of course we must be just."

He looked solemn as he uttered those words, but immediately brightened up. "Aha! What have we here?" A waiter, heavily burdened, had approached the table, and the fat man sniffed appreciatively. "Oysters!" he said.

"Flown in from Antwerp," said M. Boucher modestly. "I think you will like them."

We began to eat the oysters.

"However," I ventured, when the oyster-eating had got well under way, "it may be that even in the Congo there is some discontent, some political stir among the Africans?"

"I would be less than frank with you," said the young man, who had not yet spoken, "if I denied that, despite all our efforts, we do occasionally find evidence of Communist propaganda at work among the Negroes."

"Yes; but apart from Communists—"

"We know, however, how to deal with agitators."

"To be just," said the fat man, smacking his lips over an oyster, "but also to be firm. That is the secret."

"The fact is," said M. Boucher, rather hastily, "we have concentrated first of all on raising the deplorably low living-standards of the people. I think you must agree, from what you have seen, that we have not been entirely without success. The future is bright: the Congo is prosperous. I myself believe that, in the not too distant future, the black people of the Congo will actually be in a position to enjoy a higher standard of living than the ordinary white working class has in Europe today."

"And yet," I suggested, "it is also true that man does not live by bread alone."

" 'Or even football stadia,' I think you may have had it in your mind to add," murmured M. Boucher, with a twinkle in his eye. "I interrupt you. Pardon. Please proceed."

"What I mean," I said, "is that the very advances of which you speak may bring you face to face with demands for political rights. You cannot educate people, even to handle machines, without opening their minds to certain other ideas."

"We do our best, however," murmured M. Boucher, dryly. "You were about to say, captain?"

"I was about to say," the captain declared, with a confident smile, "that if our friend here wishes to see what happens when political theory is pushed ahead of economic reality, he ought to cross the river and examine the colonial policy of our French neighbors."

M. Boucher laughed. "The French Negroes who visit Léopoldville," he explained to me, "scoff at our Negroes, puffing out their chests and proclaiming themselves to be 'citizens of France.' When *our* Negroes cross the river in their turn, however, and visit French territory, they do not fail to note that the living-conditions of those 'French citizens' are vastly inferior to their own."

"Among the Negroes of Léopoldville," said the captain, "the term 'French citizen' has become a swearword. To call a man that is to indicate that he is a low fellow."

"I will tell you a story," said M. Boucher. "The Léopoldville Negro football team was beaten by the Negro football team of Brazzaville. Our team then played against a Negro team from Rhodesia. But a victory by Léopoldville would have left Brazzaville the final victor. Rather than allow French Negroes to score such a triumph, our men deliberately lost to the Rhodesian Negroes."

"Yet," said the fat planter, "the French Negroes, ragged and wretched as they are, have, theoretically, a vote. Ours have not."

"That is the point," said the captain.

"Whites here do not have a vote either," said M. Boucher, "so you might say that, after all, we have complete equality."

371

He looked at me ironically. "White and black alike, we are all the servants of Brussels."

"Or rather of Baron Empain and the big bankers," said the fat man recklessly. "Also of the monopolists. I am of course not a Socialist, but there are times when it seems to me that the rich men who sit in Brussels skim off the cream that we produce by our sweat." He looked wistfully at his pile of empty oyster-shells, and patted his stomach.

"To return to the Negroes," said M. Boucher, "they at least have no reason to complain against the so-called monopolists. They are protected by the state, which taxes the companies heavily to provide for their development, and also devotes a large share of its own profits to their welfare. These schools and hospitals which you have seen would scarcely be possible other-wise. The Negroes, through taxation, contribute only six per cent of the Congo's revenue. But they receive eighty per cent of the state's expenditure. How is this miracle performed? Be-cause more than half of the proceeds from every ton of copper we sell is spent on the advancement of the Negro."

"Tell me more," I said, "about your *évolués*."

"I do not care for *évolués*," said the planter, "and I will tell you why. The people of my district are simple people. They send their children to school, because they are told that this is the correct thing to do. A child shows promise, is made much of, is promoted, is sent here to Léopoldville, to a secondary school, and so on. What happens? The child grows to be a man, be-comes an *évolué*. He is wholly cut off from his former life; he despises his father and mother as savages and wishes to have no more to do with them. This is not creating an elite; it is creating rootless people, misfits who may well become dan-gerous. They do not wish to work with their hands, they wish to become lawyers. I say: by all means improve the conditions of the people, teach them to be better workers, but do not put false ideas into their heads."

"An admirable philosophy," said M. Boucher. "Unfortunately ideas are like germs, they float in the air. Vaccination prevents smallpox. Better, I think, to attempt to create a Negro bourgeoisie who will be passably loyal to our ideas than to try to stop them from having ideas at all, which I fear would be an impossible task."

"In Kenya," I said, "there is the Mau Mau. Is there a danger of the Congo being similarly affected?"

"We have of course our secret societies," said the captain. "They are not, at the moment, political. Some we tolerate, others we stamp out."

"Or try to," said M. Boucher politely.

"It is very difficult for any white man to penetrate the Negro mind in its primitive state," said the captain frankly. "Secret societies would appear to fulfill some need. While they remain innocuous we do not greatly object. But it is like a growth; who knows when or how it may not suddenly become malignant? Against such possibilities we remain constantly on guard."

I had tended to dismiss the captain, with his small mustache, pink-and-white complexion, and slightly vacuous air as being pretty innocuous himself. He now looked directly at me with his blue eyes, and in them I caught a glint of steel. Behind the eyes I glimpsed an acute mind at work.

"Here in the Congo," said the captain, "we are engaged in a crucial experiment. Like all such experiments, it is highly dangerous. We are tampering with the souls as well as the bodies of men." He smiled. "Did you ever read a story by the English writer H. G. Wells called 'The Island of Dr. Moreau'? Dr. Moreau tried to turn panthers into men. Here in the Congo we are all Moreaus. In saying this I intend no disparagement of the blacks. I merely point out to you that their customs, which are centuries old, include witchcraft, fetishism, devil-worship, slavery, and cannibalism. Quite apart from those aspects which to our way of thinking are strikingly repugnant, tribal society is constituted on a pattern as different from our own as that of a society of ants.

"We have been in the Congo scarcely fifty years. Even in that period we have imposed on those people utterly revolutionary ideas in the sphere of religion, thrust them into a new and bewildering world, forced a completely different economic pattern upon them, and turned many of them into tool-users: people who, before we burst in upon them, had no knowledge even of the wheel.

"Suppose a race of Martians, not dissimilar to us but technologically much in advance of us, and with an entirely different social, political, and economic structure, with which naturally would be bound up a different pattern of morals and emotional attitudes—suppose such creatures invaded the earth. The impact would scarcely be greater than we have had on the Congo Negroes. That they have succeeded in adjusting themselves to it at all is surprising; that so many of them have actually appeared to assimilate it speaks volumes for the Negro's intelligence and adaptability.

"But the experiment still continues, is only in its infancy; and one cannot yet talk of final success. There are still bound to be many difficult mental and emotional adjustments to be made. There are also bound to be resistances, for this is how the human mind works, be it black or white. We for our part must believe in the experiment, must have faith in the rightness of what we are doing. If we did not, assuredly we would go mad, or commit suicide in sheer self-disgust. As I said before, to tamper with the souls as well as the bodies of men is dangerous. If we falter, if we lose courage, if the knife slips, we destroy ourselves as well as the patient. Therefore, despite setbacks, we go on. . . .

"But meanwhile the experiment must be safeguarded, at all costs. It is at this point," said the captain simply, "that I disagree with those who would have us introduce the ordinary democratic concepts. We are told that we should hasten to give the Negroes a free and equal vote, teach them political philosophy, invite them to form their own forums of public opinion. Does a doctor ask the patient who has been placed in his care to tell him the medicines he shall prescribe? Are such matters put to the vote among the inmates of a hospital? If human beings are primarily social animals, then, rightly or wrongly, we are quite rapidly making these people over into what is literally a new type of man, as surely as a surgeon who performs a leucotomy

374

changes the nature of his patient. If we are wrong, God help us; but if we are right, it is we who must remain in control of the experiment and must accept all responsibility for it. We have in any case now embarked upon it and there can be no turning back.

"It follows that we must prevent, and if necessary suppress, all attempts to take the business out of our hands. We shall find ourselves dealing from time to time with fools, idealists, knaves, religious fanatics, political reformers, attempted interference from outside, and strong instinctive resistances from the remnants of the old society which is now dying and which cannot now be revived but still spasmodically struggles against us. There will be people who understand very well what we are doing and do not like it, and people who do not understand it at all, but who resent it. Against all such we wage war, not ruthlessly if we can avoid that, but certainly relentlessly. If that suggests to your mind the all too familiar apparatus of the police state, I cannot help it. It is not, of course, 'democratic.' But I for my part do not feel that the normal democratic techniques would, at this stage, be of much assistance to us in what we are trying to do."

The captain became conscious that he had made an inordinately long speech. He flushed slightly, and drank down his wine with a slightly defiant gesture of finality. "I fear I have bored you. At any rate I must certainly go. It is much later than I thought."

The fat planter, who had fallen into a light doze induced by too many oysters and too much wine, woke up with a start and said hastily that he, too, must depart. We shook hands all round. When they had gone, I found M. Boucher regarding me with a slightly quizzical eye.

"Very interesting," I said. "Who in fact is the 'captain'?"

"During the war," said M. Boucher carefully, "he was in Political and Military Intelligence. I have no reason to believe that he has changed his occupation."

I was not very much surprised.

: 4 :

BEFORE GOING to bed that night I went for a walk. The hour was late, and the streets, ghostlily lit by orange-colored lamps, were almost deserted. I felt rather like a ghost myself.

I pondered over what I had heard and on the things I had seen. M. Boucher, a sophisticate, had spoken lightly of bread and circuses, in the form of food rations and football stadia. But the captain had gone deeper. Granting his assumptions, what worried me was what he eventually hoped to achieve. Sooner or later politics had to come into the equation, and I could not help feeling that he and his like were closing their eyes to that fact. The British in West Africa were advancing to meet the problem by turning Negroes into voters and legislators. In South Africa, Malan either hoped to keep the Negroes as helots by simply arming his police with Sten guns, or else toyed halfheartedly with vague notions of a drastic, total divorce between white and black. But the Belgians plainly fitted into neither category. Here the Negroes were obviously being uplifted, but at the same time there was almost no provision for their political training. The Belgians were not out to repress, but at the same time they seemed determined to run things their way, with no interference tolerated from either within or without. The Congo furnace, well stoked with uranium, was probably the hottest thing in Africa, and might conceivably be the brightest as well, but who could tell what internal tensions the furnace might be building up for the future? The crude forces of awakening black nationalism would take little heed of the delicacy of the "experiment" if they once got under the Belgians' guard.

Meanwhile, however, I did not think I would care to be an "agitator" in the Congo—or even a Negro who had developed a curiosity about political democracy. I recalled the captain's words: "It follows that we must prevent, and if necessary sup-

376

press, all attempts to take the business out of our hands." The "experiment" came before everything else. If the captain were any criterion, the "experiment" had loyal servants.

I turned and walked back through the deserted streets, under the ghostly orange lamps, to the hotel.

377

XXV

FRENCH EQUATORIAL AFRICA: BLACK FRENCHMEN

I CROSSED THE Congo in a ferryboat. The trip took only a few minutes and cost a few francs. There were no formalities.

When in Johannesburg I had made inquiries about this crossing from Belgian to French territory, heads were shaken and lips were pursed. The young woman who handled such inquiries, acting on behalf of the Government of France, wore pince-nez and a tight bun. She said severely that the request was *très difficile*. First of all I had to get a visa, which took time. Also I would have to produce a certificate from the South African police to prove I had never been guilty of any crime involving "moral turpitude."

In order to get this document I had to go to the South African police and have my fingerprints taken. These were presumably checked against the records of known criminals. Finally the police presented me with a clean bill of health, obligingly furnishing several copies.

When I went down to the quay in Léopoldville to cross the Congo to Brazzaville, I carefully carried all my documents with me. But for all the use they were to me I might as well have left them in Johannesburg. Nobody seemed interested in me or my papers. The ferryman did not seem to care if I lacked a visa or even if I reeked of moral turpitude. He simply gave me a ticket for the boat and paid no further attention to me.

Most of the passengers on the ferryboat were Negroes. They had a holiday air. There were several six-plug girls in bright cotton dresses, and a number of stout ladies carrying laden baskets. A young Negro steadily ate his way through a bunch of bananas, and a fat man with a shiny black face carefully folded his ticket and tucked it through the ring he wore on his forefinger, before falling into a light doze. The ring was of gold and had a stone the size of a walnut. I decided he was probably a capitalist.

In midstream we passed another ferryboat, crowded, and going the other way. The French city of Brazzaville and the Belgian city of Léopoldville look defiantly at each other across the swirling brown water of the Congo. There is considerable rivalry between them. When Léopoldville built its first ten-story block, Brazzaville proceeded to erect one too, being careful to situate it where Léopoldville could not possibly overlook it. The two buildings directly face each other. Léopoldville still holds the lead, but Brazzaville is expanding faster. The white population of Léopoldville climbed from 6,000 in 1945 to 12,000 in 1951, and the black population from 100,000 to 250,000. The respective figures for Brazzaville, in the same period, are a jump from 1,000 to 7,000, and from 25,000 to 100,000.

In Léopoldville, they had told me that I would find Brazzaville to be sleepy and far behind the times. "It is a wretched, tumbledown sort of place," said my friends with cheerful vindictiveness. "The French are so indolent that as they sit in the open over their coffee, the creamy blossoms of the frangipani trees fall into their cups, and they are too lazy to remove them before drinking." Brazzaville proved to be rather different from this fanciful picture.

An enthusiastic young Frenchman offered to drive me round in his car and I gladly accepted his offer. We visited a brand-new electric power plant, and watched giant scoops busily excavating an entire hillside to make way for a new dam. A good deal of building was going on. On the outskirts of the town there were pretty bungalows, painted blue, green, and pink, for Europeans.

"The truth is," my guide confided, "the French Congo is benefiting financially from France's troubles in the Far East.

Formerly we were starved for funds, but now a lot of money is being invested."

I had heard a good deal about the French policy of education, but even so I got a slight shock when we visited a large secondary school and I looked in through the window of a classroom. Negro boys were sharing desks with white girls. Rather hesitantly, I asked my guide how this was working out.

"Quite well," he said cheerfully, "except that the white pupils are a little resentful at the moment; the Negroes are on the whole doing better than they are. This is because some of the white children thought they would score higher marks than the Negroes automatically and so did not try very hard. Now they are on their mettle and determined to win."

Despite the joint-education policy, Brazzaville, like Léopoldville, is really two cities, one white and one black. The black city is called Poto-Poto, and I found the contrast very marked. The people of Poto-Poto, or a select minority of them, might send their children to the same school as the whites; but the great majority of them were still living in mud and reed huts. The Negroes of Léopoldville, I thought, were certainly better housed.

But at the juncture of the two racially separate cities there stood a vast building that took my breath away. It was the Cathedral of St. Anne of the Congo, but it was like no other cathedral I had ever seen. Massively built, with a great arched doorway of stone and powerfully buttressed walls, it stood there amid the tall dark trees with an almost savage splendor. I thought it was less a church than a hymn in stone to the spirit of the Congo, and said so.

The young Frenchman smiled.

"But that is exactly what it is! It seeks to blend the spirit of the Congo with the spirit of Christianity. Look at the entrance: of what does it remind you?"

The great stone door rose to a sharp point at the apex of its arch. It was vaguely Gothic, and yet he was right; it reminded me, tantalizingly, of something very different.

"It looks," I said hesitantly, "like a Congo canoe raised on end, with the top of the door as the prow."

He nodded. "That was the intention. Now let us go inside."

The interior of the cathedral was vast, and cool. At the far end, behind the altar, was a painting covering most of an entire wall. Despite its size it was a fairly conventional religious scene. What chiefly attracted my attention was the stone platform that jutted out high above my head, seemingly suspended in mid-air so that the heavy stone appeared to float.

"That is where the choir take their places during services," he said. He was evidently enjoying my bewilderment.

"It must be a large choir," I said.

"Yes. There are two hundred, all Africans. The cathedral can hold a congregation of five thousand. The congregation is of course mixed. A color-bar would not be tolerated." He shook his head. "I wish you could hear a service. You see, we carry cultural assimilation very far. In addition to the choir and an organ, we have introduced tom-toms!"

I visualized the cathedral filled with five thousand white and black worshippers, the black choir, two hundred strong, on their stone platform suspended over the heads of the congregation, the organ, and the tom-toms, and agreed that a religious service that combined all those elements must be quite a thing.

From the cathedral we went back into Poto-Poto. My guide led me along a path between the reed huts until we came to a very large hut standing by itself in a clearing. It had a straw roof and flimsy bamboo walls and looked like some sort of tribal meeting hall.

"It is in fact the school of painting, directed by Monsieur Lods," said the young Frenchman, with a good deal of awe in his voice.

M. Lods was a thin, eager man with an untidy mop of hair, and he and Paul Gauguin, who, as I have already observed, would have loved the Congo, would have got along very well with each other. The work being done within those flimsy bamboo walls, under that unpretentious thatched roof, seemed to me to make the output of most modern artists look sickly and anemic.

It was explained to me that the aim of the school was less to teach Negroes how to paint than to encourage them to express themselves on paper and canvas. This of course is not a new idea, but in the Poto-Poto school of indigenous painting the results had certainly been startling. I had been told often enough in Africa that no white man really knew what went on inside a black African's mind. Here was that mind expressing itself not in fumbling words and through a language barrier, but in a medium far more direct and uninhibited. Looking at the paintings M. Lods produced, I found myself suddenly in a world of strange form and flashing color utterly unlike anything I had ever known. It was a world at once beautiful and grotesque, imaginative and yet rooted in some experienced reality beyond my own ken. It almost had the touch of another planet about it. There were figures recognizably human, yet oddly fourth-dimensional. Above all, the colors, which were what impressed most, hinted strongly that these artists could actually see more in the spectrum than met any non-African's eye. There was an obvious relationship, I thought, with those strangely moving "Bushman paintings" which have been found in caves in many parts of Africa, and which in turn are plainly akin to the paintings found in caves at Altamira in Spain, and elsewhere in Europe. But none of these had the power to transport me into a quite different world: this stuff did. For the first time I experienced a dim but genuine understanding of what my young French friend called "the spirit of the Congo." And it had nothing to do with electric power plants, ten-story buildings, or jute-bag mills. One thing was certain: these people were, in their own remote and alien world, intensely alive. Removed from it they might be like tropical fish that lose their brilliance out of the water.

We thanked M. Lods, who seemed pleased that we had shown interest, and retraced our steps to my friend's car. Half an hour later we were seated on the terrace of Air France's sumptuous establishment in Brazzaville, sipping cocktails and watching the big four-engine planes come in from Dakar.

: 2 :

BRAZZAVILLE, I afterwards discovered, might or might not be a true indication of what the French were doing in Africa. There were other aspects of French colonial rule that were less encouraging.

French Africa consists of two enormous chunks of territory: French West Africa, which sprawls over almost two million square miles, and French Equatorial Africa, which covers just under one million square miles. There are 30,000 whites in French West Africa, and it is significant that half of them live in Dakar. Moreover, since the Second World War Dakar has grown at a speed and to a pattern which seem to have little relation to the development of backward French Africa. The rate of building in Dakar is prodigious; but most of the new buildings are military installations. Most whites are in uniform.

"The fact is," I was told frankly, "France is afraid of a third World War and what it would do to Europe. If another war comes, Frenchmen will fall back on Africa as their base."

Dread and detestation of military conscription are chiefly responsible for the steady emigration of Negroes from French Africa into the British territories of the Gold Coast and Nigeria, I was also told.

"There are other factors," said a Frenchman who was highly critical of his country's policies. "Talk about advancing the Negroes and turning them into 'black Frenchmen,' who apart from their skin color will be in every way the equals of white Frenchmen, remains mostly talk. The reality is somewhat different. Whatever may be the lofty ideals of politicians in Paris or of high-placed colonial officials who write books on the subject, the fact remains that in the eyes of most minor colonial officials—and it is they who actually administer French Africa—the role of the Negro is to fight for France, grow cotton under compulsion for France, and pay taxes to France. Negroes who won't fight, don't grow enough cotton, or can't pay their taxes

383

are made to build roads. French Africa is still full of petty white tyrants who have the power of life and death over the Negroes in their remote districts, and who use that power ruthlessly."

Top-ranking French colonial administrators—for example, Robert Delavignette, former High Commissioner for the French Cameroons—paint a brighter picture than that, but even they speak, regretfully, of the continued existence of "press-gangs" and "slavers" in French Africa.

"Of course," I was told by an Englishman who lived in Nigeria but knew French Africa well, "the French have a tough problem. They simply don't have the money to develop their enormous territory. And even if they had, it would take some developing. The French govern twenty million Negroes, a good many of them cannibals. Not long ago some of the cannibals cooked and ate their Senator, who was rash enough to leave Paris to visit them. Fellow was a Communist, though," the British empire-builder added, as if he felt this helped explain and possibly even justify their action.

Negroes in French Africa have risen to high and responsible posts. Always in theory, and surprisingly often in practice, there is no color-bar. I thought the contrast between this and the admitted deficiencies of French rule over large, backward areas constituted a riddle that might be worth trying to resolve, but when I mentioned it to a Frenchman he was merely amused. "There is no riddle at all. France is poor; the Frenchmen in the colonial service are miserably paid. France must have the money the Negroes pay in taxes, must have their labor, and must have them as soldiers. The colonial bureaucrats sweating it out in the jungle are compensated for their low pay by being given autocratic powers. They employ those powers, brutally, to raise their self-esteem, and at the same time to extract the money, the labor, and the military service that France requires.

"As for the few favored Negroes who are raised to the status of 'citizens,' have you never heard of 'divide and rule'? We do not shoot our black agitators unless we are absolutely compelled to; we prefer to send them as deputies to Paris, knowing that there they will quickly become as corrupt as all the other deputies. That is the system—and it works!"

There is no cynic like a French cynic.

: 3 :

BUT NOT all Frenchmen are cynics.

Probably the best book ever written about France's colonies in Africa—or, for that matter, the best book ever written about any part of "colonial" Africa—is Robert Delavignette's *Freedom and Authority in French West Africa*, published by the Oxford University Press for the International African Institute. M. Delavignette was formerly High Commissioner for the French Cameroons. He writes from first-hand knowledge, and with considerable charm. He also has idealism, but no illusions.

Discussing French West Africa, Delavignette has pointed out that the territory is neatly divided into 118 *cercles*; thus the French passion for method and tidiness is from the beginning imposed on the sprawling African scene. Each *cercle* must contribute, in men, money, and labor, toward the 175,000,000 francs of poll tax and cattle tax, and the 21,000,000 days of labor service, which in the period of which Delavignette was writing were required to maintain French West Africa as a going concern.

He himself coined the phrase "black peasants" to describe Africans, and is wryly amused by what followed. "It gave an outlet to a certain sentimental feeling for former slaves, while it reassured the modern slavers who at first had been a little anxious. Peasants—no danger there; one can go on in the old way. And what an alibi! What could be more bucolic? Instead of dealing in cotton or niggers, one can go in for black peasants."

Delavignette well describes the bewilderment of Frenchmen, accustomed to farmers who used oxen and plows, when confronted with Africans who had no plows and whose oxen were in herds. The bewilderment became all the greater when it was perceived that Africans worked their fields in age-groups, combined the tracing of a furrow with a ritual dance, and regarded the animal sacrificed to determine whether the right field had been chosen as much more important than the draft oxen that helped to do the actual work. Labor was communal and drew its inspiration from drums and tom-toms.

The commandants of *cercles* were there to build roads, collect taxes, and maintain law and order. Each of those tasks presented its own perplexities. To build roads, with almost no money—Delavignette wittily compares France's African colonies to natural daughters whom the mother refuses to legitimize by awarding them dowries—it proved necessary to conscript labor. To collect taxes, it was necessary to cajole, or compel, the black peasants to grow cash crops—often to the detriment of food crops. To maintain law and order seemed easy—until a commandant found himself faced with such a set of circumstances, common in Africa, as a person accused of witchcraft (not recognized as a crime at all in the French Code) who freely owned up to the crime and obviously expected to be punished for it.

Some of the administrators rebelled against the things they had to do. Delavignette instances Richard Brunot, a Governor of the Ivory Coast, who was recalled and disgraced—his inquisitors sarcastically asked him if he imagined he was Jesus Christ—because he denounced forced labor and what was euphemistically known as "organized voluntary work."

The important thing to realize is that the French system could, and can, be defended. The roads had to be built, or there would certainly have been no law and order—from which the Africans undoubtedly did and do benefit. But, with money lacking, the only way to build roads was by forced labor, since the "black peasants" were certainly not prepared to offer their services free of charge. The French, like other colonists in Africa, marched into the Dark Continent and conquered large tracts of it with little or no real military force (Delavignette illuminatingly contrasts the earlier colonization efforts of other powers with Italy's "total war" against Abyssinia in the 1930's; a war that did end in the Abyssinian Emperor's defeat, but which also ruined Italy—times had changed). But, once in possession, the French, like others, found their conquest unwieldy and not very rewarding. The breakup of the African primitive society proceeded apace, yet almost unintentionally. Road-building meant taking away the young men and disrupting the traditional village life; the compulsory growing of cash crops, for export, introduced the African willy-nilly to a whole world of new values.

How to build up new peasant communities to replace the ones that were thus destroyed? Financial stringency still limits the answer to a series of very modest proposals. Delavignette proposed (in 1950) "small public works" to raise the standard of life in the villages: "a cemented well provided with a pump and a separate drinking trough for animals; a granary protected from termites." He sees a future for African producers' co-operatives, and for group marketing.

There is nothing wrong with those proposals; but they do indicate somewhat sharply the practical limits to rapid reform in those parts of Africa which have little to offer to attract out-side capital. On the credit side of the ledger, there is the French abhorrence—at any rate in principle—of a color-bar. Africans *can* become "black Frenchmen." This may save French Africa from the political convulsions that appear to be in store for other and richer parts of the continent. Man, and most certainly African man, does not live by bread alone. If the French can begin to back away from their present temptation to conscript Africans for military service, as they have conscripted them for road-building, France may retain the loyalty of her black subjects far more effectively than the Boers are likely to do with their Bantu. And, if only because of that heartening absence of a really oppressive color-bar, France in Africa surely deserves both the sympathy and the material support of other and wealthier nations.

387

XXVI

PORTUGUESE AFRICA:
PORTUGUESE PING-PONG

MANY PEOPLE, mostly South Africans, visit Lourenço Marques, the big town that the Portuguese have built in their east African colony of Mozambique. But few of the visitors penetrate deeper into Mozambique than that, and fewer still go to Angola, the other Portuguese African colony, on the west coast. Consequently the world knows little about Portuguese Africa, and the Portuguese themselves do not appear unduly anxious to add to the world's scanty stock of knowledge.

This does not prevent a good deal of speculation about what goes on in the areas of Africa under Portuguese control.

One day I sat on the terrace overlooking the open-air swimming-pool of the elegant and up-to-date Polana Hotel in Lourenço Marques. A South African, who claimed to know a good deal about Portuguese Africa, told me how the Portuguese "keep the coons in their place," and illustrated what he meant with the fascinating story of the Ping-pong bat.

"There's no 'native' crime here," he said confidently. "It isn't like Johannesburg. And I'll tell you why.

"When the Portuguese catch a nigger stealing, they don't shove him in jail, where he'll be better fed than he would be otherwise. They beat him with a thing like a Ping-pong bat, with holes in it. First they beat him on the palm of the left hand, until the hand swells up. Then they beat him on the palm of the right hand. Then on the sole of his left foot, then on the sole of his right foot. The point is that it's extremely painful,

388

but it doesn't leave any scars. After that he's sentenced for theft and put to work on the roads. Yes, the Portuguese certainly know how to handle their natives!"

Lourenço Marques, otherwise a rather dull town on the east coast of Africa, stages bullfights for pleasure-seeking South Africans to watch; and Portuguese East Africa also supplies much of the Negro labor required to work the South African gold mines. So the South Africans and the Portuguese are good neighbors.

The Portuguese nevertheless indignantly deny the Ping-pong bat story. Their version is that they have no color-bar whatever and, far from treating Africans harshly, hold wide open to them the door to full equality. In other words, Negroes in Portuguese Africa are, at any rate theoretically, black citizens.

But in the meantime, my Portuguese friends hastily explained to me when I pointed out some obvious divergences between their theory and their practice, the vast majority of the 9,000,000 Negroes in the two widely separated halves of Portuguese Africa are still "raw"; as one Portuguese put it in conversation, "they require guidance and discipline, just as children do."

The emphasis would appear to be on discipline. Portugal's handful of black *évolués* have a vote, which is about as much use to them as it is to the 120,000 whites in Portuguese Africa, meaning that they have the pleasure and privilege of voting for the administration of Dr. Salazar. But the education of most of the Negroes is limited to teaching them to speak (but not necessarily to write) Portuguese, so that when the boss shouts an order they can understand it. The Lourenço Marques housing scheme for its Negroes puts Johannesburg to shame. Rows of neat homes are arranged in the pattern of the spokes of a giant cartwheel, with an agreeable open space in the center. "You will find no shantytowns here," said a Portuguese with pride. He added thoughtfully: "It is also of course easy to get at any trouble quickly and quell it." A handful of men with machine-guns, which whites have and Negroes haven't, could control marching mobs in any of those geometrically planned avenues. The Portuguese think the white people of Johannesburg are mad to leave scores of thousands of Negroes living in crowded warrens with narrow, winding alleys where white soldiers and policemen could be ambushed.

Any adult male Negro may be compelled by Portuguese law to work for a white master for at least six months of every year, or else to produce a minimum quantity of prescribed crops on his own land. Negroes who don't are put to work on road-making, and get no pay. The same fate awaits Negroes who fail to pay their poll taxes. Negro labor is also the chief export of Portuguese East Africa. Between 60,000 and 80,000 Negroes are successfully encouraged each year to leave their land and their families and to go to work in South Africa's gold mines and coal mines. The Portuguese reward for managing to persuade this number of Negroes to work outside their own country is a guaranteed 47½ per cent share of the traffic between the Rand gold mines and the coast, this traffic having to pass through the Portuguese East African port of Lourenço Marques despite the obvious natural advantages of the South Africans' own port at Durban. The Portuguese also collect "passport fees," taxes, and other dues from the migrating Negro mine workers, both when they are leaving and when they return. To ensure that they *do* return, the Portuguese have an arrangement with the mines whereby an appreciable proportion of the Negroes' pay is transferred to the Portuguese authorities, to be paid to the Negroes only when they come back, and of course paid only in escudos.

Portugal controls over 300,000 square miles of East Africa and nearly half a million square miles of West Africa. These two Portuguese African possessions, Mozambique and Angola, are on opposite sides of the African continent, Mozambique on the Indian Ocean, and Angola on the Atlantic. Both consist mainly of bush, infested by tsetse fly. Portugal's African conquests, the earliest in Africa, date back to the fifteenth century. The Portuguese hoped to find vast gold and silver mines, but were disappointed.

"Nevertheless," said a Portuguese colonial official, "it would be a grave error for other powers to dismiss our African possessions as of no account." The reason he gave me was simple:

the Portuguese hold some key ports. In East Africa they have Lourenço Marques and Beira, and in West Africa they have Lobito, Luanda, and Mossamedes. Communications are one of Africa's biggest problems, and good ports are few and far between. Northern Rhodesia's copper mines, the Belgian Congo's copper, cobalt, tin, and uranium mines, and South Africa's gold and diamond mines, all urgently require outlets to the sea. The Portuguese are in a good bargaining position. There is also the strategic aspect. The defense of Africa calls for a rail link between the Atlantic and Indian Oceans. Such a rail link exists. It starts at Lobito and runs east to Vila Texeira de Sousa, then through the Belgian Congo, both the Rhodesias, South Africa, and Mozambique, ending at Lourenço Marques and Beira. In other words, the Portuguese control both ends, and the ports at either end. Portugal cannot possibly be left out of any scheme for Pan-African defense.

The Portuguese blandly use their possession of the ports, and their willingness to export "their" Negroes, to win trade and other concessions from their wealthier neighbors. But they would be shocked by a suggestion that this might be construed as blackmail. They missed the minerals they started out to look for, so they make the most of their other natural advantages: that is all.

: 2 :

THE TWO Portuguese colonies of Mozambique and Angola are almost classic examples of what "colonialism" has meant both for Africa and for Europe. Taken together, the two colonies are more than twenty times the size of Portugal itself; but there are only 120,000 whites there—not all of them Portuguese. And white immigration, even from Portugal, is not encouraged, though in Angola itself there is much land that would probably be suitable for white settlement.

The question that springs to mind is: what are the Portuguese doing in Africa at all?

They came in search of silver and gold. These hopes were disappointed. But, like other colonizing powers in Africa, Portugal found the conquest of enormous areas to be possible with an astonishing minimum of military force. Disease killed many of the invaders, but African resistance to white conquest was almost nonexistent. Developing the conquered area has proved much more difficult. The Portuguese have long had an air of requiring all their strength just to hang on to what they gained. The outside world has shown very little interest in Portuguese Africa. Vernon Bartlett has pointed out that, in 1953, one of the best newspaper clipping libraries in London had added only one clipping about Portugal's African colonies since 1923. This is partly due to the fact that the Portuguese have been extremely secretive about their own achievements—or lack of them. Portuguese Africa is generally regarded as about the most backward part of the continent.

But, before passing judgment, it is necessary to inquire just what is meant by "backward." It is fairly obvious that certain abuses do exist in Portuguese Africa, as elsewhere. It is equally obvious that the Portuguese are by no means proud of them. Most of them arise, not from evil intention, but from lack of financial resources. Portugal "sells" black labor to the Union of South Africa. But, at the same time, the Portuguese are not upholders or loud declaimers of the virtues of a color-bar, as South Africa certainly is. On the contrary, the Portuguese, at any rate in theory, do not have a color-bar, though they do have civilization tests. Nor does this appear to be wholly a case of hypocrisy being the tribute that vice pays to virtue. If the Portuguese had the means, they would undoubtedly try to raise the living-standards of the Africans in their territories to higher levels; if Portugal should ever broaden its area of political freedom, this will almost certainly include Africans. Meanwhile, the Portuguese do conscript black labor where they feel they must, but on the whole the Africans are left pretty much to their own devices.

The Portuguese have plans for developing their two African colonies. These remain largely on paper, but this is because the money has not yet been found, not because the Portuguese lack energy or are not in earnest about their development schemes. And the plans may not always remain on paper. Mozambique has some extremely rich soil; Angola has diamonds and gold as well as copper. If the money could be raised, Portuguese Africa might forge ahead with quite remarkable speed—and with a "native policy" better adapted to current realities than Malan's *apartheid*. The Portuguese tortoise may one day begin to catch up with the South African hare.

XXVII

GOLD COAST: "LEAD, KINDLY LIGHT"

THE NEGRO immigration officer at the airport of Accra, capital of the Gold Coast, was as obsequious as if we were both in South Africa, he black, I white. "Please, may I see your passport, sir?" he pleaded nervously, peering sad-eyed through his grille while the beads of perspiration came from under his peaked cap and ran down a black cheek bearing the tiny scars of tribal markings. But the coal-black customs officer had as cold an eye as customs officers everywhere. Briskly professional, he asked me to open up my baggage. He examined it, then brought down his piece of chalk with one clean slash, like a conductor finishing a symphony. "All right!" he snapped.

I had entered the hot little office from a pitch-black night, splashed with blotches of yellow light where the Clipper stood with stilled propeller blades on the concrete apron. After these formalities I passed through a big, bare room and so into the night again, where a taxi was waiting.

The hotel smelled of lush vegetation. There was a big open courtyard where people sat drinking at little tables. The courtyard was dimly lit by small colored electric bulbs strung sparsely on a sagging string. When I passed through with my bags, nobody seemed curious or even looked up.

The hotel-owner was a Greek. His office was in an outside hut, which contained a black safe, a white refrigerator, and a desk heaped with moldering ledgers. After signing the register I stumbled away from this oasis of light, across a dark yard, to a row of rooms in an annex. My room had barred windows with

394

no curtains, a large broken mirror, a wash basin and a towel-rail, a single dim bulb in the ceiling, a bed draped with a white mosquito net, and a two-door wooden wardrobe smelling strongly and cleanly of camphor. The wardrobe was tightly wedged between the wall and the foot of the mosquito-netted bed.

Morning brought unhappy consciousness of a body soaked in perspiration, and a glare of damp white clouds which made a backcloth for very green trees. It also brought Samson, a small black man with broad shoulders and knobbly bare knees, who bore a pot of strong black tea and four lumps of sugar jostling a cup in a white saucer. I discovered later that all the hotel waiters —in fact, nearly all the men of Accra—were small, with broad shoulders, bow-legs, and knobbly knees. They looked like English professional football-players except that all of them were black. The women of Accra, on the other hand, were tall and slim. They wore bright, cotton print dresses and looked like furled striped umbrellas.

The Gold Coast is about the size of Oregon. It hangs on the map of tropical Africa like a strip of damp wallpaper. Christopher Columbus visited the Gold Coast ten years before he discovered America and helped build the Portuguese fortress called St. George of the Mine. Gold has been coming out of the Gold Coast since 1483. Today, more famous for its cocoa, the Gold Coast is itself a bursting political pod. The black population is 4,500,000; the white population only 5,000. Accra, the capital, is a town of 150,000 people.

The streets of Accra looked as if all the junkmen in the world had set up in business there. On the crowded verandas of tumble-down houses, barefooted men in their shirt-tails furiously worked sewing-machines. The "shops" were mostly tables in the open air, ranged along the sidewalks. The tables were heaped with patent medicines (a favorite was "brain-pills"), kerosene lamps, matches, candles, loaves of bread, tins of baby-powder, hairpins, brooches, watches, suitcases, shoes, shirts, hats, combs, mirrors, razor blades, soap, bottles of mucilage, and trays of cheap earrings. The traders were statuesque women, swathed in yards and yards of bright cotton. The favorite colors were purple, plum, green, crimson, white, and blue. These bright dresses also had stripes, circles, triangles, whorls, birds, flowers, fish, the signs of the zodiac, and portraits of the late King George VI. The women also wore bright head-scarves shaped into turbans, and large earrings and thick bracelets.

The short, stocky, ugly black men, who looked like English professional football-players, wore open-neck shirts, colored blue, green, or maroon, and with the tails generally hanging outside their trousers; or else they wore short-sleeved, turtle-necked smocks with thin colored stripes, which accentuated their breadth and shortness and turned them into capless baseball-players. Less frequently, the men wore flowing robes of peacock colors, draped round them loosely like togas and worn off one shoulder, so that they looked like cut-down Roman emperors.

This colorful pageant of pedestrians flowed along the streets, past Accra's peeling white buildings. Through the mass of walkers cut speeding, hooting taxis, and large, lumbering green-painted buses. The taxis were all small English Morris Oxfords; and they had not one driver, but two. While one man drove for a spell, the other slept. Scores of these little taxis cruised swiftly round and round the streets all day and most of the night, constantly honking and looking for fares. To secure a taxi, you stood by the roadside with uplifted hand, bawling: "Service!" A taxi was bound to squeal to a halt beside you in a few minutes. This is probably the only resemblance between Accra and New York.

Accra also has a harbor, a lighthouse, two white-painted prisons, eight cinemas, and twelve recently appointed, gorgeously pretty, black police girls, in smart black uniforms. This probably makes it a pleasure to be arrested. In fact, the police girls were appointed because most petty criminals are women. In Accra, women do nearly all the pickpocketing and shoplifting, as well as most of the trading.

Over most of Africa women have a chattel status. They do the hard work while the men sit around smoking their pipes, drinking their beer, and discussing village politics. But in the Gold

Coast and also in Nigeria the women were not content simply to bear children and carry headloads. They went into business. The result today is that instead of carrying headloads, they own and operate trucks. Politics are left to the men, but the women handle the cash. From such humble beginnings as buying and selling handfuls of dried peas, some of them have built up businesses worth thousands of dollars. The United Africa Company is one of the biggest and shrewdest trading concerns in the world; but, at the very doors of its stores, Gold Coast "mammies" calmly sell the same goods as it does—at cut prices. Gold Coast men do not resent the economic independence of their women. They simply grab as large a share of the profits as their wives will let them have—and go on talking politics.

My five-foot taxi-driver wore a broad-brimmed soft hat, a gold wrist-watch, and a brown and gold toga with one chocolate-colored shoulder left bare. He was also smoking a filter-tipped cigarette. His assistant driver relaxed with his eyes shut, and his woolly head rolled to the taxi's motion as if he were dead but *rigor mortis* had not yet set in.

We drove past a filling station called the Trust in God Motor Works, and an optician's shop called the Mark of Zorro. The newspaper office I wanted to find turned out to be hidden in a back yard surrounded by narrow alleys. The editorial office overlooked the yard, in which one woman, naked from the waist up, was breast-feeding her baby, and two other women were cooking a mountain of rice in a huge iron pot and boiling tomato soup in a large caldron.

Accra has seven newspapers, six of them dailies. All are published in English. One, the *Graphic*, is owned by the British *Daily Mirror*, and has a similar, carefully copied make-up. The others are mostly political broadsheets. The Gold Coast politicians own, edit, or are in other ways connected with these newspapers, and are constantly suing one another for defamation. When I was in Accra, Dr. J. B. Danquah, the leader of the opposition, was suing one paper for thirty thousand pounds. Constant litigation keeps the black lawyers of Accra exceptionally busy—and prosperous. One lawyer was alleged (by his wife, who was suing for a divorce) to earn forty-five thousand dollars a year. The average wage in Accra is six dollars a week. The basic minimum wage of a black civil servant is fifty cents a day.

There is no color-bar on the Gold Coast. In Accra white and black use the same hotels, bars, and cinemas, eat at the same tables, ride in the same buses and taxis, and bathe on the same beaches. They drink and dance together, and occasionally inter-marry. In Accra's crowded streets, the radio loud-speakers and phonographs bawl dance music all day long, competing with the honking of the taxis and the bleating of goats in back yards. At night, white and black visit night-clubs with names like Weekend in Havana.

To get into Weekend in Havana I paid forty cents. The dance floor was open to the stars, and surrounded by wooden benches, rickety chairs, and tables on an earthen floor, and towering ramparts of beer-cases. Colored electric bulbs were strung overhead. Occasionally, apparently just for the fun of the thing, someone let off a rocket that burst in splendor against the night sky. The Negro band played *High Life*, a sort of samba, beloved of all Gold Coasters. The leader stood out in front in his shirtsleeves, tremoloing on a trombone. Englishmen danced with Negro girls, Negro men with English girls.

The Gold Coast's version of the samba must be a big strain on traditional English shyness. The Negro girls, with their bright scarves round their heads, became bundles of jigging but-tocks and breasts.

Everybody drank whisky, gin, or beer, but each time I ordered a round, I had to pay fourteen cents per glass over and above the price of the drinks; when I left this money was refunded. The reason was that so many glasses got broken, falling off the rickety tables. The dancing commenced at eight p.m. and went on until about half past two in the morning. Nobody got drunk, raped, or murdered.

I found it very difficult not to be cheerful in the company of the boisterous Gold Coasters. When mixing with the Negroes, even the English came out of their shells. But when they were

398

by themselves, they promptly went back into them. In Accra's hotels and clubs Englishmen who were not entertaining Africans sat sadly apart, not speaking to one another except when spoken to. At the end of two days the man with whom I shared a table for breakfasts, lunches, and dinners had unburdened himself to this extent:

Me: "Been here a long time?"

He: "Oh, quite."

Me: "It's an interesting country, isn't it?"

He: "Oh, quite."

Me: "What do people here do with themselves in the evenings?"

He: "Well, there's the club."

: 2 :

MOST ENGLISHMEN, I was told, do not believe that Gold Coast Africans can run the Gold Coast. Yet the swift transition from colonial rule to something very like self-government has been accepted by the British with remarkable tameness. For this there seem to be various reasons.

One is the stout backing given to the experiment by high British officials, including the Governor, Sir Charles Arden-Clarke. When the Governor's order to release Kwame Nkrumah from cell No. 9 in the white-walled Jamestown Prison came through on February 12, 1951, the Director of Prisons resigned in disgust. Nkrumah, in his prison cell, had polled, in the elections to the Legislative Council, a record 20,780 votes as candidate for Accra; it was obvious that the jailbird was designed for a high post in the new Government (he was appointed Leader of Government Business and is now Prime Minister). The irate Director of Prisons said stiffly: "I am not prepared to take orders from one of my former inmates." But an unsympathetic British colleague remarked dryly: "From now on, we British will have to get used to that sort of situation."

When the new Government led by Kwame Nkrumah came

into power, the British offered the eight African Ministers specially built, elegantly designed houses in Accra befitting their new station in life. Nkrumah and his colleagues loftily turned the offer down, and the houses are now occupied by upper-grade African civil servants.

But rising all over Accra are imposing new Ministry buildings, designed by the British architect Maxwell Fry: they are more imposing than any other Government buildings anywhere else in tropical Africa. Fry also designed Accra's Community Centre for Africans. It is a large, airy building which has, among other amenities, doors painted blue, plum, and chrome yellow, a bas-relief over the entrance of umbrella-bearing Ashanti chiefs, and a handsome reproduction of Salvador Dali's *Crucifixion*.

The Community Centre is run with tender and anxious care for African welfare by a young, specially imported upper-class Englishman who had previously been busy conferring similar delights on British workers in England's new garden cities. The Accra Community Association, which runs the Centre, publishes what it calls "an occasional news-letter," *Neighbour*. Some of the Centre's offerings are a wee bit astonishing. Subjects of lectures given when I was in Accra included "Prospects for Gold Coast Literature" and "Techniques of Economic Planning." The Centre also staged one-act plays, with such titles as *The Death-Trap*. African women are genially invited to come and be taught rug-making and raffiawork, and sewing-classes are conducted by the Seventh Day Adventist Mission.

At the Centre's top level, intellectual calls to intellectual, and they speak the same somewhat gloomy language, whatever the color of the skin. Sean Graham, director of the Gold Coast Film Unit, was starkly asking readers of *Neighbour:* "Where does our duty lie? To make a propaganda picture showing a model nurse doing her duty in a model way . . . or to show nursing as an honourable profession which is at the moment shot through with sloth, corruption and indifference to human suffering?"

Graham's chief criticism of "the most popular film shown on

the Gold Coast so far" (a film called *The Boy Kumasnu*) was that the film's prostitute was too pretty.

Also writing in *Neighbour*, J. K. Ahwoi, founder of the Wiawso Sefwi Community Centre, explained: "The people of the Gold Coast are naturally sociable and they delight in holding village and public meetings. . . . In the rural areas the men gather under the shady branches of a specially planted tree in the main village street and talk together after the day's hard work on the farms, on such topics as the scanty rains and the consequent poor yield of crops; the scarcity of meat in the village and the fruitless search of hunters in the bush. Relapsing into silence, they play draughts and marbles."

What less sophisticated Gold Coasters make of all this is not too clear. When I visited the Centre one evening, a few couples were nervously trying out modern dance steps in the big main hall, to phonograph records, and a number of men were poring over magazines in the reading-room. But lectures on such subjects as trade-unionism are said to be well attended, though one lecturer confided to me: "When I try to tell them how to run a union in terms of industrial legislation and workmen's compensation, they say: 'Yes, but how do we set about throwing out the imperialists?' "

The chief of the Gold Coast Government's well-organized Public Relations Department is a monocled Britisher, Major Jimmy Costello. I found his outer office decorated with big wall-maps. One, spattered with big red, yellow, and green disks, showed the progress of the radio rediffusion program. There are about twenty thousand rediffusion centers throughout the country (most Negroes being too poor to purchase an individual radio set). Broadcasts are in several African languages, as well as in English; they are mostly educational. One program that has been very well received gives intelligible summaries of the Gold Coast Parliament's proceedings, with scrupulously fair coverage of opposition speeches. Costello was hoping by this means to get the people so used to the (at present somewhat unfamiliar) idea of fair play for all parties that when the British finally go, the belligerently feuding Gold Coast politicians may be restrained from vilifying, boycotting, banning, and banishing one another.

Another of Costello's wall-maps showed, district by district, the progress of the "cutting out" campaign. Cutting out means the elimination of diseased cocoa trees, afflicted with swollen shoot. This disease threatens the industry on which the Gold Coast still mainly depends for its livelihood. Cutting out was the most unpopular of the British administration's many unpopular measures. It was made compulsory, and was resented by farmers, who saw only a loss of income by the destruction of trees which, though suffering from swollen shoot and certain to spread the blight, were still good for another two seasons' crops before they finally died.

Nkrumah's party, the Convention People's Party (CPP) included among its promises an end of cutting out by compulsion. This suited the farmers very well. But, once in power, the CPP saw swollen shoot making drastic inroads on the current cocoa crop, entailing a loss of hundreds of thousands of pounds. Taking his courage in both hands, Nkrumah restored compulsory cutting out, with penalties for farmers who refused to co-operate. Now the campaign is working well. But a British official said: "If *we* had tried to do it, there would have been riots."

A third large wall-map in Costello's office showed the progress of the mass education campaign, which is conducted by means of traveling loud-speaker vans and mobile cinema units. Most Gold Coasters—at least two thirds—cannot yet read or write. Outside the post office in Accra, I saw professional letter-writers doing a roaring trade, though Accra has the highest literacy rating in the country.

: 3 :

I WATCHED CPP supporters in Accra stage a monster procession. They marched twice round the straggling town, like the

Israelites marching round the walls of Jericho, except that the CPP trumpets played jazz most of the time.

To the samba strains of *High Life*, the procession jived its way along the streets, with their open drains, tall palms and stumpy almond trees, hovels, canoes, and fishing-nets. Small children danced like dervishes, some of them with still tinier tots strapped to their backs. Fat mammies joyfully undulated. The bandsmen blew and thumped. Some women, while they danced, balanced on their heads trays of chewing gum and candies, which they sold to passers-by. Men, women, and children wore red paper caps with white and green paper ribbons—the colors of the CPP.

The procession started from the Arena, a drab square of vacant ground where Nkrumah launched his CPP on June 12, 1949, and where he still makes his most important open-air speeches. It marched past the white walls of Jamestown Prison, where Nkrumah was once detained and where, during his imprisonment, CPP supporters gathered daily to sing:

Kwame Nkrumah's body lies a-mouldering in the jail,
But his soul goes marching out.

This time, passing the prison, the crowd shouted: "Freedom!" the CPP's catchword, and gave the unresponding walls the CPP salute, which consists in raising the right forearm with the palm facing outwards.

Keeping pace with the procession was a motor-car, painted garishly in red, white, and green. Perched on the roof, wearing a striped smock with short sleeves and a two-foot-high red paper hat with the letters CPP, rode plump, bespectacled E. K. Barnor, the party's financial secretary and chief comic. Clutching a hand microphone, he bawled to the crowd to keep to one side to let honking taxis, lumbering green buses, and black traffic cops on motor-bikes pass through.

The procession went on for four hours. Long before it was over, the men's colored shirts, smocks, and togas were sweat-

403

soaked. But the women continued to look cool and flower-like in their cotton print dresses, earrings, and bangles.

As the procession passed the Jamestown Prison for the second time, the jazzing, jiving crowd suddenly went mad. They came to a halt, blocking and filling the street, waving wildly. Some got hold of palm branches, torn from roadside trees, and waved these.

Through the forest of waving hands and green palm-leaves Kwame Nkrumah came riding. He was standing up in an open car, but the car was completely invisible because of the crowd. Only the upper half of him could be seen. So, like the animated bust of a Roman emperor, wearing a black-and-white striped, turtle-necked smock, his head bare, he passed slowly through the cheering crowd. The smock emphasized his broad shoulders. Out of the turtle-neck of the smock his head rose like an ebony sculpture. His thick cap of woolly black hair made his high forehead seem higher. He held a white handkerchief in one hand and waved it. The band played *High Life* with a new kick in it. Grinning, Nkrumah jigged his broad shoulders in rhythm with the jazz. The crowd roared its approval. The animated bust moved on. A Gold Coaster, shaking with excitement, turned and grabbed me by the arm. "You see," he said emotionally, "it is real—real! Real democracy. He is one of us, one with us—a man of the people. And," he added, seeming to think it a logical corollary, "you must understand now that you have seen: we *can* govern ourselves!"

Nkrumah was billed to speak the next day, a Sunday. I drove to the Arena in one of Accra's miniature taxis. The taxi-driver wore a leopard-spotted toga that left bare one muscular, chocolate-colored shoulder: it was like being driven by Tarzan. His co-driver was a youth of fifteen or sixteen, wearing a white shirt and a tall conical hat.

In the middle of the Arena was a bare wooden platform on which stood wooden chairs and a table. There was a microphone on a tripod and loud-speakers on poles. The poles were decorated with red, white, and green paper streamers. The party's comedian and financier, Barnor, was present, wearing his two-foot-tall red-paper hat. Round the edges of the platform, peering up hopefully at the still vacant dais and the empty chairs, an all-black crowd was beginning to gather. I was the only white person present. The Arena itself was without shade of any kind, but round its perimeter were houses, a church, a few palm trees. Little boys, determined to see the show, climbed into the branches of a flamboyant tree and stayed there throughout the proceedings, hanging like fruit. A huge Negress wore a red-paper CPP cap perched on top of her red turban, a white blouse, and yards and yards of bright-green skirt.

After a long wait the CPP Youth League entered the Arena: girls and boys in red caps, white shirts, and green skirts or shorts. The girls wore in addition earrings and necklaces, and were all extremely pretty.

The boys and girls were led in by a brass band. More branches of the CPP Youth League filed in. Another brass band turned up, the bandsmen wearing white suits and black ties and looking like waiters. By this time the crowd filled the whole Arena, and the seats round the edges of the platform were all occupied, but the platform itself remained vacant. When the top CPP leaders at last began to arrive, the crowd stood and gave the Freedom salute. Then they sang a hymn, *Strong in Thy Strength Make This Land Free.* The CPP leader, G. K. Amegbe, said a prayer, beginning "Our Heavenly Father," and ending "Our Saviour Jesus Christ," before introducing the first speaker, the Minister of Education and Social Welfare, Kojo Botsio.

A large, burly man, wearing the standard carnival red-paper cap, a sleeveless striped smock, khaki trousers, and brown shoes, Botsio had little to say and looked bored. After a few conventional words he passed the microphone to Kofi Baako, chairman of the CPP Information Bureau. A small man with small ears, a long, smooth face, and a steep nose, Baako wore a red cap and a long blue smock, with golden embroidery and very wide, long sleeves; he looked like a brisk African Merlin. Addressing the crowd as "Fellow Ghanians," [1] he vigorously attacked the CPP's political opponents and rivals, the Ghana Congress Party, led by Dr. Danquah, as "existing only on paper—a 'Ghost Concept Party'—intellectual, treacherous liars." Nkrumah, said Baako, had "made political organization a science. Until the arrival of this young man, we did not know a political party should have a flag, should have bands. Our opponents said these tactics were Communistic; now they have adopted them themselves." The crowd listened to his harangue good-humoredly. At its conclusion they gave the CPP salute and cried: "Freedom!"

Baako was followed by the Minister of Commerce, forty-year-old Agbeli Gbedemah, a broad-shouldered, broad-faced man who wore a white cap with the letters "PG" on it (for "prison graduate"), a white shirt whose tails hung outside cream-colored trousers, and brown shoes.

Gbedemah also attacked the Danquah party. "These critics are intellectuals, university lecturers, gray-haired professors. Despite their great intellect," said Gbedemah sarcastically, "they must learn to work with the people, through the CPP. There is no doubt that we shall be the ones who will deliver the goods. With your continued support, we shall achieve self-government. We are prepared to pay the supreme price if need be, so that our children can say: 'People of Africa, under Kwame Nkrumah, blazed a trail for the black people of the whole world to follow.' What is happening in Kenya and South Africa should steel us to make our country free. We on the Gold Coast shall be an inspiration to the people of Kenya and South Africa."

When Gbedemah sat down, mopping his brow but immedi-

---

[1] Ghana was a great Negro kingdom that existed in the West Sudan and is supposed to have attained a high level of civilization until conquered by Moslems in the eleventh century. The theory is that the defeated Ghanians retreated south down the valleys of the Niger and Volta rivers to the Gold Coast. Dr. Joseph Danquah, the Gold Coast's first leading nationalist, revived the term "Ghana" as the proposed name for a free, independent Gold Coast.

ately looking bored, the CPP organizing secretary, a man named Welbeck, who wore a white cap, a red zipper shirt, and flannel trousers, went to the microphone and began to urge the crowd to buy copies of the CPP magazine, *Freedom*, and badges bearing Nkrumah's portrait (twenty-eight cents each). Pretty Youth League girls in red-paper caps circulated among the crowd, selling the magazines and badges and also collecting donations to the party. When a girl had filled her cap with money, she came up to the platform, and the money was emptied on the wooden table and counted. Most of the donations took the form of Gold Coast pennies: large silvery coins with holes in the middle. Some people donated banknotes, but wrote their names carefully on the back; the names were read out over the microphone amid applause. Gbedemah donated fifteen dollars. The bandsmen, who were dressed like waiters, struck up the lively jazz tune of *High Life*. People began to jig.

There was considerable confusion on the platform, with people talking and two men loudly counting the money and arranging the coins in piles on the table. In the midst of all this, and while the band still played, Kwame Nkrumah arrived, almost unnoticed. He climbed up on the platform from the back and remained seated there. He wore a white cap, a white, short-sleeved shirt, white trousers, and black shoes.

The meeting had now lasted over three hours. The light was beginning to fade and would soon go fast. Nkrumah's white cap, and the blurring of his features in the gathering dusk, made him look like India's Nehru.

While the men still loudly counted the money (the total take was $160), Nkrumah advanced modestly to the microphone. He had to call for quiet. He spoke strongly and incisively, but calmly. "The first thing I want to say," he told the crowd, "is that I wish to be known simply as Kwame Nkrumah. Please leave out the 'Doctor' and the 'Honorable.'"

He raised his voice. "Friends and countrymen—party members: Freedom! All this weekend, we have been celebrating Independence Day: a day of remembrance and dedication. Let us now sing our hymn." The crowd began to sing *Lead, Kindly Light*.[2]

After the singing of the hymn, Nkrumah went on: "It is not easy to organize a party in a colonial territory when there are constant attempts to divide the people. The age-old principle of imperialism is 'divide and rule.' Imperialism must be destroyed. The history of this African continent will be changed by our acts and decisions. Let us forget our petty jealousies, our local hates. Let us make Ghana the place where freedom for Africa was born.

"We have reached a point in the struggle where there can be no turning back. Your trust will never be misplaced. A point comes where the reactionaries oppose the march of the common people. But stand firm. The goal is near. Be united, in the name of God." He concluded, obviously referring to the Danquah party: "Those who should be with us are, because of jealousy, against us, and are thus playing into the hands of the imperialists."

The dusk had now thickened. The crowd had an air of wanting to go home. Nkrumah, a dim white silhouette, moved back from the microphone. The crowd began quickly to disperse.

: 4 :

Sir Charles Arden-Clarke is one of the most experienced and is quite likely the best of Britain's governors in Africa. He was formerly High Commissioner for the three British protected territories of Bechuanaland, Basutoland, and Swaziland, the post later held by Sir Evelyn Baring.

Sir Charles shocked South Africans by having natives to tea at his headquarters in Mafeking. He is a close personal friend of Tshekedi Khama, and on visits to England entertains Tshekedi and other distinguished Africans at Athenæum Club in Lon-

---

[2] This became the hymn of Nkrumah's split-away movement, the CPP, in 1949. In the 1950 troubles, some CPP members were arrested by the British for singing *Lead, Kindly Light*, which by that time had assumed considerable political significance.

don. In Accra I found him sitting behind a big desk in romantic Christianborg Castle, with a picture of Winston Churchill glowering over his left shoulder, the roar of the Atlantic surf in his ears, and moldering sixteenth-century cannon on the ramparts below.

The castle is old and huge. There are deep dungeons, which once held slaves. A Portuguese governor is buried in a court-yard gateway (a cannon was melted down and poured over his corpse). The castle is a maze of corridors, inner courtyards, and enclosed gardens. It is guarded by stiffly saluting, coal-black sentries, and it contains sumptuous reception rooms whose walls are lined with full-length portraits in oils of British royalty. Amid this grandeur the Governor sits at his desk in his shirtsleeves, with a loose shirt button peering round the edge of his crumpled old school tie, while he chain-smokes cigarettes from a tin and knocks the ash into a brass bowl.

According to Sir Charles, Nkrumah is both sincere and able. Nkrumah, the Governor believes, is anxious to make the Gold Coast experiment work, as an example and inspiration to other Negro peoples in Africa, and to convince whites that Negroes can rule themselves in their own countries. Thus Nkrumah looks far beyond the Gold Coast.

The relation between Sir Charles as Governor and Nkrumah as Prime Minister could have been acutely embarrassing. For it was Sir Charles who was directly responsible for sending Nkrumah to prison. When Nkrumah threatened late in 1949 to launch a general strike, the Governor issued a blunt warning (the two men had never met) that if he did, Nkrumah would be arrested. This in fact happened, though the Governor was very careful to ensure that Nkrumah got a fair trial and was allowed to appeal to the Privy Council against the sentence the Accra court passed. The appeal failed, and Nkrumah went to jail. But the CPP carried on and eventually swept the polls at elections held under a new Constitution.

The Governor then had to make a tricky decision. He cut short Nkrumah's sentence, freed him forthwith, and let the newly elected Assembly put him at the head of the Gold Coast

Government, second only to the Governor himself. The two men met for the first time at the subsequent initial meeting of the new Cabinet, which Nkrumah headed. Nkrumah's first words to the Governor were to assure him that he felt no bitterness whatever. Since then the two have worked closely together.

The Cabinet meets at the Governor's castle, on the seashore; they sit in the big, newly decorated Cabinet room directly adjoining Sir Charles Arden-Clarke's office, under portraits of bewhiskered British governors dating back to 1840. The Governor listens, makes occasional suggestions, but does not attempt otherwise to influence the Cabinet's decisions.

The Governor admitted, when I asked him, that old Christianborg Castle was romantic. But he pointed out that the white-walled edifice is kept constantly damp by the spray of the Atlantic rollers that thunder day and night against its sea-walls. "I had to have electric fires installed in every cupboard to keep my clothes from going moldy," he added. On the Gold Coast, damp shoes are apt to grow green fungus overnight.

While Nkrumah, in his cell in Jamestown Prison, was making fishing nets and reflecting on the power of imperialism, Komla Agbeli Gbedemah, who was deputy chairman of CPP, organized the CPP to fight in the forthcoming elections to be held under the new constitution. Gbedemah had been sentenced to six months' imprisonment (for "publishing false news"). Immediately on his release, and by agreement with Nkrumah, he assumed acting chairmanship of the party.

To prepare the people for the elections, the Government sent out fifteen educational teams, which covered 22,000 miles. They gave lectures and showed movies in 1,300 towns and villages, played 250 phonograph records, and distributed 500,000 leaflets in six languages. This was not to tell the people for whom to vote, but merely to instruct them in the procedure of voting. Loud-speaker vans toured mud-hut villages, where chiefs and people, sitting beneath gaudy umbrellas, first listened to hot-jazz records to warm them up, then heard the well-worn record of the voting instructions. Because so many of the voters were illiterate, competing candidates were allotted pictures of elephants, cocks, or fish to represent them. On election day these pictures were pasted on the sealed ballot-boxes. To open the ballot-boxes, seven hundred special screwdrivers were ordered from Britain for electoral officers.

The CPP was not behindhand in its own preparations. Gbedemah and his organizers toured the towns and villages with bright-painted loud-speaker vans. Whole districts were bedecked with CPP red, green, and white flags. CPP supporters gave one another the Freedom salute: the forearm raised with the palm forward and all five fingers extended to represent the Five Freedoms.

To ensure against anyone's voting twice, electoral officers made each voter press his or her thumb on an inkpad fitted into the lid of a cigarette tin. The ink, specially imported like the screwdrivers, left a purple stain that the most persistent washing could not remove for three days.

The result of the elections was a landslide for the CPP. Everywhere fluttered the victorious CPP colors. All CPP meetings closed with *Nearer, My God, to Thee,* fervently sung. Nkrumah, still in jail, was freely and frequently compared with Jesus Christ.

When, as a consequence of all this, Nkrumah was set free, he put on a white cap with the letters "PG" for "prison graduate" on it, a pair of sandals, and a peacock-green toga. Thus attired, he went to the Accra Arena and, while vultures circled lazily in the blue sky overhead, addressed a cheering crowd of fifty thousand.

His speech differed remarkably from previous utterances. He had gone to prison calling the new Constitution a fraud; now he told his thousands of supporters that it would be to the benefit of the Gold Coast to give the Constitution a fair trial. He further announced: "I would like to make it absolutely clear that I am a friend of Britain. I desire for the Gold Coast the status of a Dominion within the Commonwealth. I am a Marxian Socialist, but not a Communist, and have never been one. I am an undenominational Christian. I stand for no racialism, no discrimination against any race or individual; but I am unalterably opposed to imperialism in any form." A typical 1948 Nkrumah speech had read: "I appeal to the Youth Front to unite our forces against the forces of tyranny, imperialism, and capitalism. Organize for redemption, make the Gold Coast a paradise! When the gates are opened by Peter, we shall sit in heaven and see our children driving their own aeroplanes, commanding their own armies."

When the new Assembly met in February 1951, there were only 8 whites among its 84 members. A new era had opened for the Gold Coast.

XXVIII

GOLD COAST: SHOWBOY

In the office of the Public Relations Department, a dilapidated building with creaking internal wooden staircases, a dusky male clerk pecked hesitantly at a typewriter, while another read a book called *The History of Kissing*, listened to the Ink Spots on the radio, and corrected the typewritten news of the day for delivery to the Accra broadcasting station. In the hot street outside, fat mammies swathed in cotton prints waddled under enormous head-loads.

I found Jimmy Costello in his office and we drove to the Ministry, a modern two-story red building. We climbed two flights of a spiral staircase, and walked along a balcony with airy offices opening off it. At her desk in the Prime Minister's outer office sat Nkrumah's pretty West Indian secretary, Miss Joyce Gittens, busily preparing for the Prime Minister's forthcoming visit to Liberia in the Liberian President's yacht. "We're taking the CPP dance band along," she said happily. "Guess we'll have a few calypsos on board."

The time was ten a.m.; Kwame Nkrumah had been up since four o'clock and in his office since seven. His office, adjoining Miss Gittens's, was a large, long, cool-looking room. Two of the long walls consisted entirely of windows. He sat at a desk facing the door. On the desk was a telephone. On the wall behind him was a huge map of the Gold Coast.

Kwame Nkrumah came from behind his desk to greet us. He was less tall than I had imagined—five feet seven—but slender. He looked about thirty-three years old, and was ac-

413

tually forty-three. He wore a white linen suit, a blue shirt, and a striped tie. We sat down at a small table with blue ashtrays, in the middle of the room, midway between the door and Nkrumah's desk. Jimmy Costello lit his pipe and polished his monocle. Nkrumah sat quietly, waiting to be asked questions. He showed only polite interest until the questions concerned politics. Then he became animated, talking quickly, making swift gestures with one hand, and frequently roaring with laughter. As he became animated, his face became more boy-ish. Despite his ten years in America, he had no trace of an American accent. His English was slightly imperfect, and some-times he groped for a word.

I asked: "What forces have most influenced your political thinking—what books, what persons, whose theories?"

Nkrumah began hesitantly: "I studied philosophy, of course; and education." He made a gesture. "Other subjects. I read many books. There are many books on philosophy," he added.

"Yes, indeed," I said.

"There was Hegel," he said triumphantly after a few mo-ments' pause for thought. "Yes, Hegel. When people ask: 'How did you come to study Marx?' I tell them it was from reading Hegel first. A natural step." He looked at me as if for confirma-tion. Then he added brightly: "And Kant, of course. Yes, there was Kant." He paused. "The Bible, too. And the French Revo-lution. Often still I read the French Revolution." (He did not stop to explain whether he meant Carlyle's, or whose.) "And then there is history. I have read Professor G. D. H. Cole's history of the British Labour Party. And I have studied Asian history. There is much important in Asian history." He paused, and concluded doubtfully: "Toynbee's history too."

"Do you agree with Toynbee?" I asked.

"Nobody does," said Nkrumah quickly and unexpectedly, and roared with laughter.

I had a delicate question to ask. "You describe yourself as being a Marxist Socialist," I said. "What does that mean?"

"It means," said Nkrumah readily, "being opposed to abrupt, violent change." He hesitated. "Like Fabians. Of course, it also

414

means being ready to take firm action," he added quickly. "Firm action when in a tight spot. But not violence. Not by violence. And of course it means Socialism." He lifted a hand and made an obscure gesture with the flat of it, as if he were demonstrating how an airplane flies. "Socialism, of course. Except that here in the Gold Coast there is not much to socialize." He threw his head back and roared with laughter. Then he went on more seriously: "That is why we must advance and have industries. Naturally, we want capital from outside for that. But there must be safeguards to see capital is for the real benefit of the people, without exploitation."

His explanation left me with the impression that he wanted to create industries primarily in order to bring the Gold Coast into line with the economic structure he had studied in the writings of Socialist theorists. Meanwhile the Gold Coast unfortunately didn't conform to the textbooks.

"Of course I am not a Communist," said Nkrumah. "We are in and with the West. But we are not happy about the split of the world into two camps, the West and Russia. For this split America and Russia are both to blame, I think. Formerly the five big powers, today America and Russia. As a result everything is split. For example, labor splits. Both the International Confederation of Free Trade Unions and the World Federation of Trade Unions wanted to get in here. The Gold Coast TUC would not affiliate to either. We do not want to take part in the splitting. The Gold Coast TUC is *independent*."

He began to talk about his arrest in 1950. "The charge was 'inciting an illegal strike.'" He grinned widely, "And, in a way, that is what we were doing, of course! But how separate politics from economics? Comes a time when the two converge."

After his release from prison, "I was suspicious, I admit it. But not bitter."

"The Prime Minister set an example to his colleagues," said Costello suddenly. "When he went with them to see the Governor he was intensely suspicious, but there was no bitterness."

Nkrumah nodded. "The Governor and I buried our differences. Now we are out to make this country better for everybody. There is co-operation on both sides. We understand each other."

With remarkable frankness Nkrumah discussed his current problems. "I think I have the confidence of the masses. The people are behind the CPP. I have just been on a four-thousand-mile trip by car. I was traveling five or six weeks. The time had to be extended because the people blocked the roads and would not let us proceed. They wanted me to stop all the time and talk to them. But about self-government they must not make me run too fast—and I must not go too slow. If I tried to stop their urge to be free they would turn on me. My job"—he made another gesture with his hand—"is to keep things level and steady."

I found the off-the-platform Nkrumah a good deal less impressive than the man the crowds cheered. He had good spirits and boyish charm, but seemed, generally speaking, unsophisticated. Of course, his popularity with the crowds had not been gained by discoursing on Hegel, or even Marx, but by mingling freely with the common people, speaking a language they understood, making highly acceptable promises, soundly trouncing his critics, allowing almost anyone to come and see him (crowds throng his house every day), shaking hands with lepers, and stepping down from his car to sit at the curb with his feet in the gutter talking to crippled beggars.

: 2 :

NKRUMAH EATS fish, but not meat. He generally rises at four a.m., reads official papers until half past six, then goes to the CPP headquarters and receives party officials and other visitors for between half an hour and two hours. Then he goes to the Ministry. He often skips lunch altogether, returning instead to party headquarters for more interviews. Most of these are now by appointment. At first, people were likely to call on him at any hour of the day or night, and he always received them; but he has had to curtail this practice.

416

"I sleep when I feel like it," Nkrumah told me. Sometimes, if he does not feel like it, he does not go to bed at all. On the other hand, he may decide to sleep in the afternoon. Recently some white friends discovered that since his return to the Gold Coast at the end of 1947, he had never visited the beach or had a sea bathe. They persuaded him to take a Sunday afternoon off and go to the beach with them. He promptly fell asleep on the sands. Most weekends, however, he spends out of Accra, visiting party branches and making speeches.

His father is dead, but his mother is still alive, aged seventy-one. She often visits him in Accra. As Prime Minister, his salary is ten thousand dollars a year. He hands over his monthly check to the CPP, and much has been made of this by his admirers. But the party pays all his bills. He seldom carries any money about with him. The CPP also pays his income tax. When he needs money, he asks for it.

He lives simply. Shortly after becoming Prime Minister, he confessed to a friend that he could not do any entertaining because he had no cutlery and no table linen beyond what was required for his own meals. A shopping expedition was hurriedly arranged. On another occasion he wanted to buy a gift for a lady and asked for advice. It was suggested that an acceptable gift would be a little golden stool, a favorite Gold Coast ornament. They are often worn as earrings. Nkrumah grinned and confessed: "I've got a whole chestful of these. But the chest is locked and my mother won't let me have the key. She's afraid I would give them all away."

Nkrumah is unmarried. He says very frankly: "Women are too difficult to manage." He also pleads that he has no time (he has no hobbies and plays no games). On the other hand, it is freely rumored in Accra that he has had several girl friends and has fathered several illegitimate children, for whose schooling he pays (the number of alleged children varies). He is, of course, the Gold Coast's most eligible African bachelor.

Nkrumah was born in 1909 in the village of Nkroful, in the district of Nzima, about 220 miles from Accra. He belongs to the Twi (pronounced *Twee*) tribe, an offshoot of the Fanti.

His father was a goldsmith, and his mother a trader. Being a goldsmith meant that his father was a man of some importance. His mother sold cigarettes, rice, sugar, matches, and other odds and ends. The family income was about fifty-six dollars a month. This was a good bit above the economic level of the average Nzima district woodcutter. Nkrumah is of course a famous man in Nkroful now, and the villagers have made up several songs about him. One, a little reproachful, begins: "He has no house in his own town." Another declares: "When Kofi was born, they thought to cast him away, but now he rules the country." The casting-away is pure fancy, but the reference to "Kofi" is interesting: Kwame Nkrumah was originally named Nwier Kofi. Nobody seems to know why he altered the name, and he himself is reticent on the point. He has no brothers or sisters.

He went to school first at a place called Hafasming, forty-nine miles from his birthplace and near the French border. It was a Roman Catholic mission school. Father George Fisher, who is still alive, thought Nkrumah a bright pupil and offered to look after him and pay for his further education. Eventually he was sent to the Government training college for teachers at Accra, but before he finished his course, the new Achimota College was opened and he transferred there. After his training he taught first at Axim, a center of the timber trade, in the Nzima district. Achimota had given him a taste for literature, and he founded and became secretary of the Nzima Literary and Cultural Association. The Roman Catholic priests were assiduous collectors of stories and legends in the vernacular, which they wrote down. Nkrumah austerely lectured his Literary and Cultural society on such subjects as orthography. He was then promoted as teacher to Elmina, where he taught boys who were training to be priests. His own political speeches, especially the earlier ones, contain frequent allusions to the saints.

While teaching at Elmina, Nkrumah was preparing himself for the English matriculation examination, papers for which are set in London. But before taking this examination he visited

Accra during the school holidays in 1934, and had talks with James Aggrey, the co-founder of Achimota College. Aggrey so impressed him that he decided to go to America. He turned down a scholarship in England which was offered to him by Archbishop Porter. An uncle who was a diamond prospector gave him enough money for his passage. He sailed in 1935 for Liverpool, on his way to the United States.

Until then he seems to have shown no interest in world affairs. (Gold Coast newspapers, even today, devote exactly one paragraph daily to "world news.") But his first letter home from the United States discussed Italy's attack on Abyssinia.

Nkrumah had only the vaguest notions of what subjects he intended to study in the United States; to various friends he mentioned teaching, journalism, law, and science. A Negro who was a close friend of Nkrumah at that time told me: "One day he would decide to be a lawyer, but the next day he would read an article about the need for scientists and decide to be a scientist." He was then twenty-six.

During his ten years in the United States, he collected the degrees of M.A., M.Sc., and B.D. from Lincoln University, Pennsylvania, was friendly with Paul Robeson and other prominent and politically minded Negroes, and was appointed president of a body called the African Students' Association of America and Canada. In 1945 he went to England, where he attended classes at the London School of Economics and studied for his bar examinations: he had finally decided to become a lawyer. But he spent so much time in obscure cafés discussing politics that he failed his bar examinations. He was serving on the committees of various Communist-run organizations, and he acquired a British Communist Party membership card. Later, back on the Gold Coast, he explained his possession of this damaging document by saying that he had merely wanted to study the structure of the Communist Party and its "organizational tactics."

In London, now thirty-six, he lived in cheap lodgings and edited a paper called *New Africa.* When the UGCC (United Gold Coast Convention) invited him home to act as their

419

secretary-general, they offered him fifty-six dollars a month and his passage money. He seems to have jumped at the chance. The job was first offered to various former fellow students of Nkrumah who were still in the Gold Coast and who had become lawyers and traders; they all turned it down as insufficiently alluring.

: 3 :

THE VERSION of Nkrumah's activities following his return to the Gold Coast that is given by those who invited him back and whom he proceeded to supplant differs, naturally, in material respects from Nkrumah's own version. The UGCC was led by Dr. Joseph Kwame Kyeretwie Boakye Danquah, who is today, as I have said, the leader of the Ghana Congress Party and leader of the political opposition to the CPP.

When I went to see Dr. Danquah in Accra, I found him a portly, stately, white-haired Negro. He was born in 1895. Danquah, who is the brother of a chief, studied at London University and became a barrister in 1926. After research in Gold Coast history at the British Museum, he rediscovered Ghana and formed the UGCC.

Danquah told me: "In 1947 the UGCC was looking for a secretary who would undertake routine organizational work and so relieve some of the rest of us of burdensome detail. The leaders of the UGCC were lawyers and professional men and led busy lives. We were not making politics a career, but promoting a cause.

"After various names had been suggested, Ako Adjei" (who had studied at Lincoln with Nkrumah, and was a Gold Coast barrister and organizing secretary of the UGCC) "proposed that we get in touch with a young man called Nkrumah, who, it was understood, was anxious to return home and was doing badly in London. So an offer was made, which Nkrumah accepted. Personally, I had never heard of him, but was prepared to accept Adjei's word that he was able and suited for the post, which was a comparatively minor one."

Danquah looked at me and went on indignantly: "Nkrumah lost no time in undermining us older leaders. He went far beyond his instructions and proceeded to organize branches, which he dominated. He organized the younger people, but for his own purposes. We stood for self-government in our time, or in the shortest possible time. Nkrumah preached 'self-government *now*.' He made himself the leader of the young men." (After his arrest in 1948, following the riots, the police found among Nkrumah's private papers, in addition to the British Communist Party membership card, the written rules of a secret society called "The Circle," whose slogan was "Service, Sacrifice, Suffering," and which named Nkrumah "The Leader.")

Danquah proceeded: "We began to hear disturbing reports that in London Nkrumah had declared himself a Communist. We asked him if this was so. He denied it, saying he had merely studied the Communists and their methods. We told him we wanted nothing to do with Communism, even as a student distraction or nursery plaything, but we accepted his denial."

"Do you think now he is a Communist?" I asked.

Danquah laughed derisively. "No, he knows nothing about Communism. He calls himself a Marxist Socialist, but he has not read even ten pages of Karl Marx."

When he was in London, Nkrumah published a pamphlet called *Towards Colonial Freedom*. It is heavy with the jargon of Marx and, like *Das Kapital*, seems to have been written mainly in the British Museum. It is also painfully half-baked.

But a glance at some of Nkrumah's Cabinet colleagues discredits the allegation, frequently heard in Danquah's circle, that Nkrumah and his friends are "uneducated." The Minister of Education, Kojo Botsio, is a B.A. of Oxford. The Minister of Health, Tommy Hutton-Mills, is a Negro barrister who was educated at Cambridge. E. O. Asafu-Adjaye, the Minister of Local Government, is a B.A., LL.B., of London; to enter the

Cabinet he gave up one of the biggest and most lucrative law practices on the Gold Coast.

Admirers as well as detractors call Nkrumah "Showboy." The painfully earnest student who wrote *Towards Colonial Freedom* also confided to friends, when he returned to the Gold Coast, that in England he had "lots of girl friends." It is not especially surprising. Kwame Nkrumah is a good-looking man, with very considerable charm.

"Why is he called 'Showboy'?" asked Dr. Busia, a fence-sitting Negro intellectual who lectures brilliantly on sociology at Achimota College in Accra. "Because he appeals to the masses and their emotions," he said, smiling. "They *love* jazz bands and flag-waving. Therefore they love Nkrumah."

There is little doubt about the bobby-soxer emotions that Nkrumah arouses. Crowds throng his two-story red-brick house in Accra; for privacy he has had to surround it with a six-foot wall topped with broken glass. The CPP headquarters in Accra are in a narrow street choked with beggars and patent-medicine purveyors. When Nkrumah arrives, he has to struggle through a hero-worshipping mob.

According to Danquah, Nkrumah is a reckless demagogue, eaten up with personal vanity. He got into power by making promises, which he then proceeded to break; in order to remain in power he has transformed himself from an agitator into a British stooge.

Danquah was naturally bitter about being "undermined"; he could not help feeling that it was he who should be sitting in the Prime Minister's office. The revolution succeeded, but the wrong man got the job.

When I asked Dr. Danquah, however, what his policy would be if he came to power, and how it would differ from the CPP's, he seemed somewhat at a loss. Like the CPP, he demands full self-government. The CPP outbid him by clamoring for "self-government now," instead of "self-government in the shortest possible time." Danquah nowadays tries to outbid the CPP by declaring that it has failed to keep its pledge. When Nkrumah proposed that the next step should be dominion status for

"Ghana" within the British Commonwealth, Danquah at once countered by demanding complete independence, with no mention of membership of the Commonwealth. He told me gleefully: "Oh, that put them on the spot!" Privately, he admits that in fact he would keep "Ghana" in the Commonwealth. "Where else could we go? Whom else could we join? We could not stand alone." Despite his attempts to outbid the CPP, Danquah is at heart a conservative; in my presence, one of his own supporters called him to his face "a real old Tory."

Danquah is a disillusioned man. He admitted, in a sudden burst of gloom, that he did not expect to see a change of power in his party's favor for "perhaps twenty years." The Danquah party consists mainly of a small group of intellectuals; they have no mass following in the country. About Danquah himself a senior British official said frankly: "He would be hopeless as Prime Minister. He has been 'agin the Government' so long that, in power, he would soon split his own party. Danquah is a professional oppositionist."

Danquah and his friends are intelligent; they have more suavity than some of the CPP leaders. Most of them are closely related to chiefs. They themselves are prosperous businessmen, well-to-do lawyers, or university lecturers.

I went to a party given in Accra by the Ghana Congress Party for the former British Colonial Secretary, James Griffiths. Everyone congregated on the flat garden-roof of a large white mansion, the opulent residence of a rich Danquah supporter, Obetsebi Lamptey, who is a lawyer. The guests filed through suites of rooms filled with rich furniture and divans covered in baby-blue satin, then ascended a broad staircase to the roof, where tea and cakes were served at little tables.

The Negro lawyers and businessmen moved around, beaming behind horn-rimmed spectacles, their heavy jowls dripping perspiration and benevolence. At the tables sat their brothers and cousins, the paramount chiefs, swathed in togas. Beside each chief was his official interpreter, grasping a tall stick with an elaborate gold carving of the chief's totem on top. The chiefs gulped down the tea, greedily consumed all the cakes in sight, and earnestly licked their fingers afterwards. The lawyers and the chiefs naturally resent the raw, urbanized democracy that the CPP mainly appeals to.

The Ghana Congress Party appeals to the higher-ranking, better-paid African civil servants, some of whom earn four thousand dollars a year. These top-ranking Africans are all educated men, like Danquah; generally speaking, they despise their lesser brethren. They have no time for the mobs who cheer Nkrumah wherever he goes.

In the Gold Coast, political parties grow as easily as cocoa trees. There is the Universal Conservative Party, the Conventional National People's Democratic Party, and an unnamed party the chief plank in whose program is "marriage with more than one woman." Like the cocoa trees, such parties are usually afflicted early with swollen shoot and die off. A CPP journalist gibed: "The slogan of the opposition groups is 'Utopia when each man has his own party.'"

: 4 :

WASHED BY milk-warm, pale-blue seas under a hot, cloud-piled sky, the humid Gold Coast is nevertheless happy and prosperous. "God is busy growing cocoa," is an easygoing Gold Coast saying.

The cocoa tree is a skinny, white-barked, big-leafed tree, which, without any tending, sprouts big tough pods containing purple beans. You plant the tree and God does the rest, except for breaking open the pods and drying out the beans. From a "load" of cocoa (sixty pounds), a farmer earns nine dollars. The Cocoa Board's financial reserve is standing at nearly $250,000,000.

All day and all night the big, crowded, beat-up "mammy-trucks," owned by Gold Coast's prosperous women traders, thundered along the twisting roads that wind through the thick-planted cocoa groves. The roads link the Gold Coast's sprawling tin towns, its seashore villages, stinking of fish, where the fisherfolk put out to sea in big dugout canoes, and its inland villages, where square mud houses nestle amid the tall palms with their fan-shaped leaves, and where purplish-brown cocoa beans and bright red peppers are spread out on the ground to dry, looking like gay carpets. The wildly driven trucks, packed with cheerful chocolate-brown humanity, bear such signs as "Praise God" and "Alone and miserable." One truck I saw had painted on its side: "With God's help, anything is possible." Another had a plaintive question: "A beautiful woman never stays with one man—why?"

Of the Gold Coast's untidy towns, with their tin shacks, peeling white buildings, and open street sewers, a South African said to me sneeringly: "They're all just shantytowns, like our Negro locations. How whites can live in them at all I fail to understand." The whites in fact live on the outskirts of the towns, in big two-story, Europeanized houses, with large, cool, high-ceilinged rooms, waited on by efficient, white-clad black servants, always standing by with trays of tall iced drinks. But when they go shopping, the Europeans still have to get out of their cars and push their way through the jostling Negro throng, wait their turn with Negroes at shop counters and in post offices, and share the cinemas, hotels, bars, and dance halls with them. I found no segregation, no zoning of the towns into "white" and "Negro" areas. Anyone, if he had the cash, could live anywhere.

"But the towns aren't the real Gold Coast," an old-time white Coaster told me scornfully. "The real Gold Coast is in the bush."

A handful of white officials still do their "tours," or spells of duty, in the bush. After a few months, I was told, they go "queer." A white man who had lived most of his life in the Gold Coast told me: "You can always recognize them by their manner. They're painfully shy, behave oddly, relapse into long silences, and go to parties only to get drunk. They come out of the bush cursing the country, but after a few days their one wish is to get back into the bush. It gets them."

Most people still believe in juju, including even some whites.

A white trader, who obviously believed it himself, told me this story: "There was a European who insulted an African. The African put a juju on him. In three months the European was stark staring mad."

To put a juju on someone, he explained, you get hold of clippings of his hair, or the scrapings of his teeth (in this instance the vengeful African bribed the white man's dentist). Then you swear a curse, and the job's done.

Another way of putting a juju on someone is to sneak into his room and place your juju in a secret place—tied underneath his chair, or under the mattress of his bed. The juju may be simply a twig, a piece of cotton, or a dead spider. But it will perform its task adequately provided you have the proper magic.

An African truck-driver, employed by the Government, had a juju put on him. He was told that within a week he would be involved in a bad accident, but not be killed; subsequently he would be in another accident and this time he *would* be killed. Within the week he crashed his truck. Though he was prepared to carry on with his job and defy the juju, the Government gave him another job, having nothing to do with trucks. An official explained: "Of course, we didn't believe in the juju, but the other Africans did and it was rather horrifying to watch them watching him and waiting for him to die; none of them would get into his truck."

I met a young Gold Coaster who was highly literate but who still believed in juju. He told me solemnly: "If we had Dr. Malan here, he would die quickly."

"You mean you would actually kill him?"

"Not directly. I would shoot an arrow into a pail of water and *will* him to die."

"What if Dr. Malan shot the arrow into the pail first and willed Nkrumah to die?" I jested.

He replied solemnly: "Malan would like to do that, but he could not. Nkrumah is stronger than Malan."

The fat "mammies" who control a big share of the Gold Coast's commerce own the fleets of trucks that go dashing recklessly day and night from one end of the country to the other. But the up-and-coming generation of Gold Coasters seemed to me to have one ambition: to become taxi-drivers. At the current rate of progress toward this goal, it seemed as if half the population would soon be driving the other half around in cabs. The bumpy roads swarmed with the tiny buzzing cars, honking their way triumphantly past the mammy-trucks. Cabmen off duty strolled the streets of Accra, hand in hand, like courting couples. Gold Coast men hold hands with one another with no trace of self-consciousness. The cab-drivers had formed themselves into regional associations; each regional organizer, called "the chief," collected the members' monthly dues, established fares, and took a handsome rake-off for his services.

In Accra the open-air cinemas, whose audiences sat in deck-chairs, were packed morning, afternoon, and evening with Negro adults and children biting on candy and breathlessly following the adventures of Hollywood cowboys, pirates, and gangsters. The two films that smashed all box-office records throughout British West Africa were *The Mark of Zorro* and *King Kong*. *Tarzan* was popular, and so was Gene Autry.

In the restaurants, Gold Coasters were consuming juicy thick steaks and large quantities of eggs. A typical meal consisted of meat, fish, eggs, bananas, and cassava, all swimming in rich gravy and with plenty of peppers.

Gold Coast Negro timber merchants travel as far afield as Dakar and Algiers to attend business conferences. They and other Gold Coasters, white and black, do much of their traveling by air. West African Airways has made air travel cheap. I found I could go anywhere in the Gold Coast or Nigeria for a few dollars. The big-bellied freight and passenger plane that flies from Accra to Lagos and Kano, in Nigeria, is called by patrons "the Pregnant Cow."

I attended a party given by a Gold Coast merchant whose home was built above his office and store. Outside, the sky deepened to a butterfly blue. The music of Mozart bled quietly from a big radio into a crowded room. Some of the guests were barefooted and squatted on the carpeted floor, drinking whisky.

The house was enormous, and sprawling. Big green lizards with yellow heads scampered up and down the outer walls. When someone pulled out a small table from a nest of tables, a family of spiders was disturbed.

The furniture was solid and Victorian; bad framed photographs hung on the walls. In the bedrooms, enameled white chamberpots peered unabashed from under high, old-fashioned iron beds. The offices downstairs were equipped with functional steel desks, glass-topped. But in the yard beside the office door, small bleating goats were tethered between the dustbins, and small naked children peed against the wall.

The radio went on playing Mozart. A guest rose to go and called for his driver. The driver failed to appear. A summoned servant explained loudly that he was in the latrine. "The latrine!" groaned the departing guest. "Always he is in the latrine." He turned to the assembled mixed company and explained: "It is something that is wrong with his belly."

After he had gone, the rest of us trooped upstairs to the flat roof, where chairs had been arranged facing a cinema screen. Our host owned a big projector, which he handled with skill. Soon, under the glittering disregarded African stars, the entranced guests were sucking in their breath while Kit Carson rode again.

The inevitable mixing of Western and African ways, with the inevitable initial result of some comic incongruities, is deplored by the more earnest Gold Coast nationalists. A shocked nationalist wrote in a letter to the Accra *Daily Graphic*: "Recently at a dance held in Kumasi, I saw an African girl turned away—by an African—because she wore our graceful and becoming native costume. She was rudely told, 'European dress only.' Such people should be banished to Siberia or the United Kingdom. Maybe this would be too harsh, you think. But something should be done."

Problems like these exercise the minds of the British Council, which is out to promote the maximum goodwill between Europeans and Africans. John Stuart Mill described Britain's colonies as a "vast system of outdoor relief for the upper classes."

Cynics today say the British Council performs the same function for otherwise unemployable British intellectuals, who are shipped off to the colonies to lecture the natives on such subjects as the inner meaning of the poetry of T. S. Eliot.

Because it takes itself with enormous seriousness, the British Council perhaps lays itself open to such gibes. In Accra a signpost pointing the way to its headquarters reads: "The British Council Is at the End of the Road." Native music and customs are zealously studied and native dancing and drumming encouraged. The Council is almost breathless with tact: in Accra it sponsored the performance of a thriller by Agatha Christie, originally entitled *Ten Little Niggers*. The Council re-named the play *Ten Little Chinamen*. Usually, however, the fare provided is on a higher mental plane; the British Council dotes on Gilbert and Sullivan, or, at a higher level still, Restoration comedy. "Just what they expect black Coasters to make of Congreve," said a white critic, "passes my humble comprehension."

But a different complaint made to me was that most Gold Coasters show distressingly little interest in culture. One educationist said rather bitterly: "All they want to know about is know-how." What he meant was that practical-minded Gold Coasters buy, borrow, and read books about the working of motor-cars, airplanes, and machine tools, in preference to Shakespeare, Wordsworth, and Keats.

Some less culturally minded observers think this an excellent sign. "Formerly," one man told me, "Negro parents scraped together hard-earned shillings to send their children to school, thinking education was the key to a higher standard of living, which was what they wanted. The kids were taught the dates of the kings of England, and learned to recite poems about dancing daffodils and sparrows in the hedgerows, which they had never seen and were never likely to. The result was that while they despised their backward parents, they learned nothing useful; the parents at least knew how to grow cocoa. The height of their ambition was to become post-office clerks so that they could be rude to humbler mortals, black and white, through the wire grille at a public counter. The Second World War was responsible for inculcating a new attitude. Gold Coasters served in the army, learned how to handle machines and drive trucks. They came back wanting to be mechanics and radio operators."

XXIX

NIGERIA:
THE SUN RISES IN THE WEST

A WHITE PILOT with a square-cut, flaming red beard walked briskly toward the Pregnant Cow. The other passengers and I straggled after him and climbed aboard.

My fellow passengers included a young African in white drill and a big sun helmet, Moslems in flowing robes, and a number of African women who carried babies strapped on their backs and balanced their luggage, wrapped in cotton, on their heads. We settled ourselves in our seats. The plane roared off the runway. The women placidly began to suckle their infants.

From Accra we flew eastward over the lagoons, fringed with palms, and the sandbars, thick with white sea-birds, of French Dahomey. The light faded rapidly as we flew, for the plane had started late. When we reached Lagos airport it was quite dark. An air-line bus was waiting to drive us to the capital of Nigeria. I sat beside the young African, who wore his sun helmet at a rakish angle. He also wore his white shirt outside his pants. He was reading an old novel by Aldous Huxley.

The houses of Lagos were like so many pumpkins, cut open and lit from within. They seemed insubstantial edifices, with yellow light pouring from their many windows. No curtains were drawn, and the occupants, I thought, must have about as much privacy as goldfish in a bowl. The bus roared past the brilliant lines of pumpkins, driven at reckless speed. In West Africa the technique of driving is to put the foot hard down

431

on the accelerator and keep it there. The bus swerved and lurched round sharp corners so that the passengers had to cling to their seats. Nobody seemed to mind. When the driver wished to stop to let passengers off, he simply shifted his foot from the accelerator and brought it hard down on the foot-brake.

From Accra I had telegraphed ahead to a Lagos hotel for accommodation, but when I inquired at the desk the clerk shook his head. "I'm sorry, we're full up."

"Didn't you get my wire?"

"Oh, yes," he agreed, smiling genially. "But we have no room."

"But I telegraphed days ago."

He nodded brightly. "Yes. We are full up."

"Well, I've got to sleep somewhere. And it's late. Can you recommend another hotel?"

He did so, and dispatched me and my bag in a cab.

We turned several corners in rapid succession and came to a halt in an alley facing a blank wall. The driver pointed to a small, dimly lit doorway, from which came muffled sounds of revelry.

Inside the doorway was a tiny office, and beyond the office a bar occupied by seamen singing bawdy songs. A fat bald man in his shirtsleeves and wearing no collar sat in the office looking gloomily at a fly-specked calendar on the wall.

"We're full up *here*," he said, "but I can put you in the annex."

"Where is the annex?"

"The boy will take you and carry your bag."

He pressed a bell, and a small Negro, about twelve years of age, appeared. He was barefoot and his single garment was a ragged shirt. He balanced my large bag on his head and walked out into the alley. I followed him, but told my cab-driver to wait.

My guide plunged into a maze of sub-alleys and we walked on for some time. It was not quite dark, for at intervals there were holes in the wall and in each hole sat a man, in rags, with a guttering candle stuck in the ground beside him. Nor was it silent, for the men in rags in the holes in the wall beat monotonously on drums made from kerosene cans. The noise of the tin drums rose from all the alleys and echoed between the high walls.

"Look," I called to my guide, "where is this annex?"

He turned, my bag still balanced on his head. "Not far now," he said, and we walked on.

Finally the boy stopped and pointed to a sagging wooden staircase that wound round the outside of a dilapidated building and vanished in the upper darkness. From its interior came the sound of further drunken revelry.

"Annex," he said simply.

A skinny hand gripped my ankle, and a man crawled out of his hole in the wall.

"You buy nice girl?" he inquired happily. "She only sixteen."

Attracted by the sound of voices, other men began to scramble eagerly out of their holes in the wall.

Firmly I retraced my footsteps, calling to my guide. I noticed that he accepted the position philosophically, and I suspected this was not the first time a walk to the annex had been in vain.

I retrieved my bag, got into the cab, and drove back to the first hotel. I planned to throw myself on the proprietor's mercy, but as I passed through the main lounge a voice hailed me. It was Stephen Watts, formerly the film critic of the London *Daily Express*. We shook hands and I explained my predicament.

"Oh, well, we'll try again," said Stephen.

When I approached the desk for the second time, the clerk swiveled his book toward me and extended a pen.

"You have a room for me?" I demanded.

"Oh, yes," he said, smiling genially. "Plenty rooms."

"You will find," Stephen said, "much to amuse you in Nigeria. I have been here three days."

433

: 2 :

LAGOS BY daylight proved to be a sprawling, sweltering waterfront town. Its narrow streets were crowded with cheerful pedestrians, hurtling cyclists, hooting taxicabs, speeding buses, and thundering trucks. The trucks, like those in the Gold Coast, had striking legends painted on their sides and on the front of their driving cabs. I found it quite an experience to leap back hastily to the sidewalk as a truck swung sharply round a corner bearing the ominous text: "Prepare to meet thy God."

I had introductions to people in Lagos, and hopefully rang a telephone number. "But of course we must meet!" said a voice cordially. "Tell you what, I'll fix up something and call you back." I expressed my heartfelt thanks.

I was about to sit down to lunch with Stephen Watts when I was called to the telephone.

"Well, now!" said the same voice, still cordial. "Let's get together. What are you doing at the moment?"

"I'm just about to have lunch."

"Pooh!" said the voice good-naturedly. "Hotel lunches are no good. Get a cab and meet me at the club."

I made my excuses to Stephen. I thought he watched me go with a sardonic eye.

It was a cross-town drive. We dived into narrow alleys, scraped the walls on both sides, and emerged triumphantly at the other end, sweeping before us small boys, bleating goats, and squawking chickens, as if the cab were a broom. Occasionally an alley proved to be a cul-de-sac. When this happened, the driver laughed good-naturedly and reversed his gears, forcing the small boys, goats, and chickens to retreat rapidly into doorways. Lagos seemed to consist mostly of alleys.

The club was an unpretentious white building of one story, sheltered from the sun by mango trees. My host, a large man in a white shirt and white shorts, led me to a long bar counter, took his seat on a tall stool, and ordered gins. Other people

434

joined us. Time passed. I was getting hungrier and hungrier. I glanced several times at my watch.

"Oh, that's all right," said my host. "I don't have to be back in my office until half past three. Have another gin."

I had another gin.

Finally he rose regretfully. "Well, I'm afraid I must be off home for lunch, if I'm to make the office on time. And, by Jove, old man, you'll have to dash too if you're going to get any lunch at your hotel. Not that hotel lunches are much good, though."

I had paid off my cab, but he was very kind. He got the bartender to produce another cab for me.

"I don't suppose," said Stephen, "that he really went home to lunch at all. But he noticed that you were hungry, and gave you an excuse to go. As far as I can discover, they never eat here; they just drink instead. That's one of the amusing things about Nigeria."

Harold Cooper, who directs Nigeria's public relations and is Nigeria's counterpart of Major Jimmy Costello on the Gold Coast—both are, of course, British colonial servants—told me other interesting things about the country.

Nigeria is more than twice as large as Japan and has a population of 30,000,000. But it has little unity. The north is ruled by emirs. The south is divided between Yorubas and Ibos. The northerners are Moslems, the southerners Christian or plain pagan. The Yorubas dislike the Ibos, the Ibos dislike the Yorubas, and the northerners dislike all southerners. Nevertheless Nigeria, like the Gold Coast, is clamoring for full self-government, meaning independence of British rule.

The handful of whites seemed sure that Nigeria would get its independence very soon, but appeared unperturbed about it. The United Africa Company, which is the world's biggest trading concern, was putting up new buildings in Lagos and was still pouring millions of pounds into the country. The company's affairs in West Africa were briskly conducted by a fifty-six-year-old Irishman, Patrick Fitzgerald, who had spent thirty years of his life "on the coast." Fitzgerald thought nothing of arriving at his office to begin the day's work at half past three in the morning, or of driving through the night to keep a business appointment hundreds of miles away at dawn. He also played cricket and polo.

I returned to my hotel after my talk with Harold Cooper, to find that Stephen Watts had mysteriously vanished. He had hurriedly paid his bill and fled, no one knew whither. I was disappointed, for he had been a cheerful companion.

I was just about to sit down to a solitary dinner when I was called to the telephone. It was my cordial club acquaintance.

"Tell me," he said heartily, "what are you doing this evening?"

"I'm just about to have dinner."

"Alone?"

"Well, yes."

"Nonsense! Join me at the club in five minutes."

I hesitated, but the idea of eating alone was not attractive. "All right."

At the club they were still drinking gin, occasionally varying it by consuming a little Scotch or some bottles of German beer. It was a mixed gathering. I was discussing the country with a girl not long out from England to whom I was introduced, when she gave a pleased exclamation: "Oh, here is my husband; he wants to meet you." We were joined by a smiling Negro, who was a local attorney.

Time passed. I had the feeling that this was where I had come in. I began to glance at my watch.

"What's the time?" asked my host.

"Half past ten," I said, thinking regretfully of the dinner I had abandoned.

"Early yet," he said. "But, I say, perhaps you're hungry?"

"You've dined already?"

"Oh, no," he said. "Much too early for me. But I'll tell you what, you have a bite."

He called the bartender, who vanished through a door and came back with a whole cold, cooked chicken on a plate. Everyone gathered round to watch me eat it. They seemed to think it was a curious performance. They went on drinking gin.

: 3 :

THROUGH A village near Ibadan stalked four monsters. They were twelve feet high, and cylinder-shaped. The men on stilts wore grinning masks, and long gowns, striped like barbers' poles, which came down to the ground and concealed the stilts. They were preceded by a solemn little black boy, pot-bellied and totally naked, who was beating a drum.

"Igunnu," my Ibo driver explained, "medicine men. They go round the villages smelling out witches."

We had driven the hundred miles from Lagos to Ibadan at an average speed of seventy miles an hour. The narrow road twisted and turned between high green walls of bamboo. Occasionally, at a sharp corner, we flashed past another Dodge truck, off the road and upside down. Once we came on a broken-down bus round which people were still gathered. The driver, the people explained, had lost his nerve. Foreseeing a head-on collision with another vehicle, he had simply leaped from his seat into the bushes by the side of the road. His bus, driverless, had avoided a collision after all, but had run into a tree. The driver, miraculously unhurt, was grinning somewhat shamefacedly, while his stranded passengers chaffed him. Nobody seemed to think the incident anything but amusing. After we had resumed our journey, I kept a close eye on oncoming trucks and buses, and noticed that several of them had their cab doors unlatched and swung open, ready for any emergency.

The chief occupation of the people of the villages through which we passed appeared to be selling hats. The open-air hat-stalls lined both sides of the road: first some straggling outposts before a village was reached, like outskirt hot-dog stands; then a thickening cluster, until, by the time we reached the village itself, the eye was blinded by hats. They were all shaped like skullcaps and made of velvet, and they were all the colors of the rainbow. There were pink hats, purple hats, white hats, blue hats, and hats striped green and white, purple and yellow, red and blue. Finally I could resist them no longer. I stopped the car and bought two. They cost less than a dollar apiece.

The villages of Nigeria must be the noisiest, most densely populated, most exuberant, and most colorful villages on earth. The narrow streets were always thronged. Buses, trucks, taxis, and private cars squeezed past one another continually, with much honking. Cyclists wove wildly in and out, ringing their bells. To add to the fun, there were no sidewalks. Each village had hundreds of little shops, and each shop was crammed with goods. They sold mirrors, combs, bracelets, ointments, patent medicines, newspapers, books, hairbrushes, and packs of cards for telling fortunes. And, of course, hats.

Ibadan, with a population of half a million, is estimated to be the biggest city in tropical Africa. Its mud hovels sprawl over seven hills, like ancient Rome. Innumerable religions have their temples in Ibadan, ranging from fetish-worship through Islam to Christianity. The temple of the God of Thunder is next door to the Methodist chapel. The chief pagan deity is a fertility goddess. Her worshippers say she has two huge breasts, shaped like water-pots and each capable of feeding sixteen children simultaneously. Her shrine consists, appropriately, of two large pots at the foot of a tree; women who want to have children pray and place kola nuts in the pots as offerings to the goddess.

Paganism is said to be dying out (Islam, however, is getting more converts than Christianity). But once a year the people of Ibadan still prance through the streets, acclaiming the fertility goddess. Small children brandish sticks shaped to represent crude sexual symbols and sing smutty songs.

My driver took me through the town to the University of Ibadan. The contrast was startling. The university was designed by Maxwell Fry, who also designed Accra's Community Centre. With a close eye on the climate and the brilliant African colors, Fry has created long flat-roofed blocks of fretted stone, which are colored in vivid reds, blues, and yellows. The university has one hundred professors and lecturers on its staff; there are four hundred students, of whom twenty are women.

The principal of the University was Sir Kenneth Mellanby, a British parasitologist who during the Second World War carried out some interesting experiments on human guinea-pigs: conscientious objectors willingly submitted themselves as subjects for his researches into the biting propensities of various types of flea. I had long wished to meet Sir Kenneth; but a number of students told me regretfully that the principal was away visiting Europe—possibly looking for more guinea-pigs.

The students were wearing spotless white flannels and gay-colored blazers. They told me they were off to play cricket. A girl student, swinging a neat skirt, walked across the quadrangle carrying a tennis racket. I thought of the fertility goddess and the twelve-foot medicine men, and drove on, past the university library, which contains seventy thousand volumes.

Many of the students were already living in Maxwell Fry's fretted blocks. Ultimately all will, as well as the members of the staff, most of whom have been imported from Cambridge and Oxford. But at the time of my visit, many of the young lecturers were still housed in "bungalows," which were in fact old wooden army huts, with bucket sanitation. I had been allotted one of the huts.

When I entered, someone else's baggage had already been moved in, and a man was sitting on the edge of a bed with his head in his hands. He sprang up with a stifled cry of terror as I walked in, then recognized me and relaxed. "Oh, it's you!" he said thankfully.

"How did you get here?" I demanded. "You vanished from Lagos without a trace. You didn't even leave a message. I searched all over for you. I—"

Stephen Watts waved me to silence with a weary hand. "I am a fugitive," he said hollowly.

"From what?"

"Chicken-pox."

He glared at me when I laughed. "It isn't funny! I must be in London in two days. D'you realize they might put me in an isolation ward for two weeks if they found out?"

"You don't look as if you had chicken-pox," I said.

439

"No, but the man I was sharing a room with had."

Returning to his hotel room in Lagos, Stephen had found a stranger installed. The stranger was in bed, and announced he was feeling unwell. Stephen insisted on calling a doctor, and the doctor diagnosed chicken-pox.

"I spent the night at the airport and caught the first plane up here," he said.

I looked round the rather bare and gloomy hut. "Have you been comfortable?"

"Well," he said gloomily, "you won't get much sleep, I can tell you that."

We found the lecturers consuming large quantities of soup, stew, potatoes, jam-roll pudding, tea, and bread. They were all extremely young and cheerful. A girl with a horse-tail hairdo was discussing the proper method of dissecting frogs. A young man with spectacles confided to me that he specialized in the study of letters and accounts of eighteenth-century Manchester business houses. I did not venture to inquire what scope he hoped to find for his specialty in West Africa.

The meal concluded, the lecturers romped out. Soon the solemn strains of Beethoven symphonies were booming from several phonographs. After the musical session, the lecturers went off to play tennis. While I perspired freely in the tropical heat, I could hear the brisk smack of balls and the sound of animated voices. There was a short interlude of quiet, while the lecturers prepared their notes for the next day's work. Dinner consisted of more soup, stew, potatoes, and pudding. After dinner someone produced a phonograph, and the lecturers performed boisterous square dances until after midnight.

"I see what you mean," I said to Stephen as we crawled under our mosquito nets, while the dance music still continued.

"You wait until morning," he said darkly.

I was awakened at six by the clashing of cymbals, the beating of drums, and what sounded like several animals in anguish.

"They have formed a university band," said Stephen as he dragged himself toward the improvised shower. "It practices every morning at this time, for an hour."

The band marched proudly round and round the huts. It had plenty of brass. There were also some bagpipe-players.

"When I first came here," said Stephen, pulling on his clothes, "I wondered what these young folk did about their sex life. I know now. They don't have any. They sublimate it."

: 4 :

IN THE bad old days in Ibadan, the witch doctors from time to time presented unpopular chiefs with the ominous gift of parrots' eggs. This was the Ibadan equivalent of the black spot in *Treasure Island*. It was a polite indication to the chief that he should retire from office. But the chieftainship was hereditary, and the only way a chief could retire was to commit suicide. If he declined to do so, he was seized and beheaded.

Political problems are now solved more amicably. Near the University of Ibadan stands the Western Nigerian House of Assembly. I drove over to watch its proceedings.

The building itself is a white edifice surrounded by cool green lawns. Its many doors and windows stood wide open. The open windows framed the blue sky, the bright green of the grass, and the fleshy branches of mango trees. A Negro policeman, wearing crisply creased shorts and a short-sleeved black shirt stood at the door of the public gallery, benevolently looking down on the heads of the politicians. Around the chamber, in high wall niches, green-painted fans gently whirred. Presiding over the Assembly, of six whites and eighty-one Negroes, was a fresh-faced man with a brisk manner, called Bill Milliken, who was born in New Zealand.

The members sat in rows at highly polished mahogany desks. Some wore Western clothing, but these had discarded their jackets and were in their shirtsleeves. Others wore flowing colored robes, and round hats, richly embroidered, of blue, white, or red. As they rose to speak, one after another, the air became thick with such phrases as "the honorable member," and "Mr. Speaker, sir." Everybody spoke in English.

Sitting on opposite benches, facing each other, were two small men who looked like black editions of Tweedledum and Tweedledee. Each had close-cropped hair, outjutting ears, and large spectacles. Each wore a long, wide-sleeved garment like a white nightgown, with richly embroidered, blue silk pajama-like trousers underneath. Except for the costumes, it was rather like watching Gandhi looking at Gandhi.

The two men were the most important members of the Western House of Assembly. One was Dr. Nnamdi Azikiwe, the leader of the party called the National Convention of Nigeria and the Cameroons (NCNC). The other was Mr. Obafemi Awolowo, leader of the Action Group.

For years Dr. Zik, as Azikiwe is popularly known, was the undisputed political boss of Nigeria's nationalist-minded southerners. An Ibo, Zik was educated in America. He returned to Nigeria full of national fervor and started a political newspaper. He now owns a whole chain of newspapers, all vituperatively political, and all written in remarkable English. An editorial in a Zik paper will frequently refer to Zik's opponents as "politically unprincipled pithecanthropuses." Zik is a powerful man, and much feared.

But a few years ago the political ball was snatched from him, at any rate temporarily, by Mr. Awolowo. A product of London University, Awolowo became a barrister of the Inner Temple. He founded the Trades Union Congress of Nigeria, and wrote, in remarkably cool and cogent language, a book pleading the cause of moderate nationalism, *Nigeria's Path to Freedom*. He formed his own political party, the Action Group, and split the hitherto solid south when elections were held under Nigeria's new Constitution. Zik still controlled the eastern half of southern Nigeria, but Awolowo's Action Group conquered the west. As he represents Lagos, which is a western constituency, Zik anomalously sits in the Western House, dominated by his rival.

I watched the two little men gazing at each other stonily, then listened for a while to the debate. It was a humdrum affair. The members were attempting to deal with the problem raised by the latest population census. This had revealed that the number of children under the age of five was double what had been estimated, thus throwing the entire educational program out of gear.

At the first opportunity I sought a talk with Awolowo, which was readily granted. He asked me to meet him in his upstairs office, and when I arrived he was already seated behind his desk. He promptly came from behind it and sat beside me.

"Dr. Awolowo," I said, "is it true you want full self-government for Nigeria by 1956?"

"Yes," he said. "Everyone, including the British, knows full self-government must come soon. I've set a definite date so that the transition can be effected smoothly."

"Apart from the British, won't the northern emirs object?"

"Not if we create an elastic, federal Nigeria, instead of trying for a rigid, unitary one," he said. "The emirs are afraid we southerners want to run their affairs for them. We don't. And we certainly shan't precipitate a crisis that might lead to partition, as in India."

"Would a self-governing Nigeria remain within the British Commonwealth?"

"Of course; and it would also remain on the side of the West, in the event of a clash with Communism."

"Suppose Nigeria found itself in a war on the same side as South Africa? The South Africans don't like the idea of self-governing Negro countries in Africa."

Awolowo grinned. "We would fight on the same side as South Africa, nevertheless; because a self-governing Nigeria would be equal in status to South Africa—and don't forget the South Africans would probably have to put up with India as an ally as well!"

Awolowo made no secret of his dislike of Zik and of Zik's methods. He regarded Zik as both unscrupulous and dangerous. He feared Zik's rabble-rousing methods might end in violence. "And," said Awolowo grimly, "even if you get self-government through violence, you may find yourself unable to end the violence after you have got self-government."

I had hoped for a talk with Zik, but when I approached him,

he excused himself and asked me if I would visit him at his home in Lagos. I said I would, and we made an appointment. When I returned to Lagos on the appointed day, I drove out to Zik's grandiose house, a four-story structure in spacious grounds. When I drove up, a guard emerged from a sentry-box at the gate and demanded to know my business. It was rather like trying to get into Buckingham Palace. When I explained that I had an appointment, the guard told me brusquely that Zik had not returned to Lagos. This was the only time I ever had a definite appointment with any politician in Africa that was not kept.

I was subsequently informed that Zik dislikes the "foreign" press, which he declares is "hostile": words very reminiscent of other nationalist leaders I had known elsewhere. But I found it a somewhat astonishing statement, in view of the agile acrobatics performed with the facts in Zik's own Nigerian newspapers.

: 5 :

THE MINISTER of Commerce in the Nigerian Government, Chudifu Nwapa, was only a few years ago an outstanding athlete at Cambridge University. He was also a member of the committee of the Cambridge Students' Union, for three years running. This does not by itself make Nwapa outstanding among his Nigerian Cabinet colleagues. The Minister of Lands, Okoi Arikpo, is a Fellow of both the Royal Anthropological Society and the Royal Economic Society.

"Nigeria," said Nwapa in a broadcast, "is a peaceful country. Thirty million Nigerians—the largest population of any country in Africa—are moving towards full self-government within the British Commonwealth. There is no color-bar, for in a Commonwealth you cannot have first-class coaches for some groups and third-class coaches for others.

"Racial tension does exist in some parts of Africa. Some people even feel that night is drawing in over the whole continent.

444

But it is the custom of us Africans to do things differently—sometimes even the wrong way round. In Africa today, the sun is rising in the west, not in the east. It is in the west that we are finding ways and means of solving the age-old problems of inter-racial co-operation. We Nigerians want to set a good example in race relations. We want to heal wounds, not to inflame them."

But others seemed to think differently. Despite Awolowo's apparent respect for the feelings of the northern emirs, and his expressed anxiety not to antagonize them, a prominent member of Awolowo's Action Group visited the ancient northern city of Kano and boldly requested the permission of the Emir of Kano to hold a meeting of southerners just outside the city gates. The Emir angrily refused.

Outside Kano, in an area called "the Strangers' Quarter," thousands of southerners, Ibos and Yorubas, live and trade. Tempers became strained. Fulanis and Hausas, all Moslems and loyal to the Emir, gathered in the city's narrow streets, outside the green-domed mosque. At a given signal, they rushed out of the city gates, brandishing swords and knives, and invaded the Strangers' Quarter.

The fighting went on for two days. Ibos and Yorubas were trapped among the great piles of groundnuts that rise like pyramids outside Kano's ancient mud walls, and there were done to death. The vultures that infest the city, protected against harm by Moslem law, sat on the walls and watched the slaughter. About fifty people were killed and many more injured before order was restored.

Awolowo unexpectedly joined hands with Zik in placing the blame for this riot on the British. The two southern politicians patched up a truce and pressed their demands for self-government. The northerners declared that if the British granted self-government before the north was ready for it, the Moslems would break off from the rest of Nigeria, and might even march south against the Ibos and Yorubas. It seemed that the path to Nigerian freedom might not be so smooth as Awolowo had once predicted.

XXX

WHERE I CAME IN

I<small>T WAS</small> time to come up for air.

The observant reader who has followed me thus far will have noticed that an attractive character called Jane tends to disappear from the narrative. While I was traveling round Africa, Jane perforce remained most of the time in Johannesburg looking after our three children. She read part of this book, criticized it freely, and complained: "You have all the fun."

"All right," I said, "let's go to Europe and have fun together for a change."

Johannesburg is a tough town for a woman to be alone in. Jane woke one morning to find that during the night someone had sawed out the lock of our front door. Fortunately there was also a stout bolt, which foiled the housebreakers. Later we moved to another house. A Negro was stabbed to death outside the front gate, and Jane found another Negro in a pool of blood in our back yard. So we transferred to a fifth-floor apartment.

Despite such incidents, many of our friends laughed at Jane's notion that Johannesburg was not a very safe place.

"I often leave my wife alone," said one man, "and she's in no danger whatever."

"How does she manage?" Jane asked.

"Well, she can handle a rifle, and keeps a gun under her pillow. And we've got two great Danes."

Jane would not know one end of a rifle from the other, neither of us has ever owned even a pop-gun, and she does not like great Danes.

When we planned our trip to Europe, I decided she should go by sea and I would fly over later and join her.

"Now you can have the adventures," I joked.

Jane shook her blond head. "I don't want adventures, I just want a nice quiet holiday."

She sailed up the east coast of Africa and three weeks afterwards I caught a Comet and met her in Venice. We sat contentedly looking at the lights reflected in the dark waters of the Grand Canal.

"Did you have a lovely voyage?" I asked.

"I didn't much care for the fire at Beira."

"What fire?"

"A tanker leaked oil and someone tossed a cigarette end overboard from another ship. Beira harbor was soon aflame. Three ships were damaged and about fifty people were killed in what I believe you writers call the conflagration."

"We writers don't," I said. "And after Beira?"

"At Mombasa a man came on board with four coffins. They contained the bodies of his wife and children, who had been slashed to pieces by the Mau Mau. He was taking them home to Europe for burial.

"One of the passengers on the ship had business to do in Nairobi, so he decided to fly up there from Mombasa and return in time to catch the ship before she sailed. He never did catch it. In Nairobi he walked up the main street and was shot dead by a Negro policeman who'd suddenly gone mad and who shot himself immediately afterwards."

"What else," I inquired, "happened on the schooner *Hesperus*?"

"Nothing really; except that at Suez we planned a trip to Cairo, but at the last minute they wouldn't let us go. People were being shot there too."

We had gone to Europe to escape for a while from Africa, but Africa insisted on following us.

At Pisa we saw the leaning tower and dutifully inspected the church. By that time we had seen a good many churches, but we never got tired of them, or of Italy. Whatever happened to

Europe—and it was obvious that some unpleasant things might —civilization had put down deep, strong roots there and had long been in flower. Africa seemed far away and very raw.

We were having an open-air lunch and watching the bright, cheerful crowd that thronged the narrow street in which we sat when a man at an adjoining table overheard something Jane said and immediately beamed on us. He was a hearty, chuckling man with a broad red face and massive hands. He was so solid and hearty that he made the thin, gesticulating Italians look flimsy.

"I'm from the Transvaal," he said. He chuckled. "This is a long way from Pretoria!"

We shook hands.

"How do you like Italy?" Jane asked.

"Well," said the hearty man, chuckling solidly, "these Italians are just like our natives! I can't think of them as Europeans; I mean *real* Europeans, like us."

"Why not?" asked Jane, awed.

"They look pretty like niggers to me," he chuckled. "Lots of the tarbrush, I expect. They live on spaghetti, just like Jim Fish and his mealie-pap." He shook his head, amused. "No, you can't call them really European."

"They seem to have managed to build a few churches," said Jane. Before I could kick her under the table, she went on: "And of course there's Michelangelo, Botticelli, Dante—"

"Oh, some of them are clever with their hands," he chuckled. "But they don't have proper European standards, all the same. Not like us." He looked round, and pointed. "Imagine that happening in South Africa."

We looked round. A street-cleaner in a blue uniform was moving slowly along, sweeping with his broom and whistling between his teeth. As we watched, he stooped to pick up a half-smoked cigarette, inspected it closely, then shrugged and stuck it in the pocket of his blue tunic before resuming his sweeping.

Our friend stopped chuckling momentarily and said: "You see what I mean? A white man sweeping streets! But the Italians

448

don't mind, you know. They're used to it. It doesn't mean any more to them to have to sweep a street than it would to one of our natives. That's why I say they're not real Europeans, like us.

"And what *I* think," he went on before we could say anything, "is that we ought to import a few of those Italians to South Africa. Why, they'd jump at the chance of being allowed in, and we could find plenty of jobs for them, now that our natives are beginning to get uppity. Italians don't mind working with their hands, they're accustomed to it, and they wouldn't cost much more than natives anyway, because they live on spaghetti and wouldn't demand high wages.

"Some people," he conceded, "don't like Italians, but what I say is, give them a chance. If our coons are going to get out of hand, we've got to get cheap labor from somewhere, and these Italians are just like our natives, only I expect they would be a lot more docile. Anyway, it's an idea, isn't it?"

We agreed, rather dazedly, that it was certainly an idea.

We did not dare to repeat this conversation to any Italian, but we mentioned it to a Frenchman we met in Paris, and he sat back and roared with laughter. When he had finished wiping his eyes, he lit a cigarette, looked across the Seine at the darkening bulk of the Louvre outlined against the evening sky, and said seriously: "It is funny, of course, but it is sad also. They have lost all contact with reality, these 'Europeans' in Africa. Why do they insist so strenuously on staying 'white'? They should solve their problem by intermarrying with the Africans, who outnumber them. My own grandmother was, I believe, a Negress, or at any rate a mulatto." He shrugged elegantly. "Do such trifles really matter?"

We shuddered to think what Dr. Malan would make of this advice, but consoled ourselves with the reflection that as our friend was a Left Bank Frenchman, his views were probably eccentric anyway.

In London an American Negress had made a smash hit out of a song called "Don't Malign Malan" and was stopping the show with it every night. South Africans visiting Britain for the

449

coronation of Queen Elizabeth, including Dr. Malan himself, felt very maligned indeed, and tended to try to turn every conversation into a protest meeting. It was not so much the song they objected to as to the fact that the Lord Chamberlain of England was allowing a colored woman to sing it in public; in South Africa she would have got three years in prison and a lashing.

There was a very strong feeling among the South Africans and Rhodesians in London that the British, and the Americans, were not even trying to understand their peculiar problems. They were very sore about it. "We come here fully prepared to be patient with them, and to explain matters to them, because of course we know they're ignorant about such things and have been misled by lying newspaper reports," a Rhodesian said plaintively. "But they just won't listen. As soon as we admit that we do have a color-bar, because we are determined to defend white civilization, they get annoyed. Personally I think that by *our* standards they're all Bolshies, including the Yanks."

The Kenya white settlers were vociferously represented in the hub of Empire by a "Truth about Kenya" organization, which, with a hawklike eye, read all the news items about Kenya printed in the British press and then pounced on editors, telling them that their foreign correspondents were obviously unashamed Negrophiles who were probably in the pay of the Kenya African Union. As the editors remained strangely unmoved, the Kenya defenders of white civilization tended to go into a sulky huddle with the South Africans and Rhodesians. When a dusky Nigerian delegation, including my old friend Dr. Awolowo, turned up in London for formal talks with the Colonial Secretary and got their pictures in the papers, it was generally conceded that the end had come. A worse blow, however, was the marriage of a daughter of Sir Stafford Cripps to a Gold Coast Negro. When the great British public showed a mild interest but expressed no disapproval, a number of white civilizers threw in their hands and began to pack their bags. They said they wanted to get back to Africa, where there was a decent color-bar and a white man was still a European.

: 2 :

Low over Egypt was a large crescent moon, as if all the sin in the world was hanging up there in the African sky. But in Nairobi it was cold and raining.

We drove into town from the airport, along Racecourse Road, past the huddled Negro slums and the crowded Indian stores. In Delamere Avenue the shiny cars were still circling round the statue of Kenya's founder, who had proclaimed it "White Man's Country." In the Kikuyu reserves near Nairobi, and up in the Aberdare forests and on Mount Kenya, the Mau Mau war was still going on.

General Sir George Erskine had been sent out from Britain to smash the Mau Mau. An energetic soldier with gray hair and cheeks as pink as a foxhunter's coat, he was building stout stone forts all over the Kikuyu reserves, rather like the blockhouses that still dot South Africa as relics of the ancient Boer War. The forts were surrounded by deep ditches filled with sharp bamboo stakes, for defense against Mau Mau warriors, and were manned by Kikuyu "Home Guards" whom Erskine had armed. Up in the Aberdares and on Mount Kenya, Kikuyu labor gangs were busy transforming old elephant tracks into military roads, and were boring and bulldozing tunnels through the jungle so that the soldiers could get at the Mau Mau hide-outs. Erskine was also using planes to bomb and strafe Mau Mau gangs.

It was a more hopeful picture than the murder and muddle I had seen on my last visit to Kenya, before Erskine arrived, when the isolated farmers were calling urgently for more military protection, and Nairobi seemed to be hiccuping indifferently in its night-clubs.

"But the white settlers don't seem especially grateful," said my perplexed Jane. "Some appear not even to like having a British general around. They keep talking about 'British interference,' as if they had been doing all right before and didn't need any outside help at all!"

451

"You don't know some of the white settlers of Kenya," I said, too lightly, for I was shortly to discover that I myself had not yet plumbed the full depths.

I left Jane to call on Wycliffe Awori, the "crocodile king" from Nyanza Province who had been connected with the Kenya African Union before the Kenya Government abruptly if belatedly proscribed that organization. I found Awori, still wearing a bow tie, seated behind a desk in a newspaper office. He had given up crocodiles as well as the Kenya African Union, and was currently publishing a newspaper whose Swahili name could be translated as the *News of the World*.

Awori was an unhappy man. He freely and indeed loudly declared his detestation of Mau Mau and its methods, and was even inclined now to look on Jomo Kenyatta as somewhat less noble than the natural savior of the Kikuyu who was being crucified by British imperialism. At the same time, he said, he and other Africans were still looking in vain for any signs of political maturity among the white settlers.

"What would you like to see them do?" I asked.

"There's still the land problem," said Awori. "Everyone knows that while the reserves are hopelessly congested, there is plenty of empty land which is in 'white ownership' but isn't being used at all. I'm not suggesting this land should just be handed over to individual Africans to use or misuse, but as there is a land problem and as it has to be tackled sooner or later, I suggest that the Government should acquire such unused land and have Africans farm it co-operatively, under proper supervision."

"And the political problem?"

Awori shrugged. "Our stand on that has never altered. I don't think we are unreasonable. The whites are a race minority who have all the political power. I don't expect them to throw it all away and leave themselves outvoted and politically helpless. But the African majority, and the Indians, who actually outnumber the whites, must have a voice too. So there ought to be political parity among the three race groups. Africans, Indians, and Europeans should each have an equal number of representatives on the Legislative Council. Then no one group could out-vote another group without forming an alliance of some sort with the third group."

"The Indians and the Africans might gang up against the Europeans," I suggested.

Awori laughed. "And European and Asian businessmen, who are both big employers of Africans, might also find they had plenty in common when Africans demanded higher wages!"

"What you're suggesting," I said, "is the same as Tanganyika will have under the new constitution there?"

"Exactly. If it works in Tanganyika, why not here?"

"Well, what do the white settlers here say about that?"

"I think you'd better ask them, not me," said Awori. He evidently did not wish to share the fate of Walter Fanuel Odede, another former KAU leader, who had been arrested and was languishing, without trial, in a detention camp on the steamy mangrove coast near Mombasa.

I left Awori brooding nervously over this possibility, and returned to find Jane talking to Hopalong Cassidy. Nairobi was full of Hopalong Cassidy types, who wore loud check shirts and had the large butts of six-guns sticking out of holsters lying snugly on their hips. They carried no lassos, however, did not roll their own tobacco, and rode the range in Jaguar motor-cars instead of on horseback. This particular Hopalong was drinking pink gin and leaning over Jane in a confidential fashion. I hastily joined them.

"This," said Jane, in a clear, careful voice, "is Mr. Peter Willis-Crauford, and he has been telling me some very *interesting* things about the future of Kenya as a white man's country."

"Hello, Peter," I said.

Mr. Willis-Crauford measured me with a cold eye. There is nothing colder than the eye of a Kenya white settler, especially one with a hyphenated name who is making up his mind whether to be rude to you or just formal. Hopalong evidently decided that as I carried no armaments, being very rude would be taking an unfair advantage, which would be un-British. At the same time I had interrupted his tête-à-tête with this promis-

453

ing blonde creature, and he plainly resented it. So he compromised.

"Have a pink gin," he said. When I accepted and was drinking it, he went on more severely: "Your wife says you're one of those newspaper fellahs."

"That's right."

"Every newspaper fellah who's come here has turned out to be a lying bastard, and I don't really suppose you'll prove the exception."

"Go on telling me about the future of Kenya," said Jane hurriedly.

Hopalong turned back to her and ignored me.

"Of course the first job is to finish off the Mau Mau. The home Government bungled that badly. The first batch of British Tommies they sent out, the Lancashire Fusiliers, were a lot of bally Bolshies. Why, some of them actually palled up with the Kikuyu!"

"I don't quite understand that," said Jane, who was listening intently, with her blue eyes the size of saucers and the general innocent air of the kind of doll you win at a carnival. "I mean, I don't know all your terms yet. Are the Kikuyu the Mau Mau, or have I got it wrong?"

"All Kikuyu are bastards whether they're Mau Mau or not," said Mr. Willis-Crauford. "All Kikuyu should be shot."

"I see. Do go on."

"Well, we *can't* shoot them all," Hopalong said moodily. "Too many of them. But we do mean to teach them a lesson."

"Oh!"

"Once the new lot of Tommies have cleared up the Mau Mau —and I must say," he added irritably, "they're taking their time about it—then of course it's entirely our show. I mean, we've got to live here: it's our country. And, as I say, we mean to teach the Kukes a sharp lesson."

"How?"

"Well, there won't be any nonsense about helping them reconstruct the reserves, which are in a mess. After all, they let the Mau Mau muck things up, didn't they? We'll put forced

454

labor gangs to work there; make them work their passage, by gad!"

His face alight with pleased anticipation of this happy prospect, he continued: "Then a lot of them are going to come crawling to us farmers begging for food and jobs, once this business is over. All right, they can have food and jobs—on our terms, of course."

Jane's wide blue eyes said: "You big, strong man!" but I had a feeling that inside she was saying something quite different. "Do go on!" she breathed.

"That's about all," said Mr. Willis-Crauford. "Except for the Indians, of course. We'll have to deal with them, too, sooner or later. This is white man's country."

The white settlers were holding a political meeting in Nairobi's big Memorial Hall. They assembled under a large Union Jack and made speeches filled with Imperial fervor. They violently attacked the Governor, Sir Evelyn Baring, and by implication General Sir George Erskine, because neither of these had displayed much enthusiasm for the settlers' plans to treat all Kikuyu men, women, and children as branded war criminals. Baring was a gentle soul who wanted to see peace restored, and Erskine was a gentleman and a professional soldier who wanted to end a war that was tying up British soldiers who might at any moment be needed elsewhere. One of the settlers said grumpily that he supposed British Tommies were all right as far as they went, but why didn't the Colonial Office send in Gurkhas? He was apparently still living in the days of the Indian Mutiny. Michael Blundell, the settlers' leader, looked as unhappy as a man who suddenly finds himself tearing down a mountain track in charge of a runaway mule team.

The settlers finally decided to demand the entry into the colony of thirty thousand more Europeans, to help keep Kenya white. At the same time they proposed a total ban on the further immigration of "Asians," meaning Indians, from India. As one settler explained, with magnificent brevity: "Hindus are not Christians."

Immigrants from decadent postwar Britain might well be

455

tainted with equalitarian notions about Negroes, so it was proposed to bring in refugees from East Germany, provided they were guaranteed to be anti-Communist, frugal, hard-working, suitably grateful to their British protectors, and not likely to ask for high wages.

I found this interesting, and possibly significant. The South African we had met in Italy had become lyrical about the possibility of importing cheap Italians. Now the Kenyans wanted cheap Germans. In the past, at various times, the whites in Africa, to maintain their own standard of living, have relied on imported Chinese coolies and imported Indian laborers, as well as on the local Negro populations. Europe's turn had evidently come at last. Given a third World War, the white settlers would probably be wanting to import cheap Russians.

"Are they always like this?" asked Jane.

"Usually," I said. "What do you make of them?"

"They're like ham actors who've been given parts in a bad film, but given all the wrong parts and the wrong lines. Everything is larger than life and twice as phony."

"Phony" seemed the operative word.

: 3 :

HEADING SLOWLY back to South Africa, we flew from Nairobi across the Serengeti Plains to Rhodesia, and down through the copper belt to Salisbury, now the capital of the new federated Dominion of British Central Africa. But the Negroes of those parts were strenuously opposing federation, which they claimed was being imposed on them by the white minority as a simple means of throttling African aspirations. The Negroes were beginning to defy the color-bar and were practicing "passive resistance," as explained to them by agitators like the Reverend Michael Scott, who had been summarily deported from Nyasaland for discussing such topics with Nyasa chiefs.

While the Negroes thus criticized and opposed federation

456

from their point of view, some whites formed a Confederate Party to oppose federation because they thought it blocked a possible alliance with Dr. Malan's white-supremacy South Africa. The Rhodesian scene was like a mad film script of *Gone with the Wind* written by someone who had not read the book.

But the Rhodesians also, we discovered, were looking abroad for cheap white labor to replace the cheap Negro labor they might be in danger of losing as "agitators" like Michael Scott taught the Africans to demand more. In Salisbury a rather pompous gentleman who looked as if he were enjoying a high standard of living told us solemnly that Rhodesia's future depended on white immigrants who, as he delicately put it, "are not having a high standard of living where they are now and will not expect one when they get here." He admitted that such immigrants were not likely to be found in Britain, where the people were drugged with the pernicious doctrine of the welfare state, but pointed out happily that Europe was still full of poor people.

While we were in Salisbury I heard that trouble had flared up in Nyasaland, so I took a bumpy plane ride across the border to Blantyre, Nyasaland's commercial capital. Some of the roads round Blantyre were blocked by fallen gum trees and telegraph poles. Armored cars were prowling, and there were soldiers in tin hats, with rifles slung on their backs.

Blantyre itself seemed peaceful. As I drove up the little main street, I noticed that the *Nyasaland Times* had built itself a brand-new office, and that the tiny town hall had a new coat of paint. But on the veranda of Ryall's Hotel I found Arthur Mapleson of the London *Daily Express*, and Colin Legum of the London *Observer*. My experience of these two is that where they are, there is trouble, and I thought: "This is where I came in."

I had not been in Nyasaland forty-eight hours before I was involved in a battle. Arthur and I drove to the village of Chitera, twenty miles from Blantyre, where the people had deposed a chief whom they apparently thought too subservient to the white man's government. Police and troops were sent to arrest the deposers and the new chief whom they had installed. Arthur and I arrived on the heels of the police and soldiers.

The village, a collection of mud huts with thatched roofs, was at the head of a slope, up which ran a narrow, rutted red road. The district commissioner, a young man who wore a brown felt hat, a tweed jacket, and khaki shorts, surveyed the position critically. He carried no weapon, not even a walking-stick.

At the head of the slope the villagers had massed, carrying bows and arrows, spears, clubs, and axes. Behind them, but out of sight, the women of the village put their hands over their mouths and shrilled like insects, urging their men on to battle.

The D.C. sent a Negro messenger up the hill to demand the surrender of the men he had come to arrest. The crowd sent the messenger back with the cheerful information that if he wanted the men he had better come and take them by force, if he could.

"Ah, well," said the young man resignedly, "in we go, I suppose."

About twenty Negro police, wearing tin hats and carrying pick-handles, gas-guns, and other weapons, advanced stolidly up the slope. They were led by two white officers, and had five rifles between them.

"The gentlemen of the press," said the D.C. pleasantly, "came here on their own and are under their own orders."

The women had stopped shrilling and, apart from the police toiling up the hill, the scene seemed peaceful. In the distance sharp-peaked mountains floated serenely as if suspended in the blue sky. A bush was bursting with white and purple flowers, and a bird sang in a tree.

When the twenty policemen and their two white officers reached the top of the hill, the villagers leaped on them with their spears and axes. Arrows whistled through the air. The five riflemen began to shoot. The second small company of police, and the handful of soldiers, remained at the foot of the hill, but began to fidget. "They'll call us if they need us," said an officer composedly. After a few minutes the shooting stopped. There was now nobody in sight at the top of the hill. Then one of the white officers appeared and raised his arm. The men who had been waiting at the foot of the hill marched on.

One of the white officers who had taken part in the brief battle was sucking his swollen hand where someone had bitten him. The other was examining a collection of captured weapons, including a long arrow with a needle-sharp point. Some of the Negro police were searching in the bushes. Presently they came back, carrying bodies. Two villagers were dead. An old man with a bullet wound in his leg lay on the ground and violently abused the police, in excellent English. He was gray-haired and half naked.

"I was just walking along when you shot me," he shouted.

"You were running towards me, waving a spear," said an officer unsympathetically.

"Hunting—I was only going hunting," shouted the old man.

"Well, you were hunting in the wrong direction."

The British in areas near Nyasaland were standing by, ready to rush in troops and planes. White farmers and missionaries had begun to evacuate their families to the two towns of Blantyre and Zomba. The threatening throb of tom-toms was heard in the night round white farms and tea estates, and Africans were greeting whites with the significant cry: "Go home, stranger: this is our land, not yours!"

The Nyasaland African Congress was supposed to be behind the agitation. Mr. Gwonde, whom I had met in Zomba, had evidently been replaced by other, more militant leaders. One of them, a young, intelligent schoolteacher, had taken to politics and been promptly fired from his post as "temperamentally unsuited to the work of teaching." He told me: "We always warned that federation really meant the imposition by force of the white man's will, and now I know I was right. If the people are crushed, it will be by the use of troops and planes from Northern and Southern Rhodesia, the two countries we fear most next to the Union of South Africa."

I visited the Blantyre Club and found that most of the whites had been hurriedly enrolled as "special police." They still sat round in open-neck shirts and khaki shorts, drinking brandy and gin, and they still talked about "dealing with the coons," but now they had rifles and spoke as if they really meant it.

"First chance I get I'm going to shoot one of the black bastards—shoot him dead," crooned a man who had already had too many gins, and he aimed an imaginary rifle and squeezed an imaginary trigger. The others laughed.

"Trouble is, we've put up with their bloody nonsense too long," said another. "I'd have shot a few a long time ago, but the D.C.'s are too damned soft and the Government is full of la-di-da." He grinned. "Anyway, they've asked for it now, and if I have my way they'll get it."

From Blantyre I went over to Zomba, the administrative capital of this British "protectorate," driving past the bright jade terraces of the trim tea estates. But there was blood on the tea leaves now. The Secretariat at Zomba had not changed since my last visit. It was still a maze of dusty creaking corridors lined with cobwebby offices. The Chief Secretary, a pale plump man named Charles Worthington Foden Footman, was the principal spider in this dusty web. The Secretary for Native Affairs was called Fox-Strangways: a relative of his had gained brief notoriety by kicking Aneurin Bevan down the steps of a London club. Both insisted that the trouble now looming over them was just the work of a handful of "agitators."

Meanwhile tribesmen were briskly deposing the Government's puppet chiefs. But this, I was told, was because the people were being "intimidated." When I asked how whole villages could be intimidated, and how many intimidators there were, they admitted that there had in fact been no *physical* intimidation as yet. "It is a sort of psychical intimidation," one of them explained. I passed that one over to the Society for Psychical Research, which could probably find plenty of good material in Zomba if they looked for it, and asked what the Government proposed to do about the situation.

The Chief Secretary said cheerfully: "I think the best way to gear ourselves to this 'flap' would be to have a 'waffle' about it once a week, what?"

Like other officials in British Africa, those in Zomba seemed to be jolly schoolboys talking an out-of-date slang rather than grown men.

Meanwhile, in the pubs and clubs of Blantyre, the white settlers of Nyasaland were in a rage because Africans wounded in clashes with the police were being admitted to hospital. They thought they should have been left where they fell, in the bush. It was, indeed, where I had come in.

: 4 :

JANE AND I had been back in Africa only a few weeks when already the familiar atmosphere was closing in on us. The Western world and its comparatively civilized values and way of life seemed like a faraway dream. Though it was my job to report the African atmosphere, and though we also tried to joke about it, it was like slipping back from sanity into nightmare.

In Johannesburg they were still talking about gold shares (and uranium shares as well now), and new creamy blocks of apartment-houses were still springing up. They also still talked about "the dreadful natives." We went to visit some very good friends of ours and found them mourning remorsefully over their wounded dog, which was slowly recovering from a bullet wound.

"I shot him," said our host. He seemed very disposed to cover himself with sackcloth and ashes. "It was accident, of course. All the same, I'll never forgive myself. Poor old Towser!" Towser heard his name and wagged a feeble tail, though his brown eyes seemed reproachful.

"How did it happen?" I asked.

"I heard a noise in the night, out in the garden, and I got out of bed, grabbed my rifle, and let fly. You see," he explained, "I thought it was just a Kaffir. I never dreamed it was poor old Towser chasing a rabbit."

The Negro shantytowns that ringed the Golden City were still there, and the murdering *tsotsi* gangs were still active, but the Government had conceived a new idea. Many thousands of

461

Negroes living in an old part of Johannesburg still had the right to own their own homes, and, as established householders, they could not be classed as vagrants and shipped off to the labor-hungry farmers the moment they became unemployed in the city. So, in the sacred name of *apartheid*, the Government decreed that they should be removed from their homes and sent to live elsewhere. These people of Sophiatown found a champion in Father Trevor Huddleston, a priest who had his church in their midst. A protest meeting was organized, and was held on a Sunday in a small Indian-owned cinema in Sophiatown. The bishop of Johannesburg sent the meeting a message of sympathy and support, and Father Huddleston addressed the gathering. The crowd consisted of respectable-looking and law-abiding Negroes, who listened quietly and attentively.

While the meeting was in progress, truckloads of police drew up in the sunny street outside. Policemen armed with rifles clumped into the foyer of the cinema, and others armed with Sten guns invaded the hall. While one kept an eye on the paralyzed audience, suggestively fingering his Sten gun, two more leaped onto the stage and arrested Yusuf Cachalia, a man who goes about welcoming arrest and would never dream of resisting it. The armed police then withdrew in triumph with their captive, having once again demonstrated that the white man was still boss.

Cachalia was released on bail, but after three weeks had passed, the police blandly announced that they had no charge to make against him. The people of Sophiatown are still waiting to be moved. No action has been taken against them, but the Government has not relented.

This incident caused no surprise and evoked almost no comment in South Africa, where people had been very effectively conditioned into acceptance of rule by baton and Sten gun.

In Cape Town the South African Parliament obediently continued to pass measures calculated to silence all opposition to the Boer Nationalists' decrees. To criticize the Government in terms stronger than those habitually employed by a decayed gentlewomen's sewing circle had become "incitement." The color-bar was further strengthened by legislation that debarred the law-courts from interfering with even its grosser manifestations. I heard Ben Schoeman, the Minister of Labor, introduce a bill that, he declared, was intended to "kill Negro trade unions."

Most white South Africans, including Nationalists, had few illusions as to where all this was going to end. But they were behaving like men who had passed the point of no return, and their one thought seemed to be to cram on still more speed. And not only in South Africa, but in most parts of the continent the racial pot appeared to be coming to the boil.

XXXI
CONTINENT IN CRISIS

While I waited for my next call to some part of the troubled continent, I thought of all I had seen and heard in many months of travel. I wanted to arrange my impressions, against the background of my years of living in Africa, into some sort of pattern. I felt in my bones I was not going to have much time, and that seemed to me symbolical, for Africa might not have much time either. Things were moving very fast.

I thought of one good friend of mine who is a district commissioner, with the absurdly appropriate name of Sanders. Mr. Commissioner Sanders's *boma*, which is the African name for any center of administration, is simply a thatched, whitewashed house surrounded by bush and near a crocodile-infested river. From the *boma*, Sanders supervises the lives of almost a hundred thousand primitive tribesmen, who live in mud villages scattered over two thousand square miles of territory. Until recently, he did so with the aid of only four African policemen, wearing pith helmets and bicycling along jungle tracks as peacefully as rural postmen.

When I discussed Africa's problems with Sanders, he laughed at my fears. "Of course Africa is changing," he said, "but not nearly as fast as you think. Now, take *my* Africans. You must admit they're a pretty peaceable lot of savages. We have the odd spot of bother with witch doctors, and it's a devil of a job persuading them to build latrines. But life is fairly tranquil. I collect the taxes, keep an eye on the witch doctors, build a few roads, and try to teach them not to destroy the soil. My chief

464

headache is their tremendous conservatism. Africans don't *want* change."

It was evening, and we were drinking our gins and tonic on Sanders's veranda. From behind the *boma* came the deep voices and soft laughter of his black policemen, and from the river, hidden by the trees, we heard a splash. Sanders smiled, a little grimly.

"That was probably a croc," he said. "Do you know, hardly a week passes without a crocodile snatching a man who has gone bathing in the river, or a woman from a village who has gone to the riverbank to wash clothes. And yet the Africans go on bathing and go on washing their clothes there. They are fatalists. Change is the last thing they desire."

But when I next visited Sanders at the *boma*, he was singing a more doleful tune. Change had burst unexpectedly upon him. The *boma* was heavily guarded. There were now many policemen, armed with rifles, and troops were being ferried across the river.

"What happened?" I asked.

The answer was, to me, a sadly familiar story, but it had shaken Sanders's deepest convictions. In another part of the country, miles from the river, Africans working for whites had gone on strike. They claimed loudly that the whites had "stolen" their land. Sanders's people worked for no white man, and their tribal lands were secure. But now Sanders's people were also shouting anti-white slogans, and there was unrest in all the villages throughout his sprawling territory.

"They attacked the *boma*," said Sanders, "and chased my four policemen into the bush. They say they won't pay any more taxes. Government insisted on sending in soldiers. Damn it, we've never *had* soldiers in my district before!"

There had been some shooting, though not much, for Sanders's people were armed only with bows and arrows. But he was less worried by what had already occurred than by what it seemed to presage for the future.

"You see," Sanders said quietly, "if I cannot rule this district with four policemen, I don't think I can rule it even with four thousand, or with forty thousand. Once my people have lost faith in the white man, I cannot rule them at all. And that is what they seem to have done."

: 2 :

THERE ARE about 134,000,000 people living in the vast arid bushlands and tropical jungles of Africa, below the great deserts. The vast majority of them are Stone Age men still. For the anthropologist, and for the isolated administrator like Mr. Commissioner Sanders, Africa still has the appearance of a great museum crammed with primitive peoples who with their quaint customs have miraculously survived unchanged into the modern age.

But this is an illusion. It is precisely because these Stone Age peoples are moving rapidly through a dangerous transition stage that there are violent upheavals and critical problems. All over the museum, even in its remotest parts, the neatly tagged exhibits are bursting out of their showcases and changing their nature. Inside the skull of the most naked warrior there is now an explosive ferment of often muddled ideas. It began—in most cases less than a century ago—when the first white missionary handed the first black savage a Bible. It was greatly accelerated when the first black men in Africa, straight out of the Stone Age, were set to work in the bowels of the earth with rock-drills to mine for gold.

The Arabs, and the earliest Europeans, shipped Africans out of their black continent as slaves. But this produced no such revolution as that which began when white men set firm foot in Africa and began to reshape the lives of its inhabitants to meet their own needs. The late nineteenth century crashed into the deserts and jungles of a Stone Age continent. White men of the new machine age came face to face with black men still naked, or wearing skins and carrying spears. And the white men, inevitably, brought ideas as well as guns and rock-drills. Inside

466

Africans' skulls those ideas are now exploding with far greater force than a deep-level mine rock-burst.

South of the Sahara, living amid the black millions, there are fewer than three million whites all told. Of these, about ninety per cent live in the Union of South Africa. The importance of South Africa cannot be overestimated. The steam engine that the white man brought into the Stone Age museum still vibrates most powerfully in South Africa. The Union produces 86 per cent of Africa's gold, 99 per cent of its platinum, 89 per cent of its coal, 60 per cent of its chrome, and 40 per cent of its asbestos, manganese, and tungsten. In all Africa south of the Sahara, most of the highways, most of the railroads, most of the factories, and most of the towns are in the Union of South Africa. The Union's national income now stands at well over £1,000,000,000; the national income of most African countries is not yet a tenth of that figure. Of all countries in Africa, the Union is the most prosperous, the most industrialized, the most advanced.

Fatally corresponding with this pre-eminence, South Africa has the largest degree of race tension on the African continent. Here relations between white and black are universally admitted, not least by South Africans themselves, to be at breaking-point. And nothing could better illustrate that it is the very fact of the white man "developing" Africa, of *not* treating it as a museum, that has produced the current racial crisis. Just because the Negroes in South Africa are relatively so far advanced, because they have had much greater access to the white man's own ideas, are they the most antagonistic to, and rouse the greatest fears among, their white rulers.

In 1952 the puzzled representative of the Philippines in the United Nations went on record with the statement that "the [racial] discriminatory measures taken in the Union of South Africa must have some reasons behind them, which ought to be studied and the causes eliminated." The main reason is unfortunately only too clear. In this, the most developed part of the African continent, the white innovator has achieved his triumph by inciting, cajoling, and compelling the African to forsake his old tribal way of life, and has then thrust a color-bar between the advancing African and the new civilized way of life to which he aspires. In South Africa, the majority of the blacks are too far out of their tribal museum to want or to be able to go back into it. But the white man has taken alarm and, while keeping the black man detribalized, refuses him admission to his own society in anything like the full sense. So the son of a chief works in the white man's kitchen, but may not enter the drawing-room.

The development of South Africa would not have been possible without the use of black labor. The astonishing dependence of the whites on their "Kaffirs" is a byword among the South Africans themselves. They tell this story against themselves:

A South African named van der Merwe visited New York at a time when Dr. Gallup was holding a poll on whether procreation was work or pleasure. Asked what he thought, van der Merwe replied unhesitatingly: "Pleasure." Asked how he was so sure, van der Merwe said: "Man, if it was work, we would have the Kaffirs do it for us."

Caliban has been a great convenience for the whites. But, now that he is threatening to break his bonds, he is belatedly recognized as a great danger. In South Africa the whites who have made such full use of his services now talk about dispensing with him altogether, which is what they mean by "total *apartheid*." But it is too late in the day for that.

: 3 :

THE MOST distant, most jungle-fast *boma* cannot now escape the changes rumbling across the African bush like the heavy, challenging beat of tom-toms. In South Africa the way was cleared for the conscription of the Negro in the white man's service by stripping him of nearly all his land. Reservations, called "reserves," were belatedly created, where the black man was supposed to lead his "own way of life": a satisfactory museum piece. But the steam engine quickly shook those "reserve" museums to pieces. Today, between 40 and 60 per cent of the able-bodied men in the South African Negro reserves are at any one time "absent"—working in the white man's cities, in his mines, or on his farms. South Africa sucks in black labor from far and near. Wedged partly or wholly in South African territory are the three British-protected, "High Commission" Negro countries of Basutoland, Bechuanaland, and Swaziland. From Basutoland 40 per cent of all the able-bodied men, from Bechuanaland 48 per cent, and from Swaziland 25 per cent are at any one time "absent"—working in the Union. The figure for Swaziland is lowest only because inside Swaziland itself much land is now in white ownership, and the whites there also require black labor. But from distant Nyasaland the Union and Southern Rhodesia between them have wrested more black workers than are employed in Nyasaland by the comparative handful of whites there. In Southern Rhodesia, which is fast building up industries like the Union's, 59 per cent of the Negro labor employed comes from beyond Southern Rhodesia's borders—from Northern Rhodesia, Nyasaland, Tanganyika, and the Portuguese colony of Mozambique.

The great tides of black migratory labor thus set in motion have effectively destroyed the Negroes' own tribal society over a large area of Africa south of the Sahara. The destruction has been spread still farther afield by white land-grabbing in other territories besides South Africa, but patterned on that in South Africa. In the Rhodesias, in Kenya, and in Nyasaland, early white settlers "bought" tracts of land, huge in comparison with the whites' numbers, both then and now, for a few bottles of gin or a few rolls of calico. Negroes were and are needed as a labor force on those lands. Once again, tribal society was disrupted.

The problem of land use in Africa is an acute one. All over the continent, white district commissioners and agricultural officers patiently try to instruct the Negroes in the proper use of Africa's thin, sun-scorched, and precarious soils. Their task is complicated by three factors: so much of the best land so often being in white ownership (and the whites who own it so often cultivating only a fraction of it); the Negroes often being overcrowded in "reserves"; and, the most recent phenomenon, Negroes actively or passively resisting soil-conservation measures simply because they are proposed by a white man.

Even without those factors the problem would be difficult. The African Negro was never a good farmer. He was primarily a hunter, who contemptuously left the cultivation of crops to his womenfolk. Land was and is held in a mystical regard, but far less because of the crops it can produce than because it contains the graves of the ancestors whom most African Negroes either fear or revere. In the same way, the Negroes are attached to their cattle, but prize a cow that is starving and diseased just as highly as one that is fat and healthy. The cow, like the land, is a symbol of something else, and is not regarded with a farmer's eye at all. The African Negroes were and are such bad farmers that twenty-two acres are commonly required for the bare subsistence of one family. Today the increases occurring in African populations pressing on soils already badly eroded and left shadeless under the consuming tropical sun by the destruction of forests threaten not simply further impoverishment, but wholesale famine.

But the whites who grabbed large tracts of land have not proved to be very successful farmers either. The Rhodesias cannot feed themselves. Kenya's white farmers had to fight a long, bitter battle against crop and cattle diseases, and much of Kenya's "White Highlands" remains uncultivated. In South Africa, since 1910, the white farmers have received £100,000,000 in subsidies from the Government, mostly contributed by taxing the gold mines, and each year the encroaching deserts eat their way deeper into farmlands eroded into dust-bowls by bad farming methods.

If South Africa had gone on being a country where Boer and Bantu cattlemen squabbled over waterholes, the history not only of the Union but of much of the rest of Africa might have been quite different. But the discovery of diamonds and gold, which sparked South Africa's economic development, completely altered the picture. The Boers themselves are rapidly ceasing to be a mainly rural folk; they are increasingly townsmen. And exactly the same is happening to the Bantu. Beginning in South Africa, much of Africa is today undergoing a crude industrial revolution. This has greatly hastened the destruction of the Africans' old, primitive tribal society. And there can be little doubt that this destruction, and the industrialization that accelerates it, will continue. There is, in Africa as elsewhere, a flight to the towns.

South Africa's mines and industries pull in black labor not only from South Africa's own Negro reservations, but from other African countries as well. The reason is simple. A Nyasa in his own country is unlikely to earn from his own land much more than will pay his taxes. If he works for a white farmer in Nyasaland, his wage will be only about £1 ($2.80) a month. But if he emigrates to South Africa and gets a job in a Johannesburg factory, he may earn as much as fifteen times that amount. The lure—of the money, of city life—is irresistible.

South Africa's neighbors protest against this migration. District officers, curators of the Stone Age museum, deplore the decay of tribal life. White farmers in those neighboring countries resent the loss of black labor. But the only way to stop the migration is for those countries to start industrializing themselves—as is in fact beginning to happen. The effect on the Negroes' traditional "way of life" will be exactly the same. Meanwhile, as long as South Africa offers the Negroes from other territories greater economic opportunities than they can find in their own countries, the stream of migratory black labor will continue to flow.

Unfortunately, coupled with the better economic chances that South Africa does undoubtedly offer, because it happens to be by far the richest country on the black continent, there is South Africa's harsh race policy. By a historical accident, gold mines and Boers coexist. The Boers actually resent the industrial development of their country, which has been financed chiefly by "foreign," English capital and which has disrupted their traditional "way of life" as well as that of the Bantu. They resent above all its effect of closely knitting into a "white" economy some millions of Negroes, and the consequent emancipating effect on the minds of those Negroes of daily intimate contact with the white man's civilization. But they have not been able to stop it. What they have succeeded in doing is to turn those millions of detribalized Negroes into a black working class quite like any working class in any European country, but at the same time to make it "anti-white" by stubbornly refusing it the normal outlets of trade-union organization and a political voice —which are reserved exclusively for whites. The result is a violent paradox that threatens to tear South Africa apart. The Boer Nationalists are trying to push back the hands of the clock and to hold their insurgent black workers in check by naked force. These workers are insurgent, not because—despite the appalling conditions in many "locations" and shantytowns— they have nothing to lose but their chains, but because they have had much closer contact with the white man's paradise of material benefits than any of their still tribal brethren.

The future of increasing numbers of Africans lies not on the land—two thirds of Kenya, a quite typical example, is at present unfit for cultivation or even for profitable ranching—or in a return to "tribalism," but in some form of industry. Even those who remain on the land will have to farm scientifically, in large units, for the whites' own experiences have shown that Africa's soils are not suited to anything resembling small peasant cultivation, and that their proper utilization requires considerable capital.

What threatens either to thwart this evolution altogether or else to turn it into a race revolution is the color-bar, which in its extremest form denies Africans the right to own property, just because they are black, and even in its milder manifestations continually pinpricks home the lesson that black men are "inferior" to white men.

: 4 :

AFRICA'S STONE AGE men have proved remarkably plastic, remarkably willing to learn. They crowd eagerly into the new age, and make the often perilous journey, if necessary on foot, into industrialized South Africa despite the Malan inscription now deeply carved over that golden gateway, which decrees: "No equality between white or black in Church or State." In the Belgian Congo, where a less harsh policy prevails, Negroes not long out of the bush drive locomotives and operate intricate machines, and the young grandson of an old, still surviving cannibal chief peers down a microscope in a laboratory. All over Africa, African children athirst for knowledge trudge ten miles each morning to the nearest poorly equipped mission school, where they squat on a bare floor and share one tattered reading-book among four pupils.

Idly watching the almost tame lions in the park outside Nairobi, or sitting on the beach at Mombasa under the melting globes of tropical stars, I have often been drawn into debate by my friend Hans Leuenberger. Hans is all for treating Africa as a vast museum, a human zoo whose inmates, tamer even than Nairobi's lions, shall be encouraged to preserve their "way of life."

"These people are perfectly happy as they are," Hans insists; "happier than we. Why force them into our crazy world?" He thinks Africans in their primitive state have an inner contentment, a psychological balance, a grave sense of truly human values, which Western man, and his Eastern imitators, have lost. He sees his tribal people, whom he knows and loves, as Adams and Eves in a Garden of Eden: blessed black innocents threatened by a white devil with a flaming sword.

Since the Mau Mau flare-up in Kenya, many of the whites there have argued that it is all the result of "pushing the African on too fast," cramming twentieth-century ideas into a confused Stone Age skull. The African, it is said, tiring of schools, lava-

473

tories, the tyranny of the clock, has sought relief from intolerable mental and emotional strain in an almost deliberate reversion to the ways of his most primitive forebears—and showing a particular relish for bloodshed, witchcraft, and abominable cruelty. In short, the African Negro is basically untamable and unteachable.

But in those parts of Africa where Negroes have been given a real chance, the facts mostly run counter to this theory. It is significant that the Mau Mau blazed up in Kenya, a country where there is much African land hunger and few real economic opportunities for blacks, where the ruling whites boast openly that it is "white man's country," and where the choice for the African is between a decaying tribal society, and becoming a proletarian clad in cast-off rags, in white (or Indian) employ. Only fifty years ago most African Negroes were literally spellbound, in the grip of superstition and their own witch doctors. It would be surprising if some did not "revert." But the Mau Mau is chiefly a product of deep frustrations. That is also why it is anti-white. Samson chose to bring the temple down in ruins rather than remain in it in chains.

Hans's view of the primitive tribal society as most conducive to Africans' happiness is open to grave doubts. That society seems to have been sagging and rotten even before the white man arrived; when he extended a little finger, the whole structure began to collapse. And few Africans really resent this collapse. What they resent is not being admitted to the white man's form of society. Detribalized Africans have no wish to be retribalized, and South African attempts to persuade them that this would be in their best interests are usually greeted with mocking laughter.

The African, as everyone knows, has a lively sense of humor, usually sarcastic. A man like Tshekedi Khama may tell his people to be proud of being black and not just to ape the white man. But this doesn't mean Tshekedi wants his people to turn their backs on a Western type of civilization and to retreat into the Stone Age. When white men, who so assiduously preached the virtues of their Christian culture when it suited them, now suddenly tell black men that they are better off without it, the Africans have no difficulty in seeing through this piece of hypocrisy. They perceive that the white man is trying to have his cake and eat it: to get black men to work for him, but not to let them share in his civilization. The spectacle fills them with cynical amusement.

"If," an African told me, "I am asked to choose between David Livingstone and Dr. Verwoerd, I choose Livingstone." Some of Africa's frightened whites are now attacking the missionaries for putting unwelcome ideas into black skulls. They are unconsciously abetted by the sentimental museum curators. It is claimed that in the optimistic glow of the late nineteenth century the missionaries stridently overemphasized the superiority of Christianity to crocodile-worship, fetishism, and juju, and thus seduced the African from allegiance to his own gods and from such indigenous delights as human sacrifice, cannibalism, and witchcraft. As viewed by a brisk, up-to-date comparative anthropologist, the Virgin Mary and the circumcision of virgins are equally worthy of study.

It is true that the missionaries have made mistakes. It was for example a typical nineteenth-century error to lay enormous stress on nineteenth-century notions of sexual morality, to equate these with the essence of Christianity, and to denounce as an unredeemed savage an African who had several wives and who stoutly refused to abandon all but one of them to death by starvation or a life of prostitution in order to square himself with the teachings of the Bible. Several African secret societies and fanatical cults have flourished on garbled versions of the Old Testament spread among the bush people by runaway mission pupils, while Christ's agony on the Cross has occasionally been made into a happy excuse for secret tortures inflicted by black religious maniacs.

But the real purpose of recent attacks on missionary work in Africa, which use such examples as a smoke-screen, is plain enough. It is to discredit the Christian teaching that in the eyes of God all men are equal, and that to discriminate against a man solely because of the color of his skin is, in the Christian view, an immoral act. Proposing legislation to put mission schools under the control of the Malan government, Dr. Verwoerd, of South Africa, toward the end of 1953 did not beat about the bush. The idea, he explained, was to ensure that "natives" received only the sort of education that would teach them they could never hope to be the equals of the white man.

: 5 :

"THE BLACK man in a white-dominated society," said Hans Leuenberger, "is equipped with X-ray eyes. He not only can study and understand the white man's techniques, but can see inside the white man's mind, penetrate his thoughts, and follow his motivations. But the white man sees only black bodies. He has never entered into the black man's thoughts, does not know what is going on in his heart, and seldom can speak his language."

But black men speak up when they find white men who will listen. What they have to say usually astonishes the whites, not because it reveals an alien turn of thought, but because it reveals how faithfully plastic Stone Age man has adapted himself to the other's civilization. The African Negro who has emerged from the tribal life does not want to go back into it. He wants more "integration," not less. He wants bread, a home, education for his children, and some degree of security. Above all, he wants to be regarded as a human being in his own right.

When the whites will not listen, the Negro takes refuge behind the language barrier. Into the white man's cities he has brought not only his colorful poetry—every African is a natural poet and born orator—but his talent for sharp wit and extreme sarcasm. In his comments on the unconscious white man he is merciless. In Johannesburg, where white and black jostle on every crowded sidewalk, the blacks hugely enjoy the privilege of being able openly to discuss the whites without the whites being any the wiser. Two Africans are unloading a truck, and a white girl, overdressed, passes by with her escort, who is twice her age. He is a fat and self-satisfied little man who looks proudly possessive. One of the Africans says to the other, in Sesuto: "Now whose white whore is that?" The other candidly replies: "She belongs to the little fat man, brother, but not for long, I'll bet. She'll soon find a more handsome lover."

"Ah," the other replies, "but the little fat man will continue to buy her things. She'll never tell him she has found another lover. He looks the sort to be easily fooled."

The two Africans burst into laughter. The two whites look at them, shake their heads in amusement, and pass on. They do not understand what the Africans have been saying. They think Africans are "quaint," but are sure they would not dare to be disrespectful. And the two Africans know this. To them it is the cream of the joke.

The whites have convinced themselves that most Africans are "just like children." They do not credit them with any ratiocinative process. A white South African girl looks at some charming pickaninnies at play, and murmurs regretfully: "What a pity they have to grow up into *Kaffirs*." When the blacks behave like adults, meaning that they assert themselves and voice their grievances, the whites are shocked and indignant. It is all the fault of "missionaries" or "agitators."

The tribal African believes in witchcraft, but otherwise is nobody's fool. He is shrewd in practical matters, and knows on which side his bread is buttered. If the agricultural demonstrator convinces him he can grow better crops by rotation, he will do so, though he may believe the rotation has little to do with it and it is in fact part of the white man's magic. The Masai live on cow's milk mixed with cow's blood, but also buy bottled beer from the Indian store. When the tribesman hitches his blanket on his shoulder and walks barefoot into town with his wives following behind, neither he nor they are unduly perplexed. They accept traffic lights, streetcars, omnibuses, telephones, elevators, and electricity without outward show of emotion. If they settle in the city, they quickly adapt themselves to its ways. Continued belief in things like witchcraft can coexist in their minds with complete practicality in everyday affairs. But Stone Age man easily becomes a snob. He wears "European" clothes, buys bicycles and phonographs, smokes cigarettes, loves Hollywood films, reads mysteries and Westerns. In Johannesburg two well-dressed Zulus passed two other Zulus recently arrived from their kraal and still wearing their bright-patterned blankets. "Look!" exclaimed one of the Europeanized Zulus. " 'Natives!' " The point is that the African Negro has absolutely no illusions about the delights of tribal life in the bush. He escapes from it whenever the chance offers, and seldom wishes to return to it.

The African Negro has accepted the white man's world. What he increasingly resents is its reluctance to accept him. He sees that in Africa almost every judge, every officer, every politician, every employer, has a white face. The whites have all the plums. The African wants a share. In other words, he now asks for equality of opportunity. Between him and this goal stands the color-bar.

The whites who live in Africa are suffering from a crisis of conscience. Everything the black man asks is based on what they taught him was right: Christianity, democracy, liberty, the pursuit of happiness. The whites feed themselves on illusions about the black man: that he is an unteachable savage, that he is a child, that he does not like change, that he ought to "develop along his own lines." But in their hearts they do not really believe any of this themselves. And they are afraid.

Fear knocks on the white man's door in South Africa, and he responds with naked force. In the Union, rebellious Africans fill the jails, but the white man has guns and fair numbers, and still seems strong. The case is different for the fewer, more scattered whites in other territories. Fear knocks on their door too, and they are far more hopelessly outnumbered. The pressures, generated mainly in South Africa, may wreck the flimsier white structures elsewhere before they produce really serious explosions in the Union itself. The current race war in Kenya is a warning for places like Nyasaland, Northern Rhodesia, and Uganda, to go no farther afield.

: 6 :

NOT ONLY do the most intelligent white people I have met in Africa realize the inevitability of change; they are anxious to speed it up, to bridge the dangerous gap and get through the perilous transition phase as quickly as possible. And these are not men of straw. I think of Governor Sir Charles Arden-Clarke in the Gold Coast, Sir John Macpherson in Nigeria, Sir Edward Twining in Tanganyika.

"But if we allow the Africans, who so greatly outnumber us, to share in our political power, they will push us out of Africa altogether." This is the favorite argument of frightened whites who realize that repression is not a solution but can think of no other way of safeguarding their own position.

In South Africa, James Njongwe told me: "There is no problem that cannot be solved peacefully if people have the will to do so." I have rarely met an African leader who was not almost pathetically eager for such a round-table discussion. So far, however, few of the whites have shown any disposition to treat such a suggestion seriously. To many or most of them, the thought of even sitting down at a conference table with an African is shocking. Yet the best of the African leaders are far from seeming unreasonable. They even recognize the whites' major difficulty: the fear of granting anything lest they lose everything. Most of them express willingness to accept for their people a franchise qualified by an education test, a property test, or both. Though most of the whites are not yet ready to negotiate with such men, they may yet be frightened into it. The danger is that either they will do so too late, in which case the "moderate" African leaders will have been replaced by mob-leaders, who could easily become Communist stooges; or else they will delay matters until their fear overwhelms them and they lash out blindly with thoroughly repressive acts in place of negotiation. If that happens, the end result will be the same; for if the "moderate" African leaders are thrown into jail, or executed,

479

their places will again be taken by far tougher elements. In Kenya, at this writing, the white settlers find themselves at war with bloodthirsty guerrilla fighters who appear to have no political ideas at all. The people with whom the settlers might have negotiated are all either in concentration camps or silenced by fear of being murdered by their own side, as "Quislings."

As the Africans have become more vocal in their demands, the whites have shifted their ground considerably, but generally in the wrong direction. *Apartheid*, as a race doctrine, is something comparatively new. On the other hand, the British moves toward self-government in West Africa, so fiercely denounced as radical and dangerous experiments, would not have surprised anyone living fifty years ago—not even Cecil Rhodes, who caused no great stir when he announced as the inevitable goal: "Equal rights for all civilized men." Such equality was then regarded not only as inevitable, but as the only thinkable outcome in Africa, following white intervention in that continent— since the whites' mission was held to be to make all men civilized as soon as possible. It is not surprising if Africans become cynically distrustful of all white men's promises, when whites hurriedly back away from even discussing those matters with the educated leaders the Africans are now producing. The irony is that there would be no such leaders if the whites had not in fact gone a long way toward fulfilling their civilizing mission. South Africa, the land of *apartheid*, has more black children in school than any other African country.

"They should have thought of that," one African said to me, "before they taught us." He added: "It isn't *we* who want a color-bar."

: 7 :

AFRICA IS becoming increasingly important to the rest of the world, both economically and politically. The world, and perhaps especially the United States, wants Africa's uranium, tin, manganese, bauxite, chromium, industrial diamonds, copper, lead, zinc, and cobalt; her palm oil, sisal, cotton, coffee, tea, tobacco, and hides and skins. Between 1938 and 1950, the Belgian Congo's dollar earnings rose from $1,000,000 to $26,000,000; Nigeria's from $3,000,000 to $37,000,000; the Gold Coast's from $6,000,000 to $64,000,000; Portuguese Angola's from $180,000 to $10,000,000; Liberia's from $1,000,000 to $14,000,000. From Durban all the way across the continent to Dakar, Africa is busily blueprinting or building new ports, railroads, oil refineries, hydroelectric schemes, towns.

Africa is also important to the world politically. It has been called "the last uncommitted continent." In 1953 Joe Murumbi, who is half Masai and half Goan Arab, and whom I met in Nairobi when he was connected with the Kenya African Union, went to India and had long talks with Nehru. It seemed to me a significant sign of the times: far more interesting than the aimless bellowings of the Kenya white settlers, who in an age of collapsing empires keep on stubbornly repeating that they are an Imperial people, innately and mystically superior to lesser breeds.

Most white settlers in Kenya have probably never even heard of Joe Murumbi. They certainly would never admit him to the Rift Valley Club. But he became the guest of Nehru, who has seen the inside of many a British jail and is now the ruler of Hindu India. Joe went to tell Nehru, and the Indian people, about the problems of the people of Africa. I doubt if their discussions took much account of the point of view of the Kenya settlers. Joe wanted to talk to Nehru about the Masai and the Kikuyu, the Wakamba and the Luo, the people of the plains and of the lakes. And Nehru, it seems, listened. Each year bright young Africans attend Indian universities, on scholarships awarded by the Indian Government, as a gesture of friendship to Africa by the Indian people.

There are 300,000 Indians in South Africa. In East Africa, penetrating deep inland all along the great arc of the Indian Ocean, there are more Indians than Europeans. Some were trading there before any white men arrived, and Indians played a major part in building the railroad that made white settlement possible in the first place. But in South Africa the Indians are legislated against as "coolies," and in Nairobi almost the first thing you see as you step off the plane at the airport are segregated lavatories, delicately set aside for "European Gentlemen" and "Asian Gentlemen" respectively. As a caustic-tongued friend of mine once remarked: "Here they even pee separately." Kenya is full of Indians, some of whom are extremely rich, but the whites do their best to pretend that Indians do not exist. I have seldom been so embarrassed as discovering in Nairobi, after accepting lavish Indian hospitality, that it was impossible for me to invite an Indian to have even a cup of coffee with me in the lounge of my hotel.

But today India has an important voice in the world. Russia and the West are both assiduously wooing Nehru. And Nehru has now openly made common cause with the peoples of Africa in their struggle against white-supremacy laws.

After seeing Nehru, Joe Murumbi went on to Egypt and had a talk with General Naguib. Thus he passed from the Hindu to the Moslem and Arab world, across the bridge that links Africa with the East. Through Joe, the hitherto voiceless millions of Africa talked familiarly to the Indian and Arab communities of the world.

I do not know whether Joe is a good or a bad ambassador. In Nairobi he denied to me that he was a Communist. But at any rate it seems to me that he is a significant phenomenon.

By their present treatment of Africans and Indians, the few whites in the last uncommitted continent may conceivably be imperiling the cause of the whole free world. They carry a burden of responsibility that few of them seem to appreciate. In the world as it is now constituted, with the balance of power so delicately poised, the way in which the whites behave in Africa toward non-whites may be taken by all non-Western peoples as an acid test of what the West's attitude is to be toward them. They could shape their own policies and make their own momentous choice between Russia and the West, accordingly. It is an odd thought that one humiliating word in Nairobi, or one act of repression in South Africa, might yet change the history of the world. Color has become crucial, and the future of Africa may decide the future of everyone on earth.

: 8 :

AFRICA FOR its further development needs material outside aid. The Belgian Congo is rich, but it is doubtful if the French for example can develop their huge African domains without assistance. It might also prove well worth while to encourage those countries like the Gold Coast and Nigeria, where black men are learning to govern themselves.

An obvious fear is that outside capital investment in Africa will mean "exploitation." But I did not find the Gold Coast's black Government nearly as afraid of that as it might have been. Both Prime Minister Nkrumah and Commerce Minister Gbedemah referred without prompting to the need for foreign investment.

The pattern of capital investment in the South African gold mines was fixed in the 1880's and '90's. But capitalism has made fewer mistakes in the more recently developed Northern Rhodesian copper belt, and in the Belgian Katanga. Improvement in those matters is progressive. It would be a pity if modern capitalism, because of past errors, lost its faith in its ability to raise living-standards in the one really undeveloped continent just when advancing Africans seem to feel that the key to a better future for them lies in bold plans for economic expansion.

Africans are increasingly resentful against those whites in Africa who refuse to treat them as partners. But they continue to look trustingly toward the United Nations, the United States, and the United Kingdom for redress of their racial grievances. They believe, most of them, in democracy, which teaches that men, even of different colors, are created equal. All they ask of the democratic countries is an assurance that democracy is going to be practiced in Africa.

There is of course no certainty that Africa will successfully pass through the present dangerous transition period without breaking down into the violence of a race war. There is no certainty that the Gold Coast and Nigerian experiments in self-government will not bog down in corruption and demagoguery. But these are chances that have to be taken. Repression certainly will not work, or not for long. It is much more likely to turn Africans' eyes and hopes toward Communism.

In my travels in Africa I have found much fear of "Communism" among the whites, but little real evidence of Communism itself among the Africans. The spearhead of African protest, however, is undoubtedly a tiny, highly dissatisfied Negro intelligentsia. Many of those educated Africans find Marxist references to the evils of "imperialism" highly congenial. On the other hand, given positions of responsibility and accepted as partners by the white race, they might quickly shrug off all Communist influence, as Kwame Nkrumah seems to have done when he became Prime Minister of the Gold Coast.

The root of the evil, for white and black alike in Africa, is the color-bar. It is a cancer that eats into the whites' own moral standards, for in their hearts they know that it cannot be defended. Its existence turns African "intellectuals," as well as ordinary colored folk, into rebels against the whole established order, filling them with anti-white feeling and forcing them to believe that the whites are the "haves" because they are white, the blacks the "have-nots" because they are black. The color-bar as it now exists threatens Africa not only with a race war, but with a class war as well.

The world, as the representative of the Philippines in the United Nations indicated, cannot ignore the fears of Africa's white minority. But neither can it decently condone the present irrational color-bar. That is why the world must find itself more in sympathy with the Belgians, the French, and the Portuguese, who at any rate in principle uphold no color-bar, than with the South Africans and with the white settlers in British East and Central Africa.

In those latter areas, outside influences should wherever possible stress the undesirability of a rigid color-bar, and might with advantage point out to the whites that they are still in a position to negotiate a reasonable settlement with insurgent Africans. For, though the Africans have the numbers, the whites still have the guns and all the political and economic power. If in those areas, where tension is greatest, white and black could sit down together to discuss their problems, it is far from unlikely that a realistic series of compromises could still be worked out through a process of genuine bargaining. The African leaders in those countries are by no means averse to such a discussion. It is the whites who thus far have refused even to consider it.

But, despite the appeals of many African Negroes, the Western world can scarcely interfere directly in Africa's internal affairs, except that the colonial offices of the countries that have "possessions" in Africa might take a much stronger line about the color-bar. This applies especially to Britain, whose Colonial Office pursues a progressive race policy in West Africa while appearing to throw all its weight behind the white settlers' color-bar policies in East and Central Africa.

There is perhaps little at this stage that America can do about Africa's race problems, important as the crisis-ridden continent is to the free world, and repugnant as many of the things being done in Africa must be to American principles. Americans are not debarred, however, from studying the position and expressing their opinions. And they ought to do so candidly, even at the risk of giving offense in some quarters. In particular, they should not be humbugged by some British pretensions to a monopoly of wisdom when it comes to shouldering the white man's burden. Kiplingism has been tried in Africa, as it was tried in India, and has failed to work. The white settlers of Kenya have little to boast about. India is now offering university scholarships to Africans. Similar American opportunities might be enlarged. Suitably qualified American Negroes who take an interest in Africa might be encouraged to investigate African affairs on the spot; they have a particular right to know what is going on there. Even Malan might hesitate to refuse to admit well-qualified and properly sponsored investigators to his country just because they happened to be black. If he did refuse them admission, he could legitimately be asked awkward questions; it is the continual boast of his official apologists both at home and abroad that South Africa has nothing to hide.

: 9 :

I MEANT to finish writing at this point, and on that note. But as I sought to arrange my thoughts, between African journeys, my mind went back over the many miles I had already covered, and the many people I had met.

I had seen deserts and jungles, witnessed tragedies and comedies, been hospitably received by loincloth tribesmen and white-plumed governors. I had been lost in an equatorial forest, and had walked into a battle between men with rifles and angry villagers armed with bows and arrows. I had never seen a snake, and hardly ever encountered a lion. I remembered the camel-thorn trees, pink flamingoes on a lake, and the white spray that hangs over the Victoria Falls, the Smoke-That-Thunders. I had crossed the Zambezi and the Congo, and flown over the snowy crest of Kilimanjaro.

I have met some remarkable characters. I thought of the bald Rhodesian colonel who drank pink gins with a shaky hand and shot buffalo; of the Turkana tribesman who wore a ball of ivory skewered through his lower lip. I recalled the King of Buganda, who wore a Grenadier Guards tie and lived in a palace behind a stockade of elephant grass; and Alan Neville, who played Bach on his hand-wound phonograph while leopards prowled on his lawn in the Tanganyika moonlight.

Certain scenes lived vividly in my mind. I thought of Charles Swart, South Africa's Minister of Justice, brandishing his cat-o'-nine-tails; and white-faced Senator Hendrik Verwoerd explaining with a deadly sincerity why there had to be *apartheid* if his Boer people were to survive. I remembered little gray Sir Ernest Oppenheimer chuckling with an old man's wry amusement as he showed me a diamond worth a king's ransom.

There was black-bearded Jomo Kenyatta, jauntily swinging his walking-stick with the carved elephant's head; and there was the golden-haired English girl at Lake Naivasha who said: "I

486

winged a Kuke!" I thought of Hosea Kutako, the leader of the Hereros, sitting under a tree sadly relating what had befallen his people; and Tshekedi Khama saying: "God helps those who help themselves."

I remembered Kwame Nkrumah being cheered by the Gold Coast crowds who waved palm leaves as he passed through them looking like a black Roman emperor in his toga; and the Gold Coast Negro who had explained how to "juju" Dr. Malan. I thought of the "mammy" trucks roaring at night over the winding roads of Nigeria, and the Liberian Consulate at Takoradi where plump Negroes in plum-colored uniforms had sat drinking whisky under a religious text proclaiming: "Christ is the Master of This House." I also recalled the Kikuyu women trudging under their heavy head-loads, and the tom-toms that beat in the jungle Cathedral of St. Anne of the Congo.

Africa was the most fascinating of the continents: the oldest, and at the same time the newest; the crossroads of the world. It was in Africa that Man may have been cradled, and from here that he set forth on his endless migrations, before the dawn of history. Where there had once been great civilizations, there were now only burning deserts; but, as the jungles were slowly cleared, new civilizations might arise. General Smuts described Africa as a great laboratory. The organized knowledge of mankind could have elbow-room for its experiments here, where scientists were already harnessing great rivers, and might one day remold whole landscapes and change climates. For as Pliny of old said, there was always something new out of Africa. Africa was plastic. It was also a laboratory for the mysteries of race. Its great-hearted, black-skinned peoples had been the very last to join in the main stream of modern history. Though a great question-mark still hung over their future, they could not go back, but must press forward, an integral part of mankind. I found myself hoping that their future would be as bright as their past had been dark. For Africa, as the first missionaries had perceived, could be the great test for Christianity, which proclaims that in the last resort all men, whatever their color, their creed, or their race, are brothers.

INDEX

INDEX

INDEX

A NOTE ON THE TYPE

This book was set on the Linotype in ELECTRA, designed by W. A. Dwiggins. The Electra face is a simple and readable type suitable for printing books by present-day processes. It is not based on any historical model, and hence does not echo any particular time or fashion. It is without eccentricities to catch the eye and interfere with reading—in general, its aim is to perform the function of a good book printing-type: to be read, and not seen.

Typography based on original designs by W. A. Dwiggins.

The book was composed, printed, and bound by Kingsport Press, Inc., Kingsport, Tennessee.

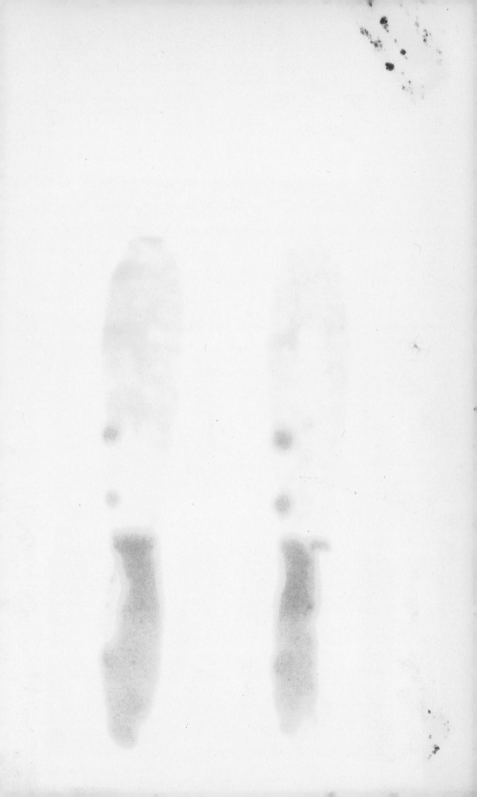

DT 12.2 .C3 c.1
Campbell, Alexander, 1912-
The heart of Africa

DATE DUE

THE HEART OF AFRICA.

Fernald Library
Colby-Sawyer College
New London, New Hampshire

GAYLORD   PRINTED IN U.S.A.